"The great strength of this rich, interesting book is that it offers the perspective of both an 'outsider' and an 'insider' for Judaism, Islam, Hinduism, and Buddhism. In the interplay between the two viewpoints, these world religions are illuminated in a fresh way for a Western Christian audience. The review questions, glossaries, and annotated bibliographies that conclude each section offer the reader the opportunity to solidify what has been learned and explore more deeply. Even in a library already stocked with world religions textbooks, this one stands out as a worthy addition."

—Kristin Johnston Largen
Associate Professor of Systematic Theology
Lutheran Theological Seminary at Gettysburg

"*World Religions in Dialogue* is that unique textbook that combines competent introduction, accessibility, and a thoughtful dialogue of insiders and outsiders in conversation. It will be a much-appreciated text for the introductory course on world religions, showing both the *what* of religions and the *how* of learning religions in an ongoing conversation."

—Francis X. Clooney, SJ
Parkman Professor of Divinity
Director of the Center for the Study of World Religions
Harvard University

# EDITOR ACKNOWLEDGEMENTS

The title of this book is *World Religions in Dialogue*, yet dialogue is always between human beings, not between religions. Dialogues with many fabulous human beings inspired me to develop this book. Ali from Ghana was the first who addressed me in dialogue, and being a former Christian he knew what he was talking about, so we had a lot to discuss. Many others followed, including the shoe salesman in Istanbul and the post office clerk in Colombo who wished me the most beautiful Buddhist blessing—the triple gem.

Catholic schools living their mission and students willing to go beyond their protected bubbles showed me how to teach world religions in an engaging fashion. Often, I have been just a facilitator for the real work that students have done with such excellent teachers in the field as Earl, Donna, Bashar, Kim, Megan, Robin, and so many others in Baltimore. The Catholic Theological Society of America's Comparative Theology section gave me the opportunity to collaborate with the excellent colleagues who have written the main parts of this book: Philip and Jan, Rita and Zeki, Aimee and Madhuri, Peter and Heng Sure. What I like most about their work is that the joy of authentic dialogue shines through in their writing. Finally, the staff of Anselm Academic helped to generate this book like the wise midwife with her maieutic techniques, beginning with Jerry Ruff and ending with Maura Hagarty. In between, there was Kathleen Walsh who was like a rock in the maelstrom of the entire project. Some of her exchanges with my colleagues made me realize how often I am but a bystander in relationships that are so much stronger than I can tell. Some of these relationships allow us to sense the divine presence in humans. Thanks to all of you, and especially to Dorris, for making me aware of that, time and again.

## Publishers Acknowledgements

Thank you to the following individuals who reviewed this work in progress:

**Frank Berna**
*La Salle University, Philadelphia, Pennsylvania*

**Cristóbal Serrán-Pagán y Fuentes**
*Valdosta State University, Valdosta, Georgia*

**Linh Hoang**
*Siena College, Loudonville, New York*

# world religions
## in dialogue

A COMPARATIVE THEOLOGICAL APPROACH

Pim Valkenberg, editor

ANSELM
ACADEMIC

Created by the publishing team of Anselm Academic.

Cover image: A Trappist monk and a Buddhist nun engage in conversation at the Second Gethsemani Encounter in 2002. © Notre Dame Archives.

The publisher gratefully acknowledges use of the following:
*Upanisads*, Oxford World's Classics, translated by Patrick Olivelle (Oxford: Oxford University Press, 1996):
Pages 154–55 (Chandogya Upanisad 6:12–13), 36 lines
Pages 268–69 and 270, 11 lines (Mundaka Upanisad 1:1:4–8, 1:2:10–11), 30 lines
Pages 272–73 (Mundaka Upanisad 2:1:7–10, 2:2:3–6), 20 lines + 23 lines (2 different selections) Total: 43 lines
Page 275 (Mundaka Upanisad 3:1:5–9), 25 lines
By permission of Oxford University Press

Excerpts from *The Ramayana: A Shortened Modern Prose Version of the Indian Epic* translated by R.K. Narayan (New York: Penguin Books, 1972), 161–62. Used by permission of Penguin, a division of Penguin Group (USA) Inc.

Excerpts from *The Laws of Manu*, trans. Wendy Doniger (New York: Penguin Books, 1991), 12–13, 77, 115, 197, 198. Reproduced by permission of Penguin Books Ltd.

Excerpt from *The Heart of Prajna Paramita Sutra,* translated by the Chung Tai Translation Committee (from the Chinese translation by Tripitaka Master Xuan Zang, seventh century). Copyright June 2002. Reprinted with permission of the Chung Tai Zen Center.

Excerpt from chapter 25 of *The Lotus Sutra*, translated by Dharma Realm Buddhist University. Copyright 1998. Reprinted with permission of Dharma Realm Buddhist University.

Printed in the United States of America

7051 (PO4300)

ISBN 978-1-59982-083-5

# CONTENTS

## PART 4: BUDDHISM  189

*Peter Feldmeier and Heng Sure*

# INTRODUCTION

# Exploring World Religions through Dialogue

*Pim Valkenberg*

## What Makes This Book Different?

Information about world religions is easy to get. While most students will search the Internet, teachers of world religions will often explore recently published texts. Regardless of approach, a wealth of information is available. So what makes this book worthwhile? More importantly, what makes this book different from other sources of information about world religions?

Like other sources, this book includes trustworthy information by well-informed scholars about the four non-Christian world religions most relevant to the Western culture of North America and Europe—namely Hinduism, Buddhism, Judaism, and Islam. Unlike many other sources, however, this book does not approach these religions from a "neutral" or an "objective" viewpoint. Instead, it presents them from the perspective of scholars immersed in religious traditions and engaged in interreligious dialogue.

This book differs from many others mainly in that it presents dialogues between Christian scholars of other religions, and Hindu, Buddhist,

Muslim, and Jewish scholars of their own religions.[1] It builds on the basic idea that the interplay between these two viewpoints—the "outsider" perspective and the "insider" perspective—offers the best way to introduce religions. The book's four parts consider Judaism, Islam, Hinduism, and Buddhism. Christianity is not included here as one of the religions discussed, but as a perspective on other religions. Each part, therefore, begins with a Christian scholar, who brings an outsider's perspective, giving an overview of the religion in question. This perspective often serves as the starting point for those who study other religions with a "Western," more or less Christian, mind-set, and this book hopes to build on their existing notions of these other religions. Next, the scholar who is an adherent of the religion in question will challenge this mind-set by providing an insider's perspective. Both work together to provide commentaries on basic texts and to reflect on the dialogue between the "insider" and the "outsider" perspectives.

This distinction between "outsider" and "insider" simplifies a more complex reality in which the "insider" is an "outsider" as well, and

---

1. Many of the contributors to this text have a connection to a Catholic university, reflecting the fact that most scholars working in the field of comparative theology (including some Protestants, Jews, Muslims, and Buddhists, as well as Catholics) do so in the institutional context of Catholic higher education.

the "outsider" is an "insider." In giving a scholarly description, "insiders" necessarily adopt an outsider's view and distance themselves from what they describe. Conversely, "outsiders" are often well acquainted with the religions they describe and as theologians they have "insider" knowledge of their own religion as well. Yet the terms *outsider* and *insider*—or their respective equivalents in anthropology, *etic* and *emic*—nonetheless offer a shorthand characterization of the two viewpoints brought into dialogue in this volume.[2] Even though most scholars would like to have their *etic* description of a world religion recognized by that religion's adherents, they would not go so far as to say that the *only* valid description of a given religion is one recognized by the adherents of that religion. Outsiders employ a specific language to describe a religion, using categories that necessarily differ from those insiders would use. Yet, those who prefer to use dialogue as an instrument of mutual understanding will always try to ensure their discourse proves acceptable to the adherents of that religion.

In the history of the study of religions, the viewpoints of insiders and outsiders have been important, but limited. Many religious insiders wrote about those different from themselves merely to defend their own religion. Therefore, they usually gave a "confessional" or "theological" viewpoint of other religions, which these "pagan" or "heretic" others generally rejected because such a viewpoint only respected criteria germane to the religion defended, not to the religion described. The image held by religious adherents about their own religion has often determined the image they had of the other. Consequently, Muslims used to speak about Jews and Christians as the "people of the Scripture" (*ahl al-kitab*) because they saw themselves as

people to whom God had given the final Scripture. Conversely, Christians talked about Muslims as "Muhammadans," thinking that the role of Muhammad in Islam would be similar to that of Christ in their own religion.

In the modern era, scholars have come to favor a more neutral, "objective" approach, free from such "confessional" biases. Using historical and literary methods, they describe religious phenomena without adding value judgments. Most modern books about world religions adopt this approach, often labeled as "the science of religions" (*Religionswissenschaft* in German) or "religious studies." Even though many scholars of religion think that a descriptive approach shows less bias and yields more "objective" knowledge, the results of such scientific descriptions have often not been acknowledged or accepted by adherents of the religions described.

While "theological" and "science of religions" approaches have been historically valuable, they describe a religion differently than an insider-scholar of a religion would. The last third of the twentieth century saw a marked rise in relationships between religions as well as an increased awareness of religious plurality. Many religions that have their origins in non-Western cultures are now represented in the Western academic world by scholars who were raised in—or later converted to—the non-Christian religions discussed in this book. Thus, they can describe their own religions in ways that open fruitful dialogue with scholars who do not share their "insider" perspective but who may be able to translate these perspectives into worldviews more familiar to students in the West. This fertile dialogue between "insider" and "outsider" perspectives informs and shapes the structure of this book.

2. For a sophisticated overview of different positions, see the volume edited by Russell T. McCutcheon, *The Insider / Outsider Problem in the Study of Religion: A Reader* (London: Cassell, 1999).

## The Term *World Religions*

Most every textbook about religions uses the term *world religions*, but the phrase has a complicated history. In the nineteenth and the early twentieth centuries, scholars of religion began to use this term to differentiate their work from the confessional approach of Christian theology, which tended to divide religions between the "true religion" (Christianity and, to a certain extent, Judaism) and "false religions" (those of "pagans," "heathen," and other "unbelievers"). In this process of differentiation, the term *world religions* was coined.[3] Yet, most scholars who used the term to allow for a larger, more nuanced array of religions within nineteenth-century scholarship did so from a decidedly confessional perspective: they agreed that Christianity was the highest religion and the fulfillment of all people's religious quests.[4] Even many of the scholars who insisted their approach was based on scientific and "objective" research, such as religious sciences pioneers Friedrich Max Müller (1823–1900) and Christian P. Tiele (1830–1902) could not avoid using concepts and classifications derived from Christian theology.[5]

In the course of the twentieth century, the "scientific" approach associated with the term *world religions* gained increasing credibility, while the idea of a confessional grading, typical of a Christian theological approach to other religions, gradually disappeared. The term *world religions* became one of the hallmarks of an "objective" comparative study of religion that coincided with a new awareness of religious plurality. Yet, there is strong evidence that the term is an invention of nineteenth-century scholarship that often serves unrecognized theological objectives by paying lip service to the idea that all religions are equal paths to the same ultimate end while nonetheless maintaining that Christianity is still the best or even the absolute way to get there. Therefore the contrast between a scientific and a theological approach to religion cannot be maintained as an absolute standard.[6]

## Different Approaches to the Study of World Religions

In one of the most influential contemporary readers on world religions, Ian Markham distinguishes four competing methodologies in the study of world religions. Two of these go back to the development of the scientific approaches outlined above. The first method—the historical-comparative method—is mainly interested in a comparison of religions based on historical research of their most important texts in their contexts; while the second method—the phenomenological method—focuses on a comparative description and interpretation of religious phenomena, such as images of God, prayer, and holy scriptures. Both methods of study

---

3. See Tomoko Masuzawa, *The Invention of World Religions* (Chicago: University of Chicago Press, 2005). In this book, she shows that the term *world religions* was, in fact, invented to underscore the relationship between Christianity and other religions of Indo-Aryan origin (Buddhism foremost) while suppressing the relationship with the other Semitic religions (Judaism and notably Islam).

4. See Masuzawa, *The Invention of World Religions*, 75–79, which mentions Frederick Denison Maurice (1805–72) and James Freeman Clarke (1810–88) as two early writers on world religions from the perspective of what they called comparative theology. On the relationship between this form of comparative theology and contemporary forms of comparative theology, see Francis X. Clooney, SJ, *Comparative Theology: Deep Learning Across Religious Borders* (Chichester: Wiley-Blackwell, 2010), 30–37.

5. See Masuzawa, *The Invention of World Religions*, 107–20; Jonathan Z. Smith, "Classification," in *Guide to the Study of Religion*, ed. Willi Braun and Russell T. McCutcheon (London: Cassell, 2000), 35–44.

6. Masuzawa, *The Invention of World Religions*, 324–28, with reference to the German theologian Ernst Troeltsch (1865–1923).

strive to be as objective as possible. The third method, which Markham calls the "confessional approach," assumes the truth of one particular faith tradition and underscores its differences with other faith traditions. Markham advocates a fourth approach, which he calls an "empathetic approach."

Markham uses John Dunne's famous metaphor of "passing over" to the point of view of religious "others" and of "coming back" to one's own point of view to characterize this methodology. This implies, first, approaching the religious tradition from the "outsider" perspective; second, it entails presenting the perspective of "a fairly orthodox adherent" of the religion in order to show this tradition in the "best possible light."[7] After this "passing over," there is a "coming back" to the original position in order to make a decision. Markham explains: "This will involve either an act of clarification or an act of modification. If one is not persuaded, then one will be in a position to clarify the reasons why one prefers the initial position; if one is persuaded to some degree, then one will find the initial position modified."[8]

In this way, Markham makes clear that historical and phenomenological "outsider" approaches to world religions can be combined fruitfully with an "insider" approach. His own "empathetic" approach aims at either confirming one's "outsider" perspective or modifying it after having been influenced by the "insider" perspective. The process of "passing over" to other perspectives and "coming back" again is similar to the "dialogical" process used in this book.

Similarly, other recent books on world religions that start from an explicitly theological perspective show that a Christian evaluation of world religions also needs to incorporate historical and phenomenological investigations of these religions.[9] These recent approaches to world religions show that the goal of an "objective" and historically correct appraisal of world religions can be integrated into a wider theological approach—one in which the shift of perspective between the "outsider," who observes a specific religion, and the "insider," who observes his or her own religion, comprises a central methodological principle. The main insight behind such an approach is that truth is best found not with a "purely scientific" approach, nor with a "purely confessional" approach, but rather through the interplay of "outsider" and "insider" approaches that blend scholarship and religious engagement.

## Comparative Theology and Dialogue

The increased awareness of religious pluralism in the last third of the twentieth century has led not only to new "insider" approaches in the study of world religions but also to new forms of theology—mainly Christian theology—that take comparative approaches to other religions very seriously. While the name "comparative theology" was used in the nineteenth century for "confessional" forms of Christian theology that saw Christianity as the epitome of world religions, the new comparative theology explicitly includes the "objective" comparative study of religions.

This new form of comparative theology makes it difficult to maintain the contrast between scientific and theological approaches to the world religions. Francis Clooney, a Jesuit

---

7. Ian Markham with Christy Lohr, eds., *A World Religions Reader*, 3rd ed. (Chichester: Wiley-Blackwell, 2009), 7.

8. Ibid., 8.

9. See Eugene Gorski, *Theology of Religions: A Sourcebook for Interreligious Study* (Mahwah, NJ: Paulist Press, 2008). Also, Karl J. Becker and Ilaria Morali, eds., *Catholic Engagement with World Religions: A Comprehensive Study* (Maryknoll, NY: Orbis Books, 2010).

scholar of Hinduism and one of the founders of present-day comparative theology, characterizes it as a form of theology that not only works "within the constraints of a commitment to a religious community . . . and a willingness to affirm the truth and values of that tradition"[10] but also learns from other faith traditions. Therefore, "comparative theology combines tradition-rooted theological concerns with actual study of another tradition."[11] Moreover, it includes the comparative study of religion, so that "the comparative theologian works first as an academic scholar, even if she also and more deeply intends the kind of religious and spiritual learning that characterizes theology richly conceived."[12] In this manner, as the subtitle of this book indicates, it is possible to use comparative theology as a new approach to world religions.

## Structure of This Book

This book proceeds from the assumption that insight into a specific religion can best be provided through dialogue between a scholar who gives an outsider approach to that religion and one who reacts to this description by giving an insider approach. Both scholars try to do justice to the "scientific" criteria of the comparative study of religion, while at the same time connecting their descriptions to their own religious backgrounds. In that sense, it would be simplistic to label the outsider approach a "scholarly" approach and the insider approach a "believer's" approach. Both approaches are scholarly, and both scholars explicitly try to relate their approach to their religious backgrounds. Yet, because one religion is the explicit subject of the

comparison while the other is only addressed implicitly some asymmetry does result.

Most theological approaches to world religions begin with the insider approach. This text, on the other hand, begins with the outsider approach because this represents the mind-set of most Western students of Judaism, Islam, Hinduism, and Buddhism, the idea being that such a mind-set can best be framed and corrected in an ongoing process of dialogue between the two points of view. In the part on Hinduism, for instance, the outsider begins by sketching how most people in the West view Hinduism—noting that the term *Hinduism* itself is a Western construct. This approach ties in with the preconceptions that some might bring to their study of Hinduism as a religion. The insider reply shows both the points where Hindus will recognize the description—for instance, because they are formed by models of Western scholarship themselves—and where they talk about their religion in different terms, such as referring to it as *sanatana dharma* ("eternal order" or "eternal duty") instead of "Hinduism." As part of this exchange, the insider may discuss some of the differences between concepts of religion shaped in his or her own tradition and concepts of religion that presuppose a Western, often Christian, point of view. In this sense, the dialogue explicitly discusses the religion called "Hinduism," while also implicitly addressing the Christian religion. This method of comparison and dialogue aims to lead readers to a better understanding of the religions discussed in this book as well as to greater insight into their own religious backgrounds.

The principles outlined above determined the content of this book. First, they led to the

10. Clooney, *Comparative Theology: Deep Learning Across Religious Borders*, 9.
11. Ibid., 10.
12. Ibid., 12.

decision to concentrate on a small number of world religions rather than discussing a greater number in less depth. The method of seeking understanding through dialogue and changing perspectives requires an extended discussion of the religions concerned. Different books on world religions may cover any number of religions since it is not at all clear what exactly a "world religion" is. Historically speaking, scholars employed the term to contrast religions with a worldwide presence from those that had relevance only in a specific cultural context; so "Hinduism" would be considered a world religion, but the religion of the Yorubas in Nigeria or the Dakotas in North America would not.

In the present situation the term *world religions* usually refers to those religions considered relevant in one's own cultural context, mixed with an awareness that they are not limited to that particular cultural context. This implies that a list of world religions drawn up in Germany might differ from such a list compiled in Romania, Mexico, or South Africa. In almost all Western cultural contexts, the list of world religions will include at least Christianity, Judaism, and Islam, and it will most likely incorporate Hinduism and Buddhism as well. Although some would argue for the inclusion of at least one of the East-Asian religions, such as Confucianism and Taoism, this text limits itself to the five religions important in every Western context.

Because this book presumes a basic knowledge of Christianity, it does not deal with Christianity in a separate part, but implicitly addresses it in all parts. This does not imply that all those engaged in the study of world religions have a thorough background in Christianity, rendering any further study of their home tradition unnecessary. However, this book supposes that most already know the basics of Christianity and thus enter the study of world religions from a Christian perspective, however vaguely articulated. Therefore, the text begins with the

religion closest to Christianity, namely Judaism, and continues with Islam as the third member of the Abrahamic family (or, in a more objective terminology, West-Asian or Semitic religions). Finally, it discusses the two great South-Asian religions that originated in India: Hinduism and Buddhism.

In this text the outsider approaches can be characterized as "Christian theological approaches"; however, they differ from the confessional approaches of the nineteenth century in not taking Christianity as the "absolute" or "highest" religion, but as the point of departure for the comparison for the outsider. Just like present-day comparative theology, these approaches are aware of their own provenance and context, are conscious of other approaches, and aim to engage in dialogue with them. In that sense, this book differs not only from "neutral" or "objective" approaches to world religions but also from traditional Christian textbooks about world religions.

The explorations of Judaism, Islam, Hinduism, and Buddhism each have the same basic structure, consisting of four chapters. In the first chapter, the outsider, who gives an *etic* approach, starts with an introduction to the religion that explicitly takes the presupposed knowledge of the readership as its point of departure. Why is it important for Christians to know about this religion? The outsider begins with a short overview of Christian approaches to that religion, of what is good or problematic about these approaches, and of avenues for future dialogue. So the exploration begins with "pictures of the other," which may sound strange for a world religions book, but highlights how one's religious background often determines one's approach.

From this point of view, the outsider discusses seven aspects of the religion, beginning with a description of what makes this religion unique and different from other religions. Often, this is phrased as "What basic question does this religion try to answer?" or "What is 'the way' this religion claims to offer?" The second aspect tackles the basic written sources of that religion, with the awareness that an outsider may take a biased approach to the sources and their canonical traditions. Third, the outsider chapter gives some history of that religion. While not comprehensive, this history surveys the most important developments, distinguishing, for instance, between "classical" and "modern" forms of that religion. The fourth aspect explores conceptions of the holy or the divine, and the fifth delves into corresponding conceptions of human beings. The sixth aspect discusses typical practices in the religion (rituals and holidays as well as ethics and social justice), and finally the outsider discusses the recent history of dialogue with that religion from the point of view of Christianity.

In the second chapter of each part the insider responds with an introduction that shows how the self-understanding of a religion (as represented by the *emic* approach) may differ from the outsider's approach. The insider's introduction more or less parallels the outsider's (following the seven points above), but may also include some response to what the outsider has written. In the last section, the insider discusses dialogue from the perspective of the non-Christian partner and offers an opinion on Christian dialogue initiatives (what is and is not helpful).

The third chapter in each part consists of a selection of texts from the most important sources of the religion under discussion along with insider and outsider commentaries. Some of the texts represent the typical interests of an outsider (for instance, "Messianic expectations" for a Christian approach to Judaism), while others reflect an insider approach (for instance, "Israel"—people, land, state—for a Jewish approach).

The two partners—insider and outsider—write the final chapter together in different ways, reflecting the divergent styles of their dialogues.

They reflect on the process of writing together—on what they learned through the dialogical process and on the most important items to continue the dialogue. Finally, each part ends with questions for discussion, suggestions for further reading, and a glossary.

The book's conclusion focuses on an essential element in the process of teaching Judaism, Islam, Hinduism, and Buddhism: learning from religious others. It discusses how the method of experiential learning—that is, learning by experiencing religious others rather than reading about them—fits well with the approach advocated in the book. This conclusion describes forms of experiential learning and presents two particular methods. The first method introduces students to religions found in their area through visits to local religious communities and subsequent reflection on these visits. The second method offers more extended experiential learning through service in these religious communities and reflection on this service-learning in papers and group presentations.

## Learning about and from Religious Others

Learning about world religions in the classical way, using textbooks and "objective" approaches to these religions, is good. However, as this book makes clear, it is better to learn not only *about* these religions but also *from* these religions and their adherents. One can do this by being attentive to the different possible approaches to world religions—both outsider and insider. Another strategy consists of becoming aware of how one's background can affect one's view of other religions and the terminology one uses. A dialogue between outsiders and insiders can show not only how adherents of other religions see their own tradition differently than do outsiders but also how outsider perceptions are often shaped by Western, often Christian, influences (including the term *world religions* itself). For this reason, it makes sense to include comparative theological perspectives as well. Finally, an exploration of other religions can be even more fruitful if it includes experiential learning. Listening to or even doing service in communities of religious others is another way to learn not only about them but also from them.

# PART 1: JUDAISM

*Philip A. Cunningham and Jan Katzew*

# CHAPTER 1

# An Outsider's Perspective

*Philip A. Cunningham*

## An Overview of Christian Approaches to Judaism

The relationship between Christianity and Judaism is unique among pairings of world religions. Of course, each bilateral interrelationship has its own distinctive features and "chemistry," but from a Christian perspective it is impossible to teach or express the Christian faith without referring to Judaism. This is true of no other religious heritage with which Christianity interacts.

### A Uniquely Intertwined Interreligious Relationship

The unparalleled interlacing of Judaism and Christianity is due to the following facts: (1) Jesus of Nazareth and the members of the earliest churches were all Jews of the late Second Temple period;[1] (2) the Christian biblical canon includes what came to be known as the "Old Testament," which more or less corresponds, though in a different order and based on different textual traditions, to the Jewish sacred scriptures: the Torah, the Prophets, and the Writings; and (3) fundamental Christian theological concepts are Jewish in origin and continue to be central to Jewish self-understanding (e.g., belief in the existence of one God, who created the world, a personal God who responds to prayer and enters into covenants of mutual responsibilities with people).

Thus, the church's relationship to Judaism is unique because it viscerally shapes Christian self-understanding. Pope John Paul II put it this way:

> [T]he Church of Christ discovers her "bond" with Judaism by "searching into her own mystery." . . . The Jewish religion is not "extrinsic" to us, but in a certain way is "intrinsic" to our own religion. With Judaism therefore we have a relationship which we do not have with any other religion. You are our dearly beloved brothers and, in a certain way, it could be said that you are our elder brothers.[2]

---

1. The late Second Temple period refers to the final decades in which the postexilic Temple in Jerusalem stood. For our purposes here, the period is defined as beginning with the start of Herod the Great's massive expansion of the Temple in 20 BCE and ending with the Temple's destruction by Roman legions in 70 CE during the first Jewish revolt against Roman rule. The terms BCE and CE (Before the Common Era and the Common Era) are widely used to delineate time periods without presuming Christian faith.

2. "Address at the Great Synagogue of Rome," April 13, 1986, §4: *ccjr.us/dialogika-resources/documents-and-statements/roman-catholic/pope-john-paul-ii/305-jp2-86apr13*. (The Christian author of this chapter is Catholic and will write about Judaism from that vantage point. Consequently, there will be citation of some pertinent Catholic documents.)

## A Conflictual Relationship

A negative and demeaning stance toward Jews and Judaism has prevailed for most of Christian history. This was not a theological inevitability, but the result of social forces.

As Christianity struggled for acceptance in the Roman Empire in the second and third centuries, it found itself negatively compared with venerable Judaism by Roman intellectuals. Christians found themselves having to defend their claims that God's promises to the people of Israel had come to fruition in the church by using Jewish scriptures as proof-texts. Since Jews could credibly assert they understood their own sacred writings better than the (mostly) former pagans who constituted Christianity, Christians had to demean Judaism in order to assert their own legitimacy. Thus from very early on, Christians universally argued they had replaced or superseded Jews as the people of God. They declared that God had cursed the Jewish people for their alleged rejection and crucifixion of Jesus. As a result, Jews were supposedly doomed to homeless wandering and shackled by a mindlessly legalistic and heartless religion.

The influence of this "supersessionism" or "theology of replacement" has been both enduring and pervasive. Biblically, for instance, Christians came to call the scriptures of ancient Israel the "Old Testament," whose single purpose was understood to prepare for and be superseded by the "New Testament." Judaism, after the coming of Christ, was thought to be obsolete.

This perspective dismissed as irrelevant the major transformation that the living tradition of Judaism underwent in the centuries after the demolition of the Jerusalem Temple by the Romans in 70 CE. Jewish scholars called rabbis refocused biblical Judaism away from the sacrificial rituals of the Temple and onto the observance of the commandments.

While few Christians today subscribe to the notion that Jews are divinely accursed, many Christians consciously or unconsciously assume they can know everything important about Judaism either by reading the Christian Old Testament or what the New Testament says about Jews. Living Judaism that has developed out of the work of the ancient rabbis escapes the horizons of Christians with such attitudes.

To really understand today's Judaism, therefore, Christians "must strive to learn by what essential traits Jews define themselves in the light of their own religious experience."[3] They must dialogue with Jews in order to learn about Judaism "from the inside," as it were. But in addition to respecting the other's perspective, inevitably participants in dialogue will also try to relate what they're learning about the other to their own frameworks and categories, otherwise the new knowledge could be so foreign as to be incomprehensible. Interreligious dialogue, in other words, is a dialectical activity between different frames of reference.

Following these principles, part 1 on Judaism begins with a chapter written by a Christian who has participated in numerous dialogues with Jews. Chapter 1 introduces Judaism to readers using Christian categories but aims to accurately represent Jewish self-understanding, even if with different emphases and nuances than Jews themselves might employ. Chapter 2 is written by a member of the Jewish community who has participated in numerous dialogues with Christians. He will respond to this chapter from that perspective. In chapter 3, both authors will present selected texts to illustrate core aspects of the Jewish tradition and will offer their respective comments on them. In conclusion, the two writers will discuss their respective sections.

---

3. Pontifical Commission for Religious Relations with the Jews, *Guidelines and Suggestions for Implementing the Conciliar Declaration "Nostra Aetate," No. 4* (1974), preamble, *ccjr.us/dialogika-resources/documents-and-statements/roman-catholic/vatican-curia/277-guidelines.*

# Distinctive Features of Judaism

## A Peoplehood

Jews understand their community as more than a "religious" one: "In dialogue with Christians, Jews have explained that they do not consider themselves as a church, a sect, or a denomination, as is the case among Christian communities, but rather as a peoplehood that is not solely racial, ethnic or religious, but in a sense a composite of all these."[4] Christians conversing with Jews for the first time may be startled to learn that an individual Jew can deny the existence of God and yet be considered a full member of the Jewish community. They may be considered by more pious Jews as not very "good" Jews, but since being accounted a part of the People of Israel is determined primarily by having been born and raised within the Jewish community, idiosyncratic beliefs do not alter that fundamental Jewish identity. Likewise, rabbinic Judaism generally tends to be more concerned with orthopraxy (correct behavior) than orthodoxy (correct belief).

## God Is One

Nevertheless, during the long evolution of Jewish culture certain religious concepts have remained normative for most Jews. Probably foremost among these is the concept expressed in Judaism's central proclamation, the Shema (named for its first word in Hebrew): "Hear, O Israel! The Lord is our God, the Lord alone [or is one or unique]" (Deut. 6:4).[5] In the Bible these words are followed by several commands that highlight their significance:

A *mezuzah* is a small box containing the words of two paragraphs of the Shema (Deuteronomy 6:4–9 and Deuteronomy 11:13–21) handwritten by a scribe. The biblical passages include the instructions to place God's commandments (mitzvot) on the doorframes of Jewish homes.

Impress them upon your children. Recite them when you stay at home and when you are away, when you lie down and when you get up. Bind them as a sign on your hand and let them serve as a symbol on your forehead; inscribe them on the doorposts of your house and on your gates. (Deut. 6:7–8)

Today, observant Jews recite the Shema twice each day, usually around sunrise and sunset. It is ideally a Jew's dying utterance and is always present in formal liturgical worship. The text of the Shema and related words are placed in small containers

---

4. National Conference of Catholic Bishops, *Statement on Catholic-Jewish Relations*, 1975, *ccjr.us/dialogika-resources/documents-and-statements/roman-catholic/us-conference-of-catholic-bishops/479-nccb1975*.

5. All biblical citations are taken from *Tanakh: A New Translation of the Holy Scriptures according to the Traditional Hebrew Text* (Philadelphia: Jewish Publication Society, 1985).

called *mezuzoth*, which are mounted on the door-frames of Jewish homes. They are also found in little cases affixed with straps called phylacteries, which are wound around the arms and foreheads of traditionally observant Jews as they pray.

Given the centrality of the Shema, it is a good place to begin an introduction to Judaism. The Hebrew word translated above as "Lord" is the Israelite holy name of God. It is derived from God's statement to Moses, which emanated from a burning bush: "And God said to Moses, 'Ehyeh-Asher-Ehyeh.' Thus you shall say to the Israelites Ehyeh sent me to you" (Exod. 3:14). The Hebrew words, meaning "I AM or I Will Be," are the basis of four Hebrew letters transliterated into English as Yhwh. Out of respect for the sacredness of God's name, Jews do not speak it. Instead, they use circumlocutions such as "the Lord" or "the Name."

The Lord is the one God of the children of Israel, the biblical patriarch first known as Jacob and later as Israel (which means in Hebrew "to grapple or wrestle with God"; see Gen. 32:23–33). The Lord is both unique—without any rival deities or powers—and indivisible. As such, the Lord is far beyond the capacities of human beings to fully grasp. Indeed, from the Jewish perspective, humans are able to know only what God has chosen to reveal to them.

Jews understand that their ancestors received a special gift of the Lord's revelation after being rescued by God from slavery in Egypt. The Torah, the "Teaching" given to Moses, says that the Lord entered into a covenant with the people of Israel at Mount Sinai (see Exod. 19-24). The Lord would be their God and they would be the Lord's people. The children of Israel understood that they should respond with gratitude for this special relationship with the Lord by seeking to observe the commandments (mitzvot) set forth in the Torah. (*Torah* narrowly refers to the first five books of the Bible [Genesis, Exodus, Leviticus, Numbers, Deuteronomy], more broadly it refers to all the biblical books, and most broadly to the scriptures and later rabbinic commentaries on them.)

A distinction is important here. Down through history, some Christian polemicists alleged that Jews were legalistically fixated on observing the commandments in a futile effort to earn divine favor. The reality is rather the reverse: in response to having been chosen by God for a covenant of mutual responsibilities and ethical imperatives, Jews interpret and seek to comply with God's will as expressed in the mitzvot.

## Jewish Messianic Expectations

The concept of a messianic age is a distinctively Jewish contribution to religious thought. The Hebrew word *mashiach,* anglicized as "messiah," means "anointed one." In biblical times, it referred to anyone appointed by God to fulfill a specific mission or role. Thus, Temple priests were anointed as such, and monarchs in the line of David were anointed kings of the Israelites. The Bible calls the Persian emperor Cyrus "God's *mashiach*" because he permitted the Jewish exiles in Babylon to return home to Judah (Isa. 45:1).

In the late Second Temple period, some Jews anticipated that God would send angelic or human agent(s) to rescue the people of Israel from foreign domination and establish peace and justice in the world. These expectations were quite varied, but there is little to no evidence that any Jews speculated about a suffering agent of God until followers of Jesus of Nazareth began to think in such terms in the first century CE.[6]

---

6. When the followers of Jesus became convinced that the Crucified One had been raised from death, they tried to understand its meaning. Being Jewish, they naturally consulted Israel's scriptures. They were particularly intrigued by Psalm 22 and passages in Isaiah that came to be called the suffering servant songs (Isa. 42:1–9; 49:1–13; 50:4–9; and 52:13–53:12). These texts discuss the fate and significance of the suffering of the righteous. Christians drew on these passages to explain the life, death, and resurrection of Jesus and so linked "messiah" and "suffering" together.

Today, all Jewish movements look hopefully toward an Age to Come in which God's peace and justice will reign. More traditional Jews understand that this new world will be somehow heralded by God's messiah or anointed agent, while more liberal Jews tend to think only in terms of a "messianic age."[7]

## The Land of Israel

Some Jews greeted the establishment of the modern State of Israel in 1948 as the unexpected healing of centuries of exile and dispersion. Part of the biblical covenant was the belief that the children of Israel would live in peace in the Land of Israel. Indeed, life on the Land can be visualized as one point on a triangular diagram of the covenantal relationship, with God and the children of Israel at the other two points. The loss of self-rule in the Land was typically seen as evidence that all was not well with Israel's relationship with God. The long years with no Jewish homeland (although Jews continued to live in the Land under others' rule) seemed to Jews everywhere a kind of exile: something seemed viscerally wrong with this picture.

The sudden resurgence of a Jewish homeland in ancient Jewish territories, especially after the horrific devastation of the Shoah, or Holocaust,[8] seemed to some Jews as evidence of divine intervention, even though many Orthodox Jews opposed the founding of the State of Israel as premature before the clear arrival of the messiah. Rabbi Henry Siegman has observed that

> The State of Israel is the result not only of modern forces of nationalism, or even of the persecution of the Jew. It is that to be sure, but it is above all a consequence of an inner need, a positive impulse working within Jewish life and history. It is the actualization of a quest for authenticity, the incarnation of the Jewish burden of otherness. The Jew is driven by a force as old as the Bible to reunite with the Land. The importance of this "internal" significance of Israel is one which Christians (and Jews) often fail to grasp.[9]

There can be no denying the importance of the Land of Israel for Jewish self-understanding. The well-being of a Jewish homeland shapes Jews' sense of security around the world. However, Jews and others do not agree about whether or how to connect biblical land promises with the existence of a nation-state in the very different geopolitical world of today.

---

7. Note these interesting statements in two Vatican documents: "[I]n underlining the eschatological [unfinished] dimension of Christianity we shall reach a greater awareness that the people of God of the Old and the New Testament are tending towards a like end in the future: the coming or return of the Messiah even if they start from two different points of view. It is more clearly understood that the person of the Messiah is not only a point of division for the people of God but also a point of convergence. . . . Thus it can be said that Jews and Christians meet in a comparable hope, grounded on the same promise made to Abraham (Gen.12:1–3; Heb. 6:13–18)"; Pontifical Commission for Religious Relations with the Jews, "Notes on the Correct Way to Present Jews and Judaism in Preaching and Catechesis in the Roman Catholic Church" (1985), II, 10, *ccjr. us/dialogika-resources/documents-and-statements/roman-catholic/vatican-curia/234-notes*. Also, "Jewish messianic expectation is not in vain. It can become for us Christians a powerful stimulus to keep alive the eschatological dimension of our faith. Like them, we too live in expectation. The difference is that for us the One who is to come will have the traits of the Jesus who has already come and is already present and active among us"; Pontifical Biblical Commission, *The Jewish People and Their Sacred Scriptures in the Christian Bible* (2001), II,A,5 - §21, *ccjr.us/dialogika-resources/documents-and-statements/roman-catholic/ vatican-curia/282-pbc-2001*.

8. Biblically, a "holocaust" is the burning of an animal sacrificed to God in prayer, which seems a grotesque way to refer to the Nazi genocide of Jews. Therefore, the Hebrew term *Shoah*, a devastating whirlwind, is often used instead.

9. Henry Siegman, "Ten Years of Catholic-Jewish Relations: A Reassessment," in the International Catholic-Jewish Liaison Committee's *Fifteen Years of Catholic-Jewish Dialogue, 1970–1985: Selected Papers* (Vatican City: Libreria Editrice Vaticana, 1988), 34.

© Josh Rinehults / iStockphoto.com

The existence of the modern nation-state of Israel in the aftermath of the Second World War has become integral to Jewish identity throughout the world.

How "God's design" for the permanence of the children of Israel relates to the rejection of any religious interpretation of the existence of the State of Israel remains unclear. Or to put it another way, just how the centrality of the Land of Israel for Jews bears on the modern nation-state of Israel according to current international law will likely remain a major topic in the ongoing dialogue among Jews as well as in interreligious dialogue with non-Jews.

The Pontifical Commission for Religious Relations with the Jews has expressed this uncertainty in this way:

Christians are invited to understand [Jewish] religious attachment [to the Land of Israel] which finds its roots in Biblical tradition, without however making their own any particular religious interpretation of this relationship. The existence of the State of Israel and its political options should be envisaged not in a perspective which is in itself religious, but in their reference to the common principles of international law. The permanence of Israel (while so many ancient peoples have disappeared without trace) is a historic fact and a sign to be interpreted within God's design.[10]

## Rabbinic Judaism: Grappling with God

As noted, the Roman destruction of the Temple in Jerusalem in 70 CE made it necessary for Jews to adapt to the loss of the central locus of their religious life. This adaptation occurred through the work of teachers known as "rabbis," who were probably somewhat indebted to the traditions of the earlier Pharisees mentioned in the New Testament. The Pharisees were a Jewish movement with some diversity of views, but they all seem to have interpreted oral "traditions of the elders" to encourage Jews to observe Temple purity practices even when not in its environs. For instance, wherever Pharisees gathered at fellowship meals, they observed the ritual purity norms required for entry to the courts of the Temple in Jerusalem. Through such practices, they reasoned, all life could be made holy. This orientation well positioned the Pharisees to begin to cope with the loss of the Temple. Even after the Temple's demise, holiness

---

10. Vatican, "Notes" (1985), VI, 25.

did not need to vanish from the world. Through study and observance of the Torah, Jews could become a nation of priests, a holy people. The rabbis venerated even those commands that were impossible to fulfill without the Temple and lauded their study. The early rabbis began putting their oral traditions into writing. The first and foundational written text was the Mishnah ("review" or "study"), assembled around 200 CE, which presents debates and discussions about living according to several categories of biblical commandments. In general terms, its six major sections consider the Torah's commands concerning agriculture, the Sabbath and festivals, marriage and divorce, civil and criminal litigation, sacrificial rites and dietary norms, and ritual purity. Commentaries on the Mishnah over the next few centuries were compiled into two editions of the Talmud ("Instruction" or "Learning"), one prepared in Palestine around 350 CE and the larger prepared in Babylon around 500 CE. This creative work ultimately defined "Rabbinic

Judaism"—a home-centered, prayerful dedication to the biblical commandments and the performance of good works. These rabbinic texts as variously interpreted and applied have set the pace for Judaism and its various movements down to the present day.

As noted, Jewish dedication to observe the Torah is not a robotic act of literalistic mindlessness. A hallmark of Rabbinic Judaism is the awareness that written texts must always be interpreted. No written text can explicitly answer every imaginable question that succeeding generations of readers will bring to it. Thus the rabbis debate with one another about the best understandings of sacred texts, seeing this disputational discourse as true to the very name "Israel"—to grapple with God. In the Talmud and in later writings, generations of sages have conversed with one another across the centuries in a constant "grappling with God" to understand the divine will. The rabbis wrote in two general styles: halakhah, which explores various

The Temple in Jerusalem shortly before its destruction by Roman armies in 70 CE. In the years after its ruin, the rabbis sought to spread holiness among the Jewish people by encouraging the study of the Torah, the offering of prayers, and the performance of the mitzvot.

legal interpretations for proper Torah obser-vance and aggadah, which is a story, legend, or anecdote to make religious or legal points. In the present day, too, the various movements within Judaism will issue responsa, which are responses to contemporary questions that draw upon the wisdom of this tradition of discussion. Debating the interpretation and meaning of sacred texts, then, has become a defining characteristic of Rabbinic Judaism that continues today.

## Forms of Modern Judaism

As the work of the rabbis demonstrates, Juda-ism's covenantal relationship with God has had different expressions over time. In addition to the different periods in biblical Israel's history, there was the tectonic shift from Temple-centered late–Second Temple Judaism to the gradual development of Rabbinic Judaism into a Torah-based, family-centered, prayerful, and delibera-tive approach to maintaining Jewish observance, identity, and solidarity.

This living process of adaptation contin-ued into modern times as Jews and other reli-gious communities in the West responded to the European Enlightenment and its philosophical and political consequences. The rise of liberal democracies in which Jews could in principle escape from the ghetto[11] and theoretically par-ticipate in society as equal citizens brought new challenges and questions.[12]

Without going into the historical details, with the arrival of more liberal forms of govern-ment founded on principles of human rights,

liberal streams of Judaism also arose. In the United States, Reform Judaism was the way of being Jewish that most fully used scientific meth-ods to study the historical and literary contexts of biblical texts. Reform Jews, therefore, generally do not subscribe to the traditional view that God dictated the Torah to Moses. Rather, the Torah was seen to have emerged from within the history of the people of Israel over time. Early Reform Judaism was especially notable for dispensing with Hebrew in favor of vernacular during wor-ship. The use of art and music, which echoed the practice of Christian neighbors, was also in evidence in Reform liturgies. To varying degrees, some Reform Jews questioned Torah commands that seemed more at home in ancient agricultural societies than in the modern world. For example, should rabbinic rules regarding the distance one could walk to synagogue on the Sabbath before it became prohibited labor prevail in a world in which one could drive a car to the synagogue without breaking a sweat? Or should certain food restrictions that developed in cultures unfamiliar with germs hold sway in today's world of pas-teurization and adequate cooking?

Grappling with such questions, Orthodox Judaism maintained that Moses received the Torah—the written Torah and the oral Torah—directly from God, who ensured that this teach-ing was faithfully transmitted down the centuries to rabbinic scribes. Therefore, the Mishnah and Talmud together with the codes of religious practice they engendered, such as the *Shulchan Arukh* (*The Set Table,* by Joseph Karo in the six-teenth century), have decisive authority in shap-ing the life of Orthodox Jews. Within Jewish

---

11. Beginning in 1555, popes, bishops, and other Christian leaders in Europe inaugurated a practice of confining Jews to walled neighborhoods called ghettos. Often locked at night, Jews so confined lived in overcrowded and unhealthy conditions. For the first papal decree concerning ghettos, see Pope Paul IV, *Cum Nimis Absurdum,* July 14, 1555, *ccjr.us/dialogika-resources/primary-texts-from-the-history-of-the-relationship/274-paul-iv.*

12. The qualifiers "in principle" and "theoretically" are used to recognize that anti-Semitism remained a potent force even in liberal democracies. While this has weakened particularly after the Shoah, animus toward Jews still resurges under certain circumstances.

Orthodoxy, there is a spectrum of views ranging from those of the modern Orthodox, who participate fully in contemporary society while maintaining Torah observance, to various groups of Chasidic Jews (*chasid* means "pious one"), who live apart and dress distinctively.

Sometimes seen as a middle road between Reform and Orthodox Judaism, Conservative or Masorti ("Traditional") Judaism is better understood as a strand of contemporary Judaism that sees the observance of the commandments as evolving and open to multiple legal (or halakhic) approaches. The Torah, for example, is understood as God's self-disclosure even if expressed by inspired people in human language. The rabbinic tradition is more authoritative for Conservative Jews than for Reform Jews, although the former feel authorized to adapt the mitzvot to changing times after careful consideration. Thus, both Reform and Conservative Jews now ordain women as rabbis. On the other hand, the use of Hebrew in Conservative worship is just as normative as for the Orthodox community.

These movements should be understood as a spectrum of approaches to living the Jewish faith today and not as static or fixed categories. Becoming more aware of the danger of assimilating into the larger society, which could result in a loss of Jewish identity, Reform Judaism is using Hebrew in community liturgies much more today than in the "classical" Reform period of the nineteenth and early twentieth centuries. In some places, it is difficult to distinguish between Reform and Conservative congregations.

Another movement called Reconstructionist Judaism developed in the United States in the 1920s–1940s. It tends to maintain Jewish traditional practices, but not for traditional reasons. Rather than seeing the Torah as God's gift to the children of Israel, Reconstructionist Jews understand it as the Jewish people's response to God's presence in all of creation. Thus the commandments or mitzvot are constructs of the Jewish people, but they should be observed because they are a systematic response to God's desire for people to be holy.

Christians and other non-Jews might see this diversity within Judaism today as contiguous with the diverse Judaisms of previous eras and evidence of Judaism's vitality and adaptability. It is important to recall that Judaism is both a "religion" and a "peoplehood." Therefore, the sense of communal responsibility and identity remains strong even among Jews for whom faith in God is unimportant and who do not formally participate in the religious practices of any of the Jewish movements.

## Humanity in God's Image

Both Judaism and Christianity recognize the One God as the Creator who creates and sustains all things. Both also strongly embrace the biblical perspective that human beings are made in the image and likeness of God (Gen. 1:26–27). In fact, this axiom is the foundation of much of the ethical thought in both traditions.

Judaism and Christianity differ significantly, however, in their respective "theological anthropologies," or how they each conceive of the relationship between God's goodness and humanity's ability to sin. The idea of a primordial Fall as the primary cause of human sinfulness, based on a certain reading of Genesis 2–3, is far less prominent in Judaism than in Christianity.

Postbiblical Judaism instead sees human behavior as resulting from the tension between two conflicting "tendencies" within each human person: the *yetzer hatov* (literally, the inclination to good) and the *yetzer hara* (literally, the inclination to evil). But the meanings of these Hebrew phrases are more subtle than literal renderings suggest.

The *yetzer hara* is better understood as the impulse to satisfy personal needs, to achieve one's desires. Without such ambition, people would not be driven to eat, build or innovate, succeed or excel. In discussing Genesis 1:31 ("And God looked at everything he had made, and found it very good"), a rabbinic commentator observed, "'good' refers to the *yetzer hatov*, but 'very good' refers to the *yetzer hara*. Why? Because were it not for the *yetzer hara* no one would build a house, take a wife, give birth, or engage in commerce."[13]

But since unrestrained ambition leads to evil deeds, it is the function of the *yetzer hatov* to channel it into constructive purposes. Rabbinic tradition sees children as lacking the impulse to good. Therefore, they need parental restriction on their desires until puberty when the *yetzer hatov* becomes active within them. For Jewish children, this coincides with their initiation into adulthood and their commitment to living according to the Torah, which enhances their inclination to the good.[14]

Thus, Judaism sees no need for a savior to rescue people from a fallen state of wretchedness. Rather, people must learn to balance their ambitions with their moral sense. The study of the Torah guides Jews in pursuing this ethical equilibrium.

## Jewish Liturgical Life

The most important holy day for Jews is the weekly observance of the Sabbath (*shabbat*). The creation narrative at the start of the book of Genesis ends as follows: "The heaven and the earth were finished, and all their array. On the seventh day God finished the work that He had been doing, and He ceased on the seventh day from all the work that he had done. And God blessed the seventh day and declared it holy, because on it God ceased from all the work of creation that He had done" (Gen. 2:1–3).

Thus, the Jewish seventh day, the Sabbath, which runs from sundown Friday to sundown Saturday, is to be set apart from the other days. On the Sabbath, Jews are to avoid everyday labor and devote themselves to prayer and reflection on the Torah. The Sabbath also anticipates the ultimate destiny of all things, the Age to Come (*olam haba*), when the peace and just rule of God will embrace all creation.

Formal Jewish congregational life also has an annual cycle of worship, which, for many Jews, proceeds through the entire text of the five books of the Torah in weekly portions. This annual cycle of biblical readings begins and ends in the early autumn with the festival of Simchat Torah (Torah Rejoicing). On this day the beginning of the book of Genesis and the conclusion of the book of Deuteronomy are read aloud. Then as the months pass, a series of major and minor holy days unfolds.

The Jewish liturgical year is based upon a lunar calendar, which requires an additional thirteenth month seven times in nineteen years to coordinate with the seasons and the solar calendar. Thus, Jewish feasts do not occur on the same day, or even necessarily within the same month, as the days on the standard solar calendar. The most important annual holy days in the Jewish liturgical year are as follows:

**Rosh Hashanah.** This holy day, which marks the start of the Jewish New Year, is the beginning of a ten-day period of reflection on the past year, known as the Days of Awe or the High Holy Days. This self-reflection then leads to repentance and prayers for the forgiveness of sins.

**Yom Kippur.** Also called the Day of Atonement, Yom Kippur is the most solemn day of the

---

13. *Genesis Rabbah*, IX, 7.

14. For more on this point, see *myjewishlearning.com/life/Life_Events/BarBat_Mitzvah/About_BarBat_Mitzvah/Age_Requirement/Good_Inclination.shtml.*

© ChameleonsEye / Shutterstock.com

A Jewish family sets up a sukkah, or tent, to celebrate the autumnal harvest festival of Sukkot.

Jewish year. The day is spent in prayer and fasting, with promises to God for future good deeds and reconciliation with fellow human beings. This holy day concludes the ten-day period of repentance known as the High Holy Days, which are celebrated in September or October.

**Sukkot (Festival of Booths).** During this autumn harvest festival, Jews eat their meals in a tent or *sukkah*, a temporary outside dwelling they build for the occasion.

**Pesach (Passover).** Celebrated in March or April, this holy day recalls the Exodus of the Israelites from slavery in Egypt. The most important event is the Seder, when the story of the Exodus is retold and foods are served that symbolize aspects of the flight from Egypt, most notably the unleavened bread or *matzah*.

**Shavuot (Festival of Weeks).** Held in May or June, and also known as Pentecost, this festival commemorates the end of the early grain harvest and Moses' receiving of the Torah on Mount Sinai.

These major holy days are accompanied by minor observances, including Simchat Torah mentioned above. Hanukkah, the festival of lights in December, marks the rededication of the Temple in Jerusalem after it had been captured by a Syrian king in the second century BCE. Tisha B'Av is a summertime commemoration of the destruction of both the First Temple (by the Babylonians) and the Second Temple (by the Romans).

## From Contempt to Fellowship

Tragically, and probably because of their organic connections, the history of relations between Christians and Jews has been mostly antagonistic. In the early centuries of the church's existence,

Christian leaders had to defend themselves against unflattering comparisons with venerable and frequently admired Judaism. In fact, some voices in the Roman intelligentsia challenged the very existence of Christianity by demanding to know why Christians, who acknowledged the divine inspiration of the Jewish scriptures by including them in their own sacred canon, did not themselves keep the commandments given in the Torah by God.[15] Such critics derided the church as a superstitious mutation of Judaism.

In response, Christian apologists sought to delegitimize the Judaism against which the church was being invidiously contrasted. Using contemporary rhetorical customs, they claimed that Jews, who had in the past been God's special people, no longer enjoyed that status, having been replaced or superseded by Christians. Drawing upon certain New Testament passages such as Matthew 27:25, these Christian leaders argued that the crucifixion of Jesus in Jerusalem had brought a divine curse upon Jews, as manifested by the destruction of the Jerusalem Temple. Moreover, they insisted that Jewish observance of the commands of the Torah was a stubborn clinging to archaic customs because the "Law of Moses" had been replaced by the universal command of Christ to love one another. This argument was supported by out-of-context readings of the New Testament letters written by Paul of Tarsus. His words about whether Gentiles joining the early churches should be required to take on full Torah observance were construed to suggest that Jews were myopically fixated on legalistic efforts to obey commands that no human being could entirely fulfill.

This basic orientation toward Jews and Judaism is today named "supersessionism," meaning that its various theological assertions are premised on the conviction that Christians have superseded Jews as God's people because of the crucifixion of Jesus, therefore making post–New Testament Rabbinic Judaism obsolete and misguided. This decisive negative stance toward Judaism developed when Christianity was inferior and weak, but it became a fixed perspective in the Christian imagination—not critiqued until the twentieth century—when the relative social status of Judaism and Christianity was reversed in the Roman Empire. After Christianity became the preferred imperial religion in the fourth and fifth centuries, it began to use its newfound legal power to weaken its Jewish rival's influence in Roman society.

Supersessionism thus became embedded in Christianity and contributed to the marginalization of Jews in the European "Christendom" that emerged after the collapse of the western Roman Empire. A certain ambivalence toward Jews prevailed in medieval Europe. While Judaism was tolerated and not suppressed, unlike all other religions in Europe, Jews were conceived of as homeless "witness people" doomed to inferior status in Christian society.[16]

It would be simplistic to draw a straight line between Christian supersessionism and the Nazi genocide of Jews in World War II. Nevertheless, after the war many Christian churches began to examine the history of anti-Jewish teaching and critiqued supersessionism in a formal and sustained way. An extremely authoritative repudiation of anti-Judaism teaching was issued by

---

15. See, e.g., R. Joseph Hoffmann, *Celsus on the True Doctrine: A Discourse against the Christians* (New York: Oxford University Press, 1987), esp. section III.

16. Augustine of Hippo was very influential in this regard. He applied Psalm 59:11 ("Do not slay them, lest my people be unmindful; with your power make wanderers of them") to Jews—Christians must not kill Jews because in their homelessness they give witness to the fate that befalls unfaithful people. In their dispersion Jews also bring the Old Testament with them, which foretells the coming of Christianity and so prepares pagans for the arrival of Christian missionaries. (See *De Civitate Dei*, ch. 46.)

the Catholic Church during the Second Vatican Council in 1965 when it declared,

> [N]either all Jews indiscriminately at that time [of Jesus], nor Jews today, can be charged with the crimes committed during his passion. It is true that the church is the new people of God, yet the Jews should not be spoken of as rejected or accursed as if this followed from holy scripture. Consequently, all must take care, lest in catechizing [teaching] or in preaching the word of God, they teach anything which is not in accord with the truth of the Gospel message or the spirit of Christ.[17]

Other churches also grappled with past hostile teachings about Jews, according to their own governance structures and procedures. Very notable is the 1994 declaration of the Evangelical Lutheran Church in America, which rejected the anti-Semitic sentiments of Martin Luther:

> In the spirit of [Martin Luther's] truth-telling, we who bear his name and heritage must with pain acknowledge also Luther's anti-Judaic diatribes and the violent recommendations of his later writings against the Jews. As did many of Luther's own companions in the sixteenth century, we reject this violent invective, and yet more do we express our deep and abiding sorrow over its tragic effects on subsequent generations. In concert with the Lutheran World Federation, we particularly deplore the appropriation of Luther's words by modern anti-Semites for the teaching of hatred toward Judaism or toward the Jewish people in our day.[18]

In the decades since World War II, a new relationship based on respect and accurate understanding has begun to grow between the Jewish and Christian communities in many parts of the world. Those involved in interreligious dialogue have had to grapple with long-lived stereotypes and caricatures widespread among both Christians and Jews because the history of hostility between them.

However, because of the developments of the past few decades, Jews and Christians today live in an unprecedented era of collaboration and dialogue. Many involved in building this new relationship draw inspiration from these words of Blessed John Paul II: "As Christians and Jews, following the example of the faith of Abraham, we are called to be a blessing for the world [cf. Gen. 12:2ff]. This is the common task awaiting us. It is therefore necessary for us, Christians and Jews, to be first a blessing to one another."[19]

---

17. Second Vatican Council, *Nostra Aetate*, "Declaration on the Relationship of the Church to Non-Christian Religions," October 28, 1965, §4, *ccjr.us/dialogika-resources/documents-and-statements/roman-catholic/second-vatican-council/293-nostra-aetate*.

18. ELCA Church Council, "Declaration of the Evangelical Lutheran Church in America to the Jewish Community," April 18, 1994, *ccjr.us/dialogika-resources/documents-and-statements/protestant-churches/na/lutheran/676-elca94apr18*.

19. John Paul II, "On the Fiftieth Anniversary of the Warsaw Ghetto Uprising," April 6, 1993, *ccjr.us/dialogika-resources/documents-and-statements/roman-catholic/pope-john-paul-ii/313-jp2-93apr6*.

# CHAPTER 2

# An Insider's Perspective

*Jan Katzew*

## The Universality and Uniqueness of Judaism: An Insider's Perspective

The dialogical format of this book enables the reader to see each religious community from the outside looking in as well as from the inside looking out. In much the same way that history is different from memory, this essay will be selective and intentional, choosing aspects of Judaism that balance its universality and its uniqueness, its ancient roots and its contemporary fruits, and its eternal relevance. The phrase "eternal relevance" is a riposte to Christian supersessionist claims that Judaism has been eclipsed, that its Testament is "Old," and that its theology has become obsolete or anachronistic. Judaism is a living tradition that represents an evolving relationship between a people and God expressed in Torah. Therefore, this essay intends to provoke questions more than to provide answers about Judaism. It aims to challenge some typical operating assumptions with the hope of facilitating a more nuanced and complex understanding of Judaism.

Both the form and the content of this chapter may prove unfamiliar. I write about Judaism Jewishly, inviting readers into a place and a time inhabited by a people that has had to learn to live as a minority, to live as a part of and yet apart from society, and that has suffered too many times as a scapegoat. I am a Reform Jew and a rabbi. Reform Judaism represents one branch on the Tree of Jewish life, a branch dedicated to egalitarianism, to inclusion, to social justice, and to progressive revelation as well as to the shared sacred values of Jewish life: God, Torah, and Israel. A Jew who identifies with Conservative, Orthodox, or Reconstructionist Judaism would likely address the same subjects from a different perspective.[1] I am but one voice in a choir that does not always sing in harmony. As a rabbi, I have accepted the sacred responsibility of being a student and teacher of Torah. I am not a dispassionate observer of Judaism. Rather I am a passionate practitioner of Judaism, who seeks to lead by example. To paint a portrait of Judaism, I will cite some Jewish beliefs and practices that I have chosen not to incorporate into my own life. This struggle is embedded in the very name *Israel*, which means "to wrestle with God."

---

1. Readers can consult *uscj.org* (Conservative), *ou.org* (Orthodox), and *rrc.edu* (Reconstructionist) to learn about these expressions of Judaism from their own sources.

# What Makes Judaism Unique

Judaism began before there were Jews. The moniker *Jew* was never applied directly to Abraham or Sarah (nee Abram and Sarai, respectively) or to any other person in the Pentateuch (hereafter referred to as Torah),[2] but their identities originate Judaism and reverberate through Jewish time. When Abraham met with the Hittite landowners of Canaan in order to bury his wife Sarah, he said, *"ger v'toshav anochi imachem,"* which means, "I am a stranger and a resident among you" (Gen. 23:4).[3] One cannot be both a stranger and a resident, yet that is precisely the dual identity of Abraham and arguably the identity of every Jew since. Rabbi Joseph Baer Soloveitchik (1903–1993), in his classic essay "Confrontation,"[4] wrote about this dialectic, the hybrid identity of a Jew seeking a dynamic equilibrium between otherness and brotherliness, counter-cultural distinctiveness and shared cultural norms.

When the Hebrew word for identity (*zehut*) was coined by Eliezer ben Yehuda in the nineteenth century, it expressed the essence of this balancing act. *Zehut* can be rendered "thisness." What makes this (*zeh*), in this case, Jew, unique? At the same time, *zehut* connotes identity in mathematics, when two sides of an equation are identical (*zehim),* thereby emphasizing the commonality between Jews and other human beings. After thousands of years, Jews are still living out the meaning of being a stranger and a resident, a unique and a universal identity. Where do we Jews diverge from the surrounding culture and where do we converge with it? In the same way that differentiation and integration are related in calculus, so are they related in life. Jews strive to be both apart from and a part of the surrounding culture and society. It is precisely in the province of a both/and dialectic and not in an either/or dichotomy, that the complexity and sanctity of Jewish life is experienced. This dialectic underlies the relationship between Jews, Judaism, and the rest of the world. A Jewish identity is complex, a hybrid composite as social as it is soulful, sometimes biological, frequently cultural, multiethnic, and especially since the advent of the State of Israel in 1948, national. Jews and Judaism defy neat definitions and therein lies an element of Jewish survival.

One manifestation of Judaism's otherness, despite its inclusion in this or any book on world religions, is that Judaism does not neatly fit the definition of a religion. Judaism is a religion, but it is not only a religion. When Ruth turns to her mother-in-law Naomi and pledges her loyalty, she says, *"Ameich Ami, v'Elohayich Elohai,"* meaning "Your people shall be my people, and your God, my God" (Ruth 1:16). To this day, proselytes invoke Ruth's words as a paradigmatic expression of embracing Judaism. It may be difficult to discern from the outside looking in, but from the inside looking out, a Jew is doubly covenanted: to a people and to God.

## Sources

Even before the Temple in Jerusalem was destroyed by the Romans in 70 CE, the authority to define Judaism was transferred from priests to rabbis. Since the rabbis lacked the divine imprimatur of a prophet and the historical authority

---

2. See Zech. 8:23 and Esther 2:5 for explicit examples of the word *Jew* in the Prophets and Writings, respectively.

3. Biblical citations throughout this chapter are taken from *The Torah: A Modern Commentary*, Revised Edition (New York: Union for Reformed Judaism Press, 2005).

4. J.B. Soloveichik, "Confrontation," in *Tradition* 6, no. 2 (1964): 5–9.

© Annie Griffiths Belt / Corbis

Two scholars study and discuss the sacred texts together. This common mode of engaging in Torah study in pairs, called *chevrutah*, meaning "friendship" or "companionship," encourages debate and the bringing of multiple perspectives to the interpretation of texts.

of a priest, they needed to establish a new strategy for defining the scope and depth of their leadership. The rabbis' method of discourse was often dialogical and dialectical; they used it to teach ethical lessons as well as to inform Jewish practice. A famous and trenchant illustration of the rabbinic method involves a prospective proselyte issuing a challenge to the Rabbis Hillel and Shammai: "Teach me Torah while I stand on one leg" (not entirely unlike this essay). Shammai dismissed the questioner as a fool whose question did not justify a substantive response. Hillel responded by saying, "Do not do unto others what you would not have them do to you. That is the whole Torah. The rest is commentary. Go and learn it!"[5] Hillel not only demonstrated the power and presence of a compassionate,

empathic teacher; he also managed to state an enduring Jewish educational principle over and above his timeless ethical teaching. "The rest is commentary, go and learn it" was not only a charge to the questioner but rather a charge to anyone who aspires to understand Judaism. Judaism is a learner-centered tradition and the learner is engaged in a lifelong pursuit of understanding and meaning-making.

To be sure, not all commentary is equal. First among equals is Rabbi Solomon ben Isaac (eleventh century), known with respect and affection as Rashi. The first Jewish book ever printed was the Bible with Rashi's commentary, emblematic of its preeminence in the field of Jewish hermeneutics. Similarly, to this day the Babylonian Talmud is printed with Rashi's commentary on

---

5. Babylonian Talmud, Tractate Eiruvin 13b (slightly adapted) in Seder Moed, vol. 2 (London: Soncino Press, 1935), 85–86.

the inside, closest to the binding, so that it will be preserved and not easily susceptible to wear and tear.

*"Eilu v'eilu divrei Elohim Hayyim"*—"These and those are words of the Living God"[6]—is the quintessential rabbinic statement on pluralism in Jewish thought. Two first-century-BCE schools of Jewish thought are represented by Hillel and Shammai, the paradigmatic dyad (*zug* in Hebrew), who reach different conclusions in the course of adjudicating principles and policies in Jewish practice. While Hillel most frequently wins these debates, Shammai establishes the validity of a minority opinion. By preserving the opinion of Shammai, the rabbis taught that a minority opinion in one case at one time can in another case and time become the majority opinion. Protecting the rights of the minority remains a challenge as we endeavor to learn from the precedent of Hillel and Shammai.

These and those: two conflicting opinions can both have validity. And some conflicting views cannot exist without the other. The phrase *eilu v'eilu*, these and those, emphasizes the incompleteness of any single opinion. The Hebrew letter *vav* that connects "these" to "those" (*eilu* to *eilu*), means "and." This conjunction is essential—uniting and complementing the two opinions without choosing one or compromising the integrity of the other. Even if one of the opinions becomes the standard of practice, both "are the words of the Living God." The debate between Hillel and Shammai is a *machloket l'shem shamayim*, "an enduring dispute in the name of heaven."[7] The sages hastened to note that not all disputes are enduring since not all disputes are for the sake of heaven, and they cite Korah's demagogic challenge of Moses' and

Aaron's leadership (Num. 16:1–40) as a case in point.[8] Nevertheless, there is ample evidence that the *machloket l'shem shamayim* is a recurring leitmotif in the symphony of Jewish thought. From the rabbis of the Talmud to the rabbis of today, principled disputes have ironically preserved and promoted Jewish life.

The Hebrew word for debate is *makhloket*, the root of which is *halek*, which means "part." To begin to understand Judaism from the inside involves accepting the idea that each perspective has a part of the whole truth. We need each other. We need community in order to accept and appreciate our differences. Truth is a mosaic. We each have a vital piece to contribute to that mosaic, yet none of us is self-sufficient. This perspective is elemental to the holy work of dialogue, intra-religious and interreligious, since dialogue is predicated on listening to and learning from, about and with the other in order to cocreate a better world.

## A History of Internal Dialogue and Dialectic: The Tree of Jewish Life

Jewish history per se has not been a Jewish preoccupation. The Passover Haggadah is a text that tells stories of the Jewish people, has thousands of versions, and is used to conduct the single most observed annual Jewish rite, the Seder. By contrast, between *Antiquities of the Jews* by Josephus in the first century and the *History of the Jews* by Heinrich Graetz in the nineteenth century, practically the only Jewish book of Jewish history is *Shevet Yehudah* by Ibn Verga in the

---

6. Ibid.
7. Mishnah Avot 5:19.
8. Ibid.

sixteenth century.[9] The dispassionate, objective pursuit of Jewish history is trumped by the passionate, subjective search for collective Jewish memory. As tendentious and even outrageous as this claim may seem on its face, it helps to reveal one of the salient differences between an outsider's and an insider's view of Judaism. In order to re-member, one must first be a member. Outsiders, so to speak, have tried to understand the "secret" of the Jews' survival. Mark Twain wrote about the Jewish people defying logic and refusing to be consigned to history.[10] But as insiders, Jews are more interested in collective memory.

The history of the Jewish people resembles one of the symbols ascribed to the Torah itself, an *eitz hayyim*, a tree of life. Judaism has adapted and grown new branches over time, especially during the nearly 2,000-year Diaspora when the Jewish people lived without political sovereignty. Some branches, such as Karaites,[11] have withered. Others, for example, Rabbinic Judaism, have grown in length and strength and borne fruit. True to the ironic and humorous aphorism that where there are two Jews there are three opinions, there are multiple contemporary expressions of Judaism. Some see this as a weakness, as evidence of internal strife within the Jewish people, a divisive intra-religious factionalism. However, this same phenomenon can also be seen as a source of strength, since each expression of Judaism is a branch on the tree of Jewish life—providing shade to its adherents

and fruit to its future. Orthodox, Reform, Conservative, and Reconstructionist all modify the noun *Jew*. As long as each of these communities remembers that it represents a part of a holy whole, diversity can be an invaluable asset. Only when one of them thinks and acts as though their part has the whole truth is there cause for serious concern.

The *makhloket,* or dispute, has multiple and powerful expressions in Jewish life. The various streams of Jewish thought and practice reflect different, and at times divergent, understandings of Jewish identity. Jews have never been a monolithic group. For example, at the time of Jesus, Pharisees and Sadducees and Essenes and Zealots offered alternative Jewish voices. This was the religious maelstrom out of which Christianity emerged. Rabbanites and Karaites and Kabbalists dominated at various points during the medieval period. In the last 200 years, especially but not exclusively in North America, the Jewish community has included Ultraorthodox,[12] Orthodox, Reform, Conservative, Reconstructionist, Renewal, and secularist forms.

To this day the Orthodox Jewish community operates on the basis of accepted halakhah, that is, Jewish law as articulated in codes such as Maimonides's *Mishneh Torah* (thirteenth century), Joseph ben Asher's *Arba'ah Turim* (fourteenth century), Joseph Karo's *Shulchan Arukh* (sixteenth century), and Moses Isserles's *Ha-Mapah* (sixteenth century) and further expounded by sages, an honorific title ascribed to the rabbis

9. Yosef Hayim Yerushalmi, *Zakhor: Jewish History and Jewish Memory* (Seattle: University of Washington Press, 1996).

10. Mark Twain, "Concerning the Jews," *Harper's Magazine,* September 1899.

11. The Karaites were a Jewish sect that rejected rabbanite authority and the divine origin of the Oral Torah (Mishna, Tosefta, Talmud) and claimed that the Tanakh (Written Torah) was the sole source of mitzvot—divine commandments. A thousand years ago, the Karaites comprised a significant proportion of the Jewish community. Now, there may be a few hundred Jews who identify as Karaites.

12. This is an uncomfortable designation. The reference is to *haredi* Jews, from the Hebrew word for "tremble/quake/dread." It describes a wide spectrum of Hasidic Jews, a branch of Judaism born in eighteenth-century Poland. For additional information about the founder of Hasidism, see the article on "Israel Baal Shem Tov" on *myjewishlearning.com.*

In Jewish synagogues, the Torah scrolls have a place of honor and prominence. This synagogue is an Orthodox one, as seen by the segregation of men and women in the assembly.

who composed authoritative works in Jewish thought and practice, in subsequent generations. The existence of many codes provides further evidence of the significance of arguments for the sake of heaven. One code may be authoritative for a particular Jewish community whereas another code with seemingly minor differences may be the binding force that unites another. Halakhah incorporates all aspects of Jewish life—social, familial, legal, ethical, ritual, spiritual, medical, educational, and theological. Halakhah is an ever-expanding universe. This halakhic process is a distinguishing if not defining characteristic of Orthodox Judaism.

In the Conservative Jewish community, a Committee on Jewish Law and Standards votes on questions of Jewish practice that emanate from the field. The committee consists of eminent and learned rabbis as well as leading members of the volunteer community who serve in an ex officio capacity. The classical texts used by the Orthodox community also play a role in the deliberations of the Conservative movement's Committee on Jewish Law and Standards. However, in the latter the balance between tradition and innovation is more weighted to modernity. For example, the proscription against driving on the Sabbath is tempered to permit driving to synagogue. Women now serve and lead congregations and communities as rabbis and cantors in the Conservative movement, but not in Orthodoxy. As the twenty-first century began, a divided committee allowed for openly gay and lesbian rabbis and cantors to study at the Jewish Theological Seminary, the primary academic seat of

Conservative Judaism, again in contrast to the practices of Orthodox Judaism. Nevertheless, Conservative Judaism represents itself as an evolving halakhic expression of Judaism.

In the Reform movement, the balance between tradition and innovation often tilts even further in the direction of modernity than in the Conservative movement. In the last generation, after having initiated the rabbinic ordination and cantorial investiture of women, the Reform movement embraced gays and lesbians as full partners in Jewish life. Furthermore, Reform Judaism has long espoused outreach, the warm embrace of intermarried families, and their acceptance into varying aspects of Jewish communal life. Halakhah does play a role in Reform Jewish life, but that role is more of a voice than a veto. Rulings of the Responsa Committee to questions of religious practice are not binding on the Reform Jewish community. They constitute a guide, not a requirement. Autonomy plays a significant and at times dominant role in the life of Reform Jews.

In the mid-twentieth century, Reconstructionist Judaism emerged primarily out of Conservative Judaism. Mordecai Kaplan wrote *Judaism as a Civilization*, which provided the cultural and theological context for an expression of Judaism that rejected chosenness as a fundamental principle and asserted the peoplehood dimension of Jewish life.[13] Peoplehood (*amiut* in Hebrew) prioritizes the secular aspects of Judaism over its sacred and religious dimension. The Reconstructionist prayer book, for example, changes the blessing prior to the reading of the Torah from "the God who has chosen us from among all the peoples" to "the God who has brought us near to divine service." The de-emphasis of Jewish religious particularity and the reemphasis on the ethnic and cultural practices of the Jewish people are emblematic of Reconstructionist Judaism.

The Reconstructionist movement often aligns itself with the Reform movement on issues of inclusion and ideology, such as the roles of women, gays and lesbians, and Zionism, the movement that advocates for Jewish sovereignty in the Land of Israel. However, theologically there are salient differences between the two movements. Reconstructionist Judaism emphasizes a God that is the power that makes for salvation, a force for good rather than a personal, providential deity. The rationale for keeping Jewish customs is therefore based on the folkways that act as a centripetal force on the people of Israel rather than the commanding voice of a transcendent being.

These multiple contemporary expressions of Judaism do not exhaust the extant alternatives, which include Haredi (or Ultraorthodox), Renewal (or neo-Chasidic), as well as a group that has been growing in North America called "just Jewish," which defies altogether the labels and modifiers of the word *Jew*. However, the array of Jewish streams illustrates a living example of *makhloket l'shem shamayim*—a dispute for the sake of heaven—proof that Judaism is alive.

## Conceptions of the Holy: Expressions of Jewish Faith

The preeminent Jewish philosopher, Moses ben Maimon (1135–1204), affectionately known as the Rambam (a moniker arrived at via an acronym) and more dispassionately known as Maimonides, proposed thirteen articles of Jewish

---

13. Mordecai Kaplan, *Judaism as a Civilization: Toward a Reconstruction of American Jewish Life* (Philadelphia: Jewish Publication Society, 1934, repr. 1994).

faith. These have been the source of controversy in Jewish thought.[14]

- The first foundation is the existence of the Creator.
- The second is God's unity.
- The third is the denial of divine corporeality.
- The fourth is God's precedence.
- The fifth is that God, may God be exalted, is the One whom it is proper to worship and to praise.
- The sixth is prophecy.
- The seventh is the superiority of the prophecy of Moses.
- The eighth is that the Torah is from Heaven.
- The ninth is the denial of the Abrogation of the Torah.
- The tenth is that God, may God be exalted, has knowledge of the acts of human beings and is not neglectful of them.
- The eleventh is that God, may God be exalted, rewards one who obeys the commandments and punishes him who violates its prohibitions; and that the greatest of God's rewards is the World to Come while the severest of God's punishments is "being cut off."
- The twelfth is the days of the Messiah, the belief in and the assertion of the truth of the Messiah's coming.
- The thirteenth is the resurrection.[15]

Writing in the twelfth century, Rambam was profoundly influenced by the Muslim milieu in which he lived. There is little, if any historical evidence that he was responding to Christian creedal statements. Other medieval Jewish thinkers proposed their own articles of faith. Still others argued against any such formulation. At various times and in various rites, Rambam's thirteen articles of faith have been included and excluded from the Siddur, the daily prayer book, where they would be read and ideally internalized by the people who used them. They were translated into the verses of a hymn, (Yigdal Elohim Chai), which commonly concludes Jewish worship to this day.[16] Nevertheless, even the great Rambam remained unable to institute a statement of essential belief into regular Jewish practice. As a result, Jews and non-Jews alike have concluded that Judaism is a religion of deed (mitzvot) rather than creed. Yet scholars such as the architect of Conservative Judaism, Solomon Schechter, argue compellingly for the falsity of such a dichotomy. Certainly, Jews have developed a nuanced, rich, and deep system of faith. However, there is no creedal articulation that has been universally accepted by Jewish people as a comprehensive statement of belief.

The Shema proclaims the uniqueness of God and of God's relationship to the people of Israel. It goes on to proclaim the acceptance of God's sovereignty, the authority of the mitzvot, and the remembrance of the Exodus from Egypt. Nevertheless, it falls short of constituting a litmus test for Jewish identity. Indeed, there are differing versions of the Shema and its blessings in the prayer books of the different branches of

---

14. Commentary on Perek Halek; the tenth (or eleventh) chapter of the Tractate Sanhedrin that begins the Mishnah is the only case in rabbinic literature that explicitly provides criteria for Jewish beliefs that lead to salvation. See Menachem Kellner, *Dogma in Jewish Thought* (New York: Oxford University Press, 1986), 10ff.

15. This reference is to bodily resurrection at the *eschaton*, the end of time as we know it. It is a subject of its own as Rambam's critics doubted the sincerity of his own belief in this foundational principle with such force that he responded by composing a special epistle exclusively devoted to this topic.

16. (Yigdal Elohim Chai) ("We praise the living God")—Rabbi Daniel ben Yehudah, thirteenth century.

the Jewish community, attesting to the diversity of belief and opinion.[17]

## Chain of Tradition

The responsibility and authority to interpret Jewish practice is embedded in revelation and an unbroken chain of tradition. "Moses received Torah from God at Sinai. He transmitted it to Joshua, Joshua to the Elders, the Elders to the Prophets, the Prophets to the members of the Great Assembly (the Sanhedrin)."[18] Rabbinic Judaism is predicated on the axiom that Moses received both the Written Torah (consisting of three parts: the Pentateuch, the Prophets, and the Writings) and the Oral Torah (which was eventually written down as two versions of the Talmud: Jerusalem—350 CE, and Babylonian—500 CE).

## Holidays

After the Bible, the Talmud (which contains the Mishnah), and the Siddur (the prayer book), the most significant book of the Jews may be the *luach*, the calendar that determines the rhythm of Jewish time. So powerful is this temporal mode that it trumps the spatial realm. Even the construction of the Tabernacle, the story of a sacred space that takes up a third of the book of Exodus, is adumbrated by the words, "Build Me a tabernacle that I may dwell among them" (25:8). God says, "among them" and not "in it." God lives in people, not in places. This perception has led Jewish thinkers to claim that time, the fourth dimension, transcends space, the third dimension. A prime example of this prioritization is

manifest in the Sabbath Kiddush, or sanctification, generally over wine or grape juice:

> Praise to You, Adonai our God, Sovereign of the Universe who finding favor in us, sanctified us with mitzvot. In love and favor, You made the holy Shabbat our heritage as a reminder of the work of Creation. As first among our sacred days, it recalls the Exodus from Egypt. You chose us and set us apart from the peoples. In love and favor You have given us Your holy Shabbat as an inheritance. Praise to You, Adonai, who sanctifies Shabbat.[19]

The intentional juxtaposition of the Creation and the Exodus, the universal and the particular, reinforces the double rationale for sanctifying time in general and Shabbat in particular. God celebrated the first Shabbat, and therefore, we imitate God when we do so, and God freed the children of Israel from slavery, thereby determining a unique destiny for the Jewish people. This conflation of themes enables the Jews to emphasize universality and uniqueness simultaneously. The first mitzvah (commandment) in the Torah explicitly addressed to the embryonic people of Israel is found in Exodus 12:2: "This month shall mark for you the beginning of the months; it shall be the first of the months for you." This refers to Nisan, the month in which the Exodus from Egypt took place. When the Jewish calendar became fixed nearly 2,000 years ago, Nisan lost its status as the first of the months, and the New Year celebration, Rosh Hashanah, was moved to the beginning of Tishrei, the seventh month according to the Torah.

---

17. For example, in the Reform movement's prayer book, *Mishkan T'filah,* the second paragraph of the Shema (Deut. 11:13–21) is not included, since it reflects a theology that is dissonant with Reform understanding and practice. See *Mishkan T'filah: A Reform Siddur* (New York: CCAR Press, 2007).

18. Mishnah Avot 1:1.

19. *Mishkan T'filah: A Reform Siddur*, 127.

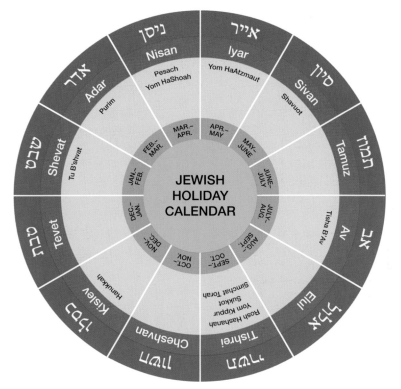

The Jewish liturgical year, showing the rough equivalences of the Jewish lunar months and the Western solar months.

The details of the Jewish calendar are remarkably complex and sophisticated.[20] The Jewish calendar is a solar and lunar hybrid, and as a result, seven times in a nineteen-year cycle a leap year occurs during which Jews add an entire month (second Adar) to the calendar. This intercalation, along with other more subtle adjustments, enables holidays to be celebrated in their appropriate seasons and to preserve the preeminent sanctity of the Sabbath. The sanctification of time is a powerful motif in Jewish life. The most complete holiday calendar in the Bible is contained in Leviticus 23. Shabbat is first among equals, and fittingly it comes first in the catalog of holidays: "On the seventh day, God had completed the work that had been done, ceasing then on the seventh day from all the work that [God] had done, Then God blessed the seventh day and made it holy, and ceased from all the creative work that God [had chosen] to do" (Gen. 2:2–3). Just as God had set aside the Sabbath and sanctified time for all people, so God spoke through Moses to the children of Israel to set aside and sanctify what has become Jewish time. Shabbat is the only holiday included in the *Aseret haDibrot* (often rendered Ten Commandments, but better translated as Ten Utterances).

---

20. See Hayyim Schauss, *The Jewish Festivals: A Guide to Their History and Observance* (New York: Schocken Books, 1996) and Irving Greenberg, *The Jewish Way: Living the Holidays* (New York: Simon and Schuster, 1993).

Next is Passover, the Feast of Matzot, which is connected by a fifty-day sacred tether to Shavuot, the Feast of Weeks. Then comes Rosh Hashanah, the day on which the shofar (the ram's horn) is sounded, followed ten days later by Yom Kippur, the Sabbath of Sabbaths, a day of physical fasting and spiritual feasting. Just five days later begins Sukkot, the Festival of Booths, as a reminder of the booths in which the Israelites lived during their trek from Egypt to Israel. Sukkot concludes with Simchat Torah (the Joy of Torah), when the last verses of Deuteronomy and the first verses of Genesis are read to reify the rabbinic axiom that the Torah is to be turned over again and again for it contains everything within it. Passover, Shavuot, and Sukkot were the three pilgrimage festivals, when people came to Jerusalem to make sacrifices at the Temple. After the Temple's destruction in 70 CE and the resulting dispersion of the Jewish people, the pilgrimage celebrations morphed from agricultural to theological as prayer replaced sacrifice.

The holidays described in the Torah have been supplemented over Jewish time. Tu B'Shvat marks the New Year for trees and serves as a reminder to celebrate the delicate ecological balance that provides us with food and drink. Purim celebrates triumph over an archetypal enemy, Haman, recounted in the book of Esther. Hanukkah celebrates the victory of the Hasmoneans over the Syrian Greeks, recorded in the Apocrypha, and the rededication of the Temple in Jerusalem. Tisha B'Av commemorates a whole series of catastrophes that have beset the Jewish people, starting with the destructions of the first and second Temples. In the twentieth century, two related events, the Holocaust and the founding of the State of Israel, led to the establishment of two holidays that punctuate the Jewish calendar, Yom HaShoah v'HaGevurah (Day of Catastrophe and Heroism) and Yom HaAtzmaut (Day of Independence). Additional minor holidays for fasting and feasting enable Jews to live in Jewish time wherever and whenever they may live.

Food plays a vital role in celebrating and commemorating Jewish time. From the prescribed (e.g., lamb on Passover) and proscribed foods (e.g., birds of prey) in the Bible, to the rabbinic disciplines of separating milk from meat, to the ethnic customs of certain foods being associated with specific holidays (e.g., dairy on Shavuot), law and lore combine to define Jewish practice.

## Prayer

The sages described prayer as *avodah she-balev* (service of the heart), a reference to the understanding that prayer replaced the sacrifices that took place in the Temple in Jerusalem. External manifestations of loyalty to God had become internalized. While prayer can and does take place in individual lives, communal prayer is normative in Jewish life. Indeed, a minyan, a group of ten,[21] is the minimum required to recite certain prayers, including the Kaddish, a doxology often recited in memory of a deceased first-degree relative. The times during the day when Jews pray are linked to the times when sacrifices were made in the Temple (morning, afternoon, and optionally in the evening). The Hebrew word most often translated as "prayer" in English, *tefillah*, comes from the root that means "assess" or "judge." *Tefillah* can be understood as a process of self-assessment, seeking to close the gap between who we are and who we could and should become in the sight of God. Prayer is but

---

21. In Orthodox communities, ten men (above the age of thirteen) are required to constitute a prayer community. In non-Orthodox circles, the ten adults can be either male or female.

one expression of *avodah*, which also includes ritual acts of faith throughout the Jewish year and indeed throughout a Jewish life.

The following excerpt is from the Mishnah, the foundation of Rabbinic Judaism. It is included in daily worship, specifically in the morning prayers:

> These are the things that are limitless,
> Of which a person enjoys the fruit of
>    this world,
> While the principal remains in the world
>    to come.
> They are: honoring one's father and mother,
> Engaging in deeds of compassion,
> Arriving early for study, morning and
>    evening,
> Dealing graciously with guests, visiting
>    the sick,
> Providing for the wedding couple,
> Accompanying the dead for burial,
> Being devoted in prayer,
> And making peace among people.
> But the study of Torah encompasses
>    them all.[22]

This text espouses infinite values, yet it also presents a taxonomy. Talmud Torah, the study of Torah, encompasses all of the previously listed virtues, presumably because study includes action.[23] The values are universal rather than explicitly or exclusively Jewish, yet they emanate from the Torah, the covenant between God and the children of Israel. The values are also humanistic, that is, they are between people, yet their basis is theological, that is, the Torah is a gift from God. This combination is a motif in Jewish thought and indeed in Jewish life. What makes any of the actions mentioned above Jewish are the intention and the contextual basis for their performance. Jews do not own goodness or diligence or piety or kindness or devotion or peace-making acumen. On the contrary, these are universally accessible virtues and abilities. They become Jewish expressions when a Jew consciously acts in consonance with them, especially as a result of Jewish learning. Talmud Torah has multiple meanings. In a narrow sense, it can refer to the study of the Torah, the Pentateuch. In its broadest sense, Talmud Torah can refer to all Jewish wisdom. The elasticity of Talmud Torah has helped to enable Jews and Judaism to survive under duress and to thrive when given the cultural oxygen to be creative.

## Mitzvah

The relationship between the God of Israel, the people of Israel, and the Torah of Israel is succinctly expressed in the blessing recited prior to a public reading of the Torah. "Praised are You, Adonai our God, Sovereign of the Universe, who has chosen us from among the peoples, and given us the Torah. Praised are You, Adonai, who gives the Torah." The Torah is a gift from God, a gift that keeps on giving, a gift that depends on the Jewish people receiving it, most explicitly and publicly on the Festival of Shavuot (Weeks).[24] Both Jews and non-Jews frequently misunderstand the role and the rule of law in Judaism. Mitzvot, divine commandments that are accepted as human obligations, represent the terms of the covenant between God and the Jewish people. According to rabbinic tradition there are 613 mitzvoth, corresponding to 365 negative

---

22. Based on Mishnah Peah 1:1.

23. See Babylonian Talmud Shabbat 40a.

24. The rabbinic name of Shavuot is *z'man matan Torateinu*—"the time of the giving of our Torah"—making it clear that God is the giver and that it is incumbent upon us to be receivers and acceptors of Torah.

A young Jewish woman at her bat mitzvah and a young Jewish man at his bar mitzvah. The reading aloud in Hebrew from the Torah scroll signifies the full entry of the young person into the observances of the commandments (mitzvot).

commandments ("you shall not") and 248 positive commandments ("you shall"). These numbers are hardly arbitrary. The number 365 corresponds to the number of full days in a solar year, and 248 was thought to correspond to the number of bones in a human body. Furthermore, 613 corresponds to the numerical equivalent of the word *Torah* (since Hebrew letters are also numbers): taf (400) plus vav (6) plus resh (200) and hay (5) equals 611, plus two commandments that the entire people of Israel heard at Mount Sinai—the first two according to the Jewish counting of the Ten Commandments—namely, (1) "I am Adonai your God who brought you out of the land of Egypt, out of the house of bondage" (Exod. 20:2), and (2) "You shall have no other gods beside Me" (Exod. 20:3).[25] According to the sages, these two commandments were heard by the children of Israel *mipee haGevurah,* "from God directly."

The commandments relate to every aspect of life—from individual to global, private and public, ritual and ethical. Nevertheless, from the inside looking out, the mitzvot are intended to create a structure, a discipline that gives meaning to life, and not a stricture, an imposition that predetermines human actions. The Talmud teaches that an action performed because it is a mitzvah is held in higher esteem than the same action that is the result of free choice.[26] This is countercultural in a society that venerates free will, but it forms an integral part of the rabbinic worldview. The mitzvot are often subdivided into *bein adam l'chavero* (between human beings—ethical) and *bein adam laMakom* (between a person and God—spiritual) as well as *sikhliot* (those rationally derivable, such as murder and stealing) and *shemiyot* (those heard directly from God, e.g., mixing wool and linen). When a Jewish boy reaches the age of thirteen he becomes Bar Mitzvah (son of the commandment), and thereby, reaches the stage of accepting responsibility and accountability. In non-Orthodox streams of Judaism, this status (Bat Mitzvah—daughter of the commandment) applies to teenage girls as well.

---

25. This counting differs from the Christian understanding that combines these two utterances into a single commandment.

26. Babylonian Talmud Avodah Zarah 3a (among many).

An evening prayer contextualizes the covenantal relationship between God and the Jewish people:

> Everlasting love You offered Your people Israel by teaching us Torah and mitzvot, laws and precepts. Therefore, Adonai our God, when we lie down and when we rise up, we will meditate on Your laws and Your commandments. We will rejoice in your Torah forever. . . . Praise to you, Adonai, who loves Your people forever.[27]

This *chatimah*, closing signature line of a blessing, leads immediately into the Shema, the proclamation of God's singularity:[28] "Hear, O Israel! The Eternal is our God, the Eternal alone." (Deut. 6:4). This declaration is literally surrounded by prayers of love, since it is followed by a paragraph that begins with the words,

> You shall love Adonai your God with all your heart, with all your soul and with all your might. Take to heart these instructions with which I charge you this day. Impress them upon your children. Recite them when you stay home and when you are away, when you lie down and when you get up. Bind them as a sign on your hand and let them serve as a symbol on your forehead; inscribe them on the doorposts of your house and on your gates. (Deut. 6: 5–9)[29]

## Israel—Still Wrestling with God

The State of Israel changed the image of a Jew from powerless to powerful in the eyes of the world including in the eyes of the Jews themselves. The "people of the book," a name given to Jews in the Qur'an, were transformed into the people capable of making the desert bloom. A subject people had become a sovereign people. Rather than waiting for God to give the Land of Israel to the people of Israel, the people of Israel were going back home to reassert their covenantal claim and realize a hope that had been latent for 2,000 years. "So long as within the inmost heart a Jewish spirit sings, so long as the eye looks eastward, gazing toward Zion, our hope is not lost—the hope of two thousand years: to be a free people in our land, the land of Zion and Jerusalem." These lyrics by Naftali Herz Imber became the national anthem of the State of Israel, a hope that did not and will not die.

The relationship between the people of Israel and the Land of Israel is intimate and ultimate. The Hebrew word used to describe the process of moving to Israel in our time and to make pilgrimage to Jerusalem to offer sacrifices in ancient times is the same word used to describe someone called to bless the Torah—*aliyah*, "ascent." The ascent is spiritual and existential, intended to depict a powerful, personal transformation. Similarly, a Jew who decides to make *aliyah*, to move to Israel, is accepted under the *chok hash'vut*, "the law of return." Even a Jew who goes physically to Israel for the first time is considered to be returning home. This characterization defies logic, yet it testifies to the transcendent power of attraction between a people, a land, and God.

The *Declaration of the Establishment of the State of Israel* provides the best articulation of her foundations and aspirations, encompassing the historical, spiritual and political spheres: "Eretz

---

27. Ahavat Olam from *Mishkan T'filah: A Reform Siddur*, 8.

28. Two of the enlarged letters in the Torah scroll are the ayin in the word *Shema* and the dalet in the word *Ehad*. These two consonants spell the word *eid* or "witness," thereby witnessing the unity and uniqueness of God.

29. The sages termed this the acceptance of the yoke of the Sovereignty of Heaven.

Yisrael was the birthplace of the Jewish people. . . . After being forcibly exiled from their land, the people remained faithful to it throughout their dispersion, and never ceased to pray for their return to it and for the restoration in it of their political freedom."[30]

Having established its essential Jewish character, the founders made explicit Israel's fundamental commitment to democracy. Having been in a minority, stateless status for nearly 2,000 years, since the destruction of the Second Temple in Jerusalem, the children of Israel clarified their intention regarding minorities in the State of Israel:

> The State of Israel . . . will foster the development of the country for the benefit of all its inhabitants; it will be based on freedom, justice and peace as envisaged by the prophets of Israel; it will ensure complete equality of social and political rights to all its inhabitants irrespective of religion, race or sex; it will guarantee freedom of religion, conscience, language, education and culture; it will safeguard the Holy Places of all religions.[31]

The *Declaration* concludes with a subtle reference to God, one left purposely ambiguous, allowing for avowedly secular understanding: "Placing our trust in the Rock of Israel,[32] we affix our signatures to this proclamation at this session of the provisional council of state, on the soil of the homeland, in the city of Tel Aviv, on this Sabbath Eve, the 5th day of Iyar 5708 (14 May 1948)."[33]

# Judaism and Christianity in Dialogue

There is a fundamental asymmetry in a Jewish-Christian dialogue—perhaps everywhere outside the State of Israel. There are approximately 13.5 million Jews in the world, and nearly 12 million of them live in either Israel (6 million) or the United States (5.8 million). Only in the State of Israel does the Jewish population constitute a majority. By contrast the American Jewish community represents less than 2 percent of the US population. This demographic reality has profoundly influenced the course of Jewish memory and destiny. Jewish survival is not taken for granted. The lessons of history, ancient and recent, have left indelible impressions on the collective memory of the Jewish people. The Jews have experienced state-sponsored anti-Semitism, exile, expulsion, and genocide. These experiences have left enduring scars and indelible memories. They have fostered a deep sense of distrust in diplomatic rhetoric and a reliance on self-determination. Since the birth of the State of Israel in 1948, the Jewish people have acquired a new image, a new identity, and a return to power. Jews have tried to live with political and military powerlessness but have learned that this combination is untenable in the contemporary world. This effort led, in part, to the nadir of Jewish history, symbolized by the crematoria in Auschwitz-Birkenau. And the murder of 6 million Jews during the Shoah,[34] more widely known as the Holocaust,

---

30. The *Declaration of the Establishment of the State of Israel* (May 14, 1948), official translation from the website of the Israel Ministry of Foreign Affairs (*mfa.gov.il*).

31. Ibid.

32. Israel's *Declaration* does not mention God explicitly. The phrase "Rock of Israel," however, lends itself to this interpretation, as it is one of the rabbinic monikers for the Divine.

33. The *Declaration of the Establishment of the State of Israel* (May 14, 1948) from the website of the Israel Ministry of Foreign Affairs (*mfa.gov.il*).

34. Hebrew for "catastrophe."

will continue to have profound, indeed incalculable, effects on Jewish life. Even as survivors, perpetrators, bystanders, and "up-standers" (an appellation that refers to those people who righteously stood up for justice and against oppression) age and die, there are those who try to erase history and deny truth, claiming the Shoah never occurred or that it has been exaggerated.

*Nostra Aetate* ("In Our Time," 1965), a Roman Catholic document from the Second Vatican Council, a council called by Pope John XXIII and overseen by him until his death in 1963 and then by his successor, Pope Paul VI, profoundly and positively changed the narrative of Catholic-Jewish relations. Two of the leading Jewish thinkers of the twentieth century, Rabbis Joseph Baer Soloveitchik and Abraham Joshua Heschel, chose differing strategies in response to the papal invitation for dialogue. Soloveitchik entitled his definitive article on the subject "Confrontation," in which "the community of the many" (Christians) confronts "the community of the few" (Jews).[35] Soloveitchik focuses on the divergence of the Jewish and Christian communities. He argues that the community of the many cannot impose its theological will on the community of the few, although he leaves room for the community of the few to engage the community of the many, outside of the theological domain, for example in the field of social justice.

Rabbi Heschel decided to accept the invitation and engage in private and public dialogue with representatives of the Catholic Church hierarchy. In May 1962 he responded to Cardinal Augustin Bea's[36] invitation to submit proposals for the document on the Catholic Church and the Jewish people. He submitted a memorandum entitled "On Improving Catholic-Jewish Relations," which in its introduction stated,

> Both Judaism and Christianity share the prophets' belief that God chooses agents through whom His will is made known and his work done throughout history. Both Judaism and Christianity live in the certainty that mankind is in need of ultimate redemption, that God is involved in human history, that in relations between man and man God is at stake, that the humiliation of man is a disgrace of God.[37]

In contrast to Rabbi Soloveitchik, Rabbi Heschel took the convergence of Judaism and Christianity as his point of departure. He emphasized the shared portion of the Venn Diagram, while acknowledging the distinctiveness of both Judaism and Christianity. Rabbi Heschel went on to make four recommendations to improve mutually fruitful relations between the Church and the Jewish community.

1. That the [Vatican] Council brand anti-Semitism as a sin and condemn all false teachings, such as that which holds the Jewish people responsible for the crucifixion of Jesus and sees in every Jew a murderer of Christ.
2. That Jews be recognized as Jews . . . and that the council recognize the integrity and the continuing value of Jews and Judaism.

---

35. Soloveichik, "Confrontation," in *Tradition* 6, no. 2 (1964). The article defies summarizing. Its language is rich, elliptical, and metaphoric. Nevertheless, "Confrontation" is an exceptionally significant statement for anyone who wishes to grapple with the nuances of Jewish-Christian relations.

36. Cardinal Bea was president of the Secretariat for Christian Unity of the Holy See. He had been asked by Pope John XXIII to compose a draft on the relationship between the Catholic Church and the Jewish people for consideration before the Council fathers.

37. *A Memorandum to His Eminence Augustino Cardinal Bea, President, The Secretariat for Christian Unity, May 22, 1962*, by the American Jewish Committee, NY.

3. That Christians be made familiar with Judaism and Jews.

4. That a high-level commission be set up at the Vatican, with the task of erasing prejudice and keeping a watch on Christian-Jewish relations everywhere.[38]

If Rabbi Heschel's perspective on the need for interreligious dialogue could be distilled to a single sentence, it would be one of his own: "No religion is an island since we are all involved with one another."[39] Heschel's thinking profoundly influenced the document that would ultimately emerge from the Vatican, *Nostra Aetate*, and open the door for a Jewish-Christian dialogue that animates this very work.[40]

There was no immediate official Jewish response to *Nostra Aetate*. The Jewish community is not organized around a central hierarchy like the Roman Catholic Church, but this fact alone does not explain the lack of a clear, univocal Jewish response to the outstretched arm of comity extended by the leadership of the Catholic Church. Written documents—even those that record official ecclesiastical rhetoric—may be necessary to change the relationship between Christians and Jews, but they are not sufficient. Confidence-building measures must support these theological claims—evidence on the ground is needed that Catholics in the pews and in catechism classes have studied the changes in attitude and belief that the Second Vatican Council has endorsed. The words of Catholic conciliation and acceptance of Judaism as an older, living sibling also need to withstand the test of time lest they die with the people who first articulated them. This skepticism from a Jewish perspective has been hardened in the crucible of historical experience. The question remains: will the words of the Roman Catholic leadership translate into the actions of the Roman Catholic membership?

It took thirty-five years until a significant Jewish response was offered in 2000 to the profound changes *Nostra Aetate* marked in Christian theology relating to Judaism. The book *Christianity in Jewish Terms* states,

> We believe that living as a minority in a still largely Christian America—and Christian West—Jews need to learn the languages and beliefs of their neighbors. . . . Jews need to learn ways of judging what forms of Christianity are friendly to them and what forms are not, and what forms of Christian belief merit their public support and what forms do not. They need, as well, to acknowledge the efforts of those Christians who have sacrificed aspects of their work and of their lives to combat Christian anti-Judaism and to promote forms of Christian practice that are friendly to Jewish life and belief.[41]

*Christianity in Jewish Terms* is a commentary on "*Dabru Emet*: A Jewish Statement on Christians and Christianity," which is predicated on the premise that changes in Christian theology

---

38. Reuven Kimmelman, "Rabbis Joseph B. Soloveitchik and Abraham Joshua Heschel on Jewish-Christian Relations," *Edah Journal* 4, no. 2 (2004), 5.

39. *Union Theological Seminary Quarterly Review* 21, no. 2 (January 1966), 6. See also *No Religion Is an Island: Abraham Joshua Heschel and Interreligious Dialogue,* ed. Harold Kasimow and Byron Sherwin (Maryknoll, NY: Orbis Books, 1991).

40. *Nostra Aetate* (Declaration on the Relation of the Church to Non-Christian Religions) proclaimed by His Holiness Pope Paul VI on October 28, 1965. *vatican.va/archive/hist_councils/ii_vatican_council/documents/vat-ii_decl_19651028_nostra-aetate_en.html.*

41. Tikva Frymer-Kensky et al., eds., *Christianity in Jewish Terms* (Boulder, CO: Westview Press, 2000), xii.

merit a significant Jewish response. The authors acknowledge their lack of official standing, noting that they represent only themselves. However, several hundred Jewish leaders subsequently signed onto the statement. *Dabru Emet* (Speak the Truth) offered eight principles or points about Christianity that its authors wanted the Jewish community to become aware of:

1.  Jews and Christians worship the same God.
2.  Jews and Christians seek authority from the same book—the Bible (what Jews call "Tanakh" and Christians call the "Old Testament").
3.  Christians can respect the claim of the Jewish people upon the land of Israel.
4.  Jews and Christians accept the moral principles of Torah.
5.  Nazism was not a Christian phenomenon.
6.  The humanly irreconcilable difference between Jews and Christians will not be settled until God redeems the entire world as promised in Scripture.
7.  A new relationship between Jews and Christians will not weaken Jewish practice.
8.  Jews and Christians must work together for justice and peace.[42]

It is not only noteworthy that thirty-five years elapsed between *Nostra Aetate* and *Christianity in Jewish Terms*. Of added significance is the asymmetry between them. The hierarchy of the Roman Catholic Church stands in stark contrast to the "ad-hocracy" assembled to develop a Jewish response. Whereas Christianity is a derivative of Judaism, and therefore, has a compelling need to assert its Jewish origin, Jews feel no such need to relate to Christianity. Nevertheless, the unprecedented opportunity for Jews to relate to Christians who seek mutual understanding and respect is worthy, if not holy.

---

42. Ibid., xvii–xx.

# CHAPTER 3

# Texts and Commentary

*Philip A. Cunningham and Jan Katzew*

## Introduction

Judaism has been justly characterized as an ongoing dance between life and Torah and back again.[1] One of the primary moves in this dance is expressed in halakhah, Jewish law, which comprises an essential part of Judaism, but only a part. The root of the word *halakhah* actually has nothing to do with law per se; rather it means "the way to walk" or "the way to go." Halakhah, therefore, is both a process and a product, a way of being and behaving in the world. Critics of Judaism through the ages have mistaken this part for the whole. The complement to Jewish law is Jewish lore, aggadah. In a classic essay, Hayim Nachman Bialik perfectly captured their rich interdependence:

> Halakhah and Aggadah are two things which are really one, two sides of a single shield. The relation between them is like that of speech to thought and emotion, or of action and sensible form to speech. Halakhah is the crystallization, the ultimate and inevitable quintessence of Aggadah; Aggadah is the content of Halakhah. Aggadah is the plaintive voice of the heart's yearning as it wings its way to its haven; Halakhah is the resting place, where for a moment the yearning is satisfied and stilled.[2]

Bialik defended the complementarity, the interdependence, and the synergy of halakhah and aggadah, especially against those who endeavored to separate them and derogate halakhah. Preserving the dialectical nature of Jewish life, Bialik argued for a recalibration of the balance of Jewish life. "Halakhah linked with Aggadah means assurance of health and a certificate of national maturity; but wherever you find Aggadah in isolation, be sure that the nation's power to act and instruments of action are weak and need medication."[3] The linkage between Jewish law and Jewish lore is nuanced and complex, but it is also critical to maintain and appreciate. It is a caricature of Judaism to portray it as a collection of laws *or* of stories. This is a false dichotomy. Rather, Judaism is the conjunction, the convergence of laws and stories. It is both, always and forever.

Passover provides a powerful illustration of how halakhah and aggadah are inextricably intertwined. At the heart of the most observed

---

1. Franz Rosenzweig, opening lecture, Freies Jeudisches Lehrhaus, Frankfurt, Germany, 1917.

2. Hayim Hachman Bialik, "Halachah and Aggadah," trans. Sir Leon Simon (London: Education Department of the Zionist Federation of Great Britain and Ireland, 1944).

3. Ibid., 26.

rite in Jewish life, the Passover Seder, are the words "It is incumbent upon a person to see himself as though he came out of Egypt." This quintessential expression of Jewish lore transcends logic, yet it is nevertheless compelling—and not only to Jews. The Exodus from slavery to freedom, as much as it is a historical memory, is also encountered as an ever-present challenge. It asks for reenactment. It suggests that all have the ability and the responsibility to empathize with the slaves who left Egypt and that we can take ourselves out of our contemporary reality and reinsert ourselves in the existential challenge of bringing those people enslaved in our world to freedom in their own land of promise.

Isaiah Berlin, in an essay entitled "Two Types of Liberty," differentiated between "freedom from" and "freedom to." This distinction is epitomized in the divine command to *free* the children *from* slavery in Egypt in order for them *to* serve God. This excerpt from the Passover ritual is emblematic of the unique/universal dialectic embedded in Jewish memory. The master story of the Jewish people, the Exodus from Egypt, is narrated as though it has an essentially universal, timeless message. All human beings are meant to be free. One can hear an echo from the blessing of God to Abram: "I will bless those who bless you, and I will pronounce doom on those who curse you; through you all the families of the earth shall be blessed" (Gen. 12:2).[4] Passover is a unique experience in Jewish memory that portends a universal experience in human destiny. Human beings are not meant to be slaves to human masters. Rather all people are intended to be servants of God. Every year at the Passover Seder, Jews reenact Passover as a reminder that the Exodus is not finished as long as there are slaves in the world. The Passover ritual

highlights the symbiotic nature of the halakhah (the rubrics of the order of the Seder) and the aggadah (its heart, its living meaning).

It was the dichotomization of halakhah and aggadah that enabled many Christians over the centuries to caricature Judaism as heartless and legalistic. It is partially to counter this tendency that this chapter presents a few biblical, rabbinic, and post-rabbinic texts. They were chosen to illustrate the nature and dynamism of the Jewish tradition. Some are longer, some are shorter, but all provide insight into key aspects of Jewish life and self-understanding.

# Text 1: *Akeidat Yitzhak*—The Binding of Isaac (Gen. 22:1–19)

Reading the following verses aloud is suggested.

## Text

Now after these events it was that God tested Avraham and said to him: Avraham! He said: Here I am. He said: Pray take your son, your only-one, whom you love, Yitzhak, and go you forth to the land of Moriyya/ Seeing, and offer him up there as an offering-up upon one of the mountains that I will tell you of. Avraham started early in the morning, he saddled his donkey, he took his two serving lads with him and Yitzhak his son, he split wood for the offering-up and arose and went to the place that God had told him of. On the third day Avraham lifted up his eyes and saw the place from afar. Avraham said to the lads: You stay here with the donkey and I and the lad will go yonder, we will bow down and then return to you. Avraham took

---

4. This biblical citation and those in the outsider's commentary are from *Tanakh: A New Translation of the Holy Scriptures according to the Traditional Hebrew Text* (Philadelphia: Jewish Publication Society, 1985). The biblical citations in the insider's commentary are from *The Torah: A Modern Commentary*, Revised Edition (New York: Union for Reformed Judaism Press, 2005).

the wood for the offering-up, he placed them upon Yitzhak his son, in his hand he took the fire and the knife. Thus the two of them went together. Yitzhak said to Avraham his father, he said: Father! He said: Here I am, my son. He said: Here are the fire and the wood, but where is the lamb for the offering-up? Avraham said: God will see for himself to the lamb for the offering-up, my son. Thus the two of them went together. They came to the place that God had told him of; there Avraham built the slaughter-site atop the wood. Avraham stretched out his hand, he took the knife to slay his son. But YHWH's messenger called to him from heaven and said: Avraham! Avraham! He said: Here I am. He said: Do not stretch out your hand against the lad, do not do anything to him! For now I know that you are in awe of God—you have not withheld your son, your only-one, from me. Avraham lifted up his eyes and saw: there, a ram caught behind in the thicket by its horns! Avraham went, he took the ram and offered it up as an offering-up in place of his son. Avraham called the name of that place: YHWH Sees. As the saying today: On YHWH's mountain it is seen. Now YHWH's messenger called to Avraham a second time from heaven and said: By Myself I swear—YHWH's utterance— indeed, I will bless you, bless you, I will make your seed many, yes many, like the stars of the heavens and like that sand that is on the shore of the sea; your seed shall inherit the gate of their enemies, all the nations of the earth shall enjoy blessing through your seed, in consequence of your hearkening to my voice. Avraham returned to his lads, they arose and went together to Be'er- Sheva. And Avraham stayed in Be'er Sheva.[5] ■

## Outsider Commentary
### *Cunningham*

Translation is commentary. Everett Fox wrote that his translation was "guided by the principle that the Hebrew Bible, like much of the literature of antiquity, was meant to be read aloud, and that consequently, it must be translated with careful attention to rhythm and sound. The translation therefore tries to mimic the particular rhetoric of the Hebrew whenever possible, preserving such devices as repetition, allusion, alliteration, and wordplay."[6] If the above translation seems foreign to you, then it has served its purpose. Rather than seek to translate the Bible into idiomatic English, Fox opted to let the English reader see and hear the Hebrew rhythm, form, and syntax. Citing earlier translators, he explained that "translations of individual words should reflect 'primal' root meanings, that translations of phrases, lines and whole verses should mimic the syntax of the Hebrew, and that the vast web of allusions and wordplays present in the text should be somehow perceivable in the target language."[7] His translation succeeds in that it makes the English rendering sound a bit foreign to native English speakers. There is nothing colloquial about it, yet it is decipherable and meaningful, both key elements in effective translation.

Examples of these principles in his translations of Genesis 22 include the following:

**YHWH.** This is a one-for-one correspondence for the four Hebrew letters of the Tetragrammaton, the "four letters" of the ineffable name of God, related to the name disclosed to Moses from the burning bush (Exod. 3:14). The Jewish tradition avoids pronouncing this name because of its holiness. In English translations it is often rendered as "Lord." Fox preserves the

---

5. Everett Fox, *The Five Books of Moses: Genesis, Exodus, Leviticus, Numbers, Deuteronomy* (New York: Schocken Books, 1995), 93–97.

6. Ibid., ix.

7. Ibid., x.

unpronounceable nature of the divine name, causing the reader to pause and wonder what to "hear"—silence, a breath. Do we insert vowels between the consonants so that we can pronounce the name of God?

**Avraham/Yitzhak instead of Abraham/Isaac.** Fox gives the English reader the sound of Hebrew names preserving the original idiom when English actually has the sounds to do so.

**Only-one.** The Hebrew is one word, so here the hyphen connects two words so that they too can imitate the Hebrew. This rendering also responds to the empirically problematic truth that Avraham had two sons, Yishmael and Yitzhak, suggesting that Avraham has an only-one that he loves.

**Offering-up.** This repeated idiom functions as a leitmotif for this biblical story. The Hebrew *olah* refers to a specific type of sacrificial offering, one that is completely consumed by fire. *Olah* is from the Hebrew root that means "to go up," so Fox decided to preserve the double entendre in English by linking the words *offering* and *up*.

**Lad.** The Hebrew *na'ar* is three letters like "lad" and refers to a youthful male. Yet, it is not the common word for "boy," so yet again Fox has endeavored to preserve the essence of the Hebrew idiom in his translation/commentary of the Torah. Taking time to compare standard English translations of this text with Fox's will help the reader uncover and discover the intentions of the translator. It will bring an increasing awareness that every translation inescapably conveys an implicit commentary. Everett Fox illustrates the interpretive power of translation as a tool for learning and teaching sacred texts. He has made a powerful, compelling argument for mastering a text in its original language by providing an English reading of the Torah that goes to great lengths to preserve the Hebrew idiom.

Apart from these translational points, as a Christian I note that this passage from the book of Genesis has been prominent in Christian traditions of interpretation, as well as Jewish. With hindsight, Christians saw in this narrative a foreshadowing of Jesus, another "only-one" who also carried the wood up the hill to the site of his sacrifice. Regrettably, many Christians thought this reading of the text was the only significant one, and so failed to benefit from the many years of profound Jewish reflection on the significance of this episode. As Rabbi Katzew's comments illustrate, Jews find much meaning in this text for their own history and self-understanding.

The numerous "blanks" in the tale offered the rabbis many opportunities to pose spiritually rewarding questions about the narrative. These include: What was Abraham thinking? Did he think that God would never really make him kill his son ("God will see to the sheep") or was he grief-stricken and despondent? Why would God need to test Abraham if God presumably knew in advance how he would respond? And perhaps most provocatively, why at the end does the text say that only Abraham returned to the servants? Where was Isaac? Was he actually sacrificed after all?

The last three questions were particularly meaningful to medieval European Jews who sometimes were threatened with death if they refused Christian baptism. Like Isaac they might be required to die for their faith in God. In some rabbinic aggadot, God actually restores the sacrificed Isaac to life, a variation on the story that would surely be comforting to oppressed Jews of later centuries.

Finally, some commentators today see in this story a Hebrew rejection of the practice of child sacrifice, which was widespread among Israel's neighbors. If so, it probably relates to the Torah commandment to offer one's firstborn son to God, but in biblical times the child owed to God was redeemed by offering an animal sacrifice instead (see Exod. 13:1–2, 11–16). Later on when the destruction of the Jerusalem Temple ended the practice of animal sacrifice, the rabbis determined that the commandment to redeem the firstborn son (*pidyon haben*) was fulfilled by making a donation to a descendant of the priestly line.

## Insider Commentary

### Katzew

In the Jewish lectionary cycle, Genesis 22 is read twice each year, at the end of the weekly portion entitled *VaYeira*,[8] and on Rosh Hashanah (on its second day in congregations that observe two days). In addition, some Jews incorporate *Akeidat Yitzhak* (the binding of Isaac) into their daily prayer in order to recount Abraham's supreme love of God.

The Jewish year begins with the birth and binding of Isaac as the Torah reading and consequently, it provides grist for the homiletical mill of rabbis throughout the world. What follows is an example of a Rosh Hashanah sermon based on *Akeidat Yitzhak*. It represents an attempt to balance the integrity of the Torah and its enduring relevance to our lives. Like the Torah itself, it is meant to be read aloud.

The following homily for the Jewish New Year assumes some familiarity with the character of Abraham. He was born first as Abram, and then he was commanded by God to leave his familiar surroundings to go on a physical and spiritual journey that would not only change identity but also considerably influence the fate and faith of the world (Gen. 12:1–9ff.). Particularly significant for Abraham's spiritual journey was his entering into a virtual negotiation with God about the fate of the people who lived in Sodom and Gomorrah (Gen. 18:16–33). In this incident, Abraham was not a passive recipient of God's judgment. Rather he was an active agent, engaged in a vigorous defense of justice and fairness. It was not always the case throughout his life.

This homiletic commentary on the *Akeidat Yitzhak* gives an example of how the Jewish community today interacts with this very influential scripture.

### "The Isaac Syndrome"

We read the same Torah portion every Rosh Hashanah, *Akeidat Yitzhak*, the binding of Isaac, and yet every year its meaning is different. God is schizophrenic, divided evenly between the judgmental *Elohim* and the compassionate *Adonai*, with each name for God mentioned five times in the story. Abraham is enigmatic. He has shown unprecedented courage in challenging God's sense of justice in wiping out Sodom and Gomorrah, yet he is obsequious and compliant when God asks him to sacrifice his son Isaac, the one he loves. Abraham's servants are incidental bit players in the unfolding drama; they are not invited to witness Isaac's binding and near-sacrifice. The angel is heroic, interrupting Abraham at the last instant and preventing him from continuing a tradition of child sacrifice that sadly persists in our own day, though the methods have evolved or devolved, depending on one's perspective. The ram is an innocent surrogate for Isaac whose presence endures in the blasts of the ram's horn, the shofar. God, Abraham, the servants, the angel, and the ram are supposed to have supporting roles in this one-act drama. The principal player, after whom the vignette is named, is Isaac. However, Isaac is hardly a compelling character. He is portrayed in the Torah as the weakest of the three links in the patriarchal chain of Abraham, Isaac, and

---

8. The Torah is divided into fifty-four Torah portions to accommodate the longest possible Jewish year, which encompasses fifty-four weeks. Each portion is named after its first distinctive or significant word, in this case "*VaYeira*," the first word in Genesis 18:1.

Jacob, plagued by a lack of sight, foresight, and insight. Rabbinic commentaries compound and solidify the inferior reputation of Isaac in relation to his father and his son, like a placeholder in a number sequence.

Isaac certainly does not need me to be his defense attorney, even though he has had more than his share of rabbinic detractors. I think his character provides a significant lens into understanding a lingering perception of the Jewish people. Abraham may have been the first Jew, but Isaac was the first Jewish victim, and the *Akeidah* set the stage for a play that is still running. The Isaac Syndrome portrays the Jews as innocent victims at the mercy of others in power. From the moment Isaac was released from his near-sacrifice, he lived with the awareness that he owed his life to his father and that only by the grace of God was he alive. This awareness had a profound effect on Isaac's life and I daresay it has had a profound effect on Jewish life, so enduring and pervasive that I think the term *Isaac Syndrome* fits.

Isaac was a model victim. He carried the wood on which he was laid. Even though he was younger and presumably stronger than his father, he allowed himself to be bound. Indeed, the rabbinic imagination posited that Isaac actually instructed his father to bind him tightly so that he would not squirm and render the offering blemished and therefore unfit for God. So pious was the rabbis' Isaac in his martyrdom that his father's sacrifice was not enough. He engaged in self-sacrifice, willingly participating in his own demise. Is this Isaac heroic, empathic, or pathetic? Were his actions an expression of the strength of his faith or the weakness of his will or both? Isaac may arouse sympathy, but I seriously doubt that he modeled behavior we should be proud to emulate. Isaac was compliant, obedient to a fault, and Isaac's descendants have struggled mightily with a world that has selectively chosen to relate to Jews as the children of Isaac

rather than the children of Abraham or at times even the children of God.

The Torah prescribed Jewish destiny with the words *Am l'vadad ysihkon*—"A people that will dwell alone" (Num. 23:9). It is an ominous status, a prophecy that I wish did not ring as true as it does even now. Even though we have all grown to expect it, I still find the global fascination with the state and people of Israel to be astounding. For a country the size of New Jersey, Israel generates news and commentary totally out of proportion to its size or population. This reality defies logic, but there is an insatiable thirst for information about the Jews, especially when we are in crisis, and the thirst seems to be particularly intense when we are perceived as victims.

In the Torah's account, Isaac was silent except for one question: "where is the lamb for the burnt offering?" Abraham responded, "God will see to the lamb for the burnt offering, my son" (Gen. 22:8). Apparently, that retort was sufficient. Isaac demonstrated such faith, in his case "blind faith," that he was resigned to his fate. Silence is only one symptom of the Isaac Syndrome. There is no attempt to speak truth to power. There is no defiance, only deference. Silence has multiple meanings—the wisdom to reflect, the pause between movements in a symphony, indecision, loneliness, and in the Isaac Syndrome, abject powerlessness. But on Rosh Hashanah we read the Bible and there is no escaping Isaac, the passive victim. Though the rabbis and poets try to recreate Isaac in their image, the original Isaac survives just as he survived his father's knife.

It is perversely understandable that anti-Semites relate to Jews as Isaac—weak, obsequious, and ready to die. They are all too willing to oblige, affirm, and exploit the status of the Jew as a victim, a sacrificial offering necessary for others to thrive. This logic enables those who hate Jews to claim they are instruments of God, continuing and completing the *Akeidah*. That anti-Semitism could be conceived of as justifiable seems preposterous on its surface, but the evidence inheres in the binding of Isaac. Isaac was a willing, complicit victim, a partner in his own sacrifice, and yet he merited the love and favoritism of his parents, human and divine. In the twisted mind of an anti-Semite, Isaac is a perfect foil, the ideal Jew waiting for Abraham to sacrifice him. The anti-Semite becomes a tragic figure, commanded by God to finish where Abraham left off. I only wish this scenario were complete fiction or at least consigned to the dustbin of history. But it is not. It is all too real. Even in places where there are no Jews there is anti-Semitism. But this perception is not inevitable. Unlike Isaac, we can count on human beings who will join us, who will support us—especially if we stand up and defend ourselves. Arguably our greatest hope for an antidote to anti-Semitism is the opportunity to build coalitions with people who are willing to see us as people, not passive, submissive victims.

Isaac on the altar fits an anti-Semitic stereotype, but I think this image is even more complex and problematic for some Jews. An Israeli poet, Haim Gouri, captures this sentiment in poignant poetry. "Isaac, as the story goes, was not sacrificed. He lived for many years, saw what pleasure had to offer, until his eyesight dimmed. But he bequeathed that hour to his offspring. They are born with a knife in their hearts."[9] Jews have tried powerlessness as a lifestyle, and trusted the powers that be. While the historical context is complex and nuanced, it is all too facile to establish a direct connection between Jewish impotence and the Holocaust, the word whose root meaning is "burnt offering." Rabbi Yitz Greenberg, former director of the US Holocaust

Memorial Museum, has written compellingly about the failure of powerlessness and the formidable yet preferable challenges intrinsic in becoming powerful, as Israel is now widely and rightly perceived. The State of Israel represents an assertion of Jewish power, and Jews and non-Jews alike who had become inured to the image of the Jew as victim have had trouble overcoming the Isaac Syndrome. The State of Israel with its nuclear deterrent does not fit the image of the Jews as victims that had taken on a life of its own since the destruction of the Temple in Jerusalem in the first century CE. Israel does not fit the mental model the world had built for the Jewish people. Israel was, is, and will likely continue to be a struggle, for us and for the rest of the world. The world can live with Isaac, who survived because the powerful were also merciful. Unlike his father and his children, Isaac lived his entire life in the Land of Israel. In this sense, he was the victor because he was always physically at home. But the price he paid for his victory was very high. He almost gave his life. He most certainly sacrificed his image as a worthy successor to the man who challenged God's justice over Sodom and Gomorrah.

The biblical Abraham listened to the voice that cried out, "Abraham, Abraham. . . . Do not lay your hand on the lad; do nothing to him; for now I know that you are one who fears God, as you did not withhold your son, your only one, from Me." This verse is the best one we have to help us understand the rationale for Isaac's victim status. The altar on Mount Moriah was a proving ground for faith. God was the teacher and Abraham was the student. The lesson plan involved a deep personal understanding of a belief in One, Good God. Like any teacher worthy of the name, God assessed Abraham

---

9. From the poem "Heritage," by Haim Gouri, trans T. Carmi, in *The Penguin Book of Hebrew Verse* (New York: Penguin Books, 1981).

by administering a test—not with a No. 2 pencil, but with a No. 1 knife. Failure meant that monotheism would die along with Isaac. Success meant they both would live. Ostensibly, Abraham passed the test and demonstrated his faith. For his part, Isaac was a quintessential victim—ready, willing, and able to accept his fate. Regrettably, history has borne witness to the fact that too many others have been willing to bind Isaac's descendants on an altar of their own design and too many of Isaac's children have not benefited from divine and human compassion. Unlike the ancient scene on Mount Moriah where the victim had the last laugh (Isaac's name in Hebrew, Yitzhak, means "he will laugh") and lived, the contemporary scene symbolized by Auschwitz resulted in the victimization of an entire people. The modern-day sacrificer of Isaac did not withhold his sword. He heard a different voice, a demonic voice that changed Jewish life forever, accelerating the birth of the State of Israel, while destroying unmercifully an utterly irreplaceable community and permanently staining world history. The Isaac Syndrome, the victimization of the Jew, lives on, but there are signs that Isaac is not taking it lying down.

## Text 2: Baba Mezi'a 59b: The Oven of Achnai

The Babylonian Talmud recounts dialogues, dialectics, and disputes that are as timeless as they are timely. As noted, contrary to popular perceptions it is not a compendium of laws and rules. Instead, halakhic arguments are often interlaced with legendary aggadah. One such case involves the oven of Achnai. From a seemingly obscure, fanciful dispute, a radical and profound truth emerges. The context is a debate over whether an oven that was not made in a single piece (but instead of a series of distinct segments with a layer of sand between) could be rendered unclean in its entirety. Rabbi Eliezer declared the segmented oven clean, but all the other sages disagreed.

### Text

On that day R. Eliezer brought forward every imaginable argument, but they did not accept them.

So he said to them: "If the *halakhah* agrees with me, let this carob-tree prove it!" Thereupon the carob-tree was torn a hundred cubits out of its place—others affirm, four hundred cubits. "No proof can be brought from a carob-tree," they retorted.

Again he said to them: "If the *halakhah* agrees with me, let the stream of water prove it!" Whereupon the stream of water flowed backwards—"No proof can be brought from a stream of water," they rejoined.

Again he urged: "If the *halakhah* agrees with me, let the walls of the schoolhouse prove it," whereupon the walls inclined to fall. But R. Joshua rebuked them, saying: "When scholars are engaged in a halakhic dispute, what right have you to interfere?" Hence the walls did not fall, in honor of R. Joshua, nor did they resume the upright, in honor of R. Eliezer; and they are still standing thus inclined.

Again he said to them: "If the *halakhah* agrees with me, let it be proved from Heaven!" Whereupon a Heavenly Voice cried out: "Why do ye dispute with R. Eliezer, seeing that in all matters the *halakhah* agrees with him!" But R. Joshua arose and exclaimed: "It is not in heaven."

What did he mean by this?—Said R. Jeremiah: That the Torah had already been given at Mount Sinai; we pay no attention to a Heavenly Voice, because Thou hast long since written in the Torah at Mount Sinai, "After the majority must one incline" [Exod. 23:2].

R. Nathan met Elijah and asked him: What did the Holy One, Blessed be He, do in that hour?—He laughed [with joy], he replied, saying, "My children have defeated Me, My children have defeated Me."[10] ■

## Insider Commentary

### Katzew

This is an incredible aggadic legend, incredible both as in highly implausible and incredible as in amazing. The idea that human reasoning, "It is not in heaven," trumps miracles and divine intervention is an extraordinary claim to make within a religious context. Furthermore, "after the majority must one incline" makes a political statement about the preferred method of arriving at decisions about religious practice. It introduces the element of democracy into the halakhic process. A single religious authority, even a divine one, can be overruled by a group.

The legendary aspect of this story is highlighted by the inclusion of Elijah, who in the biblical account had been taken up to heaven in a chariot (2 Kings 2:11), and therefore, did not die a natural death. In later rabbinic lore, the rabbis engage him regularly in dialogue. Nevertheless, this passage instructs readers about not only the power of rabbinic imagination but also their understanding of rabbinic authority. Rabbis were not mere passive inheritors or conduits of truth; they were active arbiters and even creators of truth. This is a story about power and its transfer from the divine to the human realm. God's response to the rabbinic claim, that is, laughter followed by an admission of defeat, would have the reader believe that God was delighted by this display of rabbinic authority and its triumph over divine will. God and the rabbis are partners, and as in any collaborative partnership, the balance of power shifts from time to time.

The term *Rabbinic Judaism* refers not only to a period of approximately seventeen centuries (from the end of the first century CE to the end of the eighteenth century CE) but also to the veritable center of the Jewish world during that period. The rabbis of the Mishnah and Talmud forged a link in a chain of religious authority and authenticity that could be tied directly to God, Moses, the priests, the prophets, and the Sanhedrin. This chain from revelation to tradition established these rabbis' credibility in the sight of God as well as in the sight of the Jewish people. The Judaism of today would be impossible to understand without learning about and appreciating Rabbinic Judaism. Actually, it is reasonable to assert that there would be no Judaism today without Rabbinic Judaism.

## Outsider Commentary

### Cunningham

This is one of my favorite rabbinic tales. It seems to me that it conveys several defining features of Jewish self-understanding.

Although not cited in the story, a Deuteronomic passage closely relates to it: "Surely, this Instruction which I enjoin upon you this day is not too baffling for you, nor is it beyond reach. It is not in the heavens, that you should say, 'Who among us can go up to the heavens and get it for us and impart it to us, that we may observe it?' . . . No. the thing is very close to you, in your mouth and in your heart, to observe it" (Deut. 30:12–14).

Sometimes Christians misunderstand Judaism's emphasis on God's divine transcendence to mean that God must seem far away to Jews. However, Jews understand that they are

---

10. Babylonian Talmud, Baba Metzia 59a (slightly adapted), Seder Nizikin, vol. 1 (London: Soncino Press, 1935), 352–53.

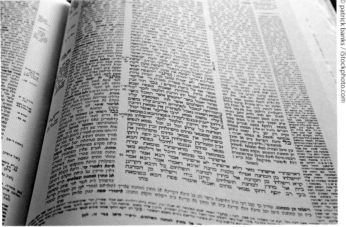

A page from the Babylonian Talmud. The central text is the Mishnah (c. 200 CE), followed immediately by the Gemarah, surrounded by authoritative commentaries on it by prominent rabbis over the centuries.

constantly "wrestling with God" (the meaning of the name *Isra-el*) by debating how best to interpret and live out the Torah in contemporary circumstances. It might be said that studying the scriptures or the Talmud in isolation would seem peculiar to most Jews. Rather, one collaborates with other Jews in grappling with Torah. The practice of *chevrutah*, working through the holy texts with a study partner (off whom one can bounce ideas about their meaning) is an example of the Jewish communal engagement with God's word in its midst.

The nearness of God's word in the Torah is, a Catholic might say, akin to a sacrament for Jews. The Torah mediates the divine Presence. In Jewish liturgies, the Torah scroll is venerated. Many Jews, for instance, will touch the Torah scroll with their prayer shawls or prayer books as it is carried through the congregation at Shabbat services.

There is a further consequence to God's commands not being in heaven but having been given into the hands of the People Israel. As this story makes clear, Jews feel that this gift of the Torah means that Jews are responsible for how they live it. They cannot simply wait for "a Heavenly Voice" to tell them the "correct" meaning of a passage. The responsibility is theirs. And even if a Heavenly Voice intervened with the amazing words, "Everything Rabbi so-and-so says is correct," the Jewish community must instead be guided by its own majority opinion because "The Torah is not in heaven." It resides in the midst of Israel.

There is occasionally a rabbinic playfulness over Israel's intimate relationship with God that also appears in this passage. When Elijah reports that God merrily exclaimed, "My children have defeated me!" the sense is not at all that God is angry or upset. Rather, God is pleased to the point of laughing in joy that his children, Israel, have taken the gift of the Torah seriously. They have assumed responsibility for being God's covenantal partners in living out a holy life. God's delight in this offers, I think, important lessons for Christians, too.

## Text 3: Babylonian Talmud Eiruvin 13b

According to rabbinic tradition, for three years in the first century there was a dispute between two different traditions of the Pharisees: Beit Hillel (the "house" or following of Hillel) and Beit Shammai. Each claimed that "The law is in agreement with our views." In the following text, the punch line comes when a *bat kol*, a voice from heaven, announced, "*Eilu v'eilu divrei Elohim Hayyim*" (These and those are the words of the Living God), adding, "but the law is in agreement with the rulings of Beit Hillel."

## Text

Rabbi Abba said in the name of Shmuel: For three years Beit Hillel and Beit Shammai debated each other. These said that the halacha follows their view and these said that the halacha follows their view. A heavenly voice went forth and declared: *These and those are words of the living God, but the halacha follows Beit Hillel.* Since both these and those are words of the living God on what basis did Beit Hillel merit to determine the halacha according to their view? Because they were relaxed and forbearing and they would study their own opinion as well as the opinion of Beit Shammai. And not only that, but they would mention the matters of Beit Shammai before their own as in the case we learned about in the Mishnah. One whose head and a majority of his body were inside the Sukkah [temporary hut built for the celebration of Sukkot] but his table was in the house [instead of the Sukkah]—Beit Shammai ruled the sukkah to be invalid whereas Beit Hillel validated it. Beit Hillel said to Beit Shammai, did not the following occur—that the elders of Beit Shammai and the elders of Beit Hillel went together to visit Rabbi Yohanan ben Hachoranis and they found that his head and a majority of his body were in the Sukkah but his table was in the house. Beit Shammai replied: Is there proof from that incident? The elders of Beit Shammai said to him: If that is how you have always conducted yourself, then you have never fulfilled the commandment of dwelling in the Sukkah in your life.

This comes to teach you that whoever humbles himself, the Holy One of Blessing will raise up and whoever exalts himself, the Holy One of Blessing will humble. Whoever searches for prominence, prominence flees from him. But whoever flees from prominence, prominence searches for him.[11] ∎

## Insider Commentary
### *Katzew*

During the Second Temple period (515 BCE–70 CE), Jewish leadership assumed the form of dyads (*zugot* in Hebrew). Beit Hillel (the school of Hillel) and Beit Shammai (the school of Shammai) represented two approaches to Jewish thought and practice. The school of Hillel seemed to win the arguments so often that the school of Shammai could be reduced to the status of a foil, an unworthy opponent present more for entertainment or providing comic relief. However, the rationale presented in tractate Eiruvin in the Babylonian Talmud comes to teach an educational and ethical principle—that how one arrives at a judgment may be at least as important as the substance of the judgment. Process and product are inextricably intertwined. Method and result are interdependent. The school of Hillel dominated Jewish thought and practice by virtue of not only the strength of their argument but also the depth of their character.

A prospective proselyte came before both Hillel and Shammai asking to have the essence of Judaism explained while standing on one foot. Shammai dismissed the questioner as an impertinent fool. Hillel responded by saying, "Do not do to another what you would not have him/her do unto you. That is the whole Torah. The rest is commentary. Go and learn it." This response encapsulates the essence of Hillel's approach to Jewish life: inclusive, accepting, engaging, and empowering. His initial impulse to a request is "yes," followed by conditions that make "yes" possible and desirable. Nevertheless, Judaism would be poorer without Shammai, without a dialogue partner, a learned opponent who keeps Hillel

---

11. Babylonian Talmud, Tractate Eiruvin 13b (slightly adapted), Seder Moed, vol. 2 (London: Soncino Press, 1935), 85–86.

honest. The rabbis noted that the schools of Hillel and Shammai interacted and intermarried. This testifies to the mutuality of their relationship. They could and did disagree, and yet they found a way to coexist. The schools of Hillel and Shammai offer insight into the realization that the Jewish people have not been monolithic, yet there is enduring hope that multiple expressions of Judaism can be symbiotic. Judaism generally and Rabbinic Judaism particularly involves a culture of multiple viewpoints on issues of shared meaning.

## Outsider Commentary

### Cunningham

Christians will hear in the closing words of this text an echo of a saying attributed to Jesus, "All who exalt themselves will be humbled, and all who humble themselves will be exalted" (Matt. 23:12). This similarity shows the common origins of Christianity and Rabbinic Judaism in the late Second Temple period. Both traditions developed ideas that were "in the air" at the time.

However, this resonance is not the most important aspect of the passage. The passage is significant in illustrating a key characteristic of Rabbinic Judaism: the value of having many different approaches and opinions on subjects of concern. The culture of discourse in Judaism is lively and vital debate. The Talmud preserves multiple perspectives because the rabbis wisely discerned that sometimes answers that work well in one situation might not be so suitable in different contexts. The majority opinion that went with one line of argument in a certain historical moment might find it preferable to embrace a different stream of thought at another time. By recording many possible options, the rabbis ensured that their conversations would continue and would be adaptable to changing circumstances.

This Jewish deliberative culture of discourse is generally quite different from the Christian one, which can tend to prefer universal and unchanging formulaic expressions of religious truths. When Jews and Christians converse, it is important for them to be aware that their respective traditions tend to talk about religious matters in different ways.

The tendency in Christianity to prefer definitive answers to theological, ethical, or liturgical questions also applies to biblical interpretation. Many public expressions of Christianity today imply there is one dominant meaning of a given scriptural text, even if there might be many ways in which that one meaning might function in an individual's life.

However, certain twentieth-century philosophical perspectives have argued that "meaning" is constructed by the dynamic interaction between a text and its diverse readers.[12] This has contributed to an understanding of biblical interpretation as a dialogue between the scriptural authors and communities of faith today, a dialogue that can produce multiple defensible "meanings" or interpretations of a text. In other words, the diversity within the Bible cannot be reduced to a dominant overarching biblical "message." As a 1993 Catholic document expressed, "No single interpretation can exhaust the meaning of the whole, which is a symphony of many voices."[13]

Interestingly, this contemporary acknowledgment of numerous biblical "voices" and "meanings" dovetails well with the rabbis' esteem for multiple perspectives and arguments. Perhaps these recent developments have contributed in our day to better understanding between the Jewish and Christian communities.

---

12. A stunning application of these approaches can be found in Sandra M. Schneiders, *The Revelatory Text: Interpreting the New Testament as Sacred Scripture* (San Francisco: HarperSanFrancisco, 1991).

13. Pontifical Biblical Commission, "The Interpretation of the Bible in the Church" (1993), III, A, 3.

## Text 4: Rav Kook, *Olat Re'aiah*

Rabbi Abraham Isaac Kook served as the Chief Ashkenazic Rabbi in Palestine from 1921 to 1935. He was a fervently Orthodox Jew, a prolific thinker and writer on halakhah,[14] as well as a Zionist who sought to build bridges between different and divergent expressions of Zionism and Judaism. He composed a commentary on the Siddur, the daily prayer book, that provides not only an enriched understanding of prayer but also insight into Rav Kook's theology and philosophy. One such insight emanates from his interpretation of a Talmudic aphorism included in the prayer book: "Disciples of the wise increase peace in the world, as it is said, 'All your children shall be taught of Adonai and great shall be the peace of your children [*banayikh*].' Read not *banayikh*, 'your children' but *bonayikh*, 'your builders.'"[15]

Torah scholarship is not purely an intellectual pursuit; rather it has a profound ethical dimension. A *talmid chacham*, one learned in Torah, is obliged to translate learning into living, and thereby increase peace in the world, literally to build a better world together. The following statement provides a commentary on this Talmudic dictum that has become part of the Shabbat worship service when selections from Torah and the Prophets are read. Rabbi Kook endeavored to explain an apparent linguistic anomaly—namely, the juxtaposition of a plural adjective (*rav* in Hebrew meaning "many") and a singular noun (*sh'lom* in Hebrew meaning "peace in the construct form").

### Text

There are those who mistakenly think that world peace can only come about when there is a unity of opinions and character traits. Therefore, when scholars and students of Torah disagree, and develop multiple approaches and methods, they think that they are causing strife and opposing shalom. In truth it is not so because true shalom is impossible without appreciating the pluralism that is intrinsic in shalom. The various pieces of peace come from a variety of approaches and methods that make it clear how much each one has a place and a value that complements one another. Even those methods

Rabbi Abraham Isaac Kook, religious Zionist leader, thinker, and author who served as the first Ashkenazic Chief Rabbi in Palestine from 1921 to 1935.

---

14. For an introduction to the Talmud, see *Back to the Sources*, ed. Barry Holtz (New York: Summit Books, 1984); and for a rich, nuanced understanding of the relationship between Jewish law and lore, see Hayim Nachman Bialik, "Halachah and Aggadah," trans. Sir Leon Simon (London: Education Department of the Zionist Federation of Great Britain and Ireland, 1944), 9ff.

15. Babylonian Talmud, Tractate Berakhot 64a on Isaiah 54:13 (slightly adapted), Seder Zeraim (London: Soncino Press, 1935), 404.

that appear superfluous or contradictory possess an element of truth that contributed to the mosaic of shalom. Indeed, in all the apparently disparate approaches lays the light of truth and justice, knowledge, fear and love of God and the true light of Torah.[16] ■

## Insider Commentary
### *Katzew*

Rav Kook's comment gives voice to the possibility that peace, the ultimate Jewish value, is the product of accepting differences rather than their disappearance. His Orthodoxy was unorthodox, in that he allowed for and even encouraged diversity of thought, if not practice. Perhaps this approach to diversity was merely tactical, a temporary suspension of discipline, but it is also possible that it was strategic, emanating from a deep understanding that uniformity is not the same as unity. The text is remarkable. It stands in opposition to religious fundamentalism. It projects humility into the conversation about what it means to lead a life in consonance with Torah. It speaks to human partiality in two senses of that word. We are partial in that we are incomplete and we are partial in that we are biased. Our opinions and interpretations are actually augmented by those of others, even and perhaps especially, when we differ from one another. The idea that dissonant views are not only tolerated but also invited and intentionally included is vital to understanding the arc of Jewish history. "Two Jews, three opinions" is a phrase that captures, albeit hyperbolically, an internal contradiction that inheres in Jewish life.

Shalom is justifiably portrayed as a quintessential Jewish value. The Levitical priestly blessing concludes, "God shall bestow favor upon you and grant you shalom" (Num. 6:25). Shalom represents the ultimate blessing; the prior ones are but prelude to the main event. The last line in the orphan's or mourner's Kaddish is also about shalom, asking God to do on earth that which God does in the heavenly domain, that is, to make peace. "Rabban Shimon ben Gamliel taught: The world depends on three things: on Justice, on Truth and on Peace."[17] This teaching provides further testimony that the rabbis regarded shalom/peace as first among equals as it is the last of the values cited. This perspective on shalom makes Rav Kook's commentary all the more meaningful. He understood shalom as a composite requiring the whole to be greater than the sum of its parts or, as in the title of a book by a leading contemporary Jewish philosopher, David Hartman, *A Heart of Many Rooms*.[18] This understanding of shalom has ramifications that extend beyond the Jewish community and may contribute to the growing understanding between Jews and Christians.

## Outsider Commentary
### *Cunningham*

This quotation from Rav Kook further develops the point of the previous text; namely, that Judaism embraces diversity of thought and values a multiplicity of ideas. It also relates diversity to the Hebrew concept of shalom.

Often translated as "peace," *shalom* means that and much more. It conveys the wholeness

---

16. *Olat Re'aiah*, a commentary on the daily prayer book by Rabbi Abraham Isaac Kook (Jerusalem: Mossad HaRav Kook, 1988), 330.

17. Mishnah Avot 1:18.

18. David Hartman, *A Heart of Many Rooms: Celebrating the Many Voices within Judaism* (Woodstock, VT: Jewish Lights Publishing, 2002).

that comes from right-relationship among people. For Kook, shalom is not the absence of difference, it is the celebration of diversity, without which interrelationship is meaningless. At a deep level, to be human is to be able to relate and to allow ourselves to be shaped by those who are different from us. People raised in isolation from other people have underdeveloped self-identities and are inhibited from fully interacting in human society. What is true on the individual level is also true on the communal plane.

Thus, the effort of many Christians to understand positively their spiritual relationship to the related religious tradition of Judaism can be understood as a "theology of shalom." It seeks right-relationship with the heritage and people that also grew out of the lineage of biblical Israel. Such shalom is, I believe, also necessary for Christianity to be at peace with itself.

# Text 5: Edmond Fleg on Jewish Identity

This self-expression of Jewish identity by Edmond Fleg (published in 1927) was made famous by Arthur Hertzberg in *The Zionist Idea: A Historical Analysis and Reader*. Fleg lived in France between the great wars of the twentieth century. At the time Franco Jewry was under the influence of the Dreyfus trial, an infamous case of treason that was fueled by anti-Semitism. The trial was covered by Theodore Herzl, a journalist who became the leader of political Zionism. Edmond Fleg sought to articulate his reasons for being Jewish. He offered a lyrical narrative of Jewish life in France, where a century earlier Napoleon had challenged the Jews to pledge their loyalty

to the state. Fleg was caught in the complex tension between universalist humanism or the drive to be accepted as a global citizen, and particularist Judaism or the desire to assert Jewish distinctiveness, a tension that persists.

## Text

I am a Jew because the faith of Israel
    demands no abdication of my mind. . . .
I am a Jew because for Israel, the world is not
    completed; we are completing it. . . .
I am a Jew because Israel places humanity
    and its unity above the nations and above
    Israel itself.
I am a Jew because, above humanity, image
    of the divine unity, Israel places the unity
    which is divine.[19] ∎

## Insider Commentary
*Katzew*

Although he came from a non-Zionist background, Edmond Fleg was influenced by his presence at the third Zionist Congress in Basel, Switzerland (1899). In learning about the Zionist enterprise, he mused about the potential rebirth of the Jewish people in Israel. But he was even more fascinated by the mission and purpose of the Jews in the Diaspora. What would be their raison d'être? More personally, what would be his own rationale for living as a Jew? At a moment when the Jewish people were engaged in an act of Jewish particularism, Edmond Fleg opted to strike a chord of Jewish universalism, thereby preserving one of the enduring dialectics in Jewish life. Rather than resolve the tension, Fleg reasserts it. Instead of going with the flow of Zionism and

19. Edmond Fleg, *Why I Am a Jew* (New York: Bloch Publishing, 1933), 93–95.

creating further momentum for the building of a sovereign Jewish state, Fleg chose to weigh in on the side of a valuable, if not invaluable Jewish Diaspora.

The tension that Fleg expressed is still palpable in the complex relationship that exists between the Diaspora and the State of Israel. The connection between them ranges from empathy to apathy to antipathy. Like two poles of an ellipse, they both attract and repel one another. They are interdependent, but yet at times seek independence from each other.

Edmond Fleg's concluding statement about the unity of the divine echoes the Shema, the quintessential statement of monotheism in the Torah. His Jewish identity is clearly religious and theological, yet he was caught up in the excitement of an expression of Judaism—Zionism—that was largely, although not exclusively, a political and secular expression of Judaism. There is poignant irony in this text and its context, irony that lives on after Edmond Fleg. Fleg wanted to have it both ways, that is, to be both a humanist and a Jew, to be accepted fully as a French citizen and a loyal Zionist. He sought a conjunction where others have and continue to see only disjunction. He wanted to demonstrate the possibility and desirability of multiple identities and the political and social environment in which he lived demanded that he choose an identity and live with the consequences.

## Outsider Commentary

### Cunningham

This profound reflection on Jewish self-identity recalls for me an important difference in perspective between the Jewish and Christian traditions over the centuries. Specifically, I am thinking of their respective attitudes toward the religious other.

Although there is an exclusivist strain that appears periodically in Jewish writings, it seems to me that the predominant Jewish stance has been an attitude that does not restrict God's love and mercy only to the children of Israel. While Christianity tended toward an absolute understanding of the ancient saying *extra ecclesiam nulla salus* (outside the church there is no salvation), Judaism never claimed that everyone had to become Jewish to be on good terms with God. Jews understood themselves to be in a special relationship with God, but that did not preclude God from having distinctive relationships with other people.

Based on the covenant God makes with Noah, and through him with all humanity, that is found in Genesis 9:8–17, the rabbis developed criteria by which any non-Jew could be considered righteous before God. These "Noahide Laws" required that non-Jews live according to just laws and avoid blasphemy, idolatry, sexual immorality, murder, theft, and eating meat cut from a living animal. Gentiles who observed these basic ethical norms would be pleasing to God.

Ironically, a recurrent Christian criticism of Jews was their living according to their own particular legal traditions and not adopting the universalism of the church, which embraced all people. However, while Christian universalism was often expressed by rejecting the possibility of salvation for non-Christians, Judaism's particular commands recognized that non-Jewish Gentiles could be righteous before God.

Another important idea conveyed by Edmond Fleg is that "faith . . . demands no abdication of my mind." Sometimes in popular discourse, people speak as if faith and reason are entirely different, or even contradictory. But although it has its mystical traditions, Judaism, especially rabbinic Judaism, places great value on the intellectual apprehension of its religious heritage. This is something Judaism shares with those Christian traditions that see faith and reason as necessarily complementary.

# Text 6: Judah Halevi,[20]
## *The Kuzari: The Book of Proof and Argument*

Written in the form of a dialogue, one of the most famous works of Jewish thought, the *Kuzari* by Judah Halevi in the eleventh century, has as its subtitle "an apology for a despised religion." Halevi defended Judaism against Aristotelian philosophy, Christianity, and Islam, three dominant influences in medieval Spain. He laid the foundation for a Judaism that espoused a combination of divine revelation and an unbroken chain of tradition, a Judaism that made up for its lack of political and military might in spiritual and ethical strength. Jewish memory transcends Jewish history. It subjectively recalls the vulnerability of a millennium ago as though it was yesterday, as though it could return tomorrow if we fail to be diligent and vigilant. The setting is an exposition before the king of the Khazars by a philosopher, a Muslim, a Christian, and a Jew of their respective traditions. The king is deciding which of them to embrace.

## Text

The Christian Scholar:

I believe in all that is written in the Torah and all the other books of the Israelites, which are undisputed, because they are generally accepted as everlasting and have been revealed before a vast multitude. Subsequently the Divinity became embodied in the womb of a noble Israelite virgin; she bore Him having the semblance of a human being, which concealed nevertheless a divinity, seemingly a prophet, but in reality a God sent forth. He is the Messiah, whom we call the Son of God, and He is the Father and the Son and the Holy Ghost. We believe in His unity, although the Trinity appears on our tongues. . . . Although we are not of Israelitish descent, we are well deserving of being called Israelites, because we follow the Messiah and his twelve Israelite companions, who took the place of the tribes. Our laws and regulations are derived from the apostle Simon (Petrus) and from ordinations taken from the Torah, which we study, for its truth and divine origin are indisputable. It is also stated in the Gospel by the Messiah: I came not to destroy one of the laws of Moses, but I came to confirm and corroborate them.[21] ■

## Insider Commentary
### *Katzew*

Judah Halevi composed the above characterization of Christianity as part of his defense of Judaism. He took the Khazar King (the spiritual seeker in the *Kuzari*) on a virtual tour of Christianity, Islam, and Aristotelian philosophy in order to arrive at a final destination of Judaism. How is Halevi's portrayal of Christianity consonant with yours? How is it dissonant or divergent? He wishes to lead the Khazar King and the reader to the following conclusions:

1. Christianity is rooted in Judaism.
2. Christianity does not deny any aspect of Judaism.

---

20. Judah Halevi lived from c. 1075–1141, and his life and work have been the subject of study ever since. Arguably the finest medieval Hebrew poet, he was also a superior physician, and he authored the *Kuzari*, one of the greatest works of medieval Jewish (anti)-philosophy. He lived most of his life in Spain and then in Egypt, although his heart and soul were intimately bound up with the Land of Israel.

21. From bk. 1, par. 4, "*The Kuzari:* The Book of Proof and Argument," in *Three Jewish Philosophers*, ed. Isaak Heinemann (New York: Atheneum, 1977).

3. Christianity adds the Trinity doctrine to Judaism.

4. Christianity adds the Incarnate Deity to Judaism.

Perhaps you can already predict Halevi's next move. Through the Khazar King, who is on a spiritual mission to find a practice that harmonizes with his thinking, Halevi accepts the first two premises and rejects the latter two. He finds the Christian doctrines of the Trinity and the Incarnate Deity illogical and irrational. Even though a millennium has passed since the writing of the *Kuzari*, these two aspects of Christianity are well nigh inscrutable and impenetrable to many, if not most, Jews. Other medieval as well as modern Jewish philosophers singled out these two fundamental tenets of Christianity as incommensurable with Judaism.

At the risk of oversimplification, one tipping point that determines the relationship between Jews and Christians is whether the emphasis is placed on the convergence articulated in the first two of Halevi's propositions or on the divergence expressed in the second pair of Halevi's propositions. If Jews and Christians can proceed along the lines of appreciative inquiry and build upon what is shared, then they can engage in dialogue. If, however, Jews and Christians choose to follow the course of mutual critique and assert their differences, then they enter the realm of dispute. Halevi's *Kuzari* is a work of religious apologetics, a vigorous defense of Judaism in the historical context of dispute and debate. While it may be naïve and perhaps dangerous to claim that the relationship between Jews and Christians has progressed beyond the need for such apologetics, there is growing evidence that a significant number of Christians and Jews are open, if not committed, to coexistence based on mutual acceptance.

There are about 13 million Jews in the world in the twenty-first century, and that demographic reality has a profound effect on Jewish-Christian relations. The Jewish people are a minority everywhere but in the State of Israel, and that fact informs essentially every aspect of Jewish life. It was true in the eleventh century and it is true in the twenty-first. The Jews may no longer need a defense of a despised religion. Nevertheless, the memory of needing such a defense lingers with the awareness that history is not necessarily restricted to the past nor is it necessarily a predictor of the future. Judah Halevi's portrait of Christianity in relation to Judaism endures. It testifies to the continual need for Jews and Christians to accept our commonalities and our differences in order to build trust.

## Outsider Commentary

### *Cunningham*

*The Kuzari* provides a window into medieval Jewish views of Christianity through the narrative of a king objectively judging among various contemporary "philosophical" options. This setting enables Judah Halevi to present Judaism on an equal footing with Christianity and Islam, compensating literarily for the enormous disparity in power and population that confronted medieval Jews.

It also illustrates the complex dynamics in play when two religious traditions that are closely related both historically and theologically interact. Although Halevi has offered a seemingly objective and nonpolemical depiction of Christianity, there are inaccuracies in his presentation. Christians, in fact, do not believe that Jesus only bore "the semblance of a human being, which concealed nevertheless a divinity," but that Jesus is both fully human (and a Jewish human being at that) and also fully divine. Nor does Halevi's fictitious Christian scholar accurately describe the Christian experience of the One God as Triune. He is, understandably, expressing Halevi's grasp of medieval Christian teaching.

How Jews and Christians comprehend one another remains challenging today. Paradoxically, the shared vocabulary and scriptures sometimes mask fundamental differences of definition and meaning. Indeed, when Jews and Christians go beyond superficial conversation into deeper discourse, they often discover a different way of relating than convergences and divergences. They find an interlacing tapestry. They hear variations on themes of greater or lesser similarity that can resonate with each other or seem unaffected by each other. What most voices stress in a particular generation of one tradition, a minority voice echoes in another generation of the other tradition.

Thus, for instance, over the centuries the theme of the degree of God's involvement in human life has generated a multiplicity of views among Jews and Christians, who can draw upon similar-sounding concepts such as holiness, divine command, word, or incarnation. The spectra of ideas that arise, it seems to me, seldom fall into neat, binary choices.

This, to me, is why Christian-Jewish dialogue is at once so attractive and so complex. It is also why Jews and Christians have much to learn from each other about what it means to be in covenant with the Holy One.

# CHAPTER 4

# Concluding Reflections

*Philip A. Cunningham and Jan Katzew*

## Shared Reflections on an Interreligious Dialogue

This section has featured observations on Judaism from a Christian "outsider" looking in on the Jewish tradition and a rabbi "insider" who lives Judaism. Dialogue involves an intentional moral stance, a conscious covenant in which two people seek shared meaning. We chose each other as partners, respecting each other's identity, neither seeking to convince or convert the other nor to engage in self-abnegation and deny our religious identities. Both of us have had prior experience in interreligious dialogue with the (br)other tradition and so have firsthand knowledge about how the two religious communities interrelate. Moreover, based on our prior professional and personal relationship, we chose to work together as a team on this project. There is no substitute for humanizing the relationship between religious communities in order to build bridges between them. Over time we grew to know one another as friends as well as representatives and teachers of Judaism or Christianity. Therefore, this project is more of a collegial dialogue rather than a scholarly debate or an academic exercise.

## The Value of Interchange

Working together has provided us with valuable exercise in switching between Jewish and Christian perspectives and in "translating" one religious culture of discourse into terms and concepts more easily appreciated by the other. What one of us perceived as essential, the other may have understood as peripheral, so it was critical to discern between principles and preferences and to give greater weight to the former. We often paused in this process to consider our readers. As much as we sought to be in dialogue with each other, we sought to engage in conversations with committed readers seeking interreligious understanding. As reflective practitioners, our task involved being aware of how we portrayed the relationship between Judaism and Christianity, seeking a balance between despair and hope, and wanting to be neither overly pessimistic nor naïvely optimistic. This process rewarded us with new insights as well as confirmations of prior observations, both of which are summarized in the following pages.

## An Asymmetrical but Organic Relationship

Through engaging in this dialogue, the historical and theological connections between our two traditions have once again become very evident to us. As religious communities with origins in biblical Israel that emerged and then diverged at the end of the Second Temple period in the first century CE, today's Jews and Christians have inherited common ways to think about God and their responsibilities in the world. We may mean very different things by the comparable words and phrases we use, but we clearly recognize significant similarities in our outlooks. We are passionate advocates of learning, generally and specifically, about the beliefs, practices, and values of different religious communities. We think Christians should learn about Judaism, and Jews should learn about Christianity, and both learn more about themselves in the process. Indeed, through the writing process we have learned at least as much about our own religious identities as we have about the other religious community. Religious life is lived in relationship—with God and with each other—and it is through these relationships that we grow spiritually. We conversed and agreed on a strategy before composing each chapter. Then, after an initial volley, we played writers' ping-pong by being tentative and tolerant, and open to revision as well as to holding our ground on points to which we were deeply committed. We sought to use a process that would model the approach to world religions we were trying to teach, that is, a clear understanding of our religious selves in relation to each other.

And yet there is a certain lack of symmetry—or maybe multiple asymmetries—in our relationship. Historically, for at least a millennium-and-a-half, Christians have been the overwhelming majority in every place where they have had Jewish neighbors. Only with the relatively recent founding of the modern State of Israel (1948) have Jews become the majority in any nation.

The disproportionate political, military, theological, and social power wielded by Christians over Jews for centuries has marked both communities in ways large and small. In a broad perspective, this imbalance of power has produced a legacy of mistrust and suspicion, which we cannot erase but can learn to accept and overcome. On a personal level, religious bridging in the United States has reached unprecedented proportions.[1] In two generations, the intermarriage rate for Jews has grown by an order of magnitude—from the single digits in 1960 to essentially half in 2010. This phenomenon has brought Jews and Christians into intimate contact and helped to demythologize the Jews in the eyes of Christians. However, it is also a most worrisome trend from a Jewish perspective as the price of religious acceptance may have been purchased at the expense of religious identity and integrity. The subject of interfaith marriage deserves significant attention and indeed there are excellent, incisive, and insightful works in this field.[2]

Yet paradoxically, the tiny minority of Jews has exerted an enormous influence on Christian self-understanding. As noted earlier, Christians cannot educate their children about their tradition without reference to Jews and Judaism for the simple reasons that (1) the Old Testament[3] is part of the Christian canon and (2) Jesus is understood as part of Israel's story. Christians have been perennially baffled by why Jews don't read these scriptures as Christians do, which perhaps explains why Christian leaders periodically became fixated on bringing Jews to baptism. It

---

1. See, e.g., Robert D. Putnam and David E. Campbell, *American Grace: How Religion Divides and Unites Us* (New York: Simon & Schuster, 2010).

2. See Sylvia Barrack Fishman, *Double or Nothing? Jewish Families and Mixed Marriage* (Waltham, MA: Brandeis University Press, 2004); Egon Mayer, *Children of Intermarriage* (New York: American Jewish Committee, 1983); and Steven Cohen and Arnold Eisen, *The Jew Within* (Bloomington: Indiana University Press, 2000).

3. Note again that the Christian "Old Testament" neither contains the exact same books nor the same order as the Jewish Tanakh (the Hebrew acronym for the Torah, the Prophets, and the Writings). Nonetheless, the presence of the scriptures of ancient Israel in the Christian Bible is a determinative influence in shaping Christian self-understanding.

is almost as though Christianity's legitimacy depended on Jewish acceptance of the Gospel. Jews do not experience this spiritual interdependence. On the contrary, Jews may relate to Christian interpretations of the Bible as retrojections, ex post facto readings that justify Christian tenets generally, and account particularly for the prefiguring of Jesus. Jews are accustomed to many conflicting interpretations of sacred texts, and indeed definitive versions of the Bible and the Talmud present divergent readings on the same page. Nevertheless, there are boundaries, interpretations that reside outside the parameters of legitimate exegesis. For Jews interpretations of the Torah that include Jesus are out-of-bounds.

While it is true that Jewish children can be raised as Jews without needing to learn about Christianity, it could be asked if it is good for Jews to be ignorant of Christianity. We respond emphatically, no! There is no compelling reason for a Jew to live devoid of a respectful understanding of Christianity. (The question as to whether Jewish self-understanding is significantly impacted by Christianity will be considered below.)

Judaism and Christianity have a long, entwined history, stitched together with theological threads of connection and contention. We wonder if the propinquity between Jews and Christians, which we hope is evident in this "insider/outsider" presentation, can be found in any other pairing of religions. While we accept the premise that it is intellectually and spiritually beneficial to learn about world religions generally, we believe that their uniquely intertwined histories provide an especially compelling rationale for Christians to learn about Judaism and for Jews to learn about Christianity. Surely Islam has close religious and historical connections with both Judaism and Christianity, but

without sharing common scriptures, perhaps the relationship with Islam is not so determinative of religious identity, particularly for Christians.

## Challenges of a New Relationship

Several times in part 1, we have alluded to the new relationship between Christianity and Judaism, a relationship that has been growing for several decades and is still, given their two-millennial history, in its childhood. As we traced the threads of the Jewish and Christian tapestry, we also became more aware of the challenges this new and positive relationship presents.

Even today, some Jews and Christians operate with inherited cultural caricatures rather than accurate portraits of each other; for instance, that Jews killed Jesus or that Christians are idolaters. Sometimes these stereotypes are unconscious, sometimes explicit. For example, there are Christians who misrepresent the rabbinic tradition as mindless legalism and Jews who distort the Christian experience of God as Triune into polytheism. We believe Jews and Christians alike should learn sensitivity to each other's perspectives, putting themselves in the other's shoes so to speak, while simultaneously retaining their own orientations and identities. The latter, however, will likely be revised in the light of more accurate knowledge of the other. As Jews and Christians learn more about each other, they will undoubtedly retain biases, but hopefully, prejudices will decrease significantly.

Specifically, Christians grapple with the meaning and vitality of Jewish covenanting with God, which important Christian leaders are coming to respect (as vividly shown in the relevant writings of Popes John Paul II and Benedict XVI).[4] Yet it remains a challenge for Christians to envision such an intimate relationship with God—one described in biblical terms

---

4. See *ccjr.us/dialogika-resources/documents-and-statements/roman-catholic*.

as "covenantal"—that does not somehow include Jesus Christ. As a recent book frames the question, "How might we Christians in our time reaffirm our faith claims that Jesus Christ is the savior of all humanity, even as we affirm the Jewish people's covenantal life with God?"[5]

The recent affirmative statements from several Christian churches that Jewish covenanting with God continues[6] challenge Jews to think anew about their traditional hopes for the future of the peoples of the world (as, e.g., in Gen. 12:3, in which God tells Abram, the future Abraham, "All the families of the earth shall bless themselves by you").[7] Could Christianity be relevant to an anticipated blessing to the peoples of the world? This question deserves further attention by Jews and Christians as they consider their self-understandings in relation to one another.

Such basic topics will take time to explore, especially since neither Christians nor Jews have many positive expressions about each other from the past to draw upon. We feel that we are witnessing the blessed beginnings of Jewish and Christian rapprochement—an epochal moment. We hope we have conveyed our excitement about this in these chapters. We want to contribute to the spirit of reconciliation and hope, because we do not take for granted that efforts at Jewish-Christian dialogue in the last fifty years will bear fruit absent constant cultivation. We want to ensure this unprecedented period does not become an ephemeral anomaly. If young Jews and Christians commit themselves to an interreligious future of mutual enhancement, this rapprochement will deepen and grow. We hope our chapters not only contribute to an ongoing narrative but also testify to the possibility and desirability of a Jewish-Christian amity that transcends mere tolerance and builds upon a foundation of mutual respect, appreciative inquiry, and spiritual growth.

## Dialogical Dynamics

Jews and Christians should have accurate knowledge about one another, and interreligious dialogue is indispensible to this goal. Moving this dialogue beyond the clarification of misunderstandings to the achievement of interreligious enrichment, however, demands great effort. Occasional ceremonial politeness is not the same as regular interaction; it is the latter that we have experienced and advocate.

We believe there is no substitute for interpersonal relationships, for friendships across religious traditions. After all, religions remain abstract systems unless embodied in people who develop trust and respect for each other. Personal friendships can work through misunderstandings or missteps, which inevitably occur, particularly in a relationship as fraught with inherited suspicions and hurts as that between Jews and Christians. We have co-taught classes in many settings, participated in formal academic interreligious dialogues, and been theological writing partners. However, over and above these tasks, we have developed a friendship and learned

---

5. Philip A. Cunningham et al., eds., *Christ Jesus and the Jewish People Today: New Explorations of the Theological Interrelationships* (Grand Rapids, MI: William B. Eerdmans, 2011).

6. To cite just a few examples: "Jews are in covenant relationship with God," 99th General Assembly of the Presbyterian Church USA, 1987; "God's covenant with the Jewish people has not been abrogated," General Synod 16 of the United Church of Christ, 1987; and "[God] made with them [Jewish people] a covenant of eternal love which was never revoked," Pope John Paul II, 1987.

7. Biblical citations taken from *Tanakh: A New Translation of the Holy Scriptures according to the Traditional Hebrew Text* (Philadelphia: Jewish Publication Society, 1985).

about each other as human beings, parents, spouses, and teachers. Through this multidimensional, evolving relationship, we have become more than colleagues, and we hope to become the norm rather than the exception.

Some people may have difficulty with religious distinctions. Putting interpersonal harmony and friendship first, they might tend to dismiss religions as divisive and attempt to relate to people as individuals rather than as members belonging to a particular religious community. They might be uncomfortable with religious topics that could cause discord, and so avoid them. History might be disregarded as unhelpfully reprising past conflicts.

There is certainly merit to forming friendships across ethnic, cultural, or religious lines. But friendships can remain superficial unless the differences among friends can be openly explored. Specifically *interreligious* friendship can unleash the universal dimensions of faith traditions to bring potent energy to actively heal the wounds of our world. In fact, we feel that it is not by avoiding religious differences but by embracing them in dialogue that people can constructively address religiously motivated bigotry or violence. Even skeptics of interreligious dialogue on theological grounds have agreed that there is reason to build coalitions among religious communities to address social justice concerns. Religion has been abused in the past, but people do not have to repeat abusive patterns. Believers can demonstrate that religion is intimately and ultimately a force for good and for God.

It seems to us that interreligious friendship thrives when there is a willingness to learn, when there is a humble recognition that no individual can know all the truth, and when each of us is seen as akin to a piece of a mosaic. In our differences, we can be complementary (as well as complimentary!). Interreligious friendship can result in reflective Jewish or Christian "practitioners" who are able to tap into the creative power of their traditions in new and life-affirming ways.

# Resources for Further Study

## Review Questions

1. Select one Jewish prayer and explain how it reflects core Jewish beliefs.
2. Why was the destruction of the Jerusalem Temple in 70 CE a pivotal moment in Jewish history?
3. Briefly describe the main "movements" or denominations of Judaism in the United States today. How do they each approach the biblical mizvoth?
4. What is the significance of the Land of Israel in the Jewish tradition? What are some issues that arise with regard to the modern State of Israel?
5. What distortions of Judaism have been prominent in Christian history?

## Questions for Reflection and Discussion

1. What are the implications of describing Jews as a people as well as a religious community?
2. What are some indications that Judaism values diversity and differences of opinion?
3. Compare the Jewish and Christian annual cycles of holy days. Are there similarities among them? How do they differ?
4. The Jewish and Christian authors of these chapters assert that "the relationship between Christianity and Judaism is unique among pairings of world religions." Assess the factors they mention in support of this judgment.
5. It has been said that Jews and Christians often use the same words but mean somewhat different things by them. What are some examples?

## Glossary

**aggadah**  Hebrew for "lore." Narrative, homiletic, and nonlegal material found in rabbinic literature.

**Akeidat Yitzhak**  Hebrew for the "Binding of Isaac." The traditional Jewish description of Genesis 22, in which God commands Abraham to sacrifice his son, Isaac.

**canon**  The list or body of texts considered authoritative or binding in some way by a particular tradition. Frequently the term is used in reference to collections of sacred or scriptural texts.

**chevrutah**  Hebrew for "study partner." A traditional rabbinic mode of study in which pairs of students explore and debate various interpretations of a text.

**Conservative Judaism**  A strand of contemporary Judaism that sees the observance of the commandments as evolving and open to multiple *halakhic* approaches.

**Dabru Emet ("Speak the Truth")**  A 2000 "Jewish Statement on Christians and Christianity" that sought to acquaint Jewish readers with post-Shoah reforms in major branches of Christianity as regards their teachings about Judaism.

**Ehyeh-Asher-Ehyeh**   Hebrew for "I Am Who I Am" or "I Will Be Who I Will Be." The sacred name revealed by God to Moses in Exodus 3:14.

**halakhah**   Hebrew for "the way of walking." The legal material found in rabbinic and post-rabbinic literature.

**Hanukkah**   An eight-day Jewish festival celebrating the rededication of the Second Temple in Jerusalem following the Maccabean Revolt against the Syrian king Antiochus IV in the second century BCE. According to tradition, the relit Temple lamp burned for eight days despite having oil sufficient for only one day.

**Israel**   Hebrew for "wrestle with God." (1) The name given to the patriarch Jacob after his overnight grappling with a mysterious supernatural entity in Genesis 32:25–31. (2) The people descended from Jacob/Israel, the children of Israel. In this sense *Israel* is the liturgical self-designation of the Jewish people today. (3) The modern nation-state.

**Mishnah**   Hebrew for "repetition." The first written expression of the "Oral Law" that forms the basis of the rabbinic textual tradition. Completed around 200 CE, it is organized in six major parts or "orders": *Zeraim* (Seeds), *Moed* (Festival), *Nashim* (Women), *Nezikin* (Damages), *Kodashim* (Holy Things), and *Tehorot* (Purities).

**mitzvot**   Hebrew for "commandments." According to rabbinic tradition, the 613 commands articulated in the Torah for the people of Israel to observe.

**Nostra Aetate (In Our Time)**   The Declaration on the Relationship of the Church to Non-Christian Religions promulgated by Pope Paul VI on October 28, 1965, in the name of the Roman Catholic bishops convened for the Second Vatican Council. The declaration was the beginning of a new, positive relationship between the Catholic Church and the Jewish people.

**olam haba**   Hebrew for "Age/World to Come." In the Jewish tradition this refers to the new epoch when the cosmos will exist in accord with God's will for creation. It is more or less equivalent with the Christian phrase "kingdom of God."

**Orthodox Judaism**   The form of Judaism that understands both the Oral and Written Torah to have been given by God to Moses on Mount Sinai and so observes the commandments according to the traditional rabbinic interpretations. There is a range of views within Orthodoxy from those who prefer to avoid much contact with the wider world (Haredi Orthodoxy) to those who engage the contemporary world while remaining traditionally observant (Modern Orthodoxy).

**Passover (Pesach)**   The seven- or eight-day Jewish celebration of the escape from slavery in Egypt. The heart of the festival occurs in Jewish homes during the Passover Meal or Seder, at which symbolic foods such as *matzah* (unleavened bread), *maror* (bitter herbs), and *charoset* (apples, nuts, and sweet wine) bring to life the events found in Exodus 3:20.

**Pharisees**   A Jewish movement in the late Second Temple period that sought to make everyday life as holy as in the Temple itself. Pharisees voluntarily practiced ritual purity at their fellowship meals even at a great distance from the Temple, where such purity rites were required, and interpreted the Torah creatively and in accord with oral traditions.

**rabbis**   Hebrew for "authoritative teachers." (1) The Jewish teachers and scholars in the early centuries of the Common Era who composed authoritative interpretations of the Torah in the major works of the Mishnah (c. 200 CE) and the Jerusalem and Babylonian Talmuds (c. 350

and c. 500 CE, respectively), and the definitive Hebrew form of the Jewish scriptures (c. 750 CE). At least partially descended from the traditions of the Pharisees, the rabbis valued multiple approaches to uncover the riches of the sacred text. (2) Jewish religious leaders today.

**Reconstructionist Judaism**  A modern Jewish movement that tends to maintain traditional practices, but not necessarily for traditional reasons.

**Reform Judaism**  A modern Jewish movement that does not subscribe to the traditional view that the Torah was directly given by God to Moses. Therefore the commands can be interpreted according to contemporary contexts and some may be deemed as obsolete.

**responsa**  Hebrew for "rulings." Responses given by legal scholars to questions posed about legal and ethical matters.

**Rosh Hashanah**  Hebrew for "Head of the Year." Marks the start of the Jewish New Year. This is the beginning of a ten-day period of reflection on the past year, known as the Days of Awe or the High Holydays. The self-reflection is to lead to repentance and prayers for the forgiveness of sins.

**Sabbath**  From the Hebrew *shabbat*, "day of rest." Observed each week by Jews from sundown on Friday to nightfall on Saturday as a day to refrain from everyday activities and to reflect on God's will. It also anticipates the joy of the Age to Come.

**Shavuot**  Hebrew for "weeks." Festival that occurs fifty days after Passover and celebrates the giving of the Torah to Moses on Mount Sinai. Its Greek name is *Pentecost*.

**Shema**  Hebrew for "Hear!" The prayer from Deuteronomy 6:4 said by Jews twice daily: "Hear, O Israel! The Lord is our God, the Lord alone."[1]

**Shoah**  A Hebrew term for the Nazi genocide of European Jews during the Second World War. It means "devastating whirlwind."

**Simchat Torah**  Hebrew for "Rejoicing with the Torah." Marks the end of the annual weekly cycle of readings from the Torah with the conclusion of the book of Deuteronomy and the start of a new cycle with the book of Genesis. It follows the feast of Sukkot in the autumn.

**Sukkot**  Hebrew for "booths" or "tents." An autumnal thanksgiving festival that lasts seven or eight days. Recalling the transient lives of the Hebrews for forty years after escaping slavery in Egypt and also the temporary shelters of workers in the fields at harvest time, Jewish families will build a sukkah or wooden shelter outdoors in which meals will be eaten during the festival.

**supersessionism**  The Christian theological claim that the church had superseded or replaced the Jewish people as God's own people because the coming of Christianity was seen as rendering Judaism obsolete and/or because God had punished Jews for the crucifixion of Jesus. This general outlook prevailed in Christianity for about eighteen centuries until systematically critiqued after World War II.

**Talmud**  Hebrew for "learning." The great rabbinic explorations and elaborations of the Mishnah that form the bases of rabbinic Judaism. Two parallel endeavors in the centers of Jewish learning in the early centuries of the Common Era produced the Jerusalem Talmud (c. 350 CE) and Babylonian Talmud (c. 500 CE).

**Tisha B'Av**  A sorrowful annual Jewish fast day that occurs on the ninth day (Tisha) of the Hebrew month of Av, recalling the destruction of both the First and Second Temples in

---

1. This biblical citation is from *Tanakh: A New Translation of the Holy Scriptures according to the Traditional Hebrew Text* (Philadelphia: Jewish Publication Society, 1985).

Jerusalem. Other tragic events in Jewish history may also be remembered, such as the expulsion of the Jews from Spain in 1492.

**Torah**   Hebrew for "teaching." (1) The first five books of the Jewish and Christian Bibles: Genesis, Exodus, Leviticus, Numbers, and Deuteronomy. (2) Can also be used in a more general sense to refer to the entire canon of Jewish scriptures, more properly named the *Tanakh*: Torah (Teaching), Nevi'im (Prophets), and Ketuvim (Writings). (3) In an extremely broad sense, it can refer to the biblical and rabbinic traditions.

**yetzer hara**   Hebrew for "evil impulse." In the rabbinic understanding, the inclination in human beings to be selfish and egotistical, but also to be ambitious and to plan for the future. Observance of the Torah's commandments is seen as the method of controlling this inclination and channeling its energies for positive purposes.

**yetzer hatov**   Hebrew for "good impulse." In the rabbinic understanding, this is the inclination in human beings to be concerned about doing the will of God, the welfare of others, and having a sense of personal and communal responsibility. It is seen as emerging at puberty.

**Yom Kippur (Day of Atonement)**   The most solemn day of the Jewish year, it concludes the ten-day period of repentance that follows Rosh Hashanah. The day is spent in prayer and fasting, with promises to God for future good deeds and reconciliation with fellow human beings.

## Annotated Bibliography

Fackenheim, Emil. *What Is Judaism? An Interpretation for the Present Age.* Syracuse, NY: Syracuse University Press, 1999.

A rich journey into liberal Jewish theology by a seminal thinker who is credited with the articulation of a 614th commandment: not to allow Hitler a posthumous victory.

Heschel, Abraham Joshua. *The Sabbath.* New York: Farrar, Straus and Giroux, 2005.

A poetic, soulful exploration of the day the sages described as a foretaste of heaven, and a penetrating look into the holiness of time over space.

Kessler, Edward. *An Introduction to Jewish-Christian Relations.* Cambridge, UK; New York: Cambridge University Press, 2010.

An excellent overview of the history of relations between Judaism and Christianity as well as the major theological questions being discussed today. Also considered are the Holocaust and the State of Israel, topics that can be difficult for Christians and Jews to discuss.

Prell, Riv-Ellen. *Women Remaking American Judaism.* Detroit, MI: Wayne State University Press, 2007.

Arguably the greatest revolution in Judaism in the last century involves the role of women in Jewish life and leadership. This volume offers firsthand testimonies and reflective essays.

Sandmel, David, Rosann Catalano, and Christopher M. Leighton, eds. *Irreconcilable Differences? A Learning Resource for Jews and Christians.* Boulder, CO: Westview, 2001.

Pairs of Jewish and Christian educators address topics of concern to both traditions and their interrelationship, including whether Jews and Christians worship the same God, sin and repentance, how we read the Bible, the meaning of Israel, and Jews and Christians working together for peace and social justice.

Sarna, Jonathan. *American Judaism: A History*. New Haven, CT: Yale University Press, 2004.

A magisterial work in sweep and depth that defines the contours of a distinctive, if not unique, expression of Judaism as it has developed in the United States.

Steinberg, Milton. *Basic Judaism*. Orlando, FL: Harvest Books, 1975.

A readily accessible, classic introduction to the foundations of Jewish thought and practice from a twentieth-century Conservative rabbi, with the breadth to include aspects of Orthodox and Reform expressions of Judaism.

Telushkin, Joseph. *Jewish Literacy: The Most Important Things to Know about the Jewish Religion, Its People, and Its History*. New York: William Morrow, 2008.

A popular yet profound work that provides insight into the rabbinic mind.

Wouk, Herman. *This Is My God*. New York, Boston, and London: Little, Brown, and Co., 1992.

The growth of Orthodox Judaism in America and beyond is a fascinating and worthy study advanced in this personal, thoughtful exposition by a magnificent writer.

## Internet Resources

Conservative Judaism: *uscj.org*

General: *Myjewishlearning.com*

Hasidic Judaism: *chabad.org*

Orthodox Judaism: *ou.org*

Reconstructionist Judaism: *rrc.edu*

Reform Judaism: *urj.org*

Jewish Theological Seminary: *jtsa.edu*

Reconstructionist Rabbinical College: *rrc.edu*

Yeshiva University: *yu.edu*

## Seminaries

American Jewish University: *aju.edu*

Hebrew College: *hebrewcollege.edu*

Hebrew Union College—Jewish Institute of Religion: *huc.edu*

### Christian-Jewish Relations

Council of Centers on Jewish-Christian Relations and Institute for Jewish-Catholic Relations of Saint Joseph's University: *dialogika.us*

International Council of Christians and Jews: *jcrelations.net*

# PART 2: ISLAM

*Rita George–Tvrtković and Zeki Saritoprak*

# CHAPTER 5

# An Outsider's Perspective

*Rita George-Tvrtković*

## Introducing Islam

I teach a course on interreligious dialogue, and the vast majority of my students say that the religion they are most eager to learn about is Islam. They come to class familiar with the stereotypes currently proliferating on the Internet and cable talk shows: that Muslims are terrorists, that Islam oppresses women, that Muslim equals Arab, that jihad means holy war, that Islam is homogeneous. But many students are rightly suspicious of these stereotypes and want to know what Islam is really about. Others come to class aware of the term *Abrahamic faiths* and hope to learn about the similarities between Christians, Muslims, and Jews.

My students reflect a general trend in American society since 9/11: the desire for basic, reliable information about Islam. What does the religion really teach? What does the Qur'an contain? Does Islam advocate holy war? Quick answers to these questions are not wanting; a Google search for the word *jihad* will produce millions of hits, including many Muslim-sponsored sites with accurate information. But most of these are buried beneath numerous Islamophobic Web pages such as *jihadwatch.org*, which appears near the top of the list and claims to "correct popular misconceptions about Islam."

So where can someone find *reliable* information about Islam? I tell my students to go talk to a Muslim—preferably several. This is actually quite possible at my university, a small Catholic institution located in Chicago's diverse suburbs, where the student body is at least 25 percent Muslim. But even in the midst of such diversity, my students know surprisingly little about Islam. For the most part, they do not ask their Muslim classmates about Islam. The mere presence of religious pluralism does not guarantee that people of different faiths will know, understand, or even talk to each other.

Many students are hesitant to broach a topic as volatile as religion with their peers and feel more comfortable learning about Islam in a more formal setting like the classroom. And in class they soon discover that Islam is as complex as Christianity, Judaism, or any other religion. Some are surprised to learn that just like Christians, Muslims practice their religion to varying degrees or not at all. And as students learn about the diverse spectrum that is Islam, they realize that despite the presence of basic "unifying" features such as the five pillars, they must be careful not to generalize. They eventually learn to ask questions that will help them to distinguish between different strains of Islam.

Just one example of Islam's diversity—a diversity that is historical, geographic, cultural,

These images illustrate some of the ways modest dress is interpreted by Muslim women: from modern jeans and long shirts to the more traditional chador.

linguistic, legal, and ritual—will be mentioned in this introduction, and that is cultural diversity. One common assumption is that Arab equals Muslim and Muslim equals Arab. While Islam was born in Saudi Arabia and flourished in capital cities such as Damascus and Baghdad, today only about 20 percent of the world's Muslims hail from the Middle East and North Africa.[1] The Arab-equals-Muslim equation is further refuted by the existence of many ancient Christian communities in the Middle East such as the Maronites of Lebanon, Copts of Egypt, and the Assyrian Church of the East in Iraq and Iran (the last of which is not even an Arab nation).

While Arabic-speaking North African countries such as Egypt, Morocco, and Algeria are easily identified as Muslim, many are unaware of the significant and ancient populations of Muslims living in sub-Saharan Africa, in countries such as Mali, Nigeria, Tanzania, Senegal, Uganda, and South Africa. But it is in Asia (and not Middle Eastern Asia) where the majority of the world's Muslims reside today. Out of a global population of roughly 1.6 billion Muslims, more than 30 percent come from South Asia (Pakistan, India, and Bangladesh) alone. Southeast Asia is also home to many Muslims: Indonesia is the most populous Muslim nation on earth with

---

1. All statistics are taken from the Pew Forum Report, "Mapping the Global Muslim Population: A Report on the Size and Distribution of the World's Muslim Population," October 7, 2009, *pewforum.org/Mapping-the-Global-Muslim-Population.aspx.*

roughly 203 million; Malaysia has significant numbers; and there are strong minority communities of Muslims in Thailand and the Philippines. Islam entered China in the middle of the seventh century CE, and today there are more than 22 million Chinese Muslims.

Finally, while pundits often juxtapose "Islam and the West," in actuality significant populations of Muslims live *in* the West. Since the mid-twentieth century there has been an increasing, visible influx of Muslim immigrants into nations such as Australia (currently 1.7% of the population), Canada (2%), the United States (0.8%), England (2.7%), Germany (5%), and France (6%). And Islam has been present in European countries such as Bosnia, Albania, and Bulgaria for more than 600 years, while Muslims of African descent began to arrive en masse to the Americas by the early sixteenth century.

## Historical Christian Approaches to Islam

Many assume that the well-publicized strife between Christians and Muslims in certain parts of the world today is inevitable, in part thanks to a history many think they know: Crusades, colonialism, terrorism. But Christian-Muslim relations have varied according to time and place. The situation in eleventh-century Cordoba differed greatly from that in eighth-century Damascus or nineteenth-century Dar es Salaam.

How have Christians throughout history viewed Islam? One of the first to write about the religion was the famous eighth-century theologian John of Damascus, a Byzantine Christian and native of Syria who had been employed by the Muslim caliph before entering monastic life. John called Islam the "still-prevailing deceptive superstition of the Ishmaelites"[2] and placed it last in a book enumerating Christian heresies. Another theologian from this era who discussed Islam was Theodore Abu Qurrah, one of the first Christians to write in Arabic.[3]

With the exception of Iberia, which had had a significant Muslim presence since the early eighth century, the rest of medieval Europe had very little accurate information about Islam until the time of the Crusades. The famous Song of Roland—an eleventh-century French epic extolling Charlemagne's victories over the Saracens[4]—epitomizes European ignorance of Islam by describing Muslims as polytheists who bow down to Apollo and even Muhammad.

But after the twelfth century, it is possible to speak of a "mainstream" medieval Latin Christian view of Islam.[5] Despite minor differences in emphasis, most Christians writing about Islam from the twelfth century on agreed that the only proper responses to Muslims were to convert them, fight them, or study them. And medieval Christians generally believed the following: Islam was a monotheistic religion with a heretical Christology; Muhammad was a lustful man, a false prophet, and the Antichrist; the Qur'an

2. For the original writings of John of Damascus pertaining to Islam, see his *De haeresibus* in *John of Damascus on Islam*, trans. Daniel Sahas (Leiden: Brill, 1972). The above quotation is on p. 132.

3. For more on early Eastern Christian engagement with Islam in general, see Sidney Griffith, *The Church in the Shadow of the Mosque* (Princeton: Princeton University Press, 2010). For Theodore Abu Qurrah, see *A Treatise on the Veneration of Holy Icons*, trans. Sidney Griffith (Leuven: Peeters, 1997).

4. *Saracens* is the medieval Latin word for Muslims. The term *Saracen* predates the rise of Islam in the seventh century; in the earlier usage it referred more broadly to the Arabs.

5. For more on medieval Christian views of Islam, see Norman Daniel, *Islam and the West* (Oxford: Oneworld, 1993), and John Tolan, *Saracens* (New York: Columbia University Press, 2002).

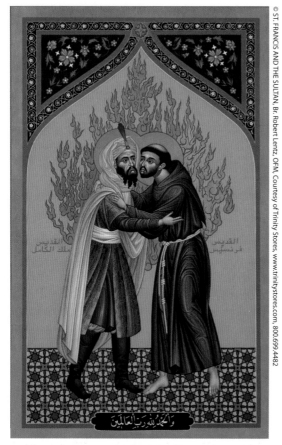

A contemporary icon by R. Lenz depicts the meeting between St. Francis and the Sultan in a positive light. The Arabic statement at the bottom reads: "Praise be to God (Allah), the Lord of the universes."

strand. Some Christians, such as Peter the Venerable, abbot of Cluny (d. 1156), actively sought out accurate information about Islam. He commissioned the first Latin translation of the Qur'an, which Europeans relied upon for roughly 400 years. Peter sought to conquer Muslims with reason, not violence. St. Francis of Assisi (d. 1226) also approached Muslims in a peaceful manner. All of Francis's biographers mention his meeting with Sultan al-Malik in Damietta, Egypt, during the Crusades. This famous encounter was traditionally viewed as proof of the saint's fervent desire to convert Muslims.[6] More recently, this event has been reinterpreted by some advocates of interreligious dialogue as a positive example of Christian-Muslim relations, as can be seen in this icon.[7] And Francis's Rule is one of the first founding documents of any Catholic religious order to devote significant space to Muslims; it contains an entire chapter entitled "On going among the Saracens and other infidels." The Dominican missionary Riccoldo da Montecroce (d. 1320) lived in Baghdad for over a decade and wrote praise-filled descriptions of seven Muslim practices he dubbed "works of perfection": devotion to study, solicitude in prayer, reverence for the name of God, hospitality, almsgiving, solemn demeanor, and fraternity. Finally, Europeans who had Muslims as neighbors during the medieval period (e.g., Christians in Iberia, Sicily, and the Balkans) had more complex and varied views of Islam than those with little or no personal experience of real-life Muslims.

was a manmade book; and the Saracens were violent, irrational, and misogynistic. Sadly, many of these stereotypes persist today.

The "mainstream" medieval view described above, however, represents only one strand among many, even if it has remained the predominant

In the early modern period (fifteenth and sixteenth centuries), the medieval missionary mind-set continued to influence Christian views of Islam, but new intellectual approaches also emerged. The sixteenth and seventeenth

---

6. The meeting is the subject of several new books. One recent scholarly study of this encounter is John Tolan, *Saint Francis and the Sultan* (New York: Oxford University Press, 2010). For more on the Franciscan encounter with Islam in general, see J. Hoeberichts, *Francis and Islam* (St. Bonaventure, NY: Franciscan Institute Publications, 1997).

7. This icon is featured on the cover of another recent book inspired by Francis and the Sultan: George Dardess and Marvin Krier Mich, *In the Spirit of St. Francis and the Sultan: Catholics and Muslims Working Together for the Common Good* (Maryknoll, NY: Orbis Books, 2011).

centuries saw an increase in Arabophilia amongst European philologists. The first printed edition of a Latin Qur'an was published in 1542, although the translation itself was the very same commissioned by Peter the Venerable in the twelfth century. By the end of the seventeenth century, several new translations of the Qur'an from the original Arabic had been produced in both English and French.

Another less positive factor affecting Western views of Islam that emerged at this time is what Edward Said has famously termed "Orientalism." A distorted view of "the East" (meaning the Middle East, not the Far East) held by Westerners, Orientalism stereotypes Middle Easterners as prurient, violent, irrational, and lazy and has influenced academia, art, economics, politics, and the popular imagination since the beginning of the colonial period.[8] While Orientalism has predominated among European and American Christians, it has generally not taken root among Asian and African Christians, who usually share a culture, language, and history with their Muslim neighbors and therefore have often had different experiences of Islam than their Western coreligionists. For example, St. Thomas Christians living in Kerala, India, have historically coexisted well with their Muslim neighbors, perhaps partly because in Kerala, Christians and Muslims both live as minorities alongside a Hindu majority.

## Unique Aspects of Islam

A religion's name often hints at its central focus. *Islam* means "submission to God's will," and this definition highlights the equal importance placed on God and the proper human response to him. The term *Islam* is preferred over the outdated *Mohammedanism*, not only because the word originates in the Qur'an and is used by Muslims

themselves but also because the latter misleadingly parallels the self-identification of Christians as followers of Christ, and incorrectly suggests that Muslims believe Muhammad to be divine.

The Qur'an considers *islam* (lowercase) to be the original human religion. As such, it addresses two fundamental questions: who is this one God to whom humans must submit, and what does submission look like, practically speaking? For Muslims, submission is demonstrated primarily through action. Some scholars speak of Islam as a religion focused more on orthopraxy ("right practice") over orthodoxy ("right belief"). Islamic orthopraxy is expressed in the "five pillars," the quintessential practices of the religion: *shahada* (declaration of faith); *salat* (prayer); *zakat* (almsgiving); *sawm* (fasting during Ramadan); and *hajj* (pilgrimage). Despite Islam's great global diversity in culture, race, and language, the international community of Muslims (*umma*) is united by submission to the one God through the practice of these same five pillars.

The first pillar, *shahada* ("I witness that there is no god but God and Muhammad is the messenger of God") can be seen as an example of orthopraxy since the beginning part of the phrase, "I witness," implies action. But the phrase also serves as an expression of orthodoxy. The first half, "there is no god but God," is a monotheistic declaration that can be affirmed not only by Muslims, but by Christians and Jews as well. While *Allah* is the Arabic word for God, Muslims often translate that word into the vernacular (*Dios, Dieu, Gott*) to emphasize that they too believe in the same one God professed by Christians, Jews, and other monotheists.

The second half of the shahada, "and Muhammad is the messenger of God," distinguishes Islam from Christianity and Judaism by identifying Muhammad as the final bringer of God's definitive revelation. For Muslims,

---

8. See Edward Said, *Orientalism* (New York: Vintage, 1978).

Muhammad is both a prophet (*nabi*) and a messenger (*rasul*). Muhammad is last in a long line of prophets with names familiar to Christians and Jews, such as Adam, Ibrahim (Abraham), and Ayoub (Job), and as such he is called the "seal" of the prophets. All messengers are prophets, but not all prophets are messengers. The relatively few messengers throughout Islamic history are distinguished by having brought a divine dispensation; Muslims therefore recognize Musa (Moses) and `Isa (Jesus) as messengers for bringing the *tawrah* and *injil*, respectively. Islam judges Judaism and Christianity in a positive light partly because these religions, like Islam, center on a single revealed book. The Qur'an calls Christians and Jews "people of the book"; they are mentioned as such in Sura 3:199, Sura 4:171, Sura 29:46–47, and elsewhere.

## Basic Sources

The Qur'an is the most authoritative source of Islamic belief and practice. Muslims revere it as the pure and uncorrupted word of God, and its centrality to the Islamic faith is such that some scholars prefer to compare the Qur'an and Jesus rather than the Qur'an and the Bible. A strong parallel is seen between the Christian doctrine of the Incarnation (the belief that Jesus is the "Word of God made flesh") and the Muslim belief in the Qur'an as the "Word of God made book," a concept that has been termed *inlibration*.

Muslims believe that the exceptional beauty of Qur'anic prose demonstrates its inherent inimitability (*i'jaz*), a quality that in turn proves its divine origin. In part due to *i'jaz*, the only true Qur'an is in Arabic; translations are considered mere commentaries. Since the majority of the world's Muslims are not native Arabic speakers, most strive to learn as much of the language as possible to enable a firsthand reading of and direct experience with the Qur'anic text.

The word *Qur'an* means recitation; in fact, the very first verse revealed to Muhammad is "Recite (or read) in the name of the Lord" (Sura 96:1). The connection between the Qur'an and recitation has special significance. Muslims believe that the Qur'an was revealed aurally to Muhammad via the angel Gabriel over twenty-two years; he memorized what he heard and conveyed it to his followers. They then recited it back to him before memorizing it themselves. While some written copies did exist during his lifetime, only after the Prophet's death were the revelations systematically compiled in book form. Since then, both memorizing and reciting the Qur'an have been praised as exemplary forms of worship. A Muslim who can recite the entire Qur'an by heart is called a *hafiz*, meaning "protector." This definition suggests that recitation is more dependable in protecting and preserving the Qur'an than reading and writing.

Islam's aural/oral approach to the Qur'an can be compared to the ancient Christian practice of *lectio divina*, where monks read and meditate upon the Bible with their whole body: eyes, ears, and mouth. Both the Islamic and Christian traditions seem to agree that silent reading is insufficient for the believer to properly internalize a sacred text.

The Qur'an consists of 114 chapters (suras), which are organized by length in descending order, with the exception of the first. The Qur'an shares much subject matter with the Bible and includes many stories about familiar figures, such as Da'ud (David), `Isa (Jesus), and Maryam (Mary), although details often differ. For example, both the Qur'an and Bible include the story in which God asks Ibrahim/Abraham to sacrifice his son. In the Bible (Genesis 22), Abraham's son is named Isaac, while in the Qur'an (Sura 37:99–109), Ibrahim's son is unnamed, though later Islamic tradition identifies the son as Isma`il (Ishmael).

Muslims and Christians accept the Qur'an and Bible, respectively, as divine revelation, but their understanding of the nature of revelation differs. Muslims believe that the Qur'an is God's literal word, with no human contribution whatsoever. In fact, Muslim tradition declares Muhammad to have been both trustworthy and illiterate; this dual identity is important, for it suggests first and foremost his reliability in conveying God's complete message, but also his inability to add anything to it. The Christian view of revelation is more complex, in part due to the fact that the biblical canon was written and compiled over many centuries and in several different languages. Christians themselves disagree about what it means when they call the Bible the inspired word of God. Some Christians acknowledge the complex interplay between God and the inspired author, with God using human language and culture to convey meaning; such a reading requires interpretation in context. Other Christians have a view of inspiration that is more Islamic in the sense that they understand the Bible as God's literal word.

Since the Qur'an is so central to Islamic faith and practice, the science of Qur'anic exegesis or interpretation (*tafsir*) has always been one of the most important branches of Islamic theology. There is as much diversity among Muslims in interpreting the Qur'an as there is among Christians in interpreting the Bible. Different exegetical schools throughout history, such as the Mu`tazili and Zahiri, have disagreed on proper Qur'anic exegesis. Another source of exegetical diversity comes from the four traditional Sunni schools of law (Hanbali, Hanafi, Shafi'i, and Maliki) plus the Shi'i Ja`fari school; all five share the same sources of law, the Qur'an being primary among them, but interpret them differently. This in turn leads to legal variances among Muslim countries, each of which adheres to a different school. Theologically they are all equally valid. Muslims believe that the Prophet said that "the diversity of my community is a mercy from God."

After the Qur'an, the second most important Islamic source is the hadith (literally meaning "saying"), a body of literature made up of individual reports that preserve the sunna (words and deeds) of Muhammad. Some Muslims consider the hadith a form of Qur'anic interpretation, since it provides examples of how Muhammad understood and actually lived out Qur'anic precepts. A hadith (plural *ahadith)* is classified as sound, good, weak, or false, depending on a variety of criteria, including the reputation of the person who originally reported it and the solidity of the chain of transmission through time. For example, a hadith recorded by the ninth-century scholar Bukhari and possessing an unbroken chain of transmission would be labeled *sahih* ("sound") and considered among the most authoritative.

## Important Historical Developments

| KEY DATES IN EARLY ISLAM | |
|---|---|
| Pre 570* | *Jahiliyya* (time of ignorance) |
| 570 | Birth of Muhammad |
| 610 | Muhammad receives first revelations |
| 622 | Hijra (Muslims migrate to Medina) |
| 630 | Mecca accepts Islam |
| 632 | Death of Muhammad |
| 632–661 | Four Rightly Guided Caliphs |
| 661–750 | Umayyad Empire |
| 680 | Battle of Karbala |
| 750–1258 | Abbasid Empire |

*All dates refer to the Common Era.

Muhammad was born in Mecca in 570 CE. Unlike the Christian calendar, which begins in the traditional year of Jesus's birth, year one of the Islamic calendar does not center on Muhammad's birth year, but on the date in which the first Islamic community (umma) was formed in Medina: 622 CE.

Muslims refer to the era into which Muhammad was born as *Jahiliyya,* the time of ignorance. His birthplace, Mecca, was a center of trade and polytheistic religion, although Islam does recognize the presence of pre-Islamic monotheists (*hanif*) at this time. The first *hanif* was Ibrahim (Abraham), who was so devoted to the one God, says Muslim tradition, that he destroyed the idols in his father's workshop.

Muhammad would regularly retreat to a cave outside Mecca to pray. When he was about forty years old, he began to receive revelations that he eventually realized came from God. Muhammad's first wife Khadija, a successful business woman fifteen years his senior, supported him and is considered the first convert to Islam.

Muhammad's message was not well received initially. So he and a small band of companions left Mecca for the town of Yathrib, which would eventually come to be known as *medinat an-nabi,* the city of the prophet, or Medina for short. This migration (*hijra*) resulted in the creation of the first Muslim community in Medina in 622. This is year one of the Islamic calendar, which is abbreviated AH, *Anno Hegirae* (in the year of the Hijra), parallel to the Christian AD, *Anno Domini* (in the year of the Lord). After a series of battles between Mecca and Medina, the Muslims finally conquered Mecca in 630, and most of its citizens converted to Islam. By the time of Muhammad's death in 632, all of Arabia was united under this vibrant new religion.

After losing their prophet, the fledgling community was led by a series of four "rightly guided caliphs," all of whom had been among Muhammad's closest companions: Abu Bakr, `Umar, `Uthman, and `Ali. Under the caliphs' leadership, Islam continued to expand. By 634, the religion had spread to Palestine and southern Iraq; by 635 it had reached Damascus, and by 638, Jerusalem. Egypt and Persia were taken in the 640s, and by the early eighth century, Islam had swept west all the way through North Africa to Spain, and east all the way to the Indus River Valley. In the first decades of its existence, Islam's swift expansion throughout the Middle East and Mediterranean was both political and religious, and involved military conquest. In later years, Islam's spread into sub-Saharan Africa, western China, and south and southeast Asia was due more to trade and Sufi missionary activity than to military action.

Concurrent with this expansion, the Muslim community experienced its first major rift. Soon after the death of the Prophet, a disagreement arose between those who wanted Abu Bakr, one of Muhammad's closest companions, to be the first caliph, and those who favored `Ali, the Prophet's cousin and son-in-law. The "partisans of `Ali" (*shi`at `Ali*), who would eventually be known as Shi'ites, believed that caliphs should only be drawn from the Prophet's family. The two sides fought the Battle of Karbala in Iraq in 680. This resulted in the death of several in `Ali's family, most notably his son Husain, and only served to exacerbate the growing split between the two factions. What began as a quarrel about leadership would eventually lead to a permanent split between Sunni and Shi'i Muslims and to the development of significant differences in theology, law, scriptural interpretation, and praxis.

Islam prospered under its first dynasty, the Umayyad, which was centered in Damascus and lasted from 661 to 750 CE. During these years, Islam stretched from Spain in the west to as far as China in the east, and the administration of this vast empire was enabled by a process of Arabization. Damascus became a center of Islamic scholarship, art, and architecture as well as government. Other cities such as Basra and Kufa (both in modern-day Iraq) emerged as centers of religious learning, and genres central to Islamic theology such as hadith, *tafsir,* and *sira* (biographies of Muhammad) developed, along with the very beginnings of *fiqh* (jurisprudence). Also at this time, a new ascetic religious lifestyle within Islam called Sufism arose as a corrective to increasingly rigid legalism and growing materialism in the Muslim community.

By the mid-eighth century, a new dynasty, the Abbasid, had emerged. It shifted the center of the Islamic world east to Baghdad. Despite other claimants to the caliphate during this time (such as the Shi'i Fatimids in Egypt), the Abbasids would rule from 750 to 1258, and under them Islam would grow and flourish. One of the most important achievements during the Abbasid period was the further development of *fiqh* and the four schools of law, which had only just been founded at the end of the Umayyad period. Furthermore, the Abbasids encouraged scholarship; the ninth-century Caliph al-Ma`mun founded the House of Wisdom in Baghdad, which served as a regional center of learning and translation. Here, scholars from all over the known world came together to discuss and translate Greek, Syriac, Arabic, Hebrew, Persian, Latin, and Sanskrit texts. Islamic philosophy and science reached a zenith during the Abbasid period, when some of the most important Muslim thinkers of all time emerged. They include Ibn Sina (known as Avicenna in medieval Europe), whose book of medicine was a standard text in European universities until the seventeenth century; al-Farabi, an influential philosopher and commentator on Aristotle; al-Khwarizmi, who made significant contributions to algebra and from whose name the word *algorithm* derives; and al-Ghazali, the great "reviver" of Islam.

Aspects of ninth-century Baghdadi scholarship were replicated in eleventh-century Iberia. In cities like Cordoba and Toledo, science, scholarship, and interreligious collaboration were fostered under Islamic rule, and tolerance was promoted at the sociopolitical level. Spain's Muslims, Christians, and Jews lived together in a relatively harmonious period known as *convivencia* (coexistence), and great philosophers such as the Jewish Maimonides and the Muslim Ibn Rushd (Averroes) flourished. Like Baghdad, Toledo became a center of learning, and the translation of Greco-Arabic texts into Latin sparked a twelfth-century renaissance that would lead to the founding of universities and a revitalization of science and philosophy in Europe.

Islamic cultures burgeoned in many parts of the world during the early modern period. For example, while Islam had reached India as early as the seventh century via northern land routes, maritime trade on the southern coasts, and Sufi missionizing throughout, it was the rise of the Mughal Empire in the sixteenth century that solidified Islam's dominance in the subcontinent. Likewise, while Islam had been established via maritime trade in southeast Asian countries such as Malaysia and Indonesia since the eighth century, Islam only eclipsed Hinduism and Buddhism in these archipelagos during the sixteenth century. Other great Muslim empires in the early modern period include the Safavids in Iran (beginning 1501) and the Ottomans in Turkey (conquered Constantinople in 1453).

The seventeenth and eighteenth centuries brought great changes to many of these powerful Islamic empires. Throughout the world, places that had formerly been under Islamic control became colonies of the West. For example, Algeria and Tunisia were colonized by the French, India by the English, and Indonesia by the Dutch.

At the same time that many Muslim empires were sinking to the nadir of power, however, revivalist movements began to emerge through-out the Islamic world. One of the first and most influential was the eighteenth-century Wahhabi movement in Saudi Arabia. The Wahhabis were critical of Sufism and popular religious practices such as the veneration of saints and their tombs, which they deemed innovations (*bid'a*). The Wahhabis preached a return to the pure, original Islam practiced in the seventh century, much in the same way that sixteenth-century Protestants stressed a return to the Bible and early church to reform Christianity. The Wahhabis implemented a strict program of reform throughout the Arabian Peninsula, condemning many Sufi practices such as saint veneration and destroying many tombs and holy sites. The Wahhabis considered these tombs, many of which had become pilgrimage sites, to be innovations that threatened to compromise the Islamic focus on one God.

While the Wahhabis certainly influenced the development of later revivalist movements, it is important to stress the distinctiveness of revivalist movements elsewhere, such as those in Africa and India. For example, nineteenth-century movements in Sudan and Nigeria did not denounce Sufism; rather, Sufism itself became the vehicle of reform. And in India there was a succession of great reformers, from the eighteenth-century Shah Wali Allah, considered by many to be the father of modern Indian Islam, to Sayyid Ahmad Khan in the nineteenth century and Muhammad Iqbal and Mawlana Mawdudi in the twentieth; ancillary to these individual reformers was the foundation of new religious societies such as the Jamaat-e-Islami. At the heart of most of these revivalist movements lay the belief that Islam was falling in power and prestige because Muslims were not faithful. Revivalists believed that the religion must be reformed and renewed if Islam was to regain its former dominance in the world.

## Conceptions of the Divine

Of the many Islamic teachings about God, the doctrine of *tawhid* (divine oneness) is possibly the most important. Islam is staunchly mono-theistic, denouncing idolatry and polytheism especially. The greatest sin of all is that of *shirk*, "associating partners with God." God's one-ness cannot be compromised, and therefore the Qur'an explicitly rejects the Christian doctrines of Trinity and Incarnation.

While Christians and Muslims disagree about the precise nature of God's oneness, they do agree about God's attributes. In fact, the 1965 Second Vatican Council document *Nostra Aetate* lists several qualities of God that both Muslims and Christians can accept: he is one, self-subsisting, merciful, omnipotent, creator, revealer, and judge. These are only some of the many divine attributes affirmed by Islam. Indeed, Muslim tradition holds that God has ninety-nine "beautiful names," including: the pure, the watchful, the nourisher, the forgiver, and the avenger. Many names demonstrate God's paradoxical and mysterious nature as merciful and just, hidden and manifest. In Islam, the name of God itself is holy, and one of the most common daily phrases uttered by Muslims is the *basmala*, "In the name of God, the Merciful, the Compassionate," which functions like the sign of the cross ("In the name of the Father, and the Son, and the Holy Spirit") for Christians, and reminds them that everything—even the most mundane acts such as writing an e-mail or getting into a car—are done in God's name. Another Muslim practice centered on the name of God is *dhikr*, which means "remembrance." Dhikr is a form of meditation, and although rooted in basic Muslim piety, it was largely popularized by the Sufis; it can be done silently with the aid of prayer beads or out loud with chanting, alone or in a group of single or mixed gender. Historically, some Sufi orders have also institutionalized dancing and/or singing as modes of dhikr.

In Islam, God alone is holy. Therefore, there is technically no such thing as a Muslim saint (the English word *saint* comes from the Latin *sanctus* meaning both "holy" and "saint"), only a "friend of God" (*wali Allah*). However, in practice Islam does recognize saint-like people, although it is not understood exactly in the same way as in Christianity. In Islam, sainthood is not by appointment (what Catholics would call "canonization"), but is only known by God and is generally hidden to the community. But there do exist *awliya* who are known in the public discourse as saints. For example, there are Sufi masters so revered that their *dargahs* (tombs) have become shrines and pilgrimage destinations. While the Wahhabis destroyed most Sufi shrines in the Arabian Peninsula in the eighteenth century, *dargahs* remain plentiful throughout the Muslim world, especially in South Asia and Africa.

## Conceptions of Human Beings

Muslims and Christians agree about one key theological concept: there is an essential distinction between the Creator (God) and creation (everything else). This ontological difference means that the relationship between God and humans is fundamentally unequal. God does not need human beings, but human beings cannot exist without God.

Both the Qur'an and the Bible acknowledge God as the creator of all and that soon after creation the first human beings disobeyed God. However, there are important differences between the Qur'anic and biblical versions of the Fall. The Qur'an describes Adam and his wife (she is not named) as equally culpable for disobeying God, and both are equally forgiven

by God (Sura 7:19–25 and 2:35–37). This differs markedly from the biblical account, which presents Eve as the instigator of the first sin (Gen. 3:1–13). The differences have many doctrinal consequences; for example, Islam rejects the notion of original sin. Also, Muslims point to their version of the Fall as proof that Islam views men and women as inherently equal; this is supported by other Qur'anic verses that further underscore male-female equality, such as those that explicitly and repeatedly address the requirements of faith to both men and women. Sura 33:35 is a good example of this:

> For Muslim men and women, for believing men and women, for devout men and women, for true men and women, for men and women who are patient and constant, for men and women who humble themselves, for men and women who give in charity, for men and women who fast (and deny themselves), for men and women who guard their chastity, and for men and women who engage much in Allah's praise, for them has Allah prepared forgiveness and great reward.[9]

Another example can be found in Sura 24:30–31, where both men and women are commanded to dress and act modestly—not just women.

Another important anthropological concept in the Qur'an is the idea that human beings have been created to be representatives of God on earth (*khalifa*). Comparable to the Christian notion of stewardship, the Qur'anic doctrine of *khalifa* can be used to support a positive Islamic environmental ethic (Sura 2:30). For example, modern-day organizations like the Muslim Green Team explicitly root their practical works with reference to Qur'anic verses on khalifa.

9. Abdullah Yusuf `Ali, *The Holy Qur-ān: English Translation and Commentary (with Arabic Text)*, 1st ed. (Kashmiri Bazar, Lahore: Shaik Muhammad Ashraf, 1934).

# Beliefs and Practices

Islam presents itself as the antidote to human forgetfulness of God and emphasizes the need for Muslims to cultivate *taqwa,* meaning "God consciousness." Muslims cultivate *taqwa* primarily by adhering to the basic practices commonly known as the "five pillars." Following the five pillars is seen as the most basic way Muslims can demonstrate their submission to God in everyday life.

As mentioned earlier, the first of the five pillars, shahada, is both a creed and an act. Whoever sincerely declares "there is no god but God, and Muhammad is the messenger of God" is considered to be a Muslim. The second pillar is *salat,* prayer. Muslims are required to pray five times a day, every day, during certain windows of time. Salat is a formalized prayer of the community that can be done anywhere (home, mosque, school, and so on). It includes the recitation of specific prayers and Qur'anic verses along with cycles of ritualized movements. Because of its formalized nature, salat is as much a creedal statement as the shahada. In addition to salat, Islam has another voluntary and more informal kind of prayer that might be said before an exam or to pray for a loved one who is ill.

The third pillar, *zakat,* is sometimes translated as "almsgiving" in English, but this does not capture all its connotations in Arabic. Zakat also means "purification" in the sense that in giving of one's wealth, one purifies both one's possessions and oneself from greed. Furthermore, the Muslim notion of zakat is semantically related to the Hebrew word *tzedakah* in Judaism, both of which suggest not voluntary charity but obligatory justice. All Muslims who are financially able are required to give 2.5 percent of their wealth annually; this is often done during Ramadan. The Qur'an (Sura 9:60) lists eight categories of people who can receive zakat (including, e.g., slaves, refugees, the debt-ridden, and the destitute), but the different legal schools disagree about whether zakat can be given only to Muslims. While most Muslims say that zakat needs to be given to a mosque or Muslim charitable organizations such as the Red Crescent, some hold that it can also be given to non-Muslim or secular charities such as Goodwill.

Muslims practice the fourth pillar, *sawm,* or fasting, during the month of Ramadan. The Islamic definition of fasting requires abstinence from all food and drink from dawn ("at the moment a white thread can be distinguished from a black thread") to dusk. Fasting also includes refraining from swearing, smoking, sex, and other activities that might distract one from a singular focus on God. Fasting is also intended to cultivate compassion for the poor, hence the link between sawm and zakat. Since Islam calls itself a moderate religion, it does not require children, pregnant or lactating women, travelers, the sick, or the elderly to fast. Those temporarily unable to fast (e.g., travelers) may make up the fast at a later date; others whose situations prevent them from fasting (such as the elderly infirm) can compensate by feeding the needy or those who are fasting.

The fifth pillar is hajj, or pilgrimage. All Muslims who are financially and physically able to travel to Mecca during the month of the hajj (Dhul Hijja) are required to do so at least once in a lifetime. The hajj gives Muslims the opportunity to connect with the worldwide umma in a unique way. Shedding usual clothes indicating nationality and socioeconomic status, all pilgrims don the same simple white garment and perform the same rituals at roughly the same time. Some Muslims find the hajj such a transformative experience that they add the title *hajji* to their names upon returning home. Malcolm X devotes an entire chapter of his autobiography to the hajj; his experience of international fraternity proved so powerful that it changed some of his

© Ahmad Faizal Yahya / Shutterstock.com

Muslim pilgrims circumambulate the *Kaba*, the holy shrine of Islam in Mecca, which is the focal point of the *hajj* (pilgrimage).

views about race and deepened his conversion to a more orthodox Islam.[10]

In addition to the five pillars, which specify duties incumbent upon individual Muslims, Islam also imposes certain obligations on the community (umma) as a whole. Among the most important is the repeated Qur'anic injunction for the umma to "command what is right, forbid what is wrong" (3:110, 7:157, 9:71, etc.). This dual decree is realized by both individuals and communities using jihad, meaning "striving in the way of God." The term *jihad* is much misunderstood given recent events, and Muslims themselves often disagree about its meaning. But many Muslims point out that according to

Muhammad, there are two kinds of jihad: the lesser jihad is an external striving for the good that can be accomplished through economic, political, persuasive, or (as a last resort), military means. But the greater jihad, says the Prophet, is an internal or spiritual striving against the evil within one's own self.

## A Living Transmission

This chapter began by noting Islam's unity and diversity. No matter what language they speak or country they inhabit, Muslims throughout the world are united in their belief in one God,

---

10. *The Autobiography of Malcolm X* (New York: Ballantine Books, 1964), ch. 17.

Mosques, reflecting the diversity within Islam, range in style from this nondescript storefront in New York City to the Ottoman-era Koski Mehmed Pasha Mosque, in Mostar, Bosnia.

his prophets, and his books, and in their practice of the five pillars. Yet there is also considerable diversity. Like Christianity, Islam is a universal, missionary religion that has spread across the globe; Christianity and Islam are now the first and second most populous religions in the world, respectively (Christianity with roughly 2 billion adherents; Islam with roughly 1.6 billion). And like Christianity, Islam is in constant conversation with local cultures, languages, peoples. As do Christians, Muslim continually ask themselves if a certain practice or attitude should be accepted as consonant with what the Qur'an says or what

Muhammad and his companions did, or if it should be rejected as an unwarranted innovation (*bid`a*). The Catholic theologian Yves Congar once described the Christian tradition as a "living transmission" that must stand in continuity with the past but also engage dynamically with the present. Given that Muslims have recognized at least one *mujaddid* (reviver or renewer) in every century since Islam's founding (e.g., al-Ghazali, d. 1111), and rely on the principle of *ijtihad* (original interpretation) to apply Islamic law to contemporary situations, Congar's definition might be an apt way to describe the Islamic tradition, too.

# CHAPTER 6

# An Insider's Perspective*

*Zeki Saritoprak*

## Islamic Worldview: A Muslim's Perspective

The Islamic worldview is a theocentric one—that is, the earth is created and prepared by God for human beings as a palace. The other planets and celestial bodies have a variety of duties, one of which is to decorate the earth for human beings. The present world is transient, but it is important because the world to come is gained in this world. Therefore, both worlds are important. The Qur'an describes this world as the urgent one and the next world as the last one. This world is temporary and the last is everlasting.

The duty of human beings on this planet is to learn and develop both spiritually and materially. The most important knowledge one can develop is the knowledge of God. Everything in the realm of Creation is considered a sign leading to the knowledge of God. From a flower to a celestial body and from the smallest living creature to the greatest one, all are considered signs from God. The human mind may not be capable of understanding God through these signs; therefore, in Islam there is a need for the coming of prophets. Prophets are those who speak on behalf of God, show what is right and what is wrong, and bring a revelation of God to humanity, generally through a scripture. There have been many prophets and messengers of God who fulfilled their duties and passed away. Muhammad, peace and blessings be upon Him,[1] is considered the final messenger of God, and the Qur'an that he brought to humanity is believed to be the final message of God to humankind.

The principles of life are detailed in the Holy Scripture. Actions are generally categorized as commanded, recommended, neutral, disapproved, or prohibited. Because religion permeates every aspect of life for Muslims, any action has to fall into one of these categories. Islam is considered a way of life and provides moral

---

* I must raise some unease with the use of the insider/outsider dialectic in this section. My objection is neither to the general principle of comparative theology as outlined in the text's introduction, nor to the possible usefulness of the insider/outsider relationship as a tool in understanding world religions. I am apprehensive for two connected reasons. The first is accuracy. As I try to show in this chapter, the original forms of the Abrahamic faiths cannot be neatly separated theologically or intellectually. Thus, I feel that the use of the terms insider and outsider is misleading at best. Second, the insider/outsider distinction can too easily be taken out of context and used to build an antagonistic relationship instead of a cooperative one. This is of particular concern for the relationship between Christianity and Islam given the current and historic geopolitical positions of adherents of the two faiths. The title "A Muslim Scholar's perspective" would better suit this chapter.

1. It is natural for a Muslim scholar to add this eulogy every time the Prophet Muhammad's name is mentioned. Though this phrase is not printed in the text each time, readers are asked to keep this in mind.

Mount Hira in Mecca, the place where Muhammad received his first revelation of the Qur'an. A line of pilgrims climbs the mountain on the right.

consciousness in the sense that an individual can evaluate his or her actions based on this framework. In fact, there is no such thing as a "profane" or worldly, nonreligious action in Islam, because every action has a spiritual consequence. Things that are generally seen as profane, such as neutral actions, can become valuable religious actions with the right intentions. In Islam intention is the spirit of action; an action therefore takes its value based on the intention behind it. A good action with a wrong intention is worthless, but a bad action may become worthy when accompanied by a good intention. Therefore, the entire realm of physicality is seen with eyes of faith and actions are measured by the principles detailed in the Qur'an and by the words, actions, and confirmations of the Prophet of Islam.

The Prophet of Islam was a human being with a unique connection to God as the receiver and conveyor of His revelation. This revelation changed the course of Muhammad's Arabian society and later of many other communities of the world. To understand the changes that he brought to humanity, one need only look to Qur'anic verses, such as "Everything that is in the heavens and on Earth praises God" (17:44).[2] This revelation was gifted to an ignorant society in which idol worshipping was strong and objects of awe and beauty—trees, flowers, the sun, the moon—were seen as insignificant phenomena. Suddenly, the Prophet Muhammad recites this verse. With this verse, he wanted to awaken the consciousness of the people of Arabia and of all humanity by providing a new

---

2. All translations of verses from the Qur'an in this chapter were made by the author.

approach to the relationship between humans and other creatures. The Qur'an blew life into the realm of Creation with this and other similar verses. One can understand from the Qur'an that every creature praises God and, in fact, Muslim mystics may go further and say that they hear the praising of these creatures. Human beings became part of this symphony through their worship of God, and the Prophet of Islam became the maestro.

Focusing on the Prophet's physical dimension may not give a real sense of his spiritual rank, but the analogy of the peacock and the egg may help in understanding how his physical and spiritual aspects can be understood together in a balanced way. If one thinks of the egg without considering the peacock, the egg might seem ugly or very weak, but in order to appreciate the peacock, which comes from this ugly egg, one must consider both at the same time. Otherwise one may have a misconception of what the egg is, and by ignoring it, one may exaggerate the situation of the peacock and consider it a deity. For this reason the Prophet of Islam is a human being who ate and drank, married and had children—all of which point to his physical dimension. However, he was able to see paradise and the throne of God while at the same time talking with others about certain worldly matters. The physical aspects of the Prophet should be balanced with his spiritual dimension. This Islamic view is applicable to the other elements of the world as well. While focusing on their physical side, one must remember the spiritual dimension of each creature as a piece of God's artwork.

Islam does not consider itself an isolated religion, unconnected to other world religions. Instead, Islam considers itself to be a continuation of the pre-Islamic revelations of God, in particular the Torah, the Psalms, and the Gospel. These early revelations were given to humankind by God, and are valid scriptures of God.

# Role of Human Beings

All human beings have been the addressees of the divine message in their spirit form before they were given bodies. In Islamic teaching, spirits of human beings were formed at the beginning of creation. Even though we have limited knowledge about the spirit itself, as the Qur'an suggests in 17:85, Islamic revelation instructs us that spirits were the addressees of God in a primordial conversation. When God asked all spirits, "Am I not your Lord?" all the spirits together said, "Yes, you are our Lord" (7:172). This indicates that all spirits of humankind initially accepted God as their Lord, but later some changed and broke this agreement.

Muslim mystics have developed a lot of literature on this first primordial conversation with God. In fact, Islam is considered to have started from that point. Given this viewpoint, Islam sees true religions of God that existed prior to Islam such as Judaism and Christianity, as "Islams" of their times. One can speak of Islam with a capital "I," which is the religion of Islam that came in a certain period of history through the message of the Prophet Muhammad. Yet accurately, one can speak of islam with a lower case "i" as any true religion of God throughout history. In light of this understanding, Muslims consider any true revelation to be islam, and anyone who submits him or herself to the will of God to be a muslim (with a lowercase "m"). Therefore, Jesus, his apostles, Moses and his helpers, theologically speaking from this perspective, were muslims.

# Basic Sources

Prophet Muhammad came and confirmed the earlier revelations and brought new things for humanity through the Islamic Holy Scripture. Therefore, just as Christians and Jews are known in the Qur'an as the "people of the book," so too

Muslims go to the mosque to perform Friday prayer in congregation. They pray shoulder-to-shoulder and prostrate themselves before God in unison.

Muslims have a book known as the Qur'an. In fact, when asked about his miracles, the Prophet of Islam would refer to the Qur'an as his greatest miracle. The Qur'an challenged the people of Arabia to present a piece of scripture comparable to the Qur'an. Historically, the people of Arabia were well known for their poetry and eloquence. When they heard the Qur'an, they were amazed by its eloquence, but had doubts about its truth. Therefore, a Qur'anic verse was revealed to Prophet Muhammad, saying, "if you are in doubt about what We have revealed [the Qur'an] to our servant [Muhammad], bring a chapter like it [the Qur'an] and invite your witnesses other than God if you are truthful" (2:23). Musaylamah was the only one who attempted to do this, and he failed. Despite his eloquence, Musaylamah was known as a false

prophet in Islam, and his attempt has become a subject of mockery.

The Holy Book has always been a key component of the spiritual life for all Muslims around the world. A regular Muslim prays five times a day and repeats the first seven verses of the Qur'an, which comprise the first chapter, at least seventeen times and, if they perform the voluntary prayers as well, as many as forty times. It is arguably the most repeated statement on earth. Many Muslims believe that the ease of memorizing the Qur'an is one of its miracles. Hundreds of thousands of people in the Islamic world today can recite the entire Qur'an by heart. Muslims begin learning the Qur'an as children and some are able to master the entire Qur'an as early as ten years old. Muslims have a great respect for the Qur'an, which they show not only through its recitation, but even in their handling and placement of the book in their homes. Generally, they do not touch the Qur'an without ritual cleansing, and they hang the Qur'an in a high place on the wall within a beautifully decorated bag made of fabric or other precious materials. The Qur'an is a source of inspiration for Muslims. Muslims, in their religious life and daily practices, refer to the Qur'an as well as the sayings of the Prophet, which are considered the most important commentary of the Qur'an. In other words, the Qur'an and its commentaries serve Muslims as a major source of inspiration in their daily lives.

The eloquence of the Qur'an has led some Muslim scholars to deem it impossible to thoroughly translate the Qur'an. This does not mean that translations are meaningless. Today almost all Islamic nations whose languages are not native Arabic have translated the Qur'an into their own languages. Muslims memorize and recite the Qur'an in its original Arabic form in their daily prayers and recitations, but because many Islamic nations are not Arabs, in order for them to understand the meaning, they must learn the language or refer to translations. Some learn Arabic and read and understand the Qur'an from the original text. Today, in the West, many English translations of the Qur'an exist. Several websites post the Arabic text of the Qur'an side by side with various translations. Rather than focus on only one translation, many Muslims compare two or more translations to better understand the meaning of a Qur'anic verse.

Because Muslims consider the meaning of the Qur'an inexhaustible, thousands of commentaries have been written. A discipline known as *tafsir* developed in the Islamic humanities. This Islamic science sets forth a methodology for the interpretation of the Qur'an known as *usul al-tafsir*. To make a valid and sensible commentary on the Qur'an, one should understand this methodology. Muslims view as invalid a commentary on the Qur'an by someone without this understanding. According to *usul al-tafsir*, there are two types of Qur'anic commentaries. One is known as *tafsir bi al-riwayah*, or commentary based on the narrations of the Prophet, and the second, *tafsir bi al-dirayah*, is commentary based on personal opinion. Commentaries can encompass the Qur'an verse by verse or they can focus only on a select number of verses that particularly address the needs of the communities.

Based on these categories, some commentators on the Qur'an are mystics. These commentaries, for example Ismail Hakki's *Ruh al-Beyan* (The Spirit of the Qur'an), emphasize the more

© Smailhodzic / Shutterstock.com

The Qur'an and hadith encourage all Muslims, both male and female, to seek knowledge. Most try to learn enough Arabic to read the Qur'an in its original language.

mystical dimension of the Qur'an. Others are more conversant in the sayings of the Prophet, so their commentaries contain many sayings of the Prophet that relate to the Qur'anic verses they are studying, which guides their interpretations. Since the Prophet is unanimously accepted as the best commentator of the Qur'an, the author uses his sayings to present a better understanding of the meaning. A good example of this is al-Tabari's commentary on the Qur'an. Other commentators of the Qur'an have a much greater interest in Islamic law and their commentaries explore Qur'anic aspects of Islamic law. Although these are not considered books of Islamic law, they can serve as guidance for legal scholars.[3] Both Abu Bakr al-Jassas's commentary, known as *Ahkam al-Qur'an* (The Laws of the Qur'an), and Al-Qur'tubi's *Ahkam al-Qur'an* (The Laws of the Qur'an) are examples of this type of commentary. The preeminent commentator of the Qur'an, however, is the Prophet himself, so regardless of a commentator's focus, he or she will refer to those sayings of the Prophet relevant to the portion of the Qur'an they are studying.

## Hadith and the Sunnah

Prophet Muhammad explained the Qur'anic verses to his community. His sayings, known as hadith or sunna, were recorded first by his companions and later by Muslim scholars throughout Islamic history. Muslims consider the two anthologies of hadith, *Sahih al-Bukhari* and *Sahih Muslim*, the most reliable references of the sayings of the Prophet. Both contain more than 10,000 of the Prophet's sayings. In addition to these anthologies, many other sources of the Prophet's sayings are available. Muslims scrutinize the sayings of the Prophet to be sure of their

reliability. When assessing the reliability of the sayings, Muslims consider the reliability of those who recorded them. For example, if the recorders are known to have weak memories, Muslims doubt the accuracy of the sayings they record.

Although the Qur'an is the final revelation and the Prophet is the final messenger of God according to Islam, Muslim scholars and saints have kept alive the dynamism of the religion throughout the centuries through various commentaries on the Qur'an. For this reason, in the Muslim tradition a particular saying of the Prophet has become a central point of Muslim revivalism: the Prophet said, "God sends for this community of Islam, at the beginning of every century, someone who renews its religion." Islamic literature refers to these people as *mujaddid*. The central role of a mujaddid is to renew the religion of Islam by acting—in their lives and teachings—as a model who gives a convincing interpretation of the Qur'an. According to Islamic theology, the Qur'an addresses all times and all people. The duty of mujaddids consists of addressing the challenging problems of their own times according to the principles of the Qur'an. They present the Qur'an to the conscience of their societies. They are not prophets, because prophethood ended with the Prophet of Islam, but they are scholars, saints, and friends of God interpreting the message of the Prophet for their time. These renewers can come from all segments of society, including administration, scholarship, and Sufi orders. For example, the Umayyad Caliph Umar Bin Abd al-Aziz was a head of the state, but many believed that he was a mujaddid. Similarly, Abu Hamid al-Ghazali was a legal scholar, jurist, and a teacher as well as a renewer in Islam, a mujaddid. An example of a mujaddid from a mystical order would be the famous Indian

---

3. It should be noted that all Islamic disciplines benefit from each other and are interconnected.

Muslim saint, known as Ahmad Sirhindi, who is credited for being the renewer in the second millennium of Islamic history.

## Central Principles of Islam

The central theme of Islam is God, which appears in the first pillar of Islam, the shahada. This statement of faith, "There is no deity but God, and Muhammad is God's messenger," is about accepting the oneness of God and the prophethood of Muhammad. The God of Islam is the Creator of the heavens and the earth. The Qur'an uses Allah as the proper Arabic name for God. Contrary to the misconception that Allah is different from or against the God of Judaism and Christianity, Allah is the same God of Jesus, Moses, Abraham, and all other prophets prior to Islam. Of the ninety-nine names used to refer to Allah in the Qur'an, the most often repeated ones are "the Most Merciful" and "the Most Compassionate." The beginning of almost every chapter of the Qur'an invokes these two names of God.

Muslims are expected to follow the way of God—to be compassionate and merciful—and to never doubt God's compassion and mercy. Islamic teaching prohibits hopelessness because of the compassion of God. Even when one's sins loom large as mountains, still there is hope and one should hope for God's mercy. Because of this divine compassion, Islam teaches that one must show kindness to the creatures of God as well. Prophet Muhammad says, "Show compassion to those on earth so that the One in Heaven will have compassion on you."[4] In Islam, as human beings have rights, so too animals have rights. The Prophet of Islam prohibited his community from putting overly heavy loads on the backs of their camels. He said that those animals are a part of communities like human beings and also had rights. That is why the Qur'an speaks of the Prophet's coming as a mercy for humankind. The verse says, "We have sent you [O Muhammad] as a mercy for all creatures" (21:107). The goal of human beings is to make the earth a paradise-like place. The Qur'an speaks of the quality of life in paradise.

## Eschatology

One of the essential themes of the Qur'an is the belief in the afterlife, which is known as *al-yaum al-achir* or the "final day." As there is an end for the life of every individual, there will be an end for the life of the planet earth. This world will be replaced with a new one, and people will be questioned about their life on earth. People who have been successful in their relationship with God, the believers, will be in paradise, and people who have failed in their relationship with God, the disbelievers, will find themselves in hell. Despite this general principle, only God can determine the final destination of an individual.

The fact that one-third of the content of the Qur'an is about the afterlife testifies to its concern about the ultimate destiny of humankind, also known as eschatology. This world is a place of preparation for the afterlife, and death is the door to the realm of eternity. Therefore, when people die, they do not dissolve into nothingness. Instead, they go to a place that is eternal and real. Every action people carry out in the current world will have consequence in the afterlife, either positive or negative. In fact, the Qur'anic chapter 99, after speaking about a mighty earthquake that brings an end to the planet (perhaps through a collision with another celestial body),

---

4. Al-Bukhari, *al-Sahih*, "al-Tawhid," 2.

speaks of the actions of human beings by saying, "anyone who has done a good with the weight of an atom will see it, and anyone who has done a bad with the weight of an atom will see it" (99:7-8). In this world, eyes are veiled to a certain extent, but in the realm of the afterlife eyes are sharp and can see the reality of things as they truly are.

While encouraging people to prepare for the afterlife, the Qur'an provides logical explanations of the resurrection of human beings. For example, it tells the story of an elite individual in Mecca who came to the Prophet with rotten bones in his hand. After scattering them on the ground, he asked, "Muhammad, how can these rotten bones be resurrected?" The Qur'an instructed the Prophet to respond, "Say [O, Muhammad] the One who made it first will revive it again, and He knows everything about His creatures" (36:79). Therefore, this current life, by itself, is a miracle. The life to come is even easier for God to make. The Qur'an also draws attention to the awakening of nature in the spring. The verse says, "Look at the works of the mercy of God. How does He revive the earth after it was dead? The One who does this will surely revive the dead, and He is all-powerful over everything" (30:50). Islam teaches that although death is not the end of life, it is an important step toward eternal life. Mystics of Islam have used the meditation on death as a way to strengthen their spirituality and detach from the comforts of this worldly life.

# Sufism

Islamic mysticism, known also as Sufism or *Tasawwuf*, is based on the spiritual dimension of Islam. Classical Sufism, as a mystical way of

life, started to be institutionalized in the eleventh century CE when Muslim mystics established their own Sufi orders. Customarily, there would be a master and pupils who followed the mystical path of the master. The path itself was called *tariqah* and the follower was called murid. In general, the word *Sufi* refers to all those following this way of life. It can be argued that the essence of Sufism was present in the time of the Prophet, although it was not named. A famous saying of the prophet is narrated and known as the source of this spiritual dimension. According to the *Hadith of Gabriel*, the angel Gabriel came to the Prophet and asked him several questions, one being about Islam. He asked, "Muhammad what is *islam*?" The Prophet responded, "*Islam* is to bear witness that there is only one God, that Muhammad is God's messenger, to perform the daily prescribed prayers, to fast during Ramadan, and to make pilgrimage." Gabriel's second question was, "What is faith, or *iman*?" The Prophet replied, "*Iman* means to believe in One God, to believe in God's angels, to believe in God's scriptures, to believe in God's messengers, to believe in the Day of Judgment, and to believe in God's plan." For his third question, Gabriel asked, "What is *ihsan*?" The Prophet replied, *ihsan* means that you should worship God as if you see Him. Even if you do not see Him, He sees you." This last question has become a foundation for Islamic spiritual life.[5]

Muslim mystics, through meditation, have tried to reach a level of spirituality in which they worship God as if they see God. Therefore, the prayer of Muslim mystics consists of not only physical postures such as bowing and prostration but also prayer in which they penetrate the deeper meaning of those rituals. Therefore in Sufism, there are two major terms: *shari'ah* and *haqiqah*. *Shari'ah* is a term used to describe the

---

5. Al-Bukhari, *al-Sahih*, "al-Iman," 37.

Bukhara, Uzbekistan, is the birthplace of one of the most authoritative compilers of hadith, Imam Muhammad al-Bukhari (d. 870).

outer aspect of Islam, which is generally Islamic law and jurisprudence. Mostly, legal scholars of Islam are concerned with this field, which includes a variety of practices of Islam, from daily prayers to trade and from fasting to freeing slaves. All these are discussed under shari'ah law. The term *haqiqah* stands for the inner dimension of Islamic practices; mostly Muslim mystics are concerned with this field. For this reason, according to Muslim mystics, performing a ritual in itself is insufficient for salvation. Rather,

one must penetrate the deeper meaning of that ritual to make sense of it. Some mystics believe that shari'ah is the shell and haqiqah is the kernel. Muslim theologians, though, have criticized the implications of this metaphor for shari'ah and haqiqah and have stated that the two entities complete each other. Shari'ah without haqiqah is incomplete, as is haqiqah without shari'ah.[6] Therefore, a certain level of tension has existed between Muslim mystics and scholars of Islamic law, primarily due to some mystical ideas about

---

6. For example, praying five times a day is shari'ah and penetrating the meaning of the prayer, that is, feeling the presence of God, is haqiqah. These two terms complement each other, as the renowned Muslim mystic Abd al-Karim al-Qushayri (d. 1072) says, "No Shari'ah unsupported by Haqiqah is acceptable and no Haqiqah unbound by Shari'ah is acceptable." Applying this principle to the example of five daily prayers, shari'ah requires that one must perform five daily prayers, and haqiqah requires that one enter into the deeper meaning of five daily prayers. One should not say, I can get that deeper meaning without five daily prayers. Similarly, one should not say that performing five daily prayers is sufficient and there is no need to penetrate the deeper meaning of prayer.

the reality of the physical world. For example, mystics like Ibn Arabi and Rumi believe in the unity of being, *wahdat al-wujud*, which suggests that there is only one real being, God, and that the rest of Creation is a shadow. Scholars of Islamic law and theology, however, focusing on Qur'anic verses, deemed this view incompatible with the Islamic theological principle that the creation of things is real and not merely a shadow. Otherwise, they argue, Qur'anic references to the heavens, earth, trees, and mountains would be meaningless because the Qur'an points to these as signs of the existence of God. The mystic response to this argument has been that they do not deny the real existence, but in comparison to the existence of God, their own existence is so weak that it does not deserve to be known properly as existence.[7]

More than a dozen Sufi orders remain in existence. Today, in many parts of the world, including Europe and the United States, Sufi orders still attract followers and practice their prayers. Some of them follow the classical style of Sufism, while others practice a more modern Sufism, which is less concerned with appearances and focuses purely on the spirit and heart.

Sufism is defined as self-annihilation of egoism in the presence of God. This does not mean that one actually annihilates him- or herself, but rather one focuses so intently on God that he or she forgets about him- or herself. Sufis are generally married and busy with their daily life, but come together on certain days for spiritual fulfillment. They come from every segment of society and are male or female. With regard to spiritual focus, Sufis can be compared to monks or nuns, but as a principle, because the Prophet of Islam was married, they imitate the Prophet and marry. Marriage, however, is not required and some remain celibate. Sufism and its practices bring tranquility and harmony to an individual's spiritual life. The Qur'anic verse that has been a source for the mystical tradition in Islam says, "Surely only through the remembrance of God hearts can rest" (13:28). This verse resonates with St. Augustine's famous quote: "You stir us so that praising may bring us joy, because you have made us and drawn us to yourself, and our heart is unquiet until it rests in you."[8] All Sufi orders aim at finding rest and tranquility in the heart, which is the center of faith and love.

---

7. It is important that this not be confused with the idea of pantheism. Pantheism and the unity of being are completely different things. Pantheism involves denying God and accepting the universe as god, while unity of being denies the universe, due to its weak existence, and accepts only the existence of God.

8. St. Augustine, *The Confessions*, trans. Maria Boulding, OSB (Hyde Park, NY: New City Press, 2008), 14.

# CHAPTER 7

# Texts and Commentary

*Rita George-Tvrtković and Zeki Saritoprak*

## Introduction

The Qur'an[1] is central to Islamic faith and practice, and Muslims believe that this book contains the literal word of God as revealed to their prophet, Muhammad, in Arabic. Technically speaking, only the Arabic text can be called the Qur'an, with translations classified as commentaries. Since Arabic is not the native language for most of the world's Muslims, most try to learn at least enough Qur'anic Arabic to read and recite a few favorite passages from the original.

As already noted in both chapters 5 and 6, Islam has a rich tradition of *tafsir* (Qur'anic interpretation). Translating the Qur'an can be seen as another form of interpretation. This chapter will use several different English translations, or rather, interpretations of the Qur'an. Sometimes two English versions of the same verses will be presented and used as the basis for commentary to demonstrate the diversity of the different translations. These differences serve as a reminder of the difficulty of scriptural interpretation in any religion and a warning against taking any verse at face value. Readers of the Qur'an cannot properly interpret a verse without knowing the Arabic original or contextualizing it

Arabic text engraved on a slab at the Baha-ud-Din Naqshband Bukhari Complex in Bukhara, Uzbekistan. The founder of the Naqshbandi Sufi order is buried here; as a result this site has become a popular pilgrimage destination.

within the overall Qur'an and the greater Islamic tradition (which includes hadith and traditional scriptural commentaries such as the famous one by al-Tabari).

---

1. The spelling *Qur'an* more accurately transliterates the Arabic into English, and hence is increasingly preferred over the older *Koran*.

To show some of the different types of interpretation, this chapter will cite a range of English translations of the Qur'an, including *The Koran Interpreted* (1955) by Cambridge University professor Arthur Arberry, a scholarly translation that remains reliable to this day; *The Holy Qur'an: Translation and Commentary* (1934) by Abdullah Yusuf ʿAli, which continues to be one of the most common translations worldwide despite some very dated commentary; and translations by the Muslim author of this chapter, Zeki Saritoprak. Other English translations not cited in this chapter but worthy of note here include *The Meaning of the Glorious Koran* (1930) by Muhammad Marmaduke Pickthall, popular during much of the twentieth century for its readability; *The Qur'an: A New Translation* (2004) by M.A.S. Abdel Haleem, a highly regarded contemporary version published by Oxford University Press; and *The Sublime Qur'an* (2007) by Laleh Bakhtiar, an Iranian-American female scholar. This last includes a new translation of one of the most problematic verses in the Qur'an, Sura 4:34, which has traditionally been interpreted as condoning wife-beating.[2] Many of these translation titles emphasize two important Muslim beliefs about the Qur'an: first, that it cannot really be translated (hence "the meaning" and "interpreted"). And second, that it is divine revelation (hence "glorious," "holy," and "sublime").

Finally, a few important details must be noted. Each of the Qur'an's 114 suras is known by a name rooted in the chapter's subject matter. For example, Sura 19 is called *Maryam* because it includes the story of Mary, the mother of Jesus (ʿIsa), while Sura 96 (the first revealed to Muhammad) is called *al-ʿAlaq* (the clot) because it says humans were created by God "from a blood clot."

Every chapter of the Qur'an except the ninth begins with the phrase, "In the name of God, the Merciful, the Compassionate," also known as the *basmala*. The *basmala* is one of the most-often recited phrases in Islam; Muslims say it multiple times a day, not only during prayer but also before beginning anything important, such as a speech, letter, or journey. Many chapters also begin with mysterious letters. For example, verse 1 of Sura 2 is "Alif Lam Mim." Islamic scholars differ on the exact meaning of these letters, but most agree that God alone knows their meaning and that their presence is a reminder of the mystical nature and divine origins of the Qur'an.

While the Qur'an is not ordered chronologically, the historical context of each verse is known based on its place of revelation, either Mecca or Medina. The Meccan or Medinan context helps the reader to contextualize the verse correctly.

Finally, this chapter presents four passages for commentary. Texts 1 and 2 are representative of verses more typically stressed by non-Muslims, while texts 3 and 4 are verses emphasized by those within the Muslim community.

---

2. The relevant section of Sura 4:34 is translated by Yusuf ʿAli as follows: "As to those women on whose part ye fear disloyalty and ill-conduct, admonish them (first), (Next), refuse to share their beds, (And last) beat them (lightly); but if they return to obedience, seek not against them Means (of annoyance): For Allah is Most High, great (above you all)." Laleh Bakhtiar's translation eliminates the English word *beat* altogether. In the introduction, xi, she argues that the Arabic word under question in 4:34 can be translated either as "beat" or "go away," and that "go away" is more accurate for two reasons: it conforms to the way Muhammad himself interpreted this verse (since tradition says he never beat his wives), and it is consistent with other verses of the Qur'an which prohibit men from injuring their wives, for example, while in the middle of a divorce (e.g., Sura 2:231). Since Islam encourages marriage, Bakhtiar asks how could it be possible that a man would be forbidden from injuring his wife when they are divorcing, but allowed to injure her when they are still married? She concludes, "the understanding of saying 'go away' is a revert interpretation to how the blessed Prophet understood it. Whoever believes in and follows the *Sunna* [words and deeds of Muhammad] should logically agree with reverting the interpretation to the way he understood it because interpreting the Arabic word *idrib* as 'beat' contradicts 2:231 and fosters divorce rather than marriage."

# Text 1: Sura 1 (*al-Fatiha, The Opening*)

## Text

v.1  In the name of Allah, Most Gracious, Most Merciful.

v.2  Praise be to Allah, the Cherisher and Sustainer of the worlds;

v.3  Most Gracious, Most Merciful;

v.4  Master of the Day of Judgment.

v.5  Thee do we worship, and Thine aid we seek.

v.6  Show us the straight way,

v.7  The way of those on whom Thou hast bestowed Thy Grace, those whose (portion) is not wrath, and who go not astray.[3] ■

## Outsider's Commentary

*George-Tvrtković*

The name of Sura 1 in Arabic, *al-Fatiha*, means "the Opening," and its placement at the very beginning of the Qur'an highlights its centrality to Islamic faith and practice. Muslims say the *Fatiha* numerous times a day during their five prayers. Some Christians have compared the *Fatiha* to the "Our Father" because the *Fatiha* is as beloved by Muslims and is as frequently recited.

Despite its short length, the seven lines of the *Fatiha* are theologically comprehensive and express some of the most central Islamic beliefs about God and the divine-human relationship. The verses begin by outlining what can be called Islam's basic "doctrine of God." Two of God's most important attributes, mercy and compassion, are listed first in line 1, and then repeated again in line 3. The translator Yusuf `Ali notes that the Arabic word *rahman* (translated here as "most gracious") is a quality unique to God, while the second and related word, *rahim* ("most merciful"), can be used to describe any human being.[4] Another important concept found in Sura 1 is that human beings owe God and God alone praise and worship; to emphasize this point, Pickthall's translation adds a parenthetical "alone" to verse 5: "thee (alone) we worship; thee (alone) we ask for help." In verse 2, God is described as the "cherisher and sustainer" of the universe (his identity as its creator is implied). The idea that God is not only creator but sustainer is consonant with the Christian notion of *creatio continua*, which means that creation does not just refer to a single moment at the beginning of time, but to a continuous process. And the use of the word *cherisher* suggests that the divine work of creation involves love.

Verse 4 underscores the Muslim belief that God holds human beings accountable for their actions and that he alone will judge them at the end of time. However, God is not only a judge at the end, but a guide on the way. In verses 5–7, God says he will show humans the "straight way," that is, the proper way to live. The Qur'anic description of Islam as a "path" in verses 5 and 7 can be seen as parallel to the biblical description of Christianity as "the Way" (e.g., in Acts 19:2), and the idea that Christians on earth are pilgrims on the road (Heb. 11:13). In the history of *tafsir*, verses 6–7 have sometimes been interpreted as a condemnation of Jews and Christians; in this view, Muslims are seen as being on "straight" or "right" path (verse 6), while non-Muslim groups such as Christians and Jews have "gone astray" and thus earned God's wrath (verse 7).

---

3. Abdullah Yusuf `Ali, *The Holy Qur-ān: English Translation and Commentary (with Arabic Text)*, 1st ed. (Kashmiri Bazar, Lahore: Shaik Muhammad Ashraf, 1934).

4. Yusuf `Ali, *Commentary*, 14.

By calling God creator, guide, and judge, the *Fatiha* describes God's all-encompassing presence, not only during the lifespan of a single person but also throughout all of human history: God promises to give guidance and grace to believers as they walk the road of life from birth to death, from creation to judgment, from the beginning of time to the end.

## Text

- v.1  In the name of God, the Most Compassionate, the Most Merciful.
- v.2  Praise be to God, the Lord of the Universes;
- v.3  Most Compassionate, Most Merciful;
- v.4  Owner of the Day of Judgment.
- v.5  Thee alone we worship, and from Thee alone we ask for help.
- v.6  Guide us to the straight path,
- v.7  The path of those on whom You have bestowed Your Bounties, and not the path of those who have received Your wrath, and have gone astray.[5] ∎

## Insider's Commentary

### Saritoprak

The first chapter of the Qur'an, The Opening or *al-Fatiha*, is considered a condensed summary of the Qur'an. Some scholars, especially of the Shafii school of Islamic law, consider the first verse to be "In the name of God, the Most Compassionate, the Most Merciful." Some other scholars consider that as a formula of blessing, but not a verse from The Opening, although it is a verse from the Qur'an mentioned in another chapter (27:30). In this line of thinking, the seventh verse is divided into two and once again the chapter is considered seven verses. My preference is that the *basmala* formula is both a verse from the Qur'an and from The Opening. As generally known, the Qur'anic verses are divided into two categories: verses revealed in Makkah and verses revealed in Medina. The verses that were revealed in Makkah (Makki verses) relate more to the existence of God, the afterlife, and eschatology. The verses revealed in Medina (Medini verses) mostly relate to social issues, prayers, and practices of Islam. A thorough interpretation of this chapter of the Qur'an requires many more pages than is allowed by the scope of this short commentary. Some scholars of eloquence such as al-Zamakhshari have elaborated on this aspect in their commentaries of the Qur'an. The following is a very brief commentary and does not claim to exhaust the meaning of the first chapter of the Qur'an.

The first verse draws our attention to the divine names—Allah, the proper name of God, then al-Rahman, the Most Compassionate, then al-Rahim, the Most Merciful. Basically the formula indicates that everything should be started with the help of Allah, who has many beautiful names such as the Most Merciful and the Most Compassionate. Muslims use this Qur'anic formula in their daily life at the beginning of a variety of occasions such as eating, drinking, reading, giving a speech, or other activities such as driving. Such a remembrance of God's name through this formula makes a connection between the actions of human beings and divine grace. That is to say, whatever positive action one does is always done through God's help. Muslims believe that not only do human beings say this, but all creatures as well. Trees are saying this formula when giving fruits as a divine gift. Animals are saying this formula when giving milk as

---

5. Translation by Zeki Saritoprak.

a divine gift. Celestial bodies are saying this formula when moving to contribute to the harmony of the universe.

The second verse discusses thankfulness for God. A God who is the Most Compassionate, the Most Merciful, who is the Giver of all bounties, deserves thankfulness. That is why the verse starts with "Praise be to God, the Lord of the Universes." Praising God is one of the goals of the creation of human beings. Any praise for any action that deserves thankfulness goes to God as well. For example, when one thanks someone for doing a favor, these thanks automatically relate to God because that action occurred due to God's help. Although the person is praised, the real praised one is God. Therefore, it is good to thank people who do favors because the Prophet of Islam said, "Those who do not present thankfulness to people are also abandoning thankfulness to God."[6]

Again, due to the importance of the divine names, the Qur'an describes God as the Most Merciful and the Most Compassionate in verse 3. The repetition of these divine names emphasizes how important it is for believers to imitate God and become a reflection of God's beautiful names. For example, if God is the Most Compassionate and the Most Merciful, as mentioned in this chapter twice, then Muslims, the first addressees of the Qur'an, are expected to be merciful and compassionate toward their fellow humans as well as other creatures.

The fourth verse mentions another attribute of God: The Owner of the Day of Judgment. This attribute reminds the readers of the Qur'an that there is a life after this life, that there will be a judgment, and that people will be accountable for what they have done on earth. There is a subtle meaning in the word *owner*, which indicates that what will happen will not be a chaotic event, but rather an orderly event controlled by

the Most Compassionate. Therefore, the verse gives hope that since God is the Most Compassionate, he will deal with human beings with his compassion and mercy, but it also gives a sense of responsibility because every action that one does on this planet will have a consequence in the next life. Islamic theological discourse emphasizes that human beings should not only be hopeful for God's mercy and compassion but also fearful about their negative actions.

God as the Most Merciful and the Most Compassionate will bring the Day of Judgment, but the question is what is the main duty of human beings on earth? The Qur'an, with the fifth verse, instructs that the foundational duty of human beings on earth is to worship God. Such worship is performed to please only God. For this reason it does not say, "We worship You," but "We worship *only* You," expressly rejecting any partners in worship to God as well as rejecting the worship of any kind of idols, including material benefits. God does not need this worship, but human beings do, therefore God teaches them how to perform their worship correctly. In many other verses the Qur'an commands people to worship God. In fact, one could argue that the first imperative word in the Qur'an is *worship*. The verse says, "O people! Worship your Lord, the One who has Created you and the people before you" (2:21). For worship, again there is a need for help and a grace from God.

The Qur'an instructs how the performer of the worship should ask God for help. This help is not only for prayer, but for any action in which a human being may be involved. That is why verse 5 instructs human beings to say, "Thee alone we ask for help." Believers should have great trust in God, that whenever they need help, God will send it. The help that comes from human beings is considered a vehicle for the help

---

6. Abu Isa Muhammad al-Tirmidhi, *Sunan al-Tirmidhi*, "al-Birr," 35.

of God and not an obstacle to it; one should always see the divine grace and help beyond the human component.

A very important prayer follows in verse 6: "Guide us to the straight path." The Qur'anic straight path is the Islamic middle way, which avoids all kinds of exaggerations. The Qur'an instructs believers to ask God for guidance to the middle way, the path in which their characters are rectified. For example, one should use character traits such as anger, desire, and intelligence according to the middle way, which is known as the straight path. To have no anger can make a person overly passive, but to have extreme anger may lead to violence and destruction. Similarly, to have no desire will make a person dull, but to have an uncontrolled or extreme desire may lead to obsession or addiction. The positive form of desire puts it in its proper place and in a balanced way. This is true for intelligence as well. To have no intelligence may lead a person to make poor choices, and to have an extreme intelligence may lead a person to deceit or pride. Therefore each character trait should be well balanced. This is the meaning of the Qur'anic straight path. This middle path is the path of those whom God has favored, as indicated in the continuation of verse 7. This group of people includes the prophets, saints, and pious people. This part of the verse refers to those opposite of the group on the straight path as those who went astray and received the wrath of the divine for their criminal actions.

The seven verses of Sura 1 is a daily prayer for Muslims, repeated in every *rak'a* or unit of the prescribed prayers. The prayer motions of standing, bowing, and prostration are considered one unit of prayer.[7] A rough calculation suggests that each Muslim individual who prays five times a day—including the voluntary prayers—repeats these approximately forty times a day. Considering 1.6 billion Muslims around the world, it can be argued that this Qur'anic chapter is the most repeated prayer on the planet.

## Text 2: Sura 4:95

### Text

> v. 95  Such believers as sit at home—unless they have an injury—are not the equals of those who struggle in the path of God with their possessions and their selves. God has preferred in rank those who struggle with their possessions and their selves over the ones who sit at home; yet to each God has promised the reward most fair; and God has preferred those who struggle over the ones who sit at home for the bounty of a mighty wage.[8] ■

### Outsider's Commentary

*George-Tvrtković*

One of the most misunderstood Islamic concepts among non-Muslims is jihad. When asked to define the word *jihad*, many non-Muslims would say "holy war," but an examination of its Arabic definition and use in the Qur'an suggests a more complex meaning. To understand the Islamic notion of jihad properly, students must first know that most Arabic words have a three-letter root; the root letters of jihad are j-h-d (جهد), meaning to endeavor, strive, or struggle. Related words include *mujtahid* (diligent or industrious), *juhd* (strain or exertion), *mujahada* (battle), and *ijtihad* (effort; also "independent judgment," a

---

7. For example, the prescribed morning prayer has two units, or cycles of motions in which Sura 1 is recited. In the same way, this is repeated in voluntary prayers as well.

8. Arthur J. Arberry, *The Koran Interpreted* (New York: Macmillan, 1955), 115.

technical term in Islamic law). Jihad's constellation of meanings does include the notion of military combat, but as can be seen from the overall context of the word in Sura 4:95, the "striving" entailed in religious jihad is much broader. This is especially evident in the phrase translated by Arberry as "struggle with their possessions and their selves." The struggle of jihad does not preclude warfare, but it also includes economic, persuasive, political, and other means.[9] Another important phrase modifying the word *jihad* here is "in the path of God" (or as Yusuf `Ali renders this line, "in the cause of Allah"), which suggests that only a struggle for a godly cause can be properly called jihad. The question then becomes, what is a godly cause? To answer this question correctly, Muslims must interpret this verse in light of other Qur'anic verses, hadith, and important scriptural commentaries.

Finally, this verse suggests that engaging in jihad, which can be defined here as "struggle in the path of God with self and possessions," is an important criterion for distinguishing between two kinds of Muslims: those who sit at home and those who exert themselves in the world. The two-tiered hierarchy is clear: God favors those willing to go out into the world and work hard for the benefit of the common good over those who are self-centered, complacent, and lazy. On this last point, Christians might see a parallel between Sura 4:95 and the New Testament parable of the talents (Matt. 25:14–30; Luke 19:12–28), in which Jesus praises the servant willing to invest what God has given him, but criticizes the servant who out of fear, laziness, and a lack of faith buries his gifts rather than using them to improve the world.

## Text

v. 95  They are not the same, those believers who are sitting at home with no legitimate excuse and those who are struggling in the way of God with their properties and themselves. God has preferred in rank those who are struggling with their possessions and themselves above those who are sitting at home; God has promised for each paradise and God has given preference with a great reward to those who are struggling above those who are sitting at home (except with an excuse).[10] ∎

## Insider's Commentary
### Saritoprak

This Qur'anic verse is about a specific event in Islamic history, but the principles that it shows have been considered important throughout the history of Islam. Originally this verse was revealed on the occasion of the Battle of Badr when the polytheists of Mecca organized a large army and marched to Medina to attack the Prophet and his community in order to bring an end to the new religion of Islam. Companions of the Prophet prepared to defend the city against the polytheists, and they emerged victorious against them. It is believed that this Qur'anic verse was revealed to praise those who participated in the war against the polytheists. When this Qur'anic verse was revealed, two companions of the Prophet, Abdullah bin Jahsh and Abdullah bin Umm Maktum, came to him and

---

9. On the basis of other Qur'anic verses and hadith, Islamic scholars further qualify proper warfare. For example, some note that it can only be defensive (22:39–40), that noncombatants must not be harmed (al-Tabari specifies women, children, and the elderly), and that those who are to be fought against are those who do not believe in God (2:190–94; 8:39; 9:29). Interpretation is required in all these qualifications, and Muslims disagree on how these verses are to be interpreted and implemented.

10. Translation by Zeki Saritoprak.

told him that they did not participate because they were blind. That is why the Qur'an made an exception and, because of their good intention, gave them the same reward as those who participated. There were still other hypocrites, who were Muslims in appearance but not in heart. They were those who did not participate and had no excuse. They sat in their homes in Medina and did not fight, so preference was given to those who did participate or who would have if not for disease.

The verse speaks of the importance of believers in the sight of God. This is because they are actively involved in good deeds. Laziness and lack of interest are considered weaknesses in human characteristics, especially when it comes to performing good deeds. The Qur'an encourages the believers by giving preference to those who are active over those who remain passive. It is interesting that the original Arabic word used here derives from the word *jihad*. The word used for the believers engaged in the struggle is *mujahidun*. The opposite word is *al-qai'dun*, the passive. The Qur'an always prefers positive action, which will be rewarded. The reward becomes even greater when the action becomes necessary either spiritually or socially. For example, in times of famine, those people actively involved in collecting food or money for people who were struggling would have greater value in the sight of God than those who would sit at home and not serve others.

This encompasses all types of struggles for goodness, including defensive and just wars. The verse speaks of many ways to participate in good deeds, such as financially supporting them. Those who are wealthy but unable to participate bodily, for example, can participate in good deeds through the establishment and financial support of educational and health institutions or centers that provide food for the needy. Those who are not wealthy, but able to participate bodily,

may still be rewarded because of their physical involvement in good deeds. The Qur'an provides opportunities for various segments in society to contribute to the betterment of the community.

# Text 3: Sura 2:285–86

## Text

v. 285 The Messenger [Muhammad] has believed in what is revealed to him from his Lord, and all believers have believed in God, His angels, His scriptures, and His Messengers. [They say,] "We do not distinguish between any of the messengers of God." They have said, "We heard and we obeyed. Our Lord, we ask for Your forgiveness, and surely the return is to you."

v. 286 Surely God does not give to any soul more than what it can bear. What the soul has earned can be for it or against it. "Our Lord! Do not make us accountable if we forget or make mistakes. Our Lord! Do not lay upon us a burden as you laid upon those before us. Our Lord! Do not charge us with something over which we have no power. Pardon us and forgive us. Have mercy upon us. You are our Supporter. Support us against the disbelieving people."[11] ■

## Insider's Commentary
*Saritoprak*

Muslims consider these two verses at the end of chapter 2 of the Qur'an a gift given to the Prophet Muhammad on his night journey (*mi'raj*). It is

---

11. Translation by Zeki Saritoprak.

believed that all Qur'anic revelations were revealed to the Prophet through angel Gabriel, with exception of these two verses. The two verses were told to the Prophet by God without the mediation of angel Gabriel. Verse 2:285 indicates the trustworthiness of the Prophet in that he thoroughly believed in what was revealed to him. It also speaks of the major articles of faith in Islam. The Prophet and all believers of Islam believe in God, which is the major principle of faith. It is also the first part of the statement of faith (shahada), which says "There is no deity but God, and Muhammad is the Messenger of God."

The verse also deals with the second article of faith, which touches on belief in angels. Muslims believe that there are innumerable angels of God, the four greatest being Gabriel, Michael, Sarafiel, and Azrael. All these angels are obedient to God and in a constant state of worship. Angels have different duties. Some of them bring revelation and inspiration to the prophets, especially the angel Gabriel, who is in charge of this duty. Some are in charge of the planet's irrigation. Angel Michael is the head of all angels who carry out this duty. Archangel Azrael, the angel of death, is the head of all angels who are charged with taking people's lives. The duty of angel Sarafiel is to blow the trumpet to start the end of human history and to blow the trumpet the second time to start the resurrection of all human beings. Angels are not God's helpers, because God does not need help, but are servants of God commanded to do certain duties, which they perform perfectly.

The verse also draws attention to more articles of faith, including belief in the pre-Islamic scriptures and pre-Islamic prophets. All Muslims must believe in the Qur'an as well as in the Torah, in the Psalms, and the Gospel because the Qur'an confirms these scriptures as divinely revealed books of God that came to humanity as a guidance and light. Similarly, Muslims must believe in all prophets before the

Prophet of Islam. The Qur'an mentions some of these, including Noah, Abraham, Ishmael, Isaac, Joseph, Moses, David, Solomon, Jonah, John the Baptist, and Jesus.

These two articles of faith connect Islam to the Jewish and Christian traditions in a way that provides a foundation for interfaith dialogue and understanding between Muslims, Christians, and Jews. In other words, just as Moses is known as the primary prophet of God for Jewish people, he is also a prominent messenger of God for Muslims. Similarly, Jesus, as the most important figure of Christianity, is also understood in Islam as a prominent messenger of God who was born miraculously of the Virgin Mary. Because Muslims consider all the prophets important and as representing the messages of God on Earth, they are asked not to distinguish between them and to believe equally in all of them. Muslims are not in a position to rank the prophets of God. Showing a great humbleness, the Prophet of Islam asked his companions to not even compare him to Moses or even to Jonah.

The verse continues to teach Muslims how they should respond to the message of God. Unlike earlier generations who heard the message of God and denied it, the Qur'an asked Muslims to hear the message and also to obey it. Therefore, merely hearing is not sufficient; obedience to the message is essential. Human beings, however, are always weak and may hear but not obey. Therefore, the verse ends with a prayer to teach Muslims how to address God when asking for forgiveness for their possible mistakes. The prayer also confirms that all human beings only temporarily live on this planet and will eventually die. Their deaths will not be eternal separation, but instead a return to God. This concept of returning to God forms an essential part of Islamic understanding of death and resurrection and is repeated in many Qur'anic verses.

The second verse (2:286) speaks of human free will and the accountability that God has put on human shoulders. Human beings are not compelled to do certain actions. Whatever they do is within their own capacities. The verse indicates a principle of Islamic theology: if God made human beings accountable for something that they were incapable of doing, it would negate the concept of free will, which is necessary for accountability. Thus, the first part of verse 2:286 gives great space for human beings to exercise their free will. It indicates that whatever they do, be it good or bad, will be counted, and they will have to take responsibility for those actions. The consequences for those actions may be seen in this world, but if not, they will be seen [in the afterlife]. As a verse in the Qur'an says, "Whoever does an atom's weight of good will see it in the afterlife. Similarly, whoever does an atom's weight of evil will see it [in the afterlife]" (99:7–8).

Since a human being has an evil, commanding soul, there will always be deviation from the right path, and therefore evil may be committed. Even such circumstances, however, leave no space for hopelessness in the Islamic theological perspective. The verse teaches that one can always ask God for forgiveness in the language of the Qur'an: "Our Lord! Do not charge us with something over which we have no power. Pardon us and forgive us. Have mercy upon us." These final statements starting with "Our Lord" have been Qur'anic prayer samples for Muslims to show how to address God and ask for forgiveness. The very final statement teaches believers how to ask for divine support for their struggle against the pressures and oppression from the people of disbelief.

## Outsider's Commentary

*George-Tvrtković*

Verses 285–86 are at the very end of the longest chapter in the Qur'an, Sura 2. The beginning of the chapter (2:2–4) states that its audience is

"those who fear God" and that its primary subject matter is faith. So it is fitting that the chapter would conclude by again addressing the same audience, "all believers," and reiterating the most fundamental articles of the Islamic faith: belief in God, his angels, scriptures, and messengers. Since these articles of faith have been revealed by God, the proper response of the believer is simply to "hear and obey" (285). The response of the Muslim believer to God's revelation parallels the proper response of a Christian believer, which can be seen for example in the prologue of the Rule of St. Benedict (addressed primarily to monks but also more broadly to all Christians), where two oft-repeated words are "listen" and "obey." The very first line of the prologue is the command "Listen!" Like Muslims, this should be the Christian's first response to God's word. The second response is to obey. If a believer does not act on what she hears then she has not truly heard it.

One line in this passage about which some Muslim scholars have argued is "We do not distinguish between any of the messengers of God." The key question is, are all God's messengers, such as Ibrahim (Abraham), Musa (Moses), and `Isa (Jesus), equal, or is Muhammad superior? This particular verse suggests that they are equal; however, elsewhere (Sura 2:253) it is said that God considers some messengers to be higher than others. The idea that Jews, Christians, and Muslims share some of the same prophets (but have different notions of what prophethood is) can either be a point of contention or an interesting starting point for constructive interfaith dialogue.

Finally, the last few lines of the passage stress God's mercy and forgiveness. Christians sometimes fail to recognize how strongly Islam emphasizes the mercy of God. Just as God's mercy is stressed throughout the Bible, for example in the Psalms (e.g., Ps. 118, "[God's] mercy endures forever") and the Gospels (e.g., Luke 6:36, "Be merciful, just as [also] your

Father is merciful"),[12] so too do these lines from the Qur'an repeatedly describe God as "merciful" and "forgiving." Furthermore, the last verse of the sura is a prayer that both stresses human accountability and God's judgment, and acknowledges human weakness and the need for God's mercy. In the list of ninety-nine names, God is called both "The Just" (*al-'Adl*) and "The Most Merciful" (*al-Rahim*), but Muslims have a reason to hope for mercy, due to a famous hadith that states, "God's mercy precedes his wrath."

# Text 4: Sura 25:63–70

## Text

v. 63  The servants of the Most Merciful, are those who are walking on earth humbly and when the ignorant address them they say "Peace."

v. 64  They are those who are spending their nights with standing and prostration for their Lord,

v. 65  and they say "Our Lord! Prevent from us the punishment of Hell.

v. 66  Surely the punishment of Hell is necessarily occurring and surely it is the worst place to stay and to reside."

v. 67  And the servants of God are those who when giving charity to their families do not waste and do not hoard, and they are between these in the middle.

v. 68  The servants of God are those who do not claim partners for Allah, who do not kill the soul God prohibits, the killing of which, with the exception of just cause. And they are those who do not

commit adultery and anyone who does will face punishment.

v. 69  The torment for him will be doubled on the Day of Judgment and he would stay in it forever, humiliated,

v. 70  with the exception of those who repent and believe and do good deeds; for those, God will change their bad deeds into good deeds and God is the Most Forgiving and Most Merciful.[13] ■

## Insider's Commentary

*Saritoprak*

These particular verses of the Qur'an discuss seven qualities of believers who are known in the Qur'an as the servants of God. In other words, they picture an ideal society made of human beings who exhibit the qualities of humility, peace, prayerfulness, supplication, charity, and repentance and who do not associate anything with God and avoid murder and adultery.

First, verse 63 speaks of humility as a prominent characteristic of believers, which can be seen symbolically in walking. In Islam, walking often serves as a good indication of humility. Believers do not walk around with chests puffed arrogantly, but consider themselves humble servants of God without harming any other creatures. They consider all other creatures as their friends in the realm of creation, and they give appropriate respect to others because they have the same Creator. In the Qur'anic story of the famous and wise man and prophet, Luqman, who is believed to have lived a millennium before the Common Era, he advised his son saying, "My son, do not turn your cheek away from people [as a sign of arrogance] and do not walk on Earth arrogantly.

---

12. Biblical citations taken from the *New American Bible*, rev. ed. © 2010, 1991, 1986, 1970, by the Confraternity of Christian Doctrine, Washington, DC.

13. Translation by Zeki Saritoprak.

Surely God does not love each arrogant boaster" (31:18).[14] Luqman's advice has been a principle in Islamic teaching; the Prophet of Islam, in various statements, praises the humble and criticizes the arrogant. For example, the Prophet says, "God exalts the one who is humble." Traditionally in Islam, the sins that come from arrogance are less forgivable than those that come from desires. Satan became Satan because of his arrogance, and he is still Satan and remains unforgiven. Adam and his wife were separated from the Garden because of their desire, and both were forgiven. Adam even went on to become a prophet of God.

The first verse of this section also emphasizes the importance of peace and nonviolence in the life of Muslims and makes a connection between humility and peace. This is a very unique aspect of the Qur'an that indicates the presence of peace as a result of humility. The flames of many conflicts and attacks come as a result of an insult. The Qur'an teaches that believers, when they receive negative comments or insults from "the ignorant," should say "Peace" and not respond in kind. The principle of responding with peace describes the daily routine of believers as well as their "nightlife." The night of the believer is a night filled with prayer. They are in constant prayer both through standing and prostrating. Some commentators of the Qur'an believe that these qualities were found in the companions of the Prophet of Islam. The Prophet himself would have had night prayer, and in fact, the Qur'an speaks of his long night prayers. It is believed that he would spend two-thirds of each night praying. Muslim mystics have taken this as an example to follow and also spend a good portion of their nights in prayer. These are voluntary prayers and additions to the prescribed five daily prayers (morning, noon, afternoon, sunset, and evening prayers), but some scholars have included the

prescribed evening prayer within the context of night prayer and substantiate its existence with this Qur'anic verse.

Verse 65 speaks of the connection between human beings and the divine, which is made through supplication. Supplication implies that whenever people need anything they can open their hearts to God and ask for what is needed. Islamic teaching encourages asking God for even the smallest things. Unlike human beings, God is more pleased the more people ask from Him. The Qur'an teaches to ask for goodness and beauty both in this world and in the afterlife. It also teaches about supplicating to God in hopes that He will prevent supplicators from experiencing the fires of hell. It is a tradition in Islam to have certain supplications after prescribed prayers, as well as in the morning and evening. The sayings and actions of the Prophet have been scrutinized and narrated carefully throughout generations up through the present. Some Muslim scholars have claimed that finding a saying of the Prophet in one of the anthologies of hadith, namely *Sahih al-Bukhari*, is like hearing the statement directly from the mouth of the Prophet. Muslims today have access to almost all these sayings of the Prophet Muhammad.

The following verses talk about the importance of charity for believers. The qualities of believers are not always theoretical, but are often action-oriented. Therefore, the believers are those who give for the betterment of human beings and for the sake of God. This includes zakat, a compulsory charity, and other voluntary charities as well. The Qur'an describes believers as those who give in a balanced way and do not waste their properties meaninglessly. The Qur'anic teaching prohibits extravagance. The Qur'an says, "Surely those who waste are the friends of satans" (17:27).[15] This can refer to

---

14. Translation by Zeki Saritoprak.

15. Translation by Zeki Saritoprak.

the waste of money, property, or time. Any kind of wasting is strongly prohibited in the Qur'an. Even charity, if not given properly, may be considered under the category of wastefulness, so it should be given carefully. A famous statement related to Abu Hanifah says, "There is no goodness in extravagance and there is no extravagance in goodness."

Interestingly, the Qur'an follows the concept of charity and avoidance of wastefulness with the belief in One God, the most essential principle in Islam. The likely reason for this sequence is to emphasize the importance of avoiding subtle *shirk*. The pagans of Mecca considered their idols as the helpers of God, which the Qur'an strongly criticized. This was called *shirk* in the Islamic theological discourse. Although the real shirk is associating someone with God, the Prophet also speaks of another type of shirk, known as subtle shirk. This relates to the actions that are done to show off rather than for the sake of God. The Prophet was greatly worried about this secret type of shirk. When asked what "secret shirk" was, the Prophet said, "It is showing off and not doing something for the sake of God, but for the sake of fame." This can be seen in some charities, making it logical and relevant to follow the concept of charity with the avoidance of shirk.

Toward the end of this segment, the verses discuss great sins in Islam: murder and adultery. The greatest sin is murder, therefore a murderer cannot be a real believer. Many Qur'anic verses talk about murder as a very grave sin. Some verses even suggest that a murderer will stay in hell forever. A verse in the Qur'an states that killing one person is akin to killing all humanity (5:32). This indicates that every human being is a universe; therefore killing one human being is equal to killing all. In the same way, saving the life of one individual is like saving the lives of all human beings. The servants of God are those who avoid the sins of murdering and committing adultery.

After all these values, a great quality of human beings is mentioned: repentance. In the Islamic teaching, God encourages people to repent. Repentance marks a positive return from a mistake. Repentance is always acceptable to God as long as one repents sincerely. One of the ninety-nine names of God is *al-Tawwab*, which means the One Who Accepts Repentance. Despite the gravity of one's sins, there is no space in Islam for hopelessness. One should remain hopeful for the forgiveness of God as long as he or she repents sincerely. Ending with repentance also draws attention to the weakness of human beings. As a result of their weakness, humans may become victims of arrogance or desire and eventually involve themselves in sinful actions. When Satan approaches humans to make them hopeless, which he always does, the open door of repentance gives hope and makes a strong case against Satan's deceit.

## Outsider's Commentary

### George-Tvrtkovic

These verses come from Sura 25, called *al-Furqan*, meaning the criterion for judgment. Much of this sura deals with issues of morality, judgment, salvation, and eschatology. Verses 63–70 list the deeds which characterize a "servant of God." Interestingly, Sura 25:63–70 stresses the *orthopraxy* of the servant (i.e., doer of God's will), in contrast to the passage discussed above (Sura 2:285–85) which stresses the *orthodoxy* of the believer.

The first deeds of the servant of God mentioned are actually more habits than deeds: a servant of God should always "walk humbly" (cf. Mic. 6:8) and greet everyone, even the ignorant, with words of peace. A servant of God is also someone whose life is characterized by constant prayer, even at night (v. 64). Finally, a servant of God is a good steward of the material goods she has been given by God; she gives precisely the right amount of charity required, and is neither stingy nor profligate (v. 67). Here, moderation is stressed (perhaps this could even be called a "green ethic"), for Islam forbids both excessive asceticism and excessive waste. Islam's preference for moderation could be contrasted with some Christian ascetic practices that, to Muslims, might seem too extreme, for example, the celibacy required of all vowed religious, the radical voluntary poverty of St. Francis of Assisi, the perpetual silence of Trappist monks. The Qur'an states that God did not prescribe monasticism (57:27) even though there is some appreciation for Christians who renounce the world (and, moreover, Sufism does contain some ascetic practices).

A servant of God avoids the three worst sins, listed in verse 68 as false worship, killing, and adultery; these three are described in verse 69 as deserving of extra punishment. The servant of God must avoid "associating partners with God," meaning that she must never worship false gods (e.g., fame or money). Furthermore, the servant of God does not commit adultery or kill (v. 68). However, there is one exception to the prohibition against killing, and that is "justice" (v. 68). This qualifier suggests that while *unjust* killing is always forbidden, there might be legitimate examples of just killing, such as in self-defense or to protect the lives of the innocent against aggressors. Just as Christians argue about the possibility of just war, so too do Muslims argue about what cases might qualify as "just killing." An example of just killing is a court's sentencing of a murderer to death. Islamic law accepts the death penalty, because of its deterrent value, as a way of upholding the Qur'an's aim to discourage the killing of human beings.

If a person fails to act as a servant of God, this passage reminds the reader repeatedly of the consequences: hell (vv. 65–66 and 68–69). But hell is not the last word. Instead, v. 70 brings the passage full circle, as the verses move from mercy, to justice and punishment, to mercy once again. If a person sins, but then "repents, believes, and does good deeds," then God will forgive that person and "change their bad deeds into good." The last line of the passage once again stresses God's forgiving, merciful nature in the superlative: he is called "the most" forgiving and "the most" merciful. Humans are accountable for their actions, but true penance (in the form of good deeds, not just mere words) can erase bad deeds. This passage is comforting, but it can also spark questions about the relationship between God's omnipotence and human freedom.

# CHAPTER 8

# Concluding Reflections

*Rita George-Tvrtković and Zeki Saritoprak*

## Reflections of an "Outsider"

*Rita George-Tvrtković*

This entire book is an exercise in interfaith dialogue. But what exactly is *dialogue*? Every interfaith relationship should begin with a clear definition of what dialogue is (and what it is not) and what the goals of the conversation are, since it is too often the case that people have different things in mind when they hear the word.

### Defining Dialogue

To begin, dialogue is not an argument. The goal of dialogue is not to prove that one religion is right and the other is wrong. Sadly, winning an argument has been the goal of most interfaith exchanges for much of history. For example, the medieval European *dialogus* genre feigned to be an authentic conversation between people of two different religions, but in actuality it was often a construct in which the Christian author put words into the non-Christian's mouth—words that denigrated the non-Christian religion and asserted the superiority of Christianity. In short, the medieval *dialogus* was a thinly veiled polemic against the other. Interfaith dialogue today has hopefully moved beyond argument.

Second, dialogue should not be an attempt to convert the other to one's own religion. If converting the other is the ultimate goal of interfaith conversation, then those conversing might soon grow disheartened when this does not occur, and wonder why they are bothering to talk at all. Third, dialogue is not an attempt to seek and affirm the lowest common denominator. When Christians and Muslims discuss their respective traditions, they might be tempted to stick with commonalities, such as belief in one God. However, Christians cannot and should not avoid explaining their belief that Christ is the Son of God, any more than Muslims should avoid explaining their belief that Muhammad is the seal of the prophets. Interfaith dialogue proves most fruitful when it not only affirms similarities, but acknowledges and examines differences (and tensions). Some important differences and difficulties that Muslims and Christians should not shy away from in dialogue include the revelatory status of the Qur'an, *tahrif* (the corruption of Christian scripture), the divinity of Christ, the prophethood of Muhammad, the Trinity, mission/*da'wah*, religious freedom, and Islamophobia. Once dialogue partners establish trust, they can and should discuss these challenging issues.

If dialogue is not an argument, an attempt to convert, or an affirmation of the lowest common denominator, then what is it? Dialogue is an honest, two-way conversation between people of faith. It is an authentic attempt to learn about another tradition and hopefully to increase respect for that tradition and its adherents (although it is possible that dialogue partners might not like, or still fail to understand, some of the things they learn about the other religion, even after extensive dialogue). Dialogue is also about building relationships of trust between individuals and communities. Building good relationships takes a long time, which means that dialogue requires commitment on all sides. Finally, the best dialogues result in a deepening of the dialogue partners' own faith. Being in dialogue with someone of another religion should ideally make the dialogue partners better practitioners of their own faith traditions.

The English word *dialogue* comes from the Greek *dia* (meaning "across") and *logos* (meaning "word" or "speech"). Therefore, the word *dialogue* is especially applicable to the long-distance conversation in which this chapter's coauthors have been engaged. It is not easy to be in dialogue with someone you have met only once, much less to discuss a topic as complex and important as religion. How has our scholarly dialogue been possible, given that we live in different time zones? "Speaking across" the miles to build an interfaith relationship can sometimes be a challenge, but it is possible if you have respect for one another, good will, flexibility, and, of course, technology.

## Recent History of Christian-Muslim Dialogue

As has been noted several times, the history of Christian-Muslim relations is complex and at times has been contentious. Since the mid-twentieth century, however, there have been many positive developments. One of the most important for Catholics is the Second Vatican Council document *Nostra Aetate* (On the Relation of the Church to Non-Christian Religions) promulgated in 1965, which articulates the first positive view of Islam at the conciliar level, the highest level of church authority. In this text, the church declares that it regards Muslims with "esteem," lists shared beliefs and practices, and encourages an honest and loving dialogue between the two religions.

The writing of *Nostra Aetate* was inspired in part by one of the most important figures in twentieth-century Catholic-Muslim relations, the French scholar of Islam, Louis Massignon (1883-1962). He not only influenced many of the framers of *Nostra Aetate* but also coined the now popular term *Abrahamic faiths*, which connects Christians, Jews, and Muslims together through a shared spiritual patrimony.[1]

Since the promulgation of *Nostra Aetate*, great strides have been made in Catholic-Muslim dialogue at both the official and grassroots levels. In the early twenty-first century, Pope John Paul II became the first pope to visit a mosque officially, and the Vatican has continued to host an annual dialogue with Muslim scholars from Cairo's al-Azhar University. In 2006, Pope Benedict XVI gave a controversial speech in Regensburg, Germany, which inspired 138 Muslim scholars to respond with a *Nostra Aetate*–like statement of their own entitled "A Common Word between Us and You," which highlights the twin commonalities of love of God and love of neighbor shared by Christians and Muslims. The website devoted to "A

---

1. Massignon was one of the first to assert that Muslims, Christians, and Jews share the spiritual patrimony of Abraham: "There in Jerusalem the Christians have Arab witness of their faith and the geographical convergence of the three Abrahamic faiths in one and the same Holy Land"; quote from "The Three Prayers of Abraham" (originally "Les trois prières d'Abraham, père de tous les croyants," 1949), in *Testimonies and Reflections*, ed. Herbert Mason, trans. Allan Cutler (Notre Dame, IN: University of Notre Dame Press, 1989), 8. See also Neal Robinson, "Massignon, Vatican II, and Islam as an Abrahamic Religion," *Islam and Christian-Muslim Relations* 2, no. 2 (1991): 182–205 (194).

Common Word" supports an ongoing dialogue; scholars and religious leaders and ordinary believers from around the world continue to post their responses to the statement.[2]

Perhaps more important than these upper-level dialogues, though, are local dialogues, which often prove more effective at changing the hearts and minds of average people. For example, in sub-urban Chicago a Catholic-Muslim women's dialogue has been meeting monthly for more than fifteen years. These women have become close friends not only because their mosque and church are within blocks of one another but also because the women themselves live in the same neighborhood. At their meetings they discuss concerns about family, school, crime, and other local issues, as well as share food, faith, and religious traditions.

## Dialogue on "A Common Word"

To give readers a sense of dialogue, the two scholars writing this chapter engage here in a brief dialogue on "A Common Word."

### Saritoprak:

The 2006 lecture of Pope Benedict XVI in Regensburg, Germany, in which he quoted a statement from Byzantine Emperor, Manuel II Palaiologos, where he spoke very negatively about the Prophet of Islam, sparked some inflammatory reactions among Muslims. As understood from his later statements, his intention was not to condemn the Prophet of Islam, but merely to quote from a historical conversation. The Pope later attempted to repair the damage he caused by visiting Turkey and praying in the Mosque with the Mufti of Istanbul. As a result of these tensions, a group of Muslim scholars sent a letter to the Pope inviting him to "a common word," a

phrase from a famous verse in the Qur'an (3:64). They defined "a common word" as loving God and loving one's neighbor. The "Common Word" initiative has become very well known among scholars of interfaith dialogue. Since 2007 this initiative has contributed to many dialogue efforts through lectures and publications as well as dialogue meetings. Though many efforts have been put forward, it would have been even more successful if the initiative had included more grassroots advocates of dialogue.

### George-Tvrtković:

In October 2012, the website associated with "A Common Word" noted the fifth anniversary of the document's publication and described the document as "the most successful Muslim-Christian Interfaith Initiative in History." But what exactly is "success"? Success can be measured on several levels. First, the original 138 Muslim signatories hail from countries as diverse as Iran, Bosnia, Nigeria, Syria, Ukraine, the United States, and Malaysia, and from backgrounds as varied as professor, editor, head mufti, *qadi* (judge), former prime minister, *alim* (traditional Islamic scholar), and ayatollah. This is quite an accomplishment, given that Muslims do not have a centralized international hierarchy of authority as do Catholics. The document serves as a response to the question often repeated in the mass media: "Why don't we hear from 'Muslim moderates'?" And finally, several Christian and Jewish scholars and organizations have written largely positive responses. In short, upper-level dialogue on "A Common Word" could be considered a success. However, in the five years between October 2007 and 2012, there were only 470,000 website hits, which is a small number in Internet terms, considering that the most popular YouTube videos often reach millions of

---

2. See *acommonword.com*.

hits within days. To be truly successful at the grassroots level, many more people from around the world must read this document, or at least be made aware of its existence.

The website states that the success of "A Common Word" is partly due to the fact that the document is built on "the most solid theological grounds possible in Muslim and Christian scriptures." These Muslim scholars deserve credit for rooting their document in scripture and for focusing on similarities. Indeed, a document entitled "A Common Word" necessarily centers on commonalities; this is its raison d'être. The document, however, may have glossed over differences too quickly. Perhaps "A Common Word" could have been stronger if it alluded at least briefly to a few differences, which would have encouraged more nuanced future dialogues. For example, Jesus does not simply reiterate Deuteronomy when he describes the greatest commandment, he also adds the idea of love of neighbor and expands further by asking and answering a new question, "Who is my neighbor?" in the parable of the Good Samaritan (Luke 10). And while Christians, like Muslims and Jews, believe in the oneness of God, their Trinitarian view of God sets them apart. A possible weakness of this critique may be that "A Common Word," like *Nostra Aetate* before it, was not meant to be the last word, but the first. A successful aspect of both documents, which are to a greater or lesser extent "magisterial," is their beginning of the dialogue on a positive note.

Another issue pertains to scriptural interpretation. The authors of "A Common Word"—all Muslim scholars—selected and interpreted verses from both the Qur'an and the Bible independent from Christian biblical scholars. It is refreshing for Christians to see which biblical verses resonate with Muslims and to learn the reasons why. Christians have been interpreting the Qur'an independent from Muslim scholars for centuries, for better or worse.[3] Many scholars who are engaged in interfaith dialogue today, however, prefer to center their conversation on a mutual interpretation of their respective scriptures. The key word here is "mutual," since interpretation of sacred texts takes on a different tenor when done together. But even an exegesis of the Bible conducted primarily by Muslims could have included some reference to Christian scholarship or even some background dialogue with Christians about, for example, which translation of the Bible would be cited in the document (such a dialogue might have in fact occurred). Why, for example, did the Muslim authors of "A Common Word" choose to cite from the New King James Version of the Bible when most Christian scholars prefer the New Revised Standard Version? Christian interpretations of the Qur'an always benefit from a consideration of Muslim interpretations; the reverse is probably true as well.

# Reflections of an "Insider"
*Zeki Saritoprak*

## The Qur'an and Dialogue

Since its first revelation, the Qur'an has been in constant dialogue with the adherents of different faiths, namely polytheists (*mushrikun*) as

---

3. Despite the preponderance of Christian polemical readings of the Qur'an throughout history, sympathetic readings of the Qur'an by Christians can also be found, for example, as early as Nicholas of Cusa (d. 1464), whose *Cribratio alkorani* simultaneously included criticism along with a more sympathetic approach, *pia interpretatio*. For more on *pia interpretatio*, see Jasper Hopkins, "The Role of *Pia Interpretatio* in Nicholas of Cusa's Hermeneutical Approach to the Qur'an," in *Miscellany on Nicholas of Cusa* (Minneapolis, MN: A.J. Banning, 1994), 39–55, and Pim Valkenberg, "Sifting the Qur'an: Two Forms of Interreligious Hermeneutics in Nicholas of Cusa," in *Interreligious Hermeneutics in Pluralistic Europe: Between Texts and People*, ed. David Cheetham et al. (Amsterdam: Rodopi, 2011), 27–48.

well as Jews and Christians, known as "people of the book" (*ahl al-kitab*). The Qur'an makes clear that Judaism and Christianity were the religions that came before Islam through divine revelation. The Torah is a revealed book of God to Moses, and the Gospel is a revealed message of God to Jesus. Though both have experienced changes through editors and translations, Muslims still have great respect for both books because they regard both as originally revealed by God. Because of this essential principle, the Qur'an calls Christians and Jews the "people of the book" and includes many verses that address the people of the book directly. If one asks, "What is an important foundation on which the Islamic understanding of dialogue is based?" the answer would perhaps be the Qur'anic verse 3:64. The verse says, "Say, O Muhammad, 'O People of the Book. Come to a common word between us and you so that we worship none but God. Also we associate no other with Him and none of us take others as lords other than God.'" The verse directly invites Christians and Jews, the people of the book, to come to a common ground. This common ground, in the Qur'anic example, is to believe in One God. The Qur'an does not limit the common ground, but begins with the first principle of believing in one God. We have just discussed how a representative group of contemporary Muslims takes this verse from the Qur'an as its point of departure in the "Common Word" initiative.

Because of this aspect of the Qur'an and Islamic reverence for people of the book, Muslims have, generally speaking, many Qur'anic verses that teach how to interact with the people of the book. For example, one verse says, "Do not argue with the People of the Book, unless it is in the way that is better, except for those People of the Book who have transgressed. You Muslims, say to them, 'We have believed in what has been revealed to us [the Qur'an] and what has been revealed to you [the Gospel and Torah].

Our God and your God is the same, and we have submitted ourselves to God'" (29:46). Another Qur'anic verse says, "And surely there are some People of the Book who believe in God and what has been revealed to you and what has been revealed to them. They are fearful of God and they do not cheapen the verses of God" (3:199). Some Qur'anic verses particularly praise Christians, for example "You [Muhammad], will find the nearest in affection to Muslims are those who say, 'Lo, we are Christians.' That is because among them there are priests and monks who are not arrogant" (5:82).

In fact, some verses even allude to salvation in the afterlife for the people of the book. A verse says, "Surely those who have believed [Muslims] and Jews and Christians and Sabaeans, if they believe in God, in the Day of Judgment, and do good deeds, they will have their reward with their Lord and they will have no fear, nor will they grieve" (2:62). Apparently this verse has three conditions for salvation: to believe in God, to believe in the afterlife, and to do good deeds.

From an Islamic theological perspective, shahada, the testimony of faith, is necessary for salvation. That is to say, one must believe in one God and in the prophethood of Muhammad from his or her heart. This is known also as the first pillar of Islam. While verse 2:62 does not directly include the belief in the prophethood of Muhammad as a necessary component of salvation, many scholars of Islamic theology have interpreted this verse as implying the necessity of that belief. In other words, when one believes in God, it also becomes necessary to believe in God's messengers. Because Muhammad is the last messenger of God, belief in him is indirectly mentioned in the first part of the verse. This essentially speaks of the first component of the testimony of faith: to testify that there is only one God. Islamic theology clearly states that the Judge in the afterlife is God, and He saves whom

He wants and punishes whom He wants. And whatever He does is justice. He never wrongs anyone. Theologians generally speak of certain principles, but cannot determine the final destination of any human being. It is God who makes that final determination. Therefore, even an individual Muslim cannot feel sure that his or her salvation is guaranteed. Accordingly, there is a balance of both hope and fear in the Islamic theology. The hope for salvation and fear of loss constitute important elements of Islamic theological discourse.

Many Qur'anic verses criticize the people of the book, Christians and Jews, for certain actions and behaviors, such as going astray, jealousy, and disbelief (see Qur'an 2:109; 98:1, 6). Despite Qur'anic criticism of these behaviors, Islamic law gives the people of the book certain privileges, through prophetic sayings that urge they be given protection when they are minorities under Islamic rule. In fact, in marriage they have some privileges in comparison to polytheists and the people who do not believe in the revelation of God. For example, according to Islamic law, a Muslim man can marry a Jewish or a Christian woman without asking them to convert to Islam, but cannot marry a polytheist. Christian or Jewish women who marry Muslim men can keep their religions if they wish and still be a good partner in marriage. The Prophet of Islam had a wife who came from the Jewish tradition named Safiyyah and a wife who came from Christianity from Egypt named Maria, who gave birth to Muhammad's son named Ibrahim or Abraham. Since the Prophet had established such a strong relationship with the people of the book, Muslims are encouraged to have positive relationships with Christians and Jews. Historically this has been the case with a few exceptions, such as the Crusades and colonialism.

Christians and Muslims have a unique relationship due to Muslims' belief in Jesus, not only as a great messenger of God but also in his miraculous birth. According to the Qur'an, an angel appeared to Mary and gave her the good news about the miraculous birth of Jesus. Mary is surprised and says, "How can I have a child without being touched by any human being?" And the angel replies, "This is the command of God. When God wants something, He just says 'Be' and it happens." Chapter 19 of the Qur'an details this story. In fact, the chapter itself is named after Mary. Muslims do not accept Jesus as the son of God, but instead they accept him as a miracle of God because of his unusual birth. In the Islamic theology of prophethood, there have been 124,000 prophets. Jesus is among the five most important prophets, the others being Noah, Abraham, Moses, and Muhammad. In the Qur'an, by using the royal pronoun "we," God says, "we have sent Jesus, the son of Mary, in the prophets' footsteps, confirming the Torah which was revealed before him. We also gave him the Gospel, in which there is guidance and light. It also confirms what was revealed before it, the Torah, and it is guidance and admonition for the pious" (5:46).

## Recent History of Muslim-Christian Dialogue

This brief introduction to the Islamic sources of dialogue sets the background against which to discuss Muslim pioneers of dialogue. One of the earliest pioneers of dialogue between Christians and Muslims is Bediuzzaman Said Nursi (d. 1960). Nursi, a devout Muslim scholar who faced some difficulties and persecution under the then ultra-secularist government of Turkey, gave a remarkable sermon in 1911 known as *The Damascus Sermon*.[4] In this sermon, Nursi speaks

---

4. Bediuzzaman Said Nursi, *The Damascus Sermon (Hutbe-i Şamiye)*, trans. Sukran Vahide (Istanbul: Sozler Yayinevi, 1991).

of his hope for Muslim and Christian relations and encourages cooperation between Muslims and Christians. In one of his early works on the commentary of the Qur'an, Nursi encouraged Muslim-Christian dialogue when he interpreted the Qur'anic verse that describes the qualities of the pious as those who believe in the revelation of the Qur'an revealed to Muhammad and the pre-Islamic revelations revealed to Moses and Jesus. The verse says, "[The pious] are those who believe in what is revealed to you [O Muhammad] and what is revealed before you and are certain in their belief of the hereafter" (2:4). Nursi comments that the language of the Qur'an is rather tender toward the followers of pre-Islamic revelations, namely Christians and Jews. According to Nursi, this verse encourages all people to accept the revelation of the Qur'an, particularly the people of the book, because the Qur'an itself is evidence and witness to the truthfulness of the Jewish and Christian scriptures. The verse declares the honorable position of those people of the book who have come to believe in the Qur'an and exhorts others to follow their example. Nursi's commentary on this verse further elaborates this point:

> O People of the Book! As you believe in the past prophets and the divine books, believe in Muhammad and the Qur'an as well. That is because the early prophets and their scriptures give good news of his coming. The proofs that show the truthfulness of those prophets and their books are truthfully and spiritually found in the Qur'an and in the personality of Muhammad. Therefore, the Qur'an is the word of God. The Prophet Muhammad, peace and blessings upon him, is the messenger of God.[5]

Nursi continued his efforts to dialogue with Christians in the 1950s in Istanbul and met with Ecumenical Patriarch Athenagoras to enhance Muslim-Christian cooperation. He even sent some of his writings to Pope Pius XII in the Vatican and received a thank-you letter of confirmation. It remains unknown whether this had an influence on the Vatican's later approach to Islam; but slightly more than ten years later, during the second Vatican Council, the Roman Catholic Church declared that it looks with esteem on the Islamic tradition.[6]

Nursi was very hopeful that cooperation between Muslims and Christians would develop and spread on a larger scale through interreligious cooperation and experience. He applauded the famous Baghdad Pact, a pact jointly signed by Turkey, Iraq, Pakistan, Iran, and the United Kingdom in 1955, since it represented intra-Muslim cooperation and was a Muslim-Christian alliance through the membership of Britain. In commenting on the Baghdad Pact, or MENTO, another name for the Middle East Treaty Organization, Nursi seemed to find in the foundation of this organization the realization of his hope for peace and positive relations between Muslims and Christians on a larger scale. He wrote a letter to the Prime Minister and the President of Turkey in 1955 in this regard:

> Your agreement with Iraq and Pakistan, God willing, will prevent the danger of nationalism. Instead of the friendship of four or five million nationalists, this agreement will bring to the country the friendship of four hundred million Muslims around the world [the population of Muslims in the world at the time], and eight hundred million Christians [the population of Christians in the world at that

---

5. Nursi, "Isarat al-I'jaz," in *Risale-i Nur Kulliyati* (Istanbul: Nesil Yayinlari, 2002), 1175.

6. Walter M. Abbott, "Nostra Aetate," in *The Documents of Vatican II* (New York: Herder and Herder, 1966), 660.1.

time] and adherents of other religions who are deeply in need of global peace. [7]

Continuing these efforts in recent times is Fethullah Gülen, another powerful Muslim voice for dialogue between Muslims and Christians.[8] Since 1994, Gülen has been a great advocate for dialogue both in Turkey and the United States. He believes that dialogue between Christians and Muslims is necessary, and he has encouraged the establishment of various institutions to promote dialogue. Many Turkish businessmen have financially supported such institutions of dialogue. It can be argued that Gülen and his movement are among the greatest investors in dialogue between Muslims and Christians, both financially and in human efforts. It would not be an exaggeration to speak of hundreds of dialogue institutions established at the encouragement of Gülen by his admirers. There are more than one hundred of these institutions in the United States alone. His meeting with John Paul II at the Vatican on February 8, 1998 created further support for cooperation between Catholics and Muslims. In addition, Muslim scholars and religious leaders, such as Mahmoud Ayoub, Seyyid Hossein Nasr, Irfan Omar, Muzammil Siddiqi, Sayyid M. Syeed, and many others, have contributed to the trend of dialogue between Muslims and Christians.

Furthermore, Muslims involved in Muslim-Catholic dialogue have contributed through various meetings and programs. For example, Midwest Catholic-Muslim Dialogue (in which I have been involved), West Coast Catholic-Muslim Dialogue, and East Coast Catholic-Muslim Dialogue all work extensively both in

academia as well as in the public sphere. Many American universities have created excellent dialogue centers to promote Muslim-Christian cooperation. For example, Georgetown University's Center for Muslim-Christian Understanding and the Macdonald Center for the Study of Islam and Christian-Muslim Relations in Connecticut are among the oldest such centers in the United States. More recently established centers include the Rumi Forum for Interfaith Dialogue in Washington, DC (where I had the honor of serving as founding president in 1999), the Niagara Foundation in Chicago, Interfaith Youth Corps, Abrahamic Alliance International, Abraham's Vision, and the Peace Islands Institute in New York. These developments have led some institutions to search for more opportunities for dialogue in academia. For example, the Claremont School of Theology campus, now Claremont Lincoln University, educates imams, rabbis, and priests; many other seminaries and theological training institutions have brought seminarians and clerics from the Abrahamic traditions together as well.

In the United States, Muslims have faced difficulties, mistrust, fear, and misguided attitudes that have created hatred against them. The media unfortunately have sometimes contributed to this trend by focusing on a small portion of the Muslim population to create a negative image of Islam. Some hate groups have even distributed free DVDs and books to cultivate more hatred against Muslims. Although the 9/11 attacks killed many Muslims as well, the media connected terrorism with the essence of Islam because the perpetrators were Arab Muslims. The silent majority of Muslims

7. Nursi, "Emirdağ Lahikasi-II," in *Risale-i Nur Kulliyati* (Istanbul: Nesil Yayinlari, 2002), 1904.

8. For additional information about Fethullah Gülen's involvement in interfaith dialogue, see Zeki Saritoprak and Sidney Griffith, "Fethullah Gülen and 'The People of the Book': A Voice from Turkey for Interfaith Dialogue," *The Muslim World* 95:3 (July 2005), 329–340, available at *webmedia.jcu.edu/nursichair/files/2012/03/2005-Fethullah-Gulen-and-the-People-of-the-Book-A-Voice-from-Turkey-for-Interfaith-Dialogue.pdf*.

suffered as a result of these prejudices. In some areas Muslims were prevented from establishing their places of worship, for example in Murfreesboro, Tennessee. In some companies, Muslim woman were prevented from wearing their head scarves, which is a part of their religious obligation. Yet, the American justice system has overturned all such discriminatory practices against Muslims.

Despite obstacles, such as Islamophobia after 9/11 and certain interest groups blemishing the face of Islam, dialogue efforts offer hope for the future of Muslim-Christian relations. These two groups come together; they share their food, especially during the month of Ramadan; and they share their community services. One can see great wisdom and common sense in most Christians and Muslims. Their shared efforts for dialogue will further marginalize the extremists on both sides. Therefore, Muslims and Christians as well as adherents of other religious traditions who work for cooperation in dialogue should constantly act for a successful mutual understanding. My hope is that through coming together, they will know each other, and through knowing each other, they will cooperate and bring harmony to their communities. An essential element of both religions is having peace, which is the priority of the Qur'an in human relationships: "peace is better" (4:128).

# Resources for Further Study

## Review Questions

1. Discuss three concrete examples of diversity in the Islamic world today.
2. Why do Muslims consider an Arabic-language Qur'an to be superior to a translation in any other language?
3. Why is Muhammad called the "seal of the prophets," and what is the difference between a prophet and messenger in Islam? Give examples of each.
4. What does it mean to say that Islam is a religion focused on orthopraxy? Discuss, using concrete examples.
5. Define *tawhid*, and explain its importance to Islamic doctrine.

## Questions for Reflection and Discussion

1. Compare and contrast Islamic and Christian ideas of God. In what ways are they similar, and where do they diverge?
2. How have various Muslims defined *jihad*, past and present? Are there any parallel concepts within Christianity?
3. Both Islam and Christianity are universal, missionary religions that together claim roughly half of the world's believers. What are the challenges and opportunities inherent in this fact?
4. What authoritative Catholic and Islamic texts (from scripture and tradition) encourage believers to respect members of the other religion? On what basis?

## Glossary

**Allah**  The Arabic word for "God" used by Muslims as well as by Jews and Christians who speak Arabic. This word contains the general Semitic word *'ilah* for a deity together with the definite article *al-*, so a literal translation would be "the (One who is) God."

**dhikr**  A form of Muslim devotion in which the devotee constantly remembers God. Dhikr can be practiced by prayer beads to repeat the ninety-nine names of God, but dhikr is particularly associated with Sufism, which is known for its more controversial dhikr practices such as singing and dancing.

**hadith**  An authoritative report of Muhammad's words. Next to the Qur'an, this is the most important source of shari'ah or Islamic law. A hadith (plural *ahadith*) has two major parts: the *matn* (text) and the *isnad* (chain of transmission). Every hadith is classified on a spectrum from sound to weak.

**hajj**  The pilgrimage to Mecca. All Muslims are required to make this pilgrimage once in their lives if they are financially and physically able; this is one of the "five pillars" or compulsory practices of Islam.

**hanif** Someone who is searching for the true God without belonging to one of the institutionalized faiths. It is used to describe pre-Islamic monotheists such as Ibrahim/Abraham.

**haqiqah** "Truth." This is a Sufi term used for the final goal of the Sufi path: the meeting with God who is the Truth. It also describes the Sufi path as a way that concentrates on inner reality.

**hijra** The migration made by Muhammad and some of his companions from Mecca to Yathrib (later renamed Medina, *Madinat un-Nabi*, "City of the Prophet") in 622 CE. The Hijra is year one of the Muslim calendar, since it marks the foundation of the first Muslim community (umma).

**i'jaz** The "inimitability" of the Qur'an. This is a term used by Muslims to describe the incomparable eloquence of Qur'anic Arabic, which for them demonstrates the book's purely divine origins.

**jahiliyya** "Ignorance" of the true faith. The term is often used to characterize pre-Islamic times and customs and sometimes used to characterize modern societies and governments that claim to be Islamic without really following the precepts of Islam.

**jihad** Arabic for "striving" or "struggle." It means to exert oneself (morally, spiritually, financially, and/or militarily) in the way of God and is sometimes translated as "holy war."

**nabi** A prophet of God. Islam recognizes a number of prophets to whom God has given messages. Some of them are known to Jews and Christians as biblical prophets, but there are nonbiblical (Arabic) prophets as well. Some prophets are also messengers (see *rasul*).

**Qur'an** An Arabic word meaning "recitation" or "reading." It is the name for the holy book of Islam revealed to Prophet Muhammad, and it comes from the first word revealed to Muhammad, *iqra* ("read" or "recite"). It also indicates that the Qur'an is meant to be read aloud.

**Ramadan** One of the twelve months of the Islamic calendar, specifically connected with the practice of strict fasting during the entire month from sunrise to sunset. It celebrates the month in which Muhammad first received revelation from God.

**rasul** A messenger of God. All messengers are prophets, but not all prophets are messengers. The word *messenger* implies the reception of a specific message or book by God. For example, Islam acknowledges Musa (Moses) and `Isa (Jesus) as messengers.

**salat** A ritualized prayer practiced five times a day and one of the five pillars of Islam. Muslims can pray their salat everywhere in a clean environment; they usually practice their afternoon prayer on Friday in the mosque (*masjid*; Arabic for place of prostration, a place where one worships God). It is one of the five pillars of Islam.

**Saracen** A medieval Latin term for "Muslim." Before the rise of Islam, the term referred to Bedouin tribes.

**sawm** Fasting during the month of Ramadan; one of the five pillars of Islam. For Muslims, fasting includes not only abstaining from all food and drink, but also from sexual relations, smoking, swearing, and so on.

**shahada** The Islamic profession of faith: "I give witness that there is no god but God and that Muhammad is the messenger of God." One of the five pillars of Islam.

**shari'ah** A term used to indicate the sacred law of Islam, which is based on the Qur'an as well as the sayings and practices of the Prophet.

**Shi'a**  Arabic for "partisans of `Ali." Muslims who believe that Muhammad appointed Ali and his descendants to lead the community; about 15 percent of the world's Muslims are Shi'a.

**Sufism**  The mystical branch of Islam, which focuses on developing a spiritual relationship between lover (Sufi) and Beloved (God). Sufism is a "path" (*tariqa*) or process that requires the assistance of a knowledgeable guide (Arabic *shaykh;* Persian *pir*). Mystical union with God is the ultimate goal.

**Sunni**  Followers of the Sunnah (words and deeds) of the Prophet as recorded in the hadith; about 85 percent of the world's Muslims are Sunni.

**sura**  A chapter of the Qur'an. There are 114 suras in all, arranged in order of length from the longest to the shortest (with the exception of the first sura).

*tafsir*  Qur'anic exegesis (interpretation). Al-Tabari, one of the greatest early exegetes, helped set the standard for this genre.

*taqwa*  Arabic for God consciousness, sometimes translated as "piety" or "fear of God." It indicates the inner dimension of faith in God.

*tawhid*  Professing the oneness of God. Muslims consider the Oneness of God as the central tenet of their faith.

*umma*  The international community of Muslims. It was first formed in 622 CE after the hijra (migration) of Muhammad and some of his earliest companions from Mecca to Medina.

*zakat*  Arabic for "purification of wealth." Also translated as "almsgiving," it is obligatory and one of the five pillars of Islam. Those Muslims who are financially able to give zakat (2.5% of their surplus wealth) often do so during the month of Ramadan.

# Annotated Bibliography

Ahmed, Leila. *A Quiet Revolution: The Veil's Resurgence, from the Middle East to America.* New Haven, CT: Yale University Press, 2011.

This book covers recent developments in Muslim women's issues around the globe, focusing on the interplay between religion, culture, and politics in the last forty years. It builds on the more sweeping historical account in the author's previous book, *Women and Gender in Islam* (1993). From a feminist and secular perspective.

Bearman, P.J., T. Bianquis, C.E. Bosworth, E. van Donzel, and W.P. Heinrichs, eds. *Encyclopedia of Islam.* 2nd ed. [Leiden:] Brill, 1960–2005. (See also the forthcoming 3rd ed., Kate Fleet, Gudrun Krämer, Denis Matringe, John Nawas, and Everett Rowson, eds. [Leiden:] Brill, 2007–. Updates yearly.)

Now beginning its third edition (the first edition commenced in 1912), this reliable and truly comprehensive encyclopedia should be one of the very first sources students consult when doing research. Entries are written by a variety of the world's leading scholars.

Ernst, Carl. *How to Read the Qur'an: A New Guide, with Select Translations.* Chapel Hill: University of North Carolina Press, 2011.

The author begins with the question "How should non-Muslims read the Qur'an?" and then provides an accessible introduction focusing on structure, historical context, development, and relationship to other texts such as the Christian Bible and Jewish Talmud. Includes the author's own translations of several passages.

Esposito, John. *Islam the Straight Path.* 4th ed. Oxford: Oxford University Press, 2010.

This compact volume is one of the most readable, logically organized introductions to Islam in print; its renowned author directs

Georgetown's Center for Muslim-Christian Understanding. Includes a useful glossary of Arabic terms. For beginners.

Gülen, M. Fethullah. *Emerald Hills of the Heart: Key Concepts in the Practice of Sufism*. Somerset, NJ: The Light, 2004.

This series of four books contains explanations of basic Sufi concepts and is Fethullah Gülen's most scholarly work. Like most of Gülen's works, the reflections were originally written as short columns in periodicals that were published to help Muslims make the connections between the tradition of Islam and the modern world. Gülen is considered by many Turkish Muslims as an important bridge builder between the world of Islam and the West.

Gülen, M. Fethullah. *Reflections on the Qur'an: Commentary on Selected Verses*. New York: Tughra Books, 2012.

This book contains an English translation of Gülen's commentaries on important verses from the Qur'an. These reflections were originally used by Gülen in teaching his students the classical commentaries on the Qur'an.

Haddad, Yvonne Yazbeck, ed. *Muslims in the West: From Sojourners to Citizens*. New York: Oxford University Press, 2002.

Building on a previous volume that focused on Muslims in America, *Muslims in the West* is a collection of essays by prominent scholars (e.g., Tariq Ramadan, Jane I. Smith, and Sulayman Nyang) on the situation of Muslims in Europe and North America.

Nursi, Bediuzzaman Said. *Letters 1928–1932*. Şukran Vahide, trans. Istanbul: Sözler Neşriyat, 1997.

Nursi, Bediuzzaman Said. *The Words*. Şukran Vahide, trans. Istanbul: Sözler Neşriyat, 1996.

These two books form the main parts of the Risale-i Nur, a topical commentary on the Qur'an. The works of Said Nursi are read by many Muslims in Turkey and abroad as a modern way to connect the Qur'an and contemporary sciences.

Rahman, Fazlur. *Major Themes of the Qur'an*. 2nd ed. Chicago: University of Chicago Press, 2009.

This is a second edition of a classic originally written in the 1980s. It remains one of the most respected introductions to Qur'anic content available.

Schimmel, Annemarie. *Islam: An Introduction*. Albany: State University of New York Press, 1992.

The author, one of the twentieth century's most prolific scholars of Islam, packs her encyclopedic knowledge into this slim volume. In addition to the basics, she manages to touch on many complex concepts not covered in the average introductory text.

Schimmel, Annemarie. *Mystical Dimensions of Islam*. Chapel Hill: University of North Carolina Press, 1975.

Students who are interested in Sufism will appreciate this magisterial and comprehensive treatment. A classic that has yet to be surpassed. For a more advanced audience.

Sells, Michael. *Early Islamic Mysticism: Sufi, Qur'an, Mi'raj, Poetic, and Theological Writings*. New York: Paulist Press, 1996.

This book brings together primary texts from a wide range of early Islamic sources. It also provides an accessible introduction to Sufism, including a brief history and an explanation of the relationship between mysticism and mainstream Islamic praxis. The five pillars in particular are well described here.

Tolan, John. *Saracens: Islam in the Medieval European Imagination*. New York: Columbia University Press, 2002.

This book replaces Norman Daniel's landmark *Islam and the West* (1960) as the standard resource for medieval Christian views of Islam. *Saracens* is organized better (chronologically), covers more centuries, and treats a wider variety of medieval authors.

Wadud, Amina. *Qur'an and Woman: Rereading the Sacred Text from a Woman's Perspective.* New York: Oxford University Press, 1999.

This is one of the few books written by a Muslim that attempts to interpret the Qur'an from both a feminist and theological perspective.

Zebiri, Kate. *Muslims and Christians, Face to Face.* Oxford, England: Oneworld, 1997.

This book is notable for its balance; the author discusses not only Christian views/distortions of Islam (a common topic) but also a variety of Muslim views/distortions of Christianity (a less common topic). Focuses on the nineteenth and twentieth centuries.

## Internet Resources

Center for Muslim-Jewish Engagement at the University of Southern California: *usc.edu/org/ cmje/religioustexts/quran/Translations*

The center has posted three different translations of the Qur'an side-by-side for study and comparison.

Dominican Institute for Oriental Studies (IDEO), Cairo: *ideo-cairo.org/*

"Interreligious Dialogue on the Internet": *groups.creighton.edu/sjdialogue/links/links.html*

Maintained by the Jesuits, this is an excellent resource not only for Christian-Muslim dialogue, but interfaith dialogue in general.

Monastic Interreligious Dialogue (MID): *dimmid.org/*

This site began as a Buddhist-Benedictine monastic endeavor, but has branched out into all areas of interfaith dialogue, including Christian-Muslim relations.

Pontifical Institute for Arabic and Islamic Studies: *en.pisai.it/*

"Theology Library: Muslim-Christian Dialogue": *shc.edu/theolibrary/muslim.htm*

Spring Hill College's extensive site.

# PART 3: HINDUISM

*Aimee Upjohn Light and Madhuri M. Yadlapati*

# CHAPTER 9

# An Outsider's Perspective

*Aimee Upjohn Light*

## Overview of Christian Approaches to Hinduism

Christian approaches to Hinduism are diverse, but tend to study sacred texts, ways of life, or philosophy. Hinduism resists the definition of religion with which one usually approaches other traditions because it is a tradition full of different, sometimes even contradictory, beliefs and practices. Both the diverse nature of Hinduism itself and Christian apprehension about studying such a broad historical reality have led scholars generally to specialize in only the sacred texts, rituals, or philosophy of Hinduism.

Less doctrinally concerned than Western religions, Hinduism is both the context for meaning in life and the product of meanings discovered, and it is sometimes codified as divinely revealed. It has no one founder, set of creeds, or foundational set of ethical precepts. Thus by choosing what part of this ancient and varied tradition to study, one runs the risk of reducing Hinduism to just a philosophy, set of practices, or specific canon. None of these approaches do justice to the myriad components that form the Hindu religion. Partial approaches may be necessary, but certainly skew the understanding of outsiders, just as studying the New Testament, Roman Catholic sacraments, or Thomas Aquinas out of context would skew the perception

of an outsider seeking to understand Christianity. Yet because Hinduism is such a vast topic—perhaps more so than most religions—a reductionist method of study seems necessary in order to tell a coherent story, rather than assemble a scattered collection of informational sound bites.

Western scholars of religions typically decide to approach the study of Hinduism by narrating its historical development; however, some proceed topically, describing various practices and texts as discrete items that seem able to be rendered intelligible in isolation. Yet, like Christianity, Hinduism integrates textual reading with ritual practice and everyday action in the world such that isolating its components fails to fully portray Hinduism as the believable and pervasive system that millions take for granted. Hinduism is experienced by Hindus as a reasonable, explanatory worldview just as Christianity is experienced by Christians as a reasonable, explanatory worldview.

As is true for all religions, Hinduism appears to its followers not as *an* option among many but as *the* option. Hindus think their religion offers the fullest, most encompassing explanation of the world and religious diversity in the world, just as Christians tend to believe Christianity offers the best explanation of the world and the multiplicity of religions. With its many gods and goddesses, who are understood as manifestations of Brahman or the ultimate, Hinduism understands the entire world as related to and frequently even manifesting the divine. Far from what is seen as polytheism by Westerners, the multiplicity of gods in Hinduism signals the pervasive presence of the One who is present throughout the world, in all facets of life. Any approach to Hinduism, whether historical or topical, should be seen as but a snapshot of a system of life so pervasive that the believability of other religions seems impossible to its members. Just as Christianity seems the only or obvious choice to many Christians, the collection of texts, beliefs, and practices labeled "Hinduism" appears to be the best and brightest choice for many followers. As with medieval and even Enlightenment Christians, Hindus generally do not know enough about other religions to consider them viable options.

The diversity of religions in the world and within Hinduism itself is better honored by the dialogical method used in this book than by a topical or historical approach. This chapter is a self-conscious simplification. Like all outsider perspectives it cannot fully capture the diversity, dynamism, and experience of Hinduism. The following overview of typical information about and approaches to Hinduism should be read in anticipation of the dialogic process that informs the rest of part 3.

Writing about a religious tradition as though it is a static system either renders it lifeless or makes it obvious that one is an outsider. The description of Hinduism in this chapter reflects the perspective of an interested outsider to the Hindu tradition, and exemplifies how Christians are taught to teach Hinduism. Until recently, training in "Eastern religions" focused on presenting facts, with great attention to dates and figures and individual beliefs, but rarely attempted to help them come alive as reasonable and sophisticated cosmologies. Instead, the training tended to presume that other religions were primitive

The OM symbol represents the primordial sound of creation. Chanting OM during meditation connects breath and sound and allows one to commune with the vibration of the universe.

and suffered from magical thinking not exhibited in Christianity, which was thought to be more advanced. Yet dialogue with Hinduism, and more importantly with Hindu friends and colleagues, has brought Hinduism alive for me and made clear that this "foreign" religion asks and answers many of the same questions as Christianity. Dialogue with trusted, respected, and most of all loved members of another religion begins the process of bringing an outsider into the fold of a religion that can otherwise only be studied theoretically. The proto-insider status received in dialogue is shared in chapter 12.

## The Hindu Way

The notion of *sanatana dharma* provides a good starting point for thinking about Hinduism; few words or practices convey so well the pervasive significance of Hinduism in the lives of its members. *Sanatana dharma* is sometimes translated as "the eternal way," with no beginning and no end. It refers to how the world is caused to be at every moment through its relationship to and dependence on the divine, and especially to how one's own existence and activity participates in this being. Adherents' participation in the way sustains the order of the world as it goes through cosmic cycles to its next stage. People are but participants in a universal whole—something modern Western individualism has perhaps lost sight of. Every aspect of Hinduism should be understood as related to the perpetuation of sanatana dharma. The creation of texts, reading of texts, meditation, caste delineations, dietary practices, rituals, stages of life, and metaphysical pronouncements all serve and should be conducted in honor of sanatana dharma.

# Sacred Texts

Hindus can choose to privilege one set of sacred texts over another. They may disagree about which are most transformative or most important, and may call beloved those containing the most voluminous or most famous stories about the deity around which their bhakti or personal devotion centers. Unlike Christianity, which considers the whole Bible—the Old and New Testaments—sacred and calls Christians to regard all the books of the Bible equally sacred and worthy of attention, Hinduism allows believers to determine for themselves the relative importance of the many Hindu texts.

## The Vedas

The Vedas are the oldest collection of writings, thought to have been written down during the first millennium BCE after centuries of oral transmission. They are primarily made up of hymns, rituals, and stories and are one of several collections considered to be pure *shruti*, or

revelation. Those who wrote the Vedas, as well as other texts considered to be shruti, are regarded as compilers or collectors rather than authors. Hindus believe that the eternal, or Brahman, literally gave the Vedas as they are; they are not considered interpreted or affected by those who took down the information.

## The Upanishads

This collection of the most mystical texts of Hinduism are also considered shruti. Unlike Vedic concern with ritual, the Upanishads' primary concern is with right relationship with Brahman, or ultimate reality. Compiled later than the Vedas, the Upanishads direct persons to look inward for transcendent reality instead of outward to ritual practice or devotion. These texts urge hearers or readers to locate Brahman inside themselves as the all-pervading reality. The body and worldly reality are impermanent and will pass away. Only by turning inward does one discover one's true self and the source of that self, joining the two at the moment of discovery. As in all religions, this mystical discovery may occur powerfully and dramatically all at once, with the insight recurring in different circumstances. The Upanishads paint a picture of spiritual practice that transcends the particular details of one's life. Mystical and esoteric, the Upanishads are frequently singled out in the West as the highest expression of Hindu spirituality.

## Ramayana

Epics are another important part of Hindu sacred literature. The epic Ramayana concerns dharma, or duty in relationship. It relates the story of Prince Rama, who is an avatar—an incarnation—of the Hindu god Vishnu.[1] Rama

---

1. The doctrine of Dasavatara, or Ten Avatars, holds that Vishnu has ten earthly incarnations, including five animal and five human forms. Each incarnation is intended to meet a particular spiritual need of that time. The last avatar, Kalki, is a mighty warrior expected to appear in the future to end the current age of moral decline known as the Kali Yuga.

is wrongly exiled by his father because of his stepmother's jealousy, but he loyally obeys his father, despite the injustice of the command. His wife, Sita, and brother, Lakshman, follow him into exile, obedient as brother and wife just as Rama is obedient as a son. Duty in the Ramayana is all about loyalty and doing as one ought, even when doing one's duty seems unjust.

## The Bhagavad Gita

The Mahabharata also teaches the reader about duty and is best-known for containing the Bhagavad Gita, or the story of Lord Krishna, another avatar of Vishnu, and the archer Arjuna. An expert marksman, Arjuna finds himself forced to engage in battle with members of his family and community. Knowing that he will triumph and have to kill people he cares about, he turns to his charioteer for support. The charioteer, God in disguise, instructs Arjuna to do his duty, withdrawing his attention from good or bad consequences. Though the text outwardly champions doing one's duty, at a deeper level it explores spiritual attitudes. Expressing the roots of karma yoga or the path of action and bhakti yoga or the path of devotion, the Bhagavad Gita urges people to relinquish the fruits of action, caring not for outcomes but offering everything to the transcendent. With this detached, transcendental understanding comes peace and joy.

## Laws of Manu

The Laws of Manu, another key Hindu text, is sometimes viewed by outsiders as antithetical in spirit to that of the Gita. The Laws originated in response to the spread of Buddhism in the second century BCE, attempting to solidify Hindu ways of life so that the newer Buddhist system would appear a radical departure from Hinduism rather than a variant of Hindu belief and practice.[2] Especially because Buddhism offered the possibility of men and women becoming monks and nuns, with greater gender and caste equality, the Laws codified gender norms and the duties of the untouchable caste. The Laws deal with social organization and rules for conduct, reinforcing caste hierarchy and responsibilities as part of dharma. Caste rigidly designates one's place in society—whether priest, worker, or untouchable. One is born into a caste and remains there for life, regardless of one's work ethics or level of education. The social and ethical norms that bind a person in his or her caste reflect and enforce a traditional patriarchal and hierarchical culture.

## The Puranas

The Puranas consist of eighteen poetic texts, divided equally into three categories, each named for a god: Brahma, Vishnu, and Shiva. The appearance of three gods explains why Christians have, until recently, spoken of a Hindu Trinity. Currently, Christians studying religion usually take care not to project their beliefs on the foreign system being studied, but until recently scholars tended to fit Hindu gods into a Christian framework. This practice misrepresents Hinduism and reflects the belief that Christianity is superior to Hinduism.

One of the most beloved texts in the Puranas is the Bhagavata Purana, which tells Krishna's life story, including the famous tale of him stealing butter as a little boy and running off to

---

2. Historians believe that the Laws of Manu and the Bhagavad Gita were written as part of a Hindu resurgence against the growing popularity of Buddhism. The Laws of Manu reflects a need to preserve the power and traditions of priestly orthodoxy, and the Bhagavad Gita influences the rise of medieval bhakti traditions. The Bhagavad Gita's teaching of acting in relinquishment also shows the clear influence of Buddhist ideals of freeing oneself of desire.

Krishna as an infant or young child is a prominent object of bhakti, and worshipers often recite stories about his mischievous antics, such as stealing butter from the neighbors' larders.

the forest to play music and wear flowers. There is perhaps no greater example of and justification for enjoying earthly pleasures than this story, immortalized in Hindu art and song.

# Historical Developments

## The Vedic Religion

The term *Vedic religion* refers to the ancient traditions that reflect the Aryan migration into the Indian subcontinent (1700-1300 BCE) and that were incorporated into what is now known as Hinduism. The Vedic religion was not a unified, monolithic tradition. It included such a diversity of beliefs and practices that one might question whether it should be thought of as a single religion at all. Though one ought never to forget that beliefs and practices in Vedic society were incredibly diverse, there are some common elements. The central ceremony in much ancient Vedic ritual life was the fire sacrifice. Controlled by Brahmins, or priests, the fire sacrifice invoked what was thought of as the breath behind all existence. This absolute reality, both formless and not entirely distinct from the self, later came to be known as Brahman. Brahman, or the absolute, proved difficult to worship because of the necessity of priestly (Brahmanic) intercession, so personal devotion to particular gods or manifestations of Brahman came to dominate Vedic practice. Because of the multiplicity of these particular manifestations, Westerners frequently misunderstood Hinduism as polytheistic. The "gods" in Hinduism are not causes of the world, but manifestations of the one cause of the world, Brahman.

## Classical Hinduism

### The Samkhya System

Samkhya is possibly the oldest philosophical system in India—yet it remains an influential school of philosophy. It predates Vedic civilization and is said to have been founded by the semimythical figure Kapila. Strongly dualistic, Samkhya holds that reality is constituted by two principles: *purusha*, the unchanging self, and *prakriti*, the changing cause of the physical world. Purusha is beyond cause, eternal and free; prakriti is the ordinary, material world. Forgetting purusha or confusing it with prakriti causes suffering. Getting back in touch with the unchanging self beyond the changing material world is the goal of spirituality.

### Yoga

Many Westerners associate Hinduism with yoga, understood as an athletic, stretching practice done in groups. Though it sometimes includes this kind of activity, *yoga* in Hinduism is a much broader term designating spiritual practice meant to discipline the egoistic self. There are many kinds of yoga, including karma yoga, bhakti yoga, jnana yoga and raja yoga. Karma yoga perhaps provides the best way to think about the true meaning of yoga since it has so little in common with Western preconceptions.

*Karma yoga* means "the way of action." One should do everything mindful of and in service to the absolute. Whether washing the dishes or morning devotion, every activity in a person's entire life should be consciously and deliberately lived in relationship with others and with God. The Bhagavad Gita's story of Arjuna and Krishna is considered the foundational text for karma yoga, as it teaches that human beings must continue to act in the world, without attachment to outcomes, in the service of God. Far from being an ascetic practice, karma yoga directs individuals to go out into the world. As in Christianity, a person should be in the world but not of the world.

Also rooted in the teaching of the Bhagavad Gita, *bhakti yoga* is the type practiced by most Hindus and may feel familiar to Jews, Christians, and Muslims for whom ritual acts of worship take place is specially designated places, with memorized prayers and ordered action. *Bhakti* means personal devotion to one's chosen deity. Bhakti yoga, then, describes the life dedicated to the divine through ritual action and prayer. In bhakti yoga the self is not transcended, but rather put at the service of the absolute, understood in particular manifestations.

*Jnana yoga* is the path of rational inquiry and the most philosophical path. The mind is the vehicle of transformation, asking and answering questions and finally coming to understand that the temporal, changing "I" or self-identity is illusory. The subject lies beyond all questioning, all temporality, all being. This is true self-discovery and brings freedom and peace.

*Raja yoga* is the oldest documented practice of clearing the mind and does so through intense concentration. Unlike the path of action, devotion, or rational inquiry, raja yoga attempts to focus a person such that ordinary reality and self-consciousness are transcended altogether. Words cannot adequately describe the state of spiritual absorption attained, but dualities vanish and the seeker becomes one with the ultimate. It is in the tradition of raja yoga that one finds the chanting of mantras to quiet the mind, ascetic practices, and breath control.

### The Bhakti Movement

The Classical Hinduism that emerged out of the Vedic tradition emphasized dharma (duty) and bhakti (devotion) over purely philosophical accounts or speculation about the nature of the absolute. The bhakti movement that arose between the second century BCE and the sixth century CE retrieved much Vedic practice as Buddhism's popularity declined. Yet these popularized ways were always punctuated by movements of sophisticated philosophical questioning and speculation. The most influential of these philosophical movements is Advaita Vedanta.

### The Advaita Movement

Advaita, even more than other philosophical movements, is perhaps the best-known Hindu school of philosophy and the one to which many Christians turn for comparative theological work. Advaita focuses on the Upanishadic teaching that atman (the principle of individuation or difference between things in the world) is one with Brahman (the principle and source of reality). Advaita Vedanta, the most influential school of Vedanta, argues that the principle of all reality is oneness. Whereas Vedanta thinking considers self-realization the proper understanding of reality and Brahman, Advaita champions thinking about the meaning of all realities being one.

Advaita's most influential figure was Shankara, who lived in the early eighth century. He held that only Brahman exists and that the visible world is a product of maya (human ignorance) about the nature of reality.

Ramanuja, a well-known follower of Shankara, developed a successful philosophical challenge to Shankara's nondualistic, unified understanding of being. Considered part of Advaita Vedanta, Ramanuja's thought balances Shankara's strong identification of reality and Brahman with an assertion of difference. According to Ramanuja, if everything is Brahman and much human understanding is wrong, then Brahman contains error and ignorance, which is an unacceptable conclusion. Ramanuja thus articulates distinction between the divine and the world and supports the essential duty of bhakti, or personal devotion to God. Bhakti restores right understanding and right relationship with God and protects against the introduction of error into the divine.

## Renaissance, Modernity, and Reform

Hinduism has arguably experienced two renaissances. The first, in response to the growing influence of Buddhism, reached the height of its popularity in the third century BCE and is responsible for many of the texts and practices that now constitute Hinduism. The second Hindu renaissance emerged in reaction to British colonization and withdrawal, an occupation that began in the early nineteenth century and ended only in 1947 with the establishment of India as its own republic.

When seen as a response to the development of Buddhism, Hinduism's first renaissance appears to owe much to Buddhism's spiritual challenge. By offering escape from the caste system through monastic life and religious practices that were accessible to all and required no priestly intercession, Buddhism challenged Hinduism to

develop a greater diversity of practices for persons in different situations. The Laws of Manu (c. 100 CE), the Yoga Sutras (c. 300 CE), and the Bhagavad Gita (c. 100 CE) all responded to the challenges of Buddhist understanding and practice, which differed from and began taking over traditional Vedic ways. While the Laws of Manu sought to retain societal structure, the Yoga Sutras responded to the attractiveness and apparent effectiveness of Buddhist meditation. The Gita advocates various yogic paths as different alternatives to the spiritual life, offering a diversity of approaches in the hopes of countering the spread of Buddhism.

In the wake of British imperial power and its eventual withdrawal, Hinduism has again experienced a visible resurgence. Beyond being the pervasive cultural influence in India, Hinduism has spread as a nationalistic as well as liberating movement. Because it has been the predominant religion of India and was countered by Christian missionary activity, Hinduism has become the symbol of a strong India, triumphant over and against imperialistic forces. Because of tension with Muslims, some Hindu nationalists have even engaged in violence. Hindu nationalism is concomitant with the spirit of pride in a culture that was seized and exploited by the West. In distinguishing Hinduness from other identities, Hindu nationals seek to define themselves largely by their differences from—and sometimes opposition to—other groups. Chiefly a response to Western colonialism and missionary activity, which resulted in large-scale Indian conversions to Christianity, Hindu nationalism is both a religious and political movement seeking to return India to its ethnic and religious heritage.

Ramakrishna (1836–1886), Vivekananda (1863–1902), and Gandhi (1869–1948) are all well-known figures associated with the contemporary Hindu renaissance: Ramakrishna for his spiritual power; Vivekananda for spreading

Vedanta and yoga to the West, starting with the World Parliament of Religions; and Gandhi for his nonviolent peace work. All three have played a role in the popularization of Hinduism outside India, especially in educated Western circles.

## Conceptions of the Sacred

Hindu understandings of the absolute are so diverse as to be contradictory. Some persons believe in a universal, personal God; others in an impersonal principle; and still others in a deity that they consider to be a manifestation of the absolute.

*Brahman* was the term used to express what was, in Vedic culture, understood as divine breath or the breath of all existence. Brahman is that which is manifested in all the gods, that which causes being. Brahman is that which is everywhere and in everything in nondualistic Advaita Vedanta. In Samkhya and bhakti yoga, Brahman is that which is different from the ordinary world. Perhaps more than anything else, Brahman reveals the radical differences in religiosity encompassed by and expressed in Hinduism—between people who believe all of the world is unified in the being of God and those who believe God is outside the world, as well as between people who believe Brahman is a personal God and those for whom Brahman is understood to be a philosophical principle.

Bhakti is the most common way of practicing Hinduism, and worship is generally categorized into three types—Vaishnavism, Shaivism, and Shaktism.[3] Vaishnavism centers on Vishnu, Shaivism centers on Shiva, and Shaktism on the mother goddess. However, many people,

especially the philosophically minded, think of and worship the absolute as a genderless, ever-present creator as well as destroyer. Not only does the ultimate cause things to come to be, it is also responsible for whatever ends, ceases, or dies. The absolute causes all that is, which is to say that the ultimate in Hinduism is frequently thought of as all-powerful and in control of history. This line of thinking may sound familiar to Christians, who think of God as creator, sustainer, and redeemer.

In addition to Brahman (understood as Vishnu, Shiva, and Devi, e.g.), there are also Krishna, Ganesh, Durga, Yama, Agni, and others.

© Malgorzata Kistryn / Shutterstock.com

Hindus often worship Ganesh, known as the remover of obstacles, when beginning a new venture.

---

3. Each of these represents a family of worship traditions, not just the worship of a single deity. Much as Vaishnavism includes the worship of different forms of Vishnu like Rama and Krishna and their consorts, Shaktism includes the worship of the mother goddess in different forms, including Lakshmi, Parvati, Kali, and Durga.

Merely listing the gods would take pages. Individual gods may serve as the primary or even sole object of worship for many, or they may be part of a pantheon understood as multiple loci of the presence of Brahman. Stories about them may be read literally or metaphorically, as teaching a lesson to or evoking an attitude in followers.

Because of the great diversity in practices and beliefs, gurus or spiritual leaders are highly important in Hinduism. Gurus share their understanding of the ultimate with their followers and teach ways of life that help produce that wisdom. Though historically Brahmins occupied the most valued place in society as teachers and priests, gurus need not come from the Brahmin caste. Westerners may have heard the term *spiritual guru*, but this phrase is redundant because a guru is always a spiritual teacher. Because of the diversity of the gods and especially because understandings of their functions—as links between the divine and everyday worlds, as actual historical figures, and as symbolic images of a divine who remains outside of time—vary so widely, who one chooses as a guru makes all the difference in one's understanding and practice of Hinduism. Christians might follow particular ministers or select churches because of particular priests, but they will learn about the same central beliefs, such as the doctrine of the Trinity and the Incarnation, and will be encouraged to love and serve others. In Hinduism, the guru one follows will radically determine not only which god one most venerates but also how one understands what a "god" even is.

## The Role of Humans

Theological anthropology has become a popular religious topic in Christianity. What is one to think of the human person? What is a person's relationship to the divine? How should the qualities and value of the person be considered, given the belief that people are created by God?

In Hinduism, one's relation to Brahman directly determines what it means to be human; thinking about oneself and thinking about God are intimately aligned. *Atman*, the primary term designating individuality or individuation, is always held in tension with Brahman. A central insight of Advaita Vedanta is that "atman is Brahman." The Upanishadic story of Uddalaka Aruni and his son illustrates this point clearly. The son returns from his religious education claiming to know everything he needs; Uddalaka Aruni teaches him otherwise using a glass of water and salt. Having dissolved the salt in the water, Uddalaka Aruni teaches the boy that there is no difference between the two, and that this is the relationship of the individual to the universal. It is in everything. Everything is in it.

Thinking about what it means to be human necessarily leads to thinking about how to live and act in the world, or ethics. Ethics in Hinduism, expressed concretely and particularly in the Laws of Manu, always results from following dharma, or duty. Acting according to one's place in society is essential and dictates what to do in any circumstance. By doing one's duty (dharma), one establishes his or her karma. Karma is the cosmic force generated by a person's actions; thus, by the law of karma, all actions have their appropriate consequence. This karmic consequence is thought to follow the person from one life to the next, determining that person's life conditions. Good karma helps one to come back as a human being in fortunate circumstances while bad karma places one farther away from not only a good life but from the conditions required to work toward *moksha*, which is the ultimate religious end or liberation from suffering and reincarnation in the world.

# Practices

Rituals pervade Hindu life. From public worship, or *puja*, led by Brahmin priests with Vedic texts, to home routine, deliberate ceremonial activity directed toward the divine is central to Hindu life. There are stage-of-life rituals that range from braiding a pregnant woman's hair to feeding a baby its first solid foods to studying scripture in preparation for marriage and death ceremonies. Yet in between these momentous occasions, or *samskaras*, which Christians might associate with sacraments, are thousands of regular practices that populate daily life. In Hinduism, home shrines and daily home rituals are a central feature. Some Hindus may have a special prayer room in their home or may set aside a corner to display statues and pictures of one's chosen deity. These are used for veneration and meditation, and worshippers may light incense and candles before them. As in public worship, making Brahman manifest in images of deities (and through senses such as smell and sight, both of which are tapped by the use of incense) is centrally important. Some may practice *prasad*, the offering of food to deities and subsequent consumption of what has then become holy, at home, but it is more often a feature of public ceremony. The diversity of approaches in daily worship and mindfulness may stem from Hinduism's emphasis on ways of life rather than on orthodoxy, which has come to dominate religious thinking and life in Christianity.

The Indian government currently recognizes sixteen Hindu celebrations as official holidays, but Hindus have many more days of celebration including the following: gods' and goddesses' birthdays; Holi, which marks the end of winter

Families may designate a room for *puja* or set aside a special area for an altar to display different icons and images that serve as visual and tangible means to connect with the deity.

and the beginning of spring; Divali, the festival of lights celebrating both (or either) the return of Rama after his exile and the New Year according to some Indian calendars; and Ganesh Chaturthi, which celebrates the son of Parvati and Shiva who was given the head of an elephant to revivify him and who now has the power to remove obstacles.

Social expectations in Hinduism remain firm and perhaps less flexible and diverse than in the modern West. Christian approaches to Hinduism tend to focus on the stringent gender roles for women, as though sexism is a thing of the past in Western culture. Many women in the West, though, continue in traditional roles, taking on the majority of childcare, for example. It remains true in Hinduism, however, that women most commonly do not work outside the home, but remain at the service of their husbands. Because of the complexity of Vedic ritual and because only men are educated to perform it, women's lack of education lowered and continues to lower their social status. Because young women were typically married to older men, women retained childlike status in their marriages. Duties of daughters toward fathers, wives toward husbands, and mothers toward sons are still taken very seriously. With the rise of women's rights movements in India and the dispersal of the Indian population throughout Europe and the United States, however, social expectations are changing.

What has not changed is the centrality of dharma. Hindus think of social order as reflecting and sustaining cosmic order, so doing one's duty—however that is construed—remains of utmost importance. Right governance and adherence to one's caste are essential to the proper working of society. Just as there is right order among different groups, there is right order in going about one's life. Unlike the West, which puts a strong emphasis and value on youth, Hinduism delineates four stages of life.[4] Rather than seeing them in opposition to one another, it views all the stages as valid and good—even sacred—times that come with differing sets of obligations. Though these stages apply specifically to the male Brahmin caste, other groups have developed similar ideas. For the Brahmins, the first stage entails being a chaste student. Having studied for roughly the first quarter of life, one is then supposed to become a householder, marrying and having children. After this second quarter of life, one begins to withdraw from the world in favor of meditation and spiritual study. Finally, for the end of life, one is to become a wandering holy person. Though few follow this trajectory to its itinerant end, the logic of activities or stations appropriate to different times of life may hold appeal as an alternative to today's growing American obsession with youth.

## Christian-Hindu Encounters

Until the early nineteenth century, Christianity and Hinduism came into contact not as partners seeking information or spiritual exchange but as competitors for devotees. Specifically, Christian missionaries sought out India as a prime location for proselytizing since Indians were learning English under the colonial rule of the British. American Southern Baptists, for example, had a booming missionary program and produced a number of Telugu-language translations of the New Testament. Knowledge of Christian

---

4. Each stage of life has its own unique set of duties, goals, and ethical norms. Unlike those in the other stages of life, for example, a householder is encouraged to pursue wealth and sexual pleasure within the bounds of marriage. These goals always carry with them certain responsibilities as well, including family caretaking and generosity toward others in society.

missionary history in India has helped fuel a return to native Hindu spiritual practice among Indians who might otherwise be less devout. This religious nationalism has become widely popular, although Indians whose families converted to Christianity under colonial rule more often remain Christian rather than converting back to Hindu devotional practice. Hinduism's emphasis on daily prayer and ritual, especially prasad offerings of food to one's deity, rather than a firm set of beliefs may be disconcerting to an Indian Christian, just as it may be to a Western Christian. While Christianity has daily prayer and devotion, Christian ritual is most often practiced only on Sunday under the leadership of an ordained person. Thus conversion back to Hinduism from Christianity may prove challenging to those Indians whose families have been shaped by the Christian primacy of mass and Sunday worship for generations.

In 1893 the guru and scholar Vivekananda introduced Hinduism to the West at the World Parliament of Religions in Chicago. Christian attitudes toward Hinduism have since undergone a radical paradigm shift. While many Christians continue to believe that Hindus must convert to Christianity to attain salvation, a significant number of Christians now either believe that Hindus can go to heaven through the practice of their own religion or that Christianity and Hinduism both somehow put one in touch with an absolute or divine that exceeds the understandings of each tradition.[5] The Roman Catholic Church's Second Vatican Council, or Vatican II (1962–1965), solidified the teaching that non-Christians could go to heaven through following their consciences and acting justly, thus connecting them to the Catholic Church.[6] This position is called "inclusivism." According to some inclusivists, from the perspective of Catholic teaching, pujas, bhakti, yogas, and the studying of Vedas, Upanishads, and other sacred texts may put the Hindu on the path to God.[7]

Beyond inclusivism, pluralists believe that at least one, if not all, other religions refer to the same absolute, are similarly right and wrong, and that no one religion has a monopoly on the truth. Enshrined in John Hick's *An Interpretation of Religion: Human Responses to the Transcendent,* pluralism eschews any one religion's claim to a monopoly on the truth. Though variously construed, pluralism is always a normative claim, going beyond a mere description of religious plurality to hold that there is good outside the bounds of one's home tradition. Clearly, Western attitudes toward Hinduism have changed dramatically since the height of missionary activity in the nineteenth century when thousands of Christians went to India, China, and the southern hemisphere with the primary purpose of converting people who were thought to be going to hell.

---

5. John Hick's work, especially *An Interpretation of Religion: Human Responses to the Transcendent* (New Haven: Yale University Press, 1989), has crept into much popular Christian spirituality. The generation of scholars who were most active in the 1980s and who are entering retirement (including Paul Knitter, Langdon Gilkey, Wilfred Cantwell Smith, and Gordon Kaufman) deeply influenced an entire generation of Christians, many of whom now believe that religions are somehow equal, even when they continue to practice their own.

6. See *Ad gentes,* nn. 3, 9, 11, Pontifical Council for Interreligious Dialogue and Congregation for the Evangelization of Peoples, *Dialogue and Proclamation,* May 19, 1991, n. 29; L'Osservatore Romano English edition, July 1, 1991, III, in which it is written "it will be in the sincere practice of what is good in their own religious traditions and by following the dictates of their own conscience that the members of other religions respond positively to God's invitation and receive salvation in Jesus Christ, even while they do not recognize or acknowledge him as their Saviour. "

7. However, others give a more strict interpretation of the Catholic teaching in these texts, saying that Hindus still need explicit faith in Christ to attain salvation.

## Efforts at Dialogue and Comparative Theology in the Twentieth and Twenty-First Centuries

Christian theology and philosophy have recently begun paying great attention to religious multiplicity. Because Christians can no longer think of themselves as the majority of the world's population, Christian understandings of God must explain how and why the majority of human beings have either lived before Jesus or in cultures where Christianity is not the dominant religion. Because Hinduism is seen by many Christians as mirroring Christianity in many ways, exploring whether and how there might be religious truth beyond the bounds of the Judeo-Christian tradition constitutes a popular topic of study. Klaus Klostermaier, a Catholic priest and professor who is one of the first to have undertaken the lifelong study of Hinduism, represents the contemporary Christian openness to not only studying, but learning from Hindu tradition and spirituality. For decades, Klostermaier has looked at Christianity and Vaishnavism for similarities in their insights about the nature of life and the divine. Just as Christianity is the practice of religion in relation to a deeply loving, personal God, Vaishnavism connects personal devotion to the divine in ways that can be understood as paralleling Trinitarian understandings of relationship between a person and God and within God's self.

Another Christian pioneer in the field of Christian-Hindu work is Hans Küng. Küng, a Swiss Catholic priest and scholar who was very influential at the Second Vatican Council and who is still writing today, does interreligious work in theology of religions, attempting to explain the diversity of religions as part of the will of God. Like Klostermaier, Küng was among the first to think about Hinduism not as an inferior, primitive religion but as a spiritual alternative to Christianity that contains wisdom and ways of life that—for the Hindu—are just as obvious, explanatory, and coherent as is Christianity for the Christian. The author of many books, Küng brought Christianity's attention to the problematic nature of its exclusive claim to truth by instead detailing a vision of God that includes the whole of humanity. Although now criticized for imposing Christian categories on Hinduism and thus misrepresenting it, Küng's work remains one of the chief reasons Christians have turned to the study of world religions. Francis Clooney, a Jesuit priest and scholar of Hindu sacred literature, is perhaps the most innovative scholar of Hinduism. The father of the popular comparative theological method known as "tradition crossing," or crossing-over between sacred texts, Clooney's work has significantly changed the methodology used by many Christian scholars doing interreligious work. Informing his reading of the Bible with the Vedas and the Upanishads and vice versa, Clooney examines how different traditions' understandings augment and transform each other—especially the understanding of one's home tradition.

Raimon Panikkar is unique among Christian-Hindu scholars. Born of a Christian parent and a Hindu parent, Panikkar was ordained a priest and only then traveled to India. Upon returning and for the rest of his life, he claimed both his Hindu and Christian heritage and did groundbreaking work in the possibility of pluralism, or the belief that many religions can be true and salvific for their members. His many books and articles have helped to transform the Christian and Hindu landscape into one in which multiple religions are considered equally good and transformative. Panikkar is without doubt one of the Christian pioneers in exploring the practice of more than one religion, a circumstance taken for granted in Asia, where it has been common for centuries.

# CHAPTER 10

# An Insider's Perspective

*Madhuri M. Yadlapati*

## Defining Hinduism: The Challenge of Transcending Christian Categories of Religion

The study of Hinduism poses several challenges for students approaching it from a Christian background. First, unlike some other religions, Hinduism largely resists definition. It cannot be defined by a historical founder, exclusive creed, or uniform catechism, and Hindus tend not to use religious language or categories of thought that Christians take for granted. For example, many Hindus are caught off guard when asked by Christians to explain what they believe. The centrality of belief, or creed, has defined Christian tradition since 325 CE, when the Council of Nicaea sought to express the meaning of Christ as Savior, an exercise that also helped define Christian orthodoxy. Unlike Christian orthodoxy, Hindu orthodoxy has been historically determined more by highly restricted access to initiation to its sacred texts, theologies, and philosophies than by definition of what is or is not correct belief.

In addition, Hindus are often confused by the Christian evangelical discussion of whether a person is saved. *Saved from what?* The Hindu goal is enlightenment, but this term is not simply a different word for salvation. The state of enlightenment or liberation promises better life circumstances than the world of suffering and continuous rebirth, but it should be seen more as a correction of ignorance or illusion than an experience of transcendence. Hinduism does not share the Christian belief in a personal God who saves people from the consequences of original sin, which are suffering and eternal death.

A third challenge arises in that Hindus do not identify themselves uniformly. Many traditional Hindus identify themselves more narrowly as Shiva devotees, Vaishnavites, followers of Vedanta, or disciples of Sai Baba or Swami Narayana, for example. These are fluid categories that resist an easy equivalence with a Christian understanding of sects or denominations, which define themselves at least in part by their difference from and rejection of other communities and theological interpretations. These particular Hindu groups do not necessarily reject the interpretations or practices of other groups in the way that many Christian denominations disagree on important interpretations of doctrine.

A reflection that can be drawn from a Hindu perspective on Christian approaches to other religions is that perhaps the definition and uniformity provided by creed, ecclesiastical institution, and clearly articulated boundaries of orthodoxy actually reflect the evangelizing

This temple in Atlanta, Georgia, has the traditional design of temples in southern India. Unlike traditional temples in India, temples in the diaspora often serve not only as places of worship but also as cultural centers with auditoriums, dining halls, and wedding facilities.

spirit of Christianity. Traditions like Hinduism, which do not seek actively to convert others (even discouraging this in some cases) and interpret their traditions more as a "way of life," are not concerned with clearly articulating religious boundaries. Definitions play a role in labeling *other* people's religions insofar as they differ from one's own and in specifying what is unique about one's tradition over and against others. This is absent from traditional mainstream Hinduism, which has instead been characterized more by its assimilation of rival worldviews (such as Buddhism) than by their definitive exclusion. Exceptions can be found in the missionary zeal of many modern reform movements (such as Arya Samaj, Vedanta Society, and ISKCON, the International Society for Krishna Consciousness) that do seek to define their precise theological outlook against other positions. In addition,

the experience of Indian diaspora (which has grown manifold in the United States following the 1965 Immigration and Nationality Act that reversed prior restrictions and facilitated unprecedented levels of immigration from Asia) will likely lead to greater Hindu self-reflection vis-à-vis other traditions. As an intrinsic part of Indian society and history, Hindus in India have often experienced their religion as an unconsciously accepted way of life. However, as the Indian diaspora grows, Hindus outside India may feel a need to impose clearer definitions upon their religion, as demonstrated by the development in recent decades of Hindu lay education in the United States, for example. Temples built by diasporic communities often serve needs different from traditional temples in India. Beyond being houses of worship presided over by priests, diasporic temples often serve as cultural centers for instruction in traditional Indian dance, music, and language. Diasporic temples in the United States regularly offer *satsang* groups for adults, which focus on the study of scripture and on meditation, and Bal Vihar youth programs.[1] Through the development of such programs, Hindu communities outside India work both to educate younger generations on ancient traditions and to build new traditions of study and practice outside the home in order to adapt to contemporary spiritual needs. For example, whereas temples in India are most often supervised by male priests, lay men and women share many responsibilities in the operations of diasporic temples. Women have recently become vitally involved in temple building, financing, and operations. Also, unlike Indian temples, which often are dedicated to a single deity, diasporic temples serve as a place of worship for people of varying backgrounds and regions of India. In all of these ways, diasporic Hindu communities are actively redefining traditional patterns of worship in a way that may in time demonstrate greater definition than has been characteristic historically of Indian Hinduism.

## Which Hindu Way?

Scholars note the variety of different, even contrary, movements that have coalesced over several millennia into one overarching family of Hindu traditions. While accurate, the scholarly emphasis on variety and difference risks missing the cohesiveness that many Hindus experience in Hindu ways of life rather than shared doctrine.

A perennial Indian story tells of six blind men who encounter an elephant. Each individual feels a different part of the elephant (a leg, the trunk, the belly, or the ear) and thus describes the animal differently (as a pillar, a snake, a great pot, or a husking basket). Hindus interpret this story as a caution against dogmatic fixation on one's own ideas about the absolute, or God. Likewise, Hinduism itself can appear as different things to different people when it is in fact all of them. For those who read the Upanishads or observe another studying the Upanishads at the feet of a teacher or guru in the traditional manner, Hinduism will appear to be a mystical, speculative philosophy that seeks to apprehend the nature of reality. For those observing pious Hindus, who perform puja daily in their homes, Hinduism will appear to be a devotional path of bhakti, in which one welcomes his or her *Ishta Devata*, or chosen deity, into a consecrated image or sculpture and honors the divine with symbolic gifts of love and devotion. For those encountering very traditional Indian Hindus, who still observe strict caste regulation, Hinduism may appear to be a traditional hierarchical culture governed by an intricate system of social rules and obligations designed to benefit social stability and order by subordinating the individual to the community. For still others familiar with the practice of yoga, Hinduism may be a means of magical self-empowerment by which one performs *tapas,* or discipline, and enjoys a growth in spiritual energy. Each of these provides an accurate description of Hinduism, and each may be found most prominently in one or more of the different texts considered sacred scripture.

## Use of Sacred Texts

In the past, the study of religion focused overwhelmingly on the "official" teachings in a tradition and its "philosophical" or intellectual content.

---

1. The Chinmaya Mission, established in 1953 in India by devotees of the Swami Chinmayananda, is a very popular spiritual renaissance movement. With more than 300 centers worldwide, this community seeks to advance the wisdom of Vedanta philosophy in a modern appropriation of the guru-student model of education and spiritual training both for adults and for children.

This is thought of as different from and as existing in tension with what may be termed "popular," "ritualistic" practice or "mythology," with a prejudice against the validity of the latter. This earlier tendency in the study of different religious traditions is being corrected with greater attention to ritual studies and popular religion. In the spirit of such correction and in the interest of taking seriously what the majority of Hindus think, understand, and practice in their tradition, this discussion of the Hindu sacred texts must begin with the great epics and the Puranas rather than with the Vedas. While the Vedas are considered shruti, or revelation simply given to humans at the beginning of the current cycle of creation, the epics are considered smriti, or remembered wisdom or tradition. The Mahabharata, one of the two great epics, is often called the fifth Veda because of its importance and value.

So what uniquely do the epics, Puranas, and Dharmasastras (legal texts about dharma, or normative behavior, including the Laws of Manu) bring to the study of Hinduism? First, they represent the spiritual knowledge most widely available to the majority of Hindus throughout history. Access to the Vedas and Upanishads was restricted to high-caste males who were initiated into a lifelong path of study. Most Hindus only encountered Vedic material when hearing the verses sung by a pujari (or Hindu priest) during a ritual service. In contrast, Hindus of every walk of life have grown up knowing the epics and mythology in great detail. Traditionally, the epics—the Ramayana and the Mahabharata (especially its most famous section, the Bhagavad Gita)—were recited or performed by traveling artists during frequent festivals that would take over the life of a village for a week or two at a time. Many Indian Hindus today remember watching the television broadcast of the Mahabharata in the 1980s. This extremely popular weekly series coincided perfectly with the spread of television sets in middle-class Indian homes. The epics are full of heroes and villains, emotional drama, political intrigue, and exemplars of faithfulness, devotion, and inscrutable morality. Therefore, these stories, and their ethical and spiritual lessons, shape Hindu values.[2]

Likewise, beginning hermeneutically with popular practice, the content of the Puranas, the mythological sources about the many different Hindu deities, is communicated through festival and ritual observance. Each holiday has a special mythological significance, and families may recite a story relevant to the holiday or about the deity being honored. The birthdays of favored deities are celebrated, while other holidays mark some great mythological victory of good over evil. In addition to these annual festivals, devout Hindus may practice vratas, or vows, one or several days every week in honor of a specific deity. Many of these vratas involve fasting from a particular food or practice, and many also require the recitation of a story that explains the origin and spiritual benefits of its observance. All in all, the many sacred days and the observance of them over time reinforce the mythological tales and the gods and goddesses themselves in the religious imagination of Hindus.

# Historical Overview: World-Maintenance and World-Transcendence

Some of the variety and diversity mentioned already stems from the focus on one or more sacred text(s) over others. Another important

---

2. The traditional mythological stories of the Puranas are today transmitted to younger generations using the form of comic books and animated cartoons. The Amar Chitra Katha series of comic books shares accounts of the many deities and their interactions, the adventures of various heroes mythological and historical, and traditional Hindu values and doctrines. Today, there is a growing corpus of animated video collections that bring these stories to life, available on television and the Internet.

factor in this variety is the tension between the two poles of world-affirmation or world-maintenance, on the one hand, and world-denial or world-transcendence, on the other. The ancient Vedas and their ritual instructions, for example, affirm and maintain the world in its harmony. Performing the fire sacrifice was, in the Vedic world (1500–500 BCE), the primary means of religious worship. One made a sacrifice and offered grains, milk, or animal flesh. As it burned away in the fire, the gift would rise up to the heavenly abode of the gods. One offered these gifts to the gods and carried out all the requisite rituals that would make the gift pleasing to the gods in order to guarantee the well-being of one's family and community.

The later focus in classical Hinduism on dharma (sacred duty, determined traditionally by age, gender, and caste) likewise provides an example of world-maintenance, because it supports the responsibilities of all members of society to each other. As long as everyone properly observes dharma, the world will run harmoniously. When the rules of dharma are not observed, resulting in social or political chaos in the world, divine intervention becomes necessary, and Vishnu, the deity of preservation, becomes incarnate in the world to correct the imbalance or chaos and restore the harmonious rule of dharma.

A third example of world-maintenance is found in the doctrine of karma.[3] The teaching of karma, that all actions have their appropriate consequences, supports the rule of dharmic responsibility. Ethically good actions result in desirable consequences and ethically bad actions result in undesirable consequences. These should not be considered rewards or punishments because they are not granted by a divine authority. Rather they should be thought of as a law of moral nature that functions even above the power of the gods. Because the law of karma holds that good actions will result in benefits in one's current life as well as in future births, it helps support the ethical norms that constitute worldly harmony and well-being.

This need to maintain the world of human experience must be seen in relation to the need to transcend this world. The Vedic Aranyakas, also known as forest treatises, are a collection of esoteric texts that explore the deeper spiritual meaning of Vedic rituals. Although originally intended for ascetics living in the forest, the ascetic life and spiritual techniques described there represent an attempt to transcend the suffering and change of worldly life. The ascetic path requires a withdrawal from society, from social and family relationships and responsibilities that define worldly life.

Another example of world-transcendence is found in the Upanishadic path of mysticism. In direct contrast to the efforts of Vedic sacrifice, the path of mysticism requires initiation into disciplined study before a guru. Unlike the Vedic world of the gods who seem very close to the natural world, the speculative philosophy of the Upanishads teaches that what is truly real, or Brahman, lies beyond what can be seen. Here one finds both a metaphysical transcendence (Brahman, the absolute reality, transcends ordinary worldly reality) and an epistemological transcendence (true knowledge or spiritual wisdom

---

3. The doctrine of karma is common to several other Indian religious traditions, including Buddhism, Jainism, and Sikhism as well, although there are differences among them. Because all actions carry consequences, karma both explains the present as a result of the past and predicts the future based on present actions. Insofar as it helps explain why things are the way they currently are, it serves at least in part as a theodicy. Insofar as it places responsibility on the individual, it echoes the teaching of free will. However, traditionally, women and lower-caste men are taught that the only way to improve their future lot is to patiently serve others in this life. Instead of compelling transformative action, then, the doctrine of karma justifies and rationalizes the social order.

requires transcendence of ordinary knowledge). The mystical path advocated in the Upanishads requires one to transcend both sense perception and intellectual understanding, because the truth of Brahman cannot be known through discursive reason, but must be experienced by the faculty of intuition.

In addition, whereas the doctrine of karma supports world-maintenance, the operation of karma itself is something to be ultimately transcended. The ultimate spiritual goal of life does not consist simply of continually improving one's birth, but of freeing oneself completely from the cycle of rebirth, known as samsara. *Moksha*, or liberation from samsara, itself transcends the karmic worldview, in which one does good to achieve good, and instead seeks to avoid accruing karma at all. The Bhagavad Gita's teaching of the four *margas*,[4] or paths, to achieve moksha recount the three paths of transcendence noted here (raja yoga, jnana yoga, and karma yoga) as well as a fourth path of bhakti yoga. Just as karma yoga teaches one to act according to one's duty without clinging to the fruits of that action, bhakti yoga teaches one to devote oneself fully and without remainder to one's chosen deity, or *Ishta Devata*. Both paths lead toward ultimate transcendence both of self and world.

## Conceptions of the Sacred

The varied Hindu descriptions of the sacred reflect a remarkable fluidity. What is divine and where is it to be found? The answer may be Brahman, the absolute reality, described in the Upanishads. It may be *Nirguna* Brahman (the absolute without attributes, suggesting an apophatic or negative theology) or *Saguna* Brahman (the absolute described with attributes). It may be the Trimurti (sometimes described as a Hindu Trinity) of Brahma the Creator, Vishnu the Preserver, and Shiva the Destroyer. It may be Lakshmi or Kali or Durga. It may be Ganesh, the remover of obstacles. In fact, Hindus have long held that there are 330 million gods, suggesting that there are as many gods as there are living beings. They may recognize the sacred in natural places like mountains, rivers, or trees, which may be divine personifications, or in a human guru, or teacher. Because of the Hindu sense of fluidity of spirit, the sacred may be found anywhere. Because of its ultimacy, the divine cannot be delimited from any particular location or image.

This raises the question of the ultimate reality of each of the gods, as well as their visual representation in paintings, stone carvings, and so on. Hindus often say that the many gods are dynamic representations of an absolute reality that transcends all representation. Where Jews and Muslims, for example, have forbidden image-making to preserve the transcendence of God and caution against a human tendency to worship what is seen, Hindus have justified the proliferation of image-making to maintain divine transcendence and recognize the limitations of and need for human visualization. Because no single image can capture the infinite and transcendent deity, Hindus use multiple images and forms. Each personification expresses a particular and partial quality or attribute of the sacred that serves the specific needs of worship. These images or statues focus the worshipper's mind during puja and serve as dynamic representations of something that inevitably transcends human understanding. Because of this transcendence, the divine needs to be theologically represented in some tangible way. It is fair to say that the very

---

4. The Bhagavad Gita's teaching on the four *margas* is often cited as support for the Hindu view that there are many paths to salvation or enlightenment. Today, it serves as a traditional theological motif for affirming the value of different religious traditions and teachings for different cultures and different individual temperaments.

© Philippe Lissac / Godong / Corbis

Many temples, including those dedicated to one primary deity, include many smaller shrines to other deities. Worshippers typically enter a temple and visit each shrine in turn, although they may choose to offer a special prayer or offering to a particular deity.

plethora of Hindu beliefs about and images of the divine shares a similar function with Jewish and Muslim refusal to image the divine—that is, Hinduism makes clear the transcendence of the absolute beyond all human categories and conceptualizations, while at the same time embracing the need to represent this transcendent absolute in tangible and meaningful ways.

## The Role of Human Beings

Discussing the role of human beings in Hindu religion involves examining two correlated trajectories. The first addresses the relationship between humanity and the divine, and the second addresses human responsibility and religious ethics. The relationship between human and divine can be described variously, depending on one's particular philosophical orientation. According to eighth-century Shankara's nondualistic philosophy, Advaita Vedanta, the human soul, or atman, is not truly separate or different from Brahman but experiences such differentiation as part of the condition of maya. According to eleventh-century Ramanuja's modified Advaita, the individual atman is distinct from Brahman, but its purpose is reunification with Brahman. In the dualism of thirteenth-century Madhva, Brahman alone possesses all perfection and directs the world, and the individual atman depends upon Brahman and seeks fulfillment in the worship of Brahman.

The modified nondualism of Ramanuja and the dualism of Madhva roughly resemble the theological anthropology of Christian orthodoxy, in that the individual soul seeks its rest in a loving relationship with God. Shankara's nondualism resembles a monistic or panentheistic worldview that Christian orthodoxy may criticize for confusing the divine nature and the world. However, within the Hindu tradition's theological and philosophical flexibility and fluidity of spirit is the suggestion that all of life carries much weight. It marries particularly well with the teachings of karma yoga and bhakti yoga taught in the Bhagavad Gita, which so pervasively influence classical Hinduism. Both karma yoga and bhakti yoga implement a self-discipline intended to transcend egoism and selfishness and instead identify with duty, or dharma, and with God. Shankara himself recommended the path of bhakti, or love and devotion, as a means of lifelong spiritual discipline.

The other trajectory in discussing the role of human beings in the world consists of religious ethics, expressed in Hinduism as dharma, or duty. It does not unfairly simplify things to call Hinduism a religion of dharma. Duties define a person's identity and responsibilities in different circumstances just as creedal formulas about one's acceptance of Jesus Christ as Lord express Christian identity. The rules of dharma are communicated in the Mahabharata, the Bhagavad Gita, the Ramayana, and the Laws of Manu.

According to these texts, performing one's duties (traditionally prescribed by gender, caste, age, occupation, and contextual relationships to others) results in the accumulation of good karma, while failure to fulfill these duties results in the accumulation of negative karma. While the law of karma functions to encourage normative behavior by promising consequences that will be borne out in the life conditions of future births, karma is not the last word in terms of religious ethics, because the goal of life is not simply to be reborn in more and more pleasant circumstances, but to be liberated from this cycle of rebirth altogether (moksha).

Hindu tradition teaches that there are four goals in human life. In addition to dharma, humans should pursue *kama* (desire or sensual and aesthetic pleasure), *artha* (material well-being, wealth, and prosperity), and *moksha* (liberation from the cycle of rebirth). Moksha is the ultimate spiritual goal of human life. While dharma, kama, and artha represent serious ethical goods, they are but penultimate spiritual goals when compared to moksha. Traditionally, only Brahmin males were considered eligible to pursue the goal of moksha, because it was presumed that they had gained enough spiritual maturity and discipline through numerous births to reach this goal of liberation. In light of the themes of world-maintenance and world-transcendence, the goals of dharma, kama, and artha all support the maintenance of harmony and well-being in the world and in one's present life, while the

Sadhus, or sannyasins (male) or sannyasinis (female), give up the worldly relationships and responsibilities of dharma to live an austere life and pursue the ultimate spiritual freedom of *moksha*. Many join an ashram community, while others live as hermits.

goal of moksha represents the transcendence of worldly life.

Hindu tradition codifies social expectations, creating a sense of orthopraxy, or correct practice, rather than the correct belief that defines Christian orthodoxy. Because religion has so pervasively marked every aspect of life, creating what is often noted as more of a Hindu "way of life" than a "religion," the function of normative ethics can be narrowly defined and restrictive. Hindu tradition, like other extant religious traditions, has developed in a patriarchal culture, and many traditional cultural and social gender norms reflect this patriarchal culture. These include a woman's presumed inability to pursue Vedic study; a woman's subordination to her father, husband, and son; and a mythologically supported cult of true womanhood that glorifies a woman's unending self-sacrifice.

The caste system also prominently reflects these deeply codified norms of responsibility, which strictly define a person's place in society. The caste system is rooted in the hierarchical order common to traditional societies around the world; it most closely resembles, for example, the medieval European feudal society. While caste no longer functions as a hereditary division of labor, it continues to operate quite centrally in Indian and Hindu society. The caste system often receives criticism from Hindus and non-Hindus alike because it can enable social prejudices against those deemed lower-caste. Caste discrimination is illegal in India, and the government has undertaken aggressive measures to tear down these traditional social restrictions, which have excluded many from institutions of power like education and government. Caste today continues to perpetuate a painful reality for many, especially when defended by some in the name of social tradition. In addition, its influence sometimes is underestimated or even denied outright by progressive Hindus who find it a backward institution and an embarrassment to their modern values of the dignity of every person and the individual's freedom to determine their own destiny. To the degree that its influence is denied in contemporary Hindu society, caste prejudice poses a similar challenge to that posed by racism in American society, because it must be recognized before people can work to right the injustices that result from it.

## Identifying Ritual Practices

The *samskaras*, festivals, and puja make the spiritual goals of life an absolutely pervasive aspect of the daily lives of Hindus. The Hindu samskaras share some resemblance to a Christian notion of sacraments in that they are seen as religiously necessary acts, but the Hindu samskaras comprehensively honor the many stages of life. The common list of sixteen samskaras includes, for example, the moment of conception, a prenatal blessing, the naming of a child, a child's first solid food, first haircut, initiation into formal study of the Vedas, marriage, and last rites. They represent opportunities to consecrate the natural stages of life and precarious transitions from one stage to another. The numerous festivals mark sacred time throughout the year and bring to life the mythological life of the sacred and one's devotional relationship to one's god or gods. Puja, or ritual worship, especially pronounces the dynamic character of devotion.[5] Homes often have a puja room or an altar. Men and women may perform puja alone, as a family, or in groups. Devout women often set up an altar in the corner of the kitchen as well and begin each day by bathing, lighting incense, and honoring

---

5. The performance of puja, while a pervasive element of Hindu practice, varies widely by interest, piety, and family and regional tradition. Some perform puja daily, whether brief or lengthy, while others perform puja only on major holy days.

Several samskaras represent key moments of child-hood development. During the Annaprasana, a baby is fed her or his first solid food, traditionally a sweet rice. Parents often invite family and friends to celebrate, and play a "game" of placing the child before several different symbolic objects, each representing a particu-lar destiny, for the child to crawl towards.

one's chosen deity. In the puja, the worshipper approaches the divine through a particular con-crete image or symbol and offers symbolic gifts of devotion. A common description of puja is that the worshipper invites God into one's home and treats God as an honored guest, offering food, water, flowers, clothing (the best of what a family has available), and then sharing the consecrated or blessed food, or prasad, among the worshipers. The puja rituals provide a dynamic and personal way to interact with a transcendent deity in tan-gible ways. Like religious practitioners in other

traditions, Hindus also participate in pilgrimage, visiting famous temples and holy sites that may be of particular significance in the mythology of one particular deity or modern-day guru.

## Christian-Hindu Encounters

It is important to acknowledge the clouded history of encounters between Christians and Hindus. Hindus continue to find themselves explaining and defending their rich iconography to Christians, some of whom condemn what they interpret as idolatry. Hindus continue to resent Christian efforts to evangelize them, particularly in India where Christian missionary work is seen as part and parcel of European imperialism, from which India freed itself only two generations ago. This suspicion of Christian missionary work has led in recent years to serious episodes of violence perpetrated by Hindu nationalists against Chris-tian nuns and other groups, which clearly defies the common perception of the great tolerance of Hinduism. Just as Christians vary on whether members of other religious communities can attain salvation, Hindus of varying tempera-ments differ on whether other religious paths are all equally valid or just partial attempts to relate to the sacred that ultimately fall within the larger canopy of religious possibility captured in Hindu theological diversity. Some may even think of non-Hindu religions as completely untrue paths for those not fortunate enough to merit birth in India to Hindu parents.

While many pioneers from the Christian tradition have engaged in their own immersive dialogue with Hindu tradition and texts, far fewer Hindus have immersed themselves thor-oughly in dialogue with Christian tradition and texts. Until recently, much of the initial Chris-tian dialogue with Hindu tradition emerged out of missionary efforts to better understand Hindu religion in order to preach the superiority of Christian religion. In contrast, Hindus have traditionally not shared this sense of evangelism that led Christians to look beyond their own religious communities. Hindu belief in dharma supports the notion of many diverse paths to spiritual liberation as well as the idea that one person's path is not necessarily the best for another. Beliefs in karma and samsara support the sense that an individual must work out his or her own enlightenment in a series of births that is unique to their identity. Together, these beliefs shape a worldview that does not seek to impose religious or doctrinal uniformity on other communities. Despite the clouded history of Christian evangelism and Hindu isolation, there is great promise of more fruitful and constructive encounters between Christians and Hindus. The work of "Hindu missions" begun by Swami Vivekananda (not attempting to convert Christians to Hinduism, but to explain and defend Hindu wisdom to culturally Western Christians) set up a process of religious apologetics that continues. However, this work of Hindu apologetics requires genuine dialogue among Hindus and Christians as well as greater Hindu study of Christian tradition, texts, and theology, especially as Hindus immerse themselves in the lives of Christian communities.

# CHAPTER 11

# Texts and Commentary

*Aimee Upjohn Light and Madhuri M. Yadlapati*

The textual excerpts included in this section represent a very small cross-section of the Hindu sacred texts, and what has been left out from the selection should be noted. For example, there follow no excerpts from the Mahabharata or from the many Puranas, both of which perhaps figure more prominently than the Upanishads in the religious lives of most Hindus, as rich sources of mythology, ethics, and devotion. The vast substance of the Vedas, with its ritual instructions, hymns, and ascetic practices also are not represented. Nevertheless, the texts included here provide a window into some of the major teachings of Hindu traditions through different styles of text.

The first set of excerpts include a single prominent verse from the Rig Veda, the oldest of what is considered Hindu revelation; verses from the mystical Upanishads; and verses from the narrative epic, the Bhagavad Gita. These very different styles of text try to express the nature of Brahman, the ultimate reality, in different ways. What stands out most prominently in these attempts are first, the pervasive challenge of describing what is considered an ineffable, transcendent reality using very limited words; and second, the tremendous religious need to affirm both the transcendence of this ineffable reality and its immanence and availability to religious experience. Therefore, while the Upanishads may emphasize the ineffability of the sacred, the Bhagavad Gita has Krishna as human avatar of the divine identifying himself with this supreme reality and offering guidance to a mere mortal Arjuna.

Other sets of textual excerpts from the epic Ramayana and the Laws of Manu demonstrate the very central Hindu concern with dharma, or sacred duty. Both these texts have played a central role in shaping social norms of traditional Hindu and Indian culture, especially because these texts have been more accessible than the Vedas and Upanishads. The final textual excerpt, taken from the Bhagavad Gita, serves as a fitting conclusion as it represents an attempt to bridge the very divergent concerns of the mystical Upanishads and the narrative epics. These verses demonstrate the tension between the goals of mystical freedom and worldly responsibility, and they promise a way for people to achieve freedom through action rather than through the renunciation of action.

## Text 1: Selections from the Rig Veda, the Upanishads, and the Bhagavad Gita

These selections explore the nature of Brahman, the ultimate reality or spirit.

## Texts

Truth is one, though sages call it by many names. (Rig Veda, bk. 1, hymn CLXIV, v. 46)

· · · · ·

What cannot be spoken with words, but that whereby words are spoken: Know that alone to be Brahman, the Spirit; and not what people here adore. What cannot be thought with the mind, but that whereby the mind can think: Know that alone to be Brahman, the Spirit; and not what people here adore. What cannot be seen with the eye, but that whereby the eye can see: Know that alone to be Brahman, the Spirit; and not what people here adore. . . . He is unknown to the learned and known to the simple. He is known in the ecstasy of an awakening which opens the door of life eternal. By the Self we obtain power, and by vision we obtain Eternity. For a man who has known him, the light of truth shines; for one who has not known, there is darkness. The wise who have seen him in every being, on leaving this life, attain life immortal. (Kena Upanishad parts 1–2)[1]

· · · · ·

I am the self abiding in the heart of all creatures; I am their beginning, their middle, and their end. I am Vishnu striding among the gods, the radiant sun among lights; I am lightning among wind gods, the moon among the stars. I am the song in sacred lore; I am Indra, king of the gods; I am the mind of the senses, the consciousness of creatures. I am gracious Shiva among howling storm gods, the lord of wealth among demigods and demons, fire blazing among the bright gods; I am golden Meru towering over the mountains. Arjuna, know me as the gods' teacher, chief of the household priests; I am the god of war among generals; I am the ocean of lakes. (Bhagavad Gita 10:20–24)[2] ∎

## Outsider Commentary
### *Light*

Christians have long perceived Hinduism as a polytheistic religion. If one understands the term *gods* in Hinduism to signify the same thing that Christians typically mean by the word *God*, then polytheism follows as the necessary conclusion. Yet the gods in Hinduism signify something very different than what is meant by God in Christianity. Far from being the source of the world, the gods are manifestations of the one source of the world, which is Brahman. Though Brahman can be understood personally or impersonally, Brahman is always one. Brahman is beyond all language, thought and images. Brahman is the source of all that is and is beyond anything, even the totality, of what one can think. Brahman, as the text reads, cannot be thought but enables thought. The wise see him in every being. ∎

These selections illustrate the monism that lies at the heart of much Hinduism, especially Hindu mysticism. It is important to distinguish monism from monotheism. Monotheism in Christianity, Judaism, and Islam signifies the oneness of God. Although primarily thought of as beyond and apart from the world, God is in the world through God's self-revelation in Jesus, to the prophets and to the Prophet, primarily in the Qur'an. Monism is the belief that the source of the world is one, but includes strong emphasis on the presence of that One throughout everything that exists. All that is is part of Brahman.

---

1. *The Upanishads*, trans. Juan Mascaro (New York: Penguin Books, 1965), 51–52.
2. *The Bhagavad-Gita*, trans. Barbara Stoler Miller (New York: Bantam Books, 1986), 94.

Everything exists in Brahman, hence the language of "I am the heart of creatures . . . , the sun . . . , Vishnu [and all the gods]."[3] The gods express Brahman's pervasive and multiple presence throughout everything that is. Brahman appears and is present differently throughout the world, but is always one.

The gods thus serve as ways to visualize Brahman's omnipresence, but also Brahman's "beyond-ness." No one god exhausts the nature of Brahman. Even the totality of all the gods cannot fully express Brahman. The gods in Hinduism function much like negative theology—or the *via negativa*—does in Christianity. The *via negativa* entails deliberate reflection on the impossibility of adequately understanding or expressing the infinite. Holding fast to the incomprehensibility of the divine and the consequent inadequacy of human knowledge, both Christianity and Hinduism offer intellectual resources for affirming the value of foreign religious traditions. Because nothing can exhaust the inexhaustible, it becomes plausible that other religions may also express, albeit differently, that which can never be entirely expressed or understood.

Coming to grips with the strong tradition of monism present in Hinduism should give Christians pause. Christianity itself is developing strong veins of eco-theology, liberation theologies, and interreligious work. Each of these directions has roots in the growing Christian awareness that God must be intimately present everywhere and in everything. Elizabeth Johnson, in her book *Quest for the Living God: Mapping Frontiers in Theologies of God* (New York: Continuum, 2007), suggests that each of these trajectories is grounded in the Christian turn from classical theism to panentheism. Though both are forms of monotheism, classical theism has dominated Christianity and thinks of God first and foremost as transcendent and beyond the world. Panentheism gives primacy to God's presence throughout the creation, only turning to questions of beyondness as a matter of speculation. Whether panentheism only bears similarities to or is identical with monism will provide a fecund topic for growing work in Christian-Hindu comparative theology. For the time being, it suffices to acknowledge that the pervasiveness of Brahman throughout all being, signified by the gods, paints a very different metaphysical picture from the polytheism Christians often understood Hinduism to be.

## Insider Commentary
### Yadlapati

These selections come from different textual sources and concern characteristic Hindu ways of speaking about the ultimate sacred reality, or Brahman. Brahman may be considered God, in the sense of an absolute and transcendent sacred reality that is the foundation of all of life, but the term *God* also suggests a very particular sort of theism that does not do justice to the comprehensive concept of Brahman. In the Vedas, Brahman is presented as the power of the gods and the ultimate enjoyer of all sacrifices. Later Hindu tradition has articulated two ways of speaking about this ultimate reality. *Nirguna* Brahman is the sacred reality described without attributes, and *Saguna* Brahman is the sacred reality described through attributes. Ultimately, of course, Brahman is only one absolute reality. That reality, though, may be described and approached in a number of ways, and the different sacred texts in Hindu tradition often focus on one or the other, if not both. The philosophical and mystical use of Nirguna Brahman resembles the *via negativa* approach of Christian mysticism.

---

3. *The Bhagavad-Gita,* trans. Sir Edwin Arnold (New York: P.F. Collier and Son, 1909–14), ch. 10, vv. 20–21.

Because Brahman transcends all particular distinguishable living forms that can be perceived, it may be best to say that Brahman is *neti, neti,* or "not this, not that." Nirguna Brahman may be emphasized in the Upanishads, which privilege a mystical, speculative philosophical approach and a direct knowledge of the sacred apart from the necessarily limiting forms of life in the world.

In contrast, the many deities in Hindu devotional tradition can be considered a true characterization of Saguna Brahman. Saguna Brahman may be approached using the terms *Isvara,* or God as personal Lord, or *Bhagavan,* or God as Supreme Lord. Thus, the devotional traditions emphasize the personal commitment to a deity as one's supreme lord. While a *via negativa* approach may emphasize the ultimate transcendence of any particular description, the *via positiva* approach captured in Saguna descriptions often emphasizes the need to describe and picture the sacred in readily recognizable and meaningful forms. It gives people something concrete to focus on, to attach themselves to. Whereas Judaism and Islam condemned image-making to uphold the divine transcendence of all particularity, Hindu tradition has encouraged image-making to affirm divine transcendence. The sacred is infinite; it cannot be restricted to any one form, but must be seen in multiple, inevitably limited shapes and forms. At the same time, the sacred can be pictured in virtually any particular form, because it is ultimately one and all-pervasive. It is the truth of any and all particular life-forms.

The selections above emphasize the diversity of possible forms of sacred reality and the

In the Bhagavad Gita, Krishna reveals his true cosmic form to Arjuna, displaying the unity of the many divine forms.

underlying identity of this sacred reality. Those more familiar with a monotheistic tradition often ask whether Hindus are monotheists or polytheists. Both assessments would be correct in some sense. Hindus do worship a number of different gods and goddesses (330 million is a commonly used figure). At the same time, all the different sacred texts emphasize the underlying unity or identity of these different deities. According to the Rig Veda, the sacred reality is ultimately one, but it may be described in a number of different ways, using a number of different names. In the Bhagavad Gita, when Krishna, the incarnate god, counsels Arjuna through his spiritual crisis, he speaks not as one particular god among several but as the ultimate single Godhead. When Arjuna asks Krishna to show him his true nature, Krishna obliges with a cosmic vision that overwhelms and terrifies Arjuna. Arjuna's description of what he sees—many heads, many arms, many mouths devouring everything—serves as an excellent illustration of what Rudolf Otto calls the "mysterium tremendum et fascinans."[4] The sacred transcends simple description or simple identifiable feeling. It is mysterious and captivates even while it terrifies; it simultaneously attracts and repels.

Ultimately, Hindu tradition upholds the characterization of Brahman above all particular forms as well as within all particular forms because of its pervasive transcendence and immanence. Brahman is the source of all life and is found in all life-forms. It is the unseen force that quickens life as well as the underlying essence of all life. Brahman is so comprehensive that it can be immanent or manifest in particular ways in all things. Because it is the true essence of all life, apprehending Brahman can yield spiritual freedom. Knowing Brahman is the goal of the spiritual quest.

# Text 2: From the Chandogya Upanishad

This text is an instructional dialogue between father and son regarding the nature of ultimate reality and human relationship to it.

## Text

"Bring a banyan fruit."
   "Here it is, sir."
   "Cut it up."
   "I've cut it up, sir."
   "What do you see there?"
   "These quite tiny seeds, sir."
   "Now, take one of them and cut it up."
   "I've cut one up, sir."
   "What do you see there?"
   "Nothing, sir."
Then he told him: "This finest essence here, son that you can't even see—look how on account of that finest essence this huge banyan tree stands here.

   "Believe me, my son: the finest essence here—that constitutes the self of this whole world; that is the truth; that is the self (atman). And that's how you are, Svetaketu."
   "Sir, teach me more."
   "Very well, son."
   "Put this chunk of salt in a container of water and come back tomorrow."
   The son did as he was told, and the father said to him: "The chunk of salt you put in the water last evening—bring it here." He groped for it but could not find it, as it had dissolved completely.
   "Now, take a sip from this corner," said the father. "How does it taste?"
   "Salty."

---

4. Rudolf Otto, *The Idea of the Holy* (London: Oxford University Press, 1958).

"Take a sip from the center.—How does it taste?"

"Salty."

"Take a sip from that corner.—How does it taste?"

"Salty."

"Throw it out and come back later." He did as he was told and found that the salt was always there. The father told him: "You, of course, did not see it there, son; yet it was always right there.

"The finest essence here—that constitutes the self of this whole world; that is the truth; that is the self (atman). And that's how you are, Svetaketu." (Chandogya Upanishad 6:12–13)[5] ∎

## Outsider Commentary

### Light

The story of Uddalaka Aruni and his son, Sveta-ketu, exemplifies and grounds much Hindu thinking about the relationship of the one and the many, or unity and difference in the world. The story also seeks to distinguish common, unreflective religiosity from genuine spirituality. These themes exist in parallel fashion throughout the Christian tradition and may already feel familiar to Christian readers with a background in philosophy or spiritual studies.

Much like the Christian doctrine of the Trinity, Hindu belief seeks to account for the experienced reality that existence is both one and diverse. While persons exist as distinct centers of consciousness with individual bodies, human beings also participate in the totality of existence. From trees to animals to cities and oceans, there is difference in the world; yet the world is also a totality that can be thought of as one. Both unity and diversity are experienced as real and must be accounted for.

The Christian Trinity locates unity and distinction in the very being of God, which then serves as the source and model of all creation. In Hindu Advaita Vedanta, Shankara, Ramanuja, and Madhva all take different positions on the question of Being as one and Being as many. For Shankara, all Being is one. Unity is the principle that causes things to be, while difference is an illusion. Ramanuja qualifies Shankara's radical nondualism by holding that both unity and difference are constitutive of reality. Madhva, the apparent pessimist among these three great thinkers, holds that only difference is real, while the appearance of unity or oneness is an illusion. Many other philosophical movements, Samkhya chief among them, think through the relationship between oneness and difference.

The story of the salt in the water represents Brahman, or the principle of unity, as salt. Water is the world in all its diversity, and Brahman is present throughout. Svetaketu, after years of religious training, does not yet have the spiritual awareness that everything that exists is permeated and constituted by Brahman. It takes a father's simple example to teach him that even atman is Brahman, that the principle of individuation is the principle of unification and vice versa. Everything, even difference, is one in Brahman.

The need for spiritual awareness is just as important to the story as the presence of Brahman throughout the world. As in the Gita, which fought the spread of Buddhism, this text includes an imbedded critique of the common religiosity prevailing at the time. Though devout persons may pursue official channels of religion—sophisticated training, ritual practice, and so forth—these practices remain meaningless without the higher spirituality toward which they point. This highlights the issue of religious hypocrisy, in which people appear outwardly pious and follow

---

5. *Upanisads*, trans. Patrick Olivelle (Oxford: Oxford University Press, 1996), 154–55, 268–69, 270, 272, 273, and 275. All quotes from the Upanishads in this chapter are taken from this translation.

all the religious rules but are inwardly angry, judgmental, and unpleasant toward other people. Uddalaka Aruni and Svetaketu make the point that organized religion without spirituality is, at best, empty. Hinduism, like Christianity, seeks to promote spirituality beyond superficial religious training and practice.

## Insider Commentary

### Yadlapati

The Upanishads form the end of the Vedas, but they stand as independent texts to be studied on their own. Written later than the Vedas, they represent a historical shift away from the external religious practices like the Vedic fire sacrifice and toward an internal quest for knowledge. The word *upanishad* means "sitting near." According to the Upanishads, one gains this higher knowledge not through the completely solitary life of the ancient ascetic who renounces society altogether, but rather through individualized study at the feet of an experienced teacher, or guru. The Upanishads display the value of mysticism and speculative philosophy, where spiritual insight involves a process of looking inward to the nature of the soul.

This chapter of the Chandogya Upanishad takes up a long series of conversations between a father and a son, in which the son, Svetaketu, seeks clarification on spiritual truths and the father teaches by means of a question-and-answer dialogue designed to bring the student to personal insight on the matter at hand. This selection and several others concern the true nature of the atman, or the self, as the underlying essence of the whole universe. Just as bees prepare honey by gathering nectar from a variety of trees and then reducing that nectar to one homogeneous whole that cannot be differentiated, all the different creatures in this world also merge in one source of life. Just as rivers flow from different directions but become one when they merge into the ocean, all the different creatures have an underlying true essence that is actually one and undifferentiated.

This dialogue between father and son explicates the common and single reality that undergirds all of life. In the living world, things appear separate and different. However, they share a common essence and at this level, they cannot even be distinguished. The object of Upanishadic study consists of seeing through these superficial differences to this underlying identity of spirit. The subjective self (oneself) and the objective self (whatever one apprehends in the world) are ultimately one and the same. Advaita philosophy articulates this as *Tat tvam asi*, or "Thou art that," meaning the absolute identity and equality

The Hindu greeting "Namaste," said with palms together, communicates the message "The divine in me honors the divine in you."

© Julian Kumar / Godong / Corbis

of the inner soul or self (atman) and the absolute reality of the universe (Brahman).

# Text 3: From the Mundaka Upanishad

The selections explain the higher and lower religious knowledge.

## Text

Two types of knowledge a man should learn—those who know Brahman tell us—the higher and the lower. The lower of the two consists of the RigVeda, the YajurVeda, the Samaveda, the Atharvaveda, phonetics, the ritual science, grammar, etymology, metrics, and astronomy; whereas the higher is that by which one grasps the imperishable. What cannot be seen, what cannot be grasped, without color, without sight or hearing, without hands or feet; What is eternal and all-pervading, extremely minute, present everywhere—That is the immutable, which the wise fully perceive. . . . [Ritualists argue] Through heat Brahman is built up; thereby food is produced. From food comes breath, mind, truth, and worlds, and immortality in rites. (Mundaka Upanishad 1:1:4–8)

. . . . .

Deeming sacrifices and gifts as the best, the imbeciles know nothing better. When they have enjoyed their good work, atop the firmament, they return again to this abject world. But those in the wilderness, calm and wise, who live a life of penance and faith, as they beg their food; Through the sun's door they go, spotless, to where that immortal Person is, that immutable self. (Mundaka Upanishad 1:2:10–11)

. . . . .

Gods, celestial beings, humans, beasts, and birds: from him in diverse ways they spring; in-breath and out-breath, barley and rice, penance, faith, and truth, the chaste life and the rules of rites: from him do they spring. The seven breaths, the seven flames, the seven oblations, the seven pieces of wood: from him do they spring. These seven worlds in which the breaths move as they lay hidden, seven by seven, within the cave: from him do they spring. From him spring all oceans and hills; from him flow rivers of all types; from him spring all plants and the sap by which he abides in things as their inmost self. All this is simply that Person—rites, penance, prayer (Brahman), the highest immortal. One who knows this, my friend, hidden within the cave, cuts the knot of ignorance in this world. (Mundaka Upanishad 2:1:7–10)

. . . . .

Take, my friend, this bow, this great weapon of upanisad; Place veneration on it as the whetted arrow, Stretch it with the thought fixed on the nature of that; that very imperishable is the target, my friend. Strike it. The bow is Om, the arrow's the self, the target is Brahman, they say. One must strike that undistracted. He will then be lodged in that. Like the arrow, in the target. That alone is the self, you must understand, on which are woven the earth, intermediate region, and sky, the mind, together with all breaths. Put away other words, for this is the dike to the immortal. Where the veins come together like spokes, in it is that one, taking birth in many ways. "It is Om"—meditate thus on this self; Good luck to you, as you cross beyond the darkness! (Mundaka Upanishad 2:2:3–6)

. . . . .

By truth can this self be grasped—by austerity, by right knowledge, and by a perpetually chaste life. It lies within the body, brilliant and full of light, which ascetics perceive, when their faults are wiped out. The real alone he wins, never the unreal. Along the real runs the path to the gods, on which the seers proceed, their desires fulfilled, to where that highest treasure of the real is found. It is large, heavenly, of inconceivable form; yet it appears more minute than the minute. It is farther than the farthest, yet it is here at hand; it is right here within those who see, hidden within the cave of their heart. Not by sight, not by speech, nor by any other sense; nor by austerities or rites is he grasped. Rather the partless one is seen by a man, as he meditates, when his being has become pure, through the lucidity of knowledge. By thought is this subtle self to be known, into which breath has entered in five ways; by the sense is laced the entire thought of people, in which, when it is pure, this self becomes disclosed. (Mundaka Upanishad 3:1:5–9) ∎

## Outsider Commentary
### Light

The Mundaka Upanishad is popular especially among Hindu practitioners inclined toward a mystical approach. Written primarily for a monastic audience, the text preaches against the mere practice of rituals, instead demanding right-knowledge through new awareness, which cannot be gained by external means. The question naturally arises where this knowledge then comes from, and the answer can only be from the text itself. Like gnosticism in early Christianity and like modern esoteric perspectivalism, both of which hold that a mystical elite share privileged access to the nature of God, Hindu spirituality inspired by the Mundaka Upanishad considers deep awareness key to the authentic spiritual life. This awareness has no relation to outward shows of devotion.

The description of right awareness has great appeal, for it might be understood as pointing toward the widespread availability of authentic spirituality among persons who do not practice organized religion. Such an interpretation could not be further from the intent of the texts. The selection from 1:2:10–11 also notes that only those who wander and beg for food come to this privileged understanding. The Mundaka, far from advocating a popularly available mystical awareness, has an elitist understanding of the divine, restricting it to the monks for whom it was written.

## Insider Commentary
### Yadlapati

As seen in the selections above, the Mundaka Upanishad attacks Vedic ritualism and contrasts a lower and higher form of knowledge. The lower one it identifies with empty ritual and actions performed in desire or attachment; these are said to result in continued rebirth in the world, whereas the higher knowledge of Brahman promises freedom from rebirth.

The selections here present Brahman as the ultimate reality, the source of all natural life, and the underlying truth of all the gods. While the Vedas tend to present Brahman as the truth of the gods, the source of nature, and the object of sacrifice, the Upanishads focus on the unseen reality of Brahman, on Nirguna Brahman, or Brahman without attributes. Although only one reality, Brahman is viewed through the use of attributes (Saguna), or without (Nirguna), and the Mundaka Upanishad clearly prefers the apprehension of Brahman without attributes. A person apprehends the immortal self by detaching oneself from the changing material universe.

According to the Mundaka Upanishad, knowledge of Brahman can be achieved through a number of means, but meditative focus is the preferred way. One reaches the target of

Brahman by aiming one's self or atman at it and using the om, or the techniques of meditation, as a bow. Again, although it focuses on the individual's spiritual progress and turning inward, this is not a solitary practice, but one performed under a guru's guidance. One trains oneself progressively to see more clearly the nature of reality and the nature of the soul. This training itself will also require right ways of living to gain a purity of purpose. The immortal self is achieved not by experience of nature or by rituals, but by thought, because this spiritual knowledge is really a self-knowledge. According to Advaita philosophy, "That art Thou"; the immortal self is none other than the reality of one's individual self. However, realizing this requires detachment and purification of the self qua individual egoistic self. A related verse in the Mundaka Upanishad mentions two birds sitting side by side on a branch. One is busy eating the fruit of the tree and enjoys the sweet fruit and suffers the bitter fruit; it is enslaved in a sense, dependent on what it finds for its own pleasure or pain. The other, not caught up in the bitter and the sweet, looks on with equanimity and peace. The Mundaka Upanishad privileges such a spiritual freedom and detachment, which can be attained through meditation.

## Text 4: From the Ramayana

This excerpt explores socially prescribed duty and the narrative treatment of gender. It appears near the end of the Ramayana, after Rama has defeated the evil demon Ravana after long years of war. After rescuing his kidnapped wife Sita, Rama accuses her of infidelity and orders her away.

### Text

A large crowd pressed around Rama. When Sita eagerly arrived, after her months of loneliness and suffering, she was received by her husband in full view of a vast public. She felt awkward but accepted this with resignation. But what she could not understand was why her lord seemed preoccupied and moody and cold. However, she prostrated herself at his feet, and then stood a little away from him, sensing some strange barrier between herself and him.

Rama remained brooding for a while and suddenly said, "My task is done. I have now freed you. I have fulfilled my mission. All this effort has been not to attain personal satisfaction for you or me. It was to vindicate the honour of the Ikshvahu race and to honour our ancestors' codes and values. After all this, I must tell you that it is not customary to admit back to the normal married fold a woman who has resided all alone in a stranger's house. There can be no question of our living together again. I leave you free to go where you please and to choose any place to live in. I do not restrict you in any manner."

On hearing this, Sita broke down. "My trials are not ended yet," she cried. "I thought with your victory all our troubles were at an end . . . ! So be it." She beckoned to Lakshmana and ordered, "Light a fire at once, on this very spot."

Lakshmana hesitated and looked at his brother, wondering whether he would countermand the order. But Rama seemed passive and acquiescent. Lakshmana, ever the most unquestioning deputy, gathered faggots and got ready a roaring pyre within a short time. The entire crowd watched the proceedings, stunned by the turn of events. The flames rose to the height of a tree; still Rama made no comment. He watched. Sita approached the fire, prostrated herself before it, and said, "O Agni, great god of fire, be my witness." She jumped into the fire.

From the heart of the flame rose the god of fire, bearing Sita, and presented her to

Rama with words of blessing. Rama, now satisfied that he had established his wife's integrity in the presence of the world, welcomed Sita back to his arms.[6] ■

## Outsider Commentary

### Light

The Ramayana, one of the most beloved epics in Hindu literature, has long been used as a model for proper behavior. A Hindu child might be told, "Be like Rama," or "Be like Sita." The text urges all persons to follow their dharma, or duty. This duty is very different for men and women.

Rama, the virtuous leader, is virtuous precisely because he followed his parents' orders. Unjustly banished by his stepmother so that her own son could become king, Rama goes into exile in the forest with his brother and wife. It is here that the demon Ravana abducts Sita.

The beginning of the story already suggests mandates for proper behavior according to one's sex. Though sons must obey their parents, wives must not only obey their husbands but also seek to make their lives comfortable. Myriad versions of the story exist, but a popular detail has Sita brushing Rama's path clean in front of him. Although she must have known that following Rama into exile in the wilds of the jungle would be dangerous, it never occurs to Sita not to accompany her husband on this perilous and unjust journey.

When discussing Sita's abduction, most versions of the story include significant detail about her humble and virtuous behavior in the presence of her captor. Sita's eyes remain down, she declares her loyalty to her husband, and she frequently is portrayed as having great confidence that Rama will come to rescue her. The story makes the point that women's duties are always to their husbands—to the point of not even looking at another man.

The way the Ramayana develops after Sita's rescue by Rama and Hanuman, the brave general of the monkey army, is significant, with great potential for both harming women in society and for their liberation, as modern readings show. Again, despite the many versions of the story, in every rendering, Sita's virtue is questioned. In the text quoted above, she is not only put into the fire to ascertain her purity (that she was not violated by another man) but enters it willingly. Perhaps a reflection of a male culture seeking to perpetuate the practice of immolating wives on their husbands' funeral pyres, the text depicts Sita as voluntarily walking into a blaze.

Regarding men's roles, the above text makes clear that while Rama believes in his wife's purity and virtue, his subjects do not. Rama tests Sita's purity not to quell his own suspicions, but those of his people. Rama's duty as a public figure trumps his duties as a husband, suggesting that a man's duties to the outside world are more important than his duties to his wife.

Many versions of the story end with Sita being swallowed up by the earth, and modern Hindu feminists have started using this unexplored detail to help create what Christian feminists call a "usable past" in a religion dominated by patriarchy. Until recently, no one has remarked that Sita exits the story never to return. In a religious system that considers reincarnation not as the ultimate religious end, but the means to that end, Sita's disappearance takes on great significance.

Moksha, or the escape from the wheel of samsara or reincarnation, means that one has finally lived so well as to eliminate the need to come back to improve karma, which is the totality of good and bad that one has engaged

---

6. R.K. Narayan, *The Ramayana: A Shortened Modern Prose Version of the Indian Epic* (New York: Penguin Books, 1972), 161–62.

The events of the Ramayana, especially Rama's defeat of the evil Ravana, are recited, illustrated, and enacted during the fall holiday of Dussehra. Modern audiences may find the dangerous fire testimony to Sita's fidelity more challenging.

in throughout existence. For Sita to disappear from the story and not be reincarnated means that she has attained the greatest virtue and has been liberated from the cycle of life. She is now in union with Brahman. That this final detail of the story has not been the subject of religious reflection until recently shows the status historically accorded to women by a tradition dominated by strict gender expectations, a tradition that also taught that women had to be reborn in male bodies to pursue the highest liberation of moksha.

## Insider Commentary
### *Yadlapati*

Up to the present time, the Ramayana teaches norms of dharmic behavior for individuals in varying relationships. It shows Rama as the ideal son who obeys his father's will despite its injustice. His brother exemplifies the perfect duty, or dharma, of a younger brother as he loyally follows Rama into exile. Hanuman exemplifies the characteristic responsibilities of an ideal friend and companion as he helps Rama rescue Sita and defeat Ravana. Sita represents the ideal wife who accompanies her husband despite the challenges and remains steadfastly pure and faithful during her captivity, at one point refusing to believe Ravana's deceptions about Rama's alleged death. Rama is also taken to embody the ideal king, willing to sacrifice his own happiness as well as his wife's to maintain even the appearance of propriety for the sake of the kingdom. Although an important source of social norms and dharmic guidance, the Ramayana, like all great epics, renders a rather complicated picture about one's conflicting duties as opposed to a simple instruction on right and wrong.

This selection appears near the end of the epic poem, after Rama has rescued his wife Sita and defeated the demon Ravana. The interaction between Rama and Sita continues to challenge the popular audience as well as scholarly commentators. Many deem Rama's accusation of infidelity patently unfair and unjustified. Some find it confusing that Rama would rescue his wife only to dismiss her so roughly afterward, while others wonder how Rama can still be considered an ideal husband and father given his unjust behavior toward his wife. Apologetic interpretations suggest that Rama had a duty to uphold social order in the kingdom and that he made the difficult decision to sacrifice his own happiness for the sake of his reputation as a righteous ruler over an orderly kingdom. Modern feminists as well as many traditional Hindu women and men focus on the extraordinary truth-test in which Sita proves her purity with divine testament. The unfairness of Rama's suspicion of Sita's fidelity is corrected by the divine testament to her virtue. She is in fact so pure that even Agni the fire god could not burn her. Such an interpretation can provide comfort and hope that divine intervention will correct human injustice.

The Hindu tradition's idealization of Sita's sexual purity raises a question of the justice of having a woman's entire value and dignity depend upon not only perfection in sexual purity until marriage and profuse fertility within the marriage, but even the reputation of sexual purity, which Rama as king values. Some feminist readers appreciate how Sita enjoys the privilege of divine defense of her purity. Sita also enjoys the last word when, in certain later variations of the Ramayana, she declares her innocence in a second truth-test and disappears into her mother, the earth. However, this does not satisfy concerns of social justice, because both of these truth-tests endanger the suspected woman's life. The story of Sita, critically interpreted, reflects the serious vulnerability of women's lives in the face of society's suspicions and accusations about their reputation (consider the disastrous accusations of witchcraft in Western history). Still, it provides a divine defense that has the potential to correct these social structures that place women in such precarious positions in the first place.

## Text 5: From the Laws of Manu

The following selections from the Laws of Manu[7] deal with socially prescribed norms and duties, specifically the subjects of caste, relationships between men and women, and the virtue of hospitality.

### Text

To protect this whole creation, the lustrous one made separate innate activities for those born of his mouth, arms, thighs, and feet. For priests, he ordained teaching and learning, sacrificing for themselves and sacrificing for others, giving and receiving. Protecting his subjects, giving, having sacrifices performed, studying, and remaining unaddicted to the sensory objects are, in summary, for a ruler. Protecting his livestock, giving, having sacrifices performed, studying, trading, lending money, and farming the land are for a commoner. The Lord assigned only one activity to a servant: serving these (other) classes without resentment. (1:87–91)

. . . . .

Men must make their women dependent day and night, and keep under their own control those who are attached to sensory objects. Her father guards her in childhood, her husband guards her in youth, and her sons guard her in old age. A woman is not fit for independence. (9:2–3)

. . . . .

No man is able to guard women entirely by force, but they can be entirely guarded by using these means: he should keep her busy amassing and spending money, engaging in purification, attending to her duty, cooking food, and looking after the furniture. . . . Drinking, associating with bad people, being separated from their husbands, wandering about, sleeping, and living in other people's houses are the six things that corrupt women. Good looks do not matter to them, nor do they care about youth; "A man!"

---

7. All quotations and citations from the Laws of Manu in this chapter are from *The Laws of Manu*, trans. Wendy Doniger (New York: Penguin Books, 1991), 12–13, 77, 115, 197, 198, respectively.

they say, and enjoy sex with him, whether he is good-looking or ugly. By running after men like whores, by their fickle minds, and by their natural lack of affection these women are unfaithful to their husbands even when they are zealously guarded here. Knowing that their very own nature is like this, as it was born at the time of creation by the Lord of Creatures, a man should make the utmost effort to guard them. The bed and the seat, jewelry, lust, anger, crookedness, a malicious nature, and bad conduct are what Manu assigned to women. There is no ritual with Vedic verses assigned to women; this is a firmly established point of law. For women, who have no virile strength and no Vedic verses, are falsehood; this is well established. (9:10–18)

·  ·  ·  ·  ·

A husband who performs the transformative ritual (of marriage) with Vedic verses always makes his woman happy, both when she is in her fertile season and when she is not, both here on earth and in the world beyond. A virtuous wife should constantly serve her husband like a god, even if he behaves badly, freely indulges his lust, and is devoid of any good qualities. Apart (from their husbands), women cannot sacrifice or undertake a vow or fast; it is because a wife obeys her husband that she is exalted in heaven. (5:153–55)

·  ·  ·  ·  ·

No guest should reside in his house without being honoured, to the best of his ability, with a seat, food, a bed, water, and roots and fruits. (4:29) ■

## Outsider Commentary
### Light

The Laws of Manu contains the most concrete regulative norms for persons according to caste and gender. Long used as a guide for social behavior, the Laws describe some of the most controversial restrictions and regulations for women's behavior and the behavior of persons in the lowest of castes and continue to be highly influential despite the Indian government's widespread program of affirmative action.

The most important question about the Laws of Manu is whether they are descriptive or prescriptive. Do they merely describe the behavior that was expected at the time of their composition or do they mandate the continued observation of these behaviors, which may prove troubling in this day and age? Depending on the answer, the Laws become either a historical relic and reminder of how much gender and caste behavior has changed or an edict calling for the continued suppression of women and Untouchables.

In Christianity, the same question of the descriptive versus prescriptive status of texts has long troubled scholars. For example, when the author of Paul's letters writes that women should be silent (1 Cor. 14:34) and cover their heads (1 Cor. 11:1–16), should churches still make sure that women do so? Many Christians consider this text descriptive. They believe Paul's directive reflects gender expectations of the time and that he incorporated them into his vision of what life in the community to which he was writing should look like. Thus Christians now do not have to follow this behavior because expectations for women have changed. Other Christians hold that Paul's directive for women to be silent and cover their heads is prescriptive—meaning that it prescribes behavior and should still be followed today.

As Hindus continue to reflect on the Laws of Manu, similar questions arise. While the duties required of a twice-born male householder to provide hospitality—a requirement certainly related to his economic security—are popularly received as normative, accounts of the significance and necessity of behaviors for women and *dalits* (a group also called the Untouchables) are widely questioned.

One of the chief examples of guidelines cited in the Laws of Manu that are now widely understood as descriptive rather than prescriptive is the delineation of women's spirituality as empty, save for activity toward their husbands' well-being (see 5:153–55, in which a woman is said to attain heaven only by serving her husband). Far from a critique made only by feminists or liberals, the Laws of Manu have elicited widespread dissatisfaction on the part of pious Hindu women whose bhakti devotion and regular reading of sacred scripture lead them to believe that their spirituality is positively comprised of specific religious activity, not just the tending of a home and the needs of their husband.

Similarly, the text, in 9:10–18, describes women as intrinsically promiscuous: "'A man!' they say, and enjoy sex with him whether he is good-looking or ugly." Both insiders to Hindu tradition and outsiders who do not view women as more promiscuous than men face the question of whether the wisdom contained in the Laws, based on this theological anthropology regarding women, can be adopted as normative. The same question of textual reception has arisen in Christianity when readers question Augustine as a source for tradition when he held that marriage must be enacted to ensure paternity.[8]

Perhaps most troubling is the description of the life of a servant, who is meant to serve others without resentment. No other duties are appropriate to those at the lowest levels of society. No other way of life but one of service is possible for these persons, and the privileges and choices open to other persons remained closed to the servant caste. Clearly written by the highest castes to justify and perpetuate their own status, the Laws of Manu have come under increasing scrutiny in a modern Hindu society where views of caste and gender have changed dramatically.

## Insider Commentary
### *Yadlapati*

Written around 100 CE, the Laws of Manu is one of the texts, along with the Bhagavad Gita, by which orthodox Vedic Hinduism reasserted itself against the challenges posed by ancient world-denying ascetic traditions and the ascendancy of the Buddhist and Jain traditions. The Gita does it by means of karma yoga and devotional bhakti, while Manu expounds the intricate details of dharma in every particular context. Dharma and the teachings of karma yoga and bhakti yoga indicate the reassessment of religious values occurring during this formative period in Hindu history. One of the primary sacred texts illustrating dharma, the Laws of Manu provides rationale for maintaining social order. It includes detailed discussion of the rules concerning caste and gender that have so pervasively determined Hindu social norms and obligations for most of Indian history. In addition to the overwhelming number of restrictions on people's behavior and interaction, the Laws of Manu articulates a wide array of admirable social recommendations, such as the one found in the verse above that enjoins all twice-born householders to observe the duty of hospitality.[9] At the same time, it articulates

---

8. See Saint Augustine's *On Marriage and Concupiscence*, bk. 1, ch. 27, in which he reduces original sin to lust, identifies lust as female and something that needs to be controlled by men, and justifies men's control over their wives. From "Medieval Sourcebook: Saint Augustine: On Marriage and Concupiscence," *fordham.edu/halsall/source/aug-marr.asp*.

9. The "twice-born" refers to the higher three *varnas*, or castes, including Brahmins or priests, Kshatriyas or rulers, and Vaishyas or merchants and farmers. The fourth and lowest *varna* consists of the Shudras, who are to be servants. Outside the *varnas* altogether are those who are entirely without caste, or the so-called Untouchables, who were renamed *Harijans* (children of God) by Gandhi.

gender norms that contemporary readers clearly find unsavory and problematic, like the selection from chapter 5 that teaches a woman must serve her husband like a god even if he lacks all good qualities. This kind of teaching has helped cement a very pervasive and traditional Hindu ideal for women of *pativratya*, by which a woman is thought to gain salvation through her unending service and devotion to her husband. The selection demonstrates, as is typical in Manu and in Hindu thinking on dharma, the paradoxical ways in which two seemingly conflicting teachings appear side by side. According to Manu, a husband must take responsibilities for his wife's happiness and a man requires his wife's participation to gain merit for certain rituals. This suggests respect for wives, but at the same time the text holds that a woman gains her salvation only in complete obedience to a husband, however immoral he may be, and can do nothing of spiritual merit on her own.

As a text that seems both to describe the social order as it is and prescribe moral behavior as it should be, Manu dwells on the divinely mandated hierarchy among the four castes: Brahmins, or priests; Kshatriyas, or warrior nobility; Vaishyas, or merchants; and Shudras, or manual laborers. According to the text, the only way to improve one's lot in life consists of following the rules set forth by dharma and accepting the particular restrictions on one's behavior in order to slowly work one's way up the caste ladder through subsequent rebirths. In this sense, Manu appears to maintain the status quo, justifying it as divinely mandated. A Shudra who refuses to serve the upper three castes of the twice-born or a woman who protests subjugation to her father, husband, or son not only offends these other people, but commits a sin against the sacred order. The dharma taught by Manu successfully exerts virtually total control because the duties prescribed for each social group help maintain that group's particular standing.

Chapter 1 of the Laws of Manu opens with the great sages approaching Manu and asking him to explain the duties of all the four castes. Written by priests, this dharma text reinforces and justifies the hierarchical caste system with priests at the top of the hierarchy. Manu explains the superiority of the priestly caste to other castes on the basis of its purity. Each caste or social class has a particular described natural order and prescribed set of duties. Whereas farmers inadvertently cause harm to small creatures of the land and rulers hunt and eat animals and therefore defile themselves, the priests alone presumably embody a state of purity and self-purification through sacrifice. This exemplifies how Manu both justifies the "lower" way of the other castes as appropriate for them and yet condemns this work as ultimately defiling in a way that justifies their continued subjugation. It problematically suggests that the other castes were created with the nature of sin or impurity and are encouraged to continue their impurity, and then are *still* criticized and punished for doing so. Thus, a ruler's impure acts of killing will maintain his impurity and justify his lower status below the priests, upon whom he relies for the all-too-necessary purification rituals. By focusing on the relative purity of different actions and different groups of people, Manu successfully reinforces the priests' spiritual status over the rulers who by all measures enjoy greater worldly power.

The text selection on women demonstrates a similar problem—women were created to be weak and impure and then are punished for it in perpetuity. Such texts prompt the queries: Who deemed these rules? Who stands to gain from these rules? The answer to both is clearly the priests and the men with authority in society. It is undoubtedly problematic that women are punished for their supposedly God-given nature. However, this reveals how dharma functions both descriptively and prescriptively. It reflects the way of nature, and the articulation of *svadharma*—that everyone must fulfill his or her own unique set of duties—helps ensure that things stay the way they are. This may well strike modern readers as a convenient priestly rationalization of the status quo that leaves no room for the moral overturning of such injustice. While some Hindu apologetics emphasize the classical turn to bhakti, and how this path of love and devotion opened a way to liberation for anyone, regardless of gender or caste, the fact remains that the rules of dharmic behavior articulated in the Laws of Manu have perpetuated a set of norms for society that have been neither criticized harshly enough within society nor entirely overturned in actuality. While the Indian government has taken bold steps to remedy gender and caste inequality with aggressive affirmative action programs and other legal actions, Hindu and Indian society remains enmeshed in these strongly hierarchical norms of social behavior.

# Text 6: Bhagavad Gita[10]

The selected verses explore the concepts of action, contemplation, and devotion.

## Texts

Be intent on action, not on the fruits of action; avoid attraction to the fruits and attachment to inaction. (2:47)

. . . . .

Perform actions, firm in discipline, relinquishing attachment; be impartial to failure and success—this equanimity is called discipline. (2:48)

. . . . .

A man cannot escape the force of action by abstaining from actions; he does not attain success just by renunciation. (3:4)

. . . . .

Action imprisons the world unless it is done as sacrifice. (3:9)

. . . . .

Content with whatever comes by chance, beyond dualities, free from envy, impartial to failure and success, he is not bound even when he acts. (4:22) ∎

## Outsider Commentary
### *Light*

The Gita offers the foundation of karma yoga and calls into question many Western assumptions about Hinduism. Christians typically know that Hinduism is a distinct religion from Buddhism, and some know that Hinduism predates Buddhism and was the religion in which Siddhartha Gautama, who became the Buddha, was raised. Few know that Buddhism deeply influenced Hindu spirituality.

As Buddhism gained popularity across the Indian subcontinent, Hinduism responded by promoting diverse practices that would address the need some Hindus tried to fill by converting to Buddhism. The Gita borrows from the Buddhist emphasis on nonattachment to action, admonishing readers to act in the world in a way that does not care about outcomes, but only about duty. The way of activity, or karma yoga, entails acting with a whole new attitude in which the outcome of one's activity is irrelevant and does not motivate one's actions. One should always perform his or her duty for

10. Selections from and references to the Gita in this chapter are taken from *The Bhagavad-Gita*, trans. Barbara Stoler Miller (New York: Bantam Books, 1986) unless otherwise noted.

duty's sake and not become a slave to the consequences of activity.

The story of Arjuna the warrior and his charioteer—Lord Krishna himself—may not resonate with Christian readers. The dynamic of a god depicted in human form can be so jarring that, as an outsider to the Hindu tradition, one misses the point of the story. In that story, Krishna tells the reluctant Arjuna that he must go into battle against part of his extended family. The story illustrates that the proper path is that which continues one's life and prescribed place in the world, even when one might want to relinquish one's duties. The parts of the Gita that prescribe the same spiritual path in theoretical language, like the passage above, may better serve to introduce Christian readers to Hindu spirituality. Directives like "relinquish attachment; be impartial to failure and success"[11] may already sound like good advice to Christians, giving the general sense that doing the right thing is sometimes hard.

The Gita is fighting ascetic practices in which the spiritual person withdraws from the world. Outlining a way of life that is neither ascetic nor attached, the Gita urges people to continue being in the ordinary world—working, being part of a family, whatever one's place in society is as determined by cast and gender—but to do so without interest or concern for what their actions accomplish.

For Catholics this path may sound familiar. The language of "in the world but not of the world" has been popular at least since Vatican II, which emphasized the idea of the church as participating in the modern world. This Christian focus on going about life but "remaining above it all" in the life of the spirit resonates with the spirituality promulgated by the Gita.

## Insider Commentary
### Yadlapati

The Bhagavad Gita presents a sophisticated set of spiritual questions on the relative value of the active life and the contemplative life in the context of a dialogue between the human Arjuna and the incarnate god Krishna. As the two warring families assemble on the battlefield, Arjuna sees many cousins, uncles, and teachers on the opposing side and breaks down at the prospect of killing family members with whom he had been raised. He refuses to fight, claiming that killing, especially the killing of family, is known universally to be a terrible sin that will be punished in multiple hells. His charioteer Krishna (who will presently reveal himself as God incarnate) counsels Arjuna through this moral and spiritual crisis by taking up the karmic relationship of action and consequence. As a result, the Gita presents not only a solution to Arjuna's immediate crisis on the battlefield but also a discussion of the merits of karma yoga, the path of dutiful and selfless action without regard for the pleasant or unpleasant consequences of those actions.

Ancient Indians were forced to choose between the worldly life of action in family and society—a life devoted to dharma or duty in one's relationships with others and with the sacred as enacted through ritual sacrifice—and the ascetic life of renunciation in the forest to pursue ultimate spiritual freedom. The Gita, however, teaches that a life in the world of dharmic obligation can also be liberating. It suggests that action and inaction both have consequences and accrue karma. True discipline lies in acting impartially, committed to one's duty without caring for the benefits or detriments that may result.

---

11. *The Bhagavad-Gita*, trans. Sir Edwin Arnold (New York: P.F. Collier and Son, 1909–14), ch. 2, v. 48.

The ancient Hindu choice between a life of action and a life of renunciation echoes the choice in Christian tradition between a life of action and a life of contemplation, as considered in the Gospel story of the interaction of Jesus with two sisters, Mary and Martha (Luke 10:38–42). In the Gospel narrative, Martha criticizes her sister for sitting idly listening to Jesus talk instead of helping her with the housework that must be done. Jesus responds by admonishing Martha and defending Mary's choice as the better one. Although traditionally interpreted as supporting the superiority of the contemplative life, contemporary Christian feminist theologians have criticized this interpretation. They instead defend Martha, who works tirelessly and yet is admonished for her supposed lack of wisdom. The domestic work of caring for and feeding a household, a task that continues to fall disproportionately on women's shoulders, has been devalued or undervalued in countless ways. Likewise, the broader "domestic" work of providing for earthly concerns and working in the world among people perhaps needs defending as a spiritual calling as well.

The instruction of karma yoga, to act dutifully and selflessly in the world while relinquishing the fruits of action, provides the framework for such a needed defense of worldly work. In addition, the traditional Hindu division of life into four stages supports the sacred value seen in the worldly life that revolves around work and family. One is first a student, then a householder, then a renunciate, and lastly a forest dweller. During the householder stage, one ought to work hard in society, earn an honest living, live charitably, and raise, support, and educate children. Such a division of life into four distinct stages, with their respective ethics and goals, appreciates the value of the worldly life of action in its appropriate time rather than devaluing it in comparison with the life of physical renunciation or spiritual contemplation.

# CHAPTER 12

# Concluding Reflections

*Aimee Upjohn Light and Madhuri M. Yadlapati*

## Reflections of an "Outsider"

*Aimee Upjohn Light*

Writing an introductory chapter on Hinduism from a Christian perspective was a challenging task, and one that made me extremely nervous. The further I advance in my own studies, the more deeply I realize the lack of uniformity within my own Christian religious tradition. Catholics disagree with Southern Baptists on many things, Lutherans of the Missouri Synod share few worship practices with Anglicans, and so forth. In fact, Presbyterians may disagree with other Presbyterians, or Pentecostals with Pentecostals. If "Christianity" is so far from being a unified religion, how does one even begin to speak of it? Combine this lack of uniformity with the plethora of Hindu beliefs and worship and I began to wonder if I could say anything at all in an introductory book.

Yet there are important developments in interreligious work that make less daunting the task of continuing in the face of irreducible diversity. Specifically, scholarship on multiple religious belonging and the nature of religious identity has contributed to the understanding that religious identity is always and everywhere complicated. The drive to distill Christian or Hindu or any other religious identity into one or several pure things is unnecessary. Only by relinquishing this monolithic and hegemonic approach can one realistically grapple with the phenomenon of religion.

Instead of thinking about "Hinduism" or "Christianity," it often proves more helpful to think about "Hinduisms" and "Christianities." In *Monopoly on Salvation? A Feminist Approach to Religious Pluralism*,[1] Jeannine Hill Fletcher applies the identity theories of Patricia Hill Collins, an African-American sociologist, and Edward Said, a Palestinian-American literary theorist and cultural critic, to the situation of being religious. Both Hill Collins and Said, as members of minority groups, analyze the ways in which representations of identity by majority populations misrepresent and oversimplify the reality of oppressed groups.[2] Instead of thinking of identities as pure, Hill Collins and Said insist that all identities result from the intersection of multiple factors. One's race, class, educational level, sexual orientation, familial situation, nationality, and so forth combine to actually constitute

---

1. Jeannine Hill Fletcher, *Monopoly on Salvation? A Feminist Approach to Religious Pluralism* (New York: Continuum, 2005).

2. See Edward Said's *Orientalism* (New York: Random House, 1978) throughout, and Patricia Hill Collins's *Black Feminist Thought: Knowledge, Consciousness and the Politics of Empowerment* (New York: Routledge, 2008).

any particular category by which one identifies him- or herself. Whether one identifies one's self primarily as "black," "white," "American," or "German," this category is made up of the intersections of all one's other categories. A person's racial identification is affected by gender and class. A person's politics are deeply affected by race and age. A person's socioeconomic position is affected by class, race, and age. Each category helps to constitute every other category. Identity is never simple. Jeannine Hill Fletcher rightly points out that contemporary society has already widely accepted this understanding of identities as hybrid—*except regarding religion.*

Hill Fletcher contends that many still hold on to the myth of a pure religious identity in which a "Christianity" or at least denominational "Presbyterianism" or "Catholicism" can be separated out from a person's other identifying factors. To extend Hill Fletcher's contention, many may also be holding on to the myth of a pure Hindu identity. If so, the variety of Hindu practices and beliefs will be confounding at best and intimidating at worst. I see now that this very tendency to cling to a myth of religious purity contributed to my hesitancy to write anything for an introductory book on Christian-Hindu comparative theology.

Writing on the subject of multiple religious belonging—the simultaneous practice of two different religious traditions, such as Buddhism and Christianity or Judaism and Islam—Peter Phan, a Catholic priest and scholar of religion, suggests that the inclination to think of religions as pure is a particularly Western phenomenon.[3] Having observed this Western tendency, Phan then goes on to show how religion in Asia works

very differently. What he and others call "multiple religious belonging" is the norm, with people being Buddhist and Christian, Hindu and Buddhist, or Buddhist with Muslim and Christian practices throughout their devotion.[4]

Thus my hesitancy or fear of reducing either Christianity or Hinduism into a pure set of beliefs and practices, and my consequent nervousness at writing anything at all, actually reflects the state-of-the-debate in Christian approaches to interreligious work. Thinking like that of Hill Fletcher and Phan, not to mention the need to do comparative theology itself, has influenced how I understand religion to such a degree that I wished to avoid reducing traditions that I considered diverse to some sort of mythic purity.

Where then did, and does, my confidence in writing come from? In this age of irreducible religious plurality and understanding of intra-religious complexity, how does one begin to write or speak? The answer, for me as for so many other scholars, lies both in the relationships that inform our reflections and in which we carry them out.

When I began studying religion in Yale's PhD program, one of the few other women in the program was Madhuri Yadlapati. She was Hindu and I was Christian by training, but we both had similar questions and in some ways similar families. We bonded over not only the reading of philosophical and theological texts but also trips to the mall and the reading of novels, as well as by reflecting on gender expectations and our own developing views of family life. Madhuri was as integral to my study of religion as any famous book or graduate seminar.

---

3. December 24, 2010, interview with *National Catholic Reporter*, "The Uniqueness of Jesus: Facing Doctrinal Questions, Peter Phan Speaks His Mind," *docstoc.com/.../the-uniqueness-of-Jesus-facing-doctrinal-questions-Peter-Phan-speaks-his-mind.*

4. Combining different religions is not a problem in Asia, as the long history of Asian studies regarding *syncretism*, or religious blending, illustrates. For an excellent survey of studies on syncretism, see Anita Leopold and Jeppe Sinding Jensen's *Syncretism in Religion: A Reader* (New York: Routledge, 2004).

Because she and I shared similar and frequently identical questions and opinions, I witnessed how Hinduism and Christianity in action led to similar ways of thinking and living in the world.

By sharing our lives, Madhuri and I learned that Hindus and Christians are extremely similar not because of any argument or analysis, but because we manifested the similarities. There is nothing more powerfully convincing than experience, and nothing as useless as an argument that one does not want to listen to. Studying theories of why religions are similar or the same is far less convincing than seeing clearly that someone from what looks like a very foreign tradition sees things the same way that you do.

The effectiveness of lived relationship and experience is an important aspect of comparative theology itself. For several generations, Christians have attempted to give a coherent theory of the relationship between the multiple religions. The Catholic Church advocated inclusivism, the position that non-Christians are unknowingly saved through Jesus. John Hick advocated pluralism, the position that all religions enable their members to reach out to the same reality, which is bigger than and encompasses our ideas of God, enlightenment, and so forth. Progress in these theoretical approaches is slow. Many scholars have given up. Widespread frustration with the self-congratulatory and imperialistic tendencies in inclusivism and with the internal inconsistencies in pluralism have led many to wonder what comes next. This quagmire has also, I believe, led to the widespread popularity of comparative theology.

Comparative theology does not attempt to argue anyone into believing in interreligious similarity. It does not try to provide a theory of how all religions do the same thing. Instead, comparative theology is akin to the Nike slogan "Just Do It!" We do not actually have to prove the similarities amongst religions to fruitfully proceed. We can inhabit Christianity and Hinduism or Christianity and Buddhism through reading their sacred texts or engaging in community ritual and belonging.[5]

Thus the process of writing this chapter could aptly be described as one of friendship. It is because Madhuri and I have reflected over time on the same things in life—career, marriage, having children, how to relate to people in our communities—that I have developed the confidence to think I might be able to take something meaningful from the Vedas and Upanishads. In looking to the passage on Sita and Rama in the Ramayana, I already had in mind the many years over which Madhuri and I reflected on changing gender expectations for women in families. In thinking about the Laws of Manu and their status in religious community, I hearkened back to conversations in graduate school about problematic Christian texts like some of those found in the Pauline literature that instruct women to remain silent with heads covered during worship.

In this chapter on Christian-Hindu comparative work, I see the reflection of two friends and scholars who, though trained in two different religions, share a worldview. How better to convince undergraduate readers that Christianity and Hinduism are related spiritual paths than the witness of two young women whose work is at times almost indistinguishable? Madhuri and I do not have to argue this point. Instead, she teaches the Trinity in university lectures while I teach Advaita.

The general observation that I hope students will take away from this reflection is that lived experience is much more useful than

---

5. That Paul Knitter, arguably the most famous theorizer of religious multiplicity, is now engaging in Buddhist-Christian belonging instead of creating universal theories of religion, is a powerful witness. See Knitter's *Without Buddha I Could Not Be a Christian* (Oxford: Oneworld, 2009).

theory. We all have trouble believing things we haven't experienced, and conversely we usually most deeply believe things we have experienced. In the study of religion, relationships and participating in other ways of life—understanding that the people practicing these other religions are people just like ourselves—is much more important than learning dates and facts. Madhuri and I already know that our religions are differing, culturally conditioned articulations of spirituality. My hope is that students will discover religious similarities in relationships for themselves.

## Reflections of an "Insider"

*Madhuri M. Yadlapati*

Collaborative partnerships challenge participants to cooperate and compromise as well as to maintain the integrity of individual contributions and the project as a whole. Our experience in co-writing an account of Hinduism dialogically has shown that this process can be very educational. Authors usually write with a particular audience in mind; they try to persuade some group of the value of a certain perspective or to share a particular set of insights they consider meaningful. They often attempt to join a conversation that is already going on, especially in the world of academic research. This project is unique, however, in the way that it involves four key academic exercises: it is rooted in the comparative study of religion, uses a dialogic model, explicitly connects the religious insider and religious outsider, and shares with readers both participants' reflections on this process.

My reflections following the co-writing of chapter 11, "Hinduism: Texts and Commentary," are the culmination of an ongoing self-consciousness about not only the process of writing and co-writing but also, and especially, what it means to contribute to the academic study of religion. This process has raised

rudimentary questions for me about what we are doing when we study and write about religion, and how we go about doing it. The following are a few of the issues that became prominent for me.

First, the process of co-writing a chapter on Hinduism raised my awareness of the methods used to study religion. Much as the study of a foreign language brings to the fore the rules of grammar used unconsciously in one's native language, the study of an unfamiliar religious tradition joined with the academic presentation of a familiar one foregrounds the methods of religious studies (e.g., historical, textual, or ritual) and the "rules" unconsciously used in the practice and study of religion. Encountering and making sense of what is relatively unfamiliar allows us to see our own, more familiar traditions with a new interpretive lens and in a broader context.

The discussion of Hinduism in relation to Christianity also pushes to the fore that different religious traditions operate by different rules: each has its own set of rules, or unique theo-*logical* apparatus, that establish its internal consistency. Scholars have long suggested that Hinduism defies conventional efforts to define it. Drawing such broadly diverse traditions as those within Hinduism into conversation with Christianity clarifies how fully the academic discipline of religious studies, born in mid-1800s Europe, stems from Western and Christian presuppositions. That every global religious tradition possesses great internal diversity is often overlooked as scholars select which teachings, practices, and historical moments to include as central identifiers of a particular tradition and which to leave to the periphery. During the process of writing, I became very conscious of the choices I had to make: focusing on the most universal Hindu teachings or practices would leave out the most unique interpretations; focusing on philosophical approaches to the sacred would risk leaving out much of the vibrant religious iconography that is so characteristic of Hinduism. Unlike

Christianity in particular, Hinduism lacks the uniformity provided by a historical founder or an agreed-upon creed. Hinduism could accurately be identified as a family of related traditions, including the theistic movements of Vaishnavism, Shaivism, and Shaktism; the non-theistic philosophical movements of Advaita and Samkhya; and the combination of and interaction between these theistic and nontheistic movements. These represent not only separate components of Hindu tradition like devotional worship, philosophical theology, and ethical norms, but even contradictory movements that remain separate throughout Hindu history. Nevertheless, because of the intimate interaction and prolonged coexistence of these diverse movements, they can be grouped together under the rubric of *Hinduism*, or *Hinduisms*. Many scholars increasingly choose the latter, plural form to acknowledge that every tradition has a multiplicity that cannot judiciously be reduced to a single teaching and set of practices.

Another major part of the co-writing process involved the identification of a religious insider and a religious outsider, which highlighted the fact that any religious tradition is itself multiple. Which Christianity? Which Hinduism? I became acutely aware during the dialogue that each of us operated with a particular vision of Hinduism and Christianity. For example, I realized the degree to which Aimee Light, my dialogue partner, was influenced by certain post–Vatican II Roman Catholic sensibilities—namely, the inclusivist-pluralist opening created by the Second Vatican Council's statements on the value of other religious traditions. In fact, this project as a whole, rooted in comparative method and dialogue, reflects the value of truly engaging non-Christians, which was affirmed in large part only in the aftermath of the Second Vatican Council. I understood this fact at the outset, but the experience of dialogical collaboration made me appreciate it on a more personal level.

The question of which Christianity or which Hinduism is being referenced calls to mind areas of interreligious dialogue that remain neglected. While the "liberals" of different religious traditions have participated in numerous spirited dialogues, these conversations often lack the unique insights brought by those who are more religiously conservative. Too often, the religiously conservative are mistaken for those who espouse the dogmatic and fundamentalist strains of their traditions, but sincere and traditional faith commitments are not necessarily rooted in dogmatism and fundamentalism. I believe a dialogical model for studying religion may help clarify the unique concerns of those who maintain such deeply traditional faith standpoints. This approach brings into conversation two particular viewpoints instead of presuming to compare two coherent systems, which can only be abstractions of a living set of interacting strands of tradition.

Writing as the Hindu "insider," I became acutely aware of the tension involved in the academic study of religion itself. What makes me an insider? What sources of authority am I using to speak for Hinduism? Am I an authoritative Hindu insider because I was born Hindu? Is the act of self-identifying as Hindu enough to give one authority? Or does one also need to participate regularly in a certain number of ritual traditions to qualify as an authority? If so, what is that number and who determines these rules? This question becomes problematic in a tradition like Hinduism that has been so loosely defined. The criterion used to determine what makes a good Hindu is often adherence not to a creedal system but to a set of ethical norms that are culturally specific explications of dharma. Am I a Hindu because my identity is formed by my duties as a daughter, granddaughter, sister, wife, mother, friend, and teacher? Because I believe that all our actions have consequences that will determine our character as well as our future circumstances?

A prioritization of practice over belief does nothing to simplify the issue. For example, many Hindus over the centuries have been vegetarian, but many have chosen not to follow this tradition, and their choice is considered equally valid. How does a norm such as vegetarianism function, and again, who decides how to apply it?

In the course of this dialogue with my friend Aimee Light, I realized that I operate from a perspective shaped by my diasporic experience and Western education in the study of religion. In certain ways, both of these experiences may be considered secondary or inauthentic qualifications; perhaps an orthodox, vegetarian Hindu living in India who has not studied religion academically, but who regularly performs puja would possess more authority to speak for Hinduism. Recent years have seen a growing concern that religious practitioners be included in interreligious dialogues, that these should not be exclusively conversations among academics. At the same time, as a Western-trained scholar, I would not want to forsake the tools gained from the academic study of religion and allow religious participants alone to determine the parameters of conversation based on their definitions of orthodoxy. We are all, adherents and scholars, limited and defined by our particular perspectives, and we all have something to gain from voicing these perspectives in collaborative conversation and from reflecting on how these perspectives are shaped. The question about what kind of authority any one individual representative has is a universal issue we ought to keep in mind when encountering any account of a religious tradition; even while it is necessary to generalize about a religious tradition, we must exercise caution that we do not universalize all the particular expressions of tradition.

The academic study of religion has much to gain from explicitly acknowledging the positions of religious insiders and religious outsiders. After all, every one of us is always simultaneously both an insider (with a perspective formed by one's religious, educational, cultural, and personal background) and an outsider (to anything that is unfamiliar to us). Students would do well to remember this as they begin to study a "foreign" religious tradition. They would do well to note the ways their particular experience and their unfamiliarity with a different tradition influence how they interpret that tradition's teachings, rules, or practices. What one community accepts as entirely natural and rational can appear strange, superstitious, or even unethical to an outsider who subjects it to the rules or theo-logic of his or her own tradition.

Looking back, the identification of religious insider and religious outsider made each of us very self-conscious about what we brought to the conversation. We often found ourselves, for example, overcompensating for our respective position as the "insider" or the "outsider" to the point that the outsider was sometimes defending Hindu norms while the insider was trying to articulate a more scholarly and so-called objective approach. In articulating the subject matter, we attempted to transcend the limitations of our individual perspectives as best we could. This process taught that the claim to objectivity only masks the particulars of one's perspective and, further, that these particularities are valuable and should be acknowledged and reflected upon.

This project of dialogical comparative study and reflection is a first step. For me, many questions remain. Questions of authority and what it means to call myself a Hindu "insider" provoke discomfort that bears a vague and alarming resemblance to that which many of us may remember from junior high: questions about who we truly are and whether we have the right to speak authoritatively on a given subject. Although these questions remain unresolved, they provide motivation to continue this conversation with others. The study of religion is a provocative and, some may say, even dangerous and subversive exercise in examining the boundaries of how we define ultimate meaning and value. Reflecting seriously on the makeup of our religious identities is a subversive act. But, given the violent clashes over religious orthodoxy around the world, it could be among the most valuable acts called for today. With any luck, the suggestion that serious reflection and questioning is potentially subversive will sound more and more ridiculous to us the more it becomes a habit. One task of education is to reflect on the boundaries each of us is given and to grow into who one is. To that end, the process of dialogical study is a rewarding educational experience that ought to be used more often. The challenges of engaging in fruitful interreligious dialogue with those of an unfamiliar tradition should not hinder anyone who approaches the task with a sincere desire to learn from the other and gain in mutual understanding.

# Resources for Further Study

## Review Questions

1. How does the study of Hinduism challenge Western and Christian categories of "religion"?
2. What do *shruti* and *smriti* suggest about the different sacred texts?
3. Describe the two renaissances that Hinduism has undergone.
4. What are the four goals of life, according to Hindu teaching?
5. How is a person's dharma constituted?
6. What central themes and moral lessons are communicated in the Mahabharata, Bhagavad Gita, and Ramayana?

## Questions for Reflection and Discussion

1. How do the collected sacred texts of Hinduism impact one's understanding of the Christian Bible, its composition, content, and use?
2. How does a Hindu view of the central goals of life differ from a Christian view of salvation?
3. To what extent does religion justify traditional social norms such as patriarchy or provide resources for their reversal or transcendence?
4. What promising venues for comparative religion and interreligious dialogue still remain untapped between Christianity and Hinduism?

## Glossary

**Advaita Vedanta**  One of the most influential and philosophical schools of Hindu thought. *Advaita* refers to the relationship of identity between the self and Brahman. Shankara and Ramanuja rank among Advaita's most influential figures.

**atman**  "Self" in Sanskrit, or the principle of differentiation. The wisdom that "atman is Brahman" is emphasized in much Advaita Vedanta, meaning that what makes the self real is its identity with the source of all reality or the divine.

**avatar**  An appearance or manifestation of the divine. Avatars may also be called "incarnations," though the significance of an incarnation is not that it is the unique or highest manifestation of the divine.

**Bhagavad Gita**  The Bhagavad Gita or simply "Gita" is part of the longer epic, the Mahabharata. The Gita is 700 verses, and is believed to have been written between the fifth and second centuries BCE. The Gita is considered smriti or remembered literature, not directly revealed by the divine.

**bhakti**  The path of personal spiritual devotion, typically taking the form of prayer and meditation to and with one's chosen Ishta Devata, or personal deity. Bhakti typically takes place in the schools of Vaishnavism and Shaivism, the dominant forms of Hindu monotheism. Bhakti often leads practitioners to create home shrines and spend time at these places of devotion daily.

**Brahman**   The name given to the one source of all being, who is sometimes understood as a personal, involved God and sometimes as an impersonal principle. Although Hindu belief about Brahman is diverse, the term always refers to the ultimate, which exceeds all human conception.

**Brahmin**   Refers to the Hindu priestly caste—those allowed to perform and govern religious ritual. One is born into the Brahmin caste and cannot join because of training, however, the number of non-Brahmin pujaris (trained priests) is increasing.

**caste**   One's position in life inherited by birth. There have traditionally been four castes (priestly, warrior, trader, and laborer). Many were left out of the caste system altogether and were referred to as *dalits*, or untouchables—meaning filth or outcasts. Though the Indian government officially abolished the caste system, most Hindus still understand themselves in terms of caste.

**dharma**   A core concept of Hinduism, it means duty. Every person has a duty to follow the obligations and rites of his or her position. Because the concept of dharma is so strong, and because following one's dharma not only keeps the universe going in an orderly direction but helps one escape from samsara, doing one's dharma according to caste perpetuates the caste system as people follow their duties according to historical group. Even though the caste system has been outlawed in today's society, it is voluntarily upheld by persons out of concern for attaining their religious ends.

**Devi**   The root form of every Hindu female goddess, to whom all trace their origin. In some forms of Hinduism, Devi is the supreme principle, while in others she is secondary or understood as the energy of the male divine.

**jnana**   A Vedic word literally meaning "knowledge." In Hinduism it refers to the knowledge gained through mystical experience. This is knowledge of the self and of how the self is identical to Brahman or the principle of all reality. Jnana is implicitly understood to be cosmic as well as self-knowledge.

**karma**   Refers to one's actions and the necessary effects of that action. The whole of reality—samsara—is caused by the totality of karma. It determines one's rebirth, whether good or bad, and dictates one's future life. Good karma is understood to help one attain a better rebirth; bad karma leads one toward a lesser rebirth, so attaining good karma is a central concern of Hindu religion.

**Laws of Manu**   An ancient text (translated into English in the 1700s) that claims to dictate the laws of society from the mouth of Manu, the creator of all humankind. The Laws describe the proper roles, duties, and rights of all persons in society and claims a divine mandate for these behaviors and stratifications. Because of the text's harsh norms for women and untouchables, some contemporary Hindus resist its status as a divinely inspired text.

**maya**   The state of illusion or ignorance, in which persons believe reality is dual. Duality refers to a difference or division between that which is finite and that which is divine or ultimate.

*moksha*   The desired religious end in Hinduism, akin to heaven in Christianity or enlightenment in Buddhism. Moksha is liberation from samsara, the cycle of rebirth.

**monism**   Although different from traditional Western monotheism, both monism and monotheism believe God is one. Yet whereas monotheism understands God as at a distance from all reality, in monism God permeates reality.

Hinduism has contained both monotheistic and monistic understandings of Brahman.

*Nirguna*  Part of the term *Nirguna Brahman* or Brahman without qualities. Nirguna is the pure, actual being of Brahman, which cannot be thought and is beyond all human categories. Nirguna Brahman serves as a placeholder for an infinite reality that cannot be conceptualized, rather than as a positive concept. Some Hindu mystics claim to have experiences of Nirguna Brahman, or Brahman beyond qualities.

**polytheism**  The belief in many gods. The polytheism of Hinduism often obfuscates (to the outsider) a deep monotheism or even monism, which understands Brahman as one and pervading the cosmos. Hinduism can be polytheistic, but to the philosophically trained Hindu, that polytheism expresses something beyond itself, namely the relationship of the ultimate to the world.

*prasad*  A gift offered to a deity. Most commonly prasad is the food placed at the feet of a statue of a god and then consumed by devotees with the understanding that food is now blessed.

*puja*  A religious ritual that involves making an offering to a god or goddess and receiving blessings in return. Pujas can take place at home, in temples, and at major festivals.

*Saguna*  Literally meaning "with qualities," it is most commonly applied to Brahman. Saguna Brahman means God, or the principle of ultimate reality, as actually experienced in ordinary categories of thought or action. Brahman in Brahman's self is beyond understanding, thus experiences of Brahman are ordinarily considered Saguna Brahman. Some consider the pantheon of Hindu gods to be Saguna Brahman, though the totality of the pantheon is understood as a mediating level of being between Nirguna Brahman and Saguna Brahman, not merely part of individuated Saguna Brahman experiences.

**samsara**  The cycle of all being—birth, death, and rebirth. Samsara is that which one seeks to escape through liberation or moksha.

*sanatana dharma*  *Sanatana* literally means "eternal," and *dharma* literally means "duty." English has no satisfactory equivalent for this term, which means much more than the sum of its two constituent parts. Sanatana dharma refers to everything that exists, pointing to all being as part of the unfolding of the universe according to the being and will of the ultimate, Brahman. By following one's dharma or duty, one participates in sanatana dharma in a heightened, more deliberate way. All persons are called to intentionally participate in sanatana dharma as the way to attain moksha, or liberation from the cycle of rebirth.

*sannyasa*  The last stage of life in which a person renounces the world, cultivating an attitude of detachment. Ordinarily, persons over fifty take on the role of Sannyasin (male) or Sannyasi (female). Hinduism defines various stages of life and activities appropriate to each. Sannyasa is the last of these stages.

**Shaivism**  The form of Hindu practice and worship focusing on Shiva as Lord and ultimate principle of being. Like other types of Hinduism that understand Brahman as personal, Shaivism is characterized by regular bhakti worship in the home, at festivals, and in pujas.

**Shaktism**  Shaktism is the Hindu practice of worshipping Brahman understood as the divine mother. In Shaktism, all other male and female gods are understood as manifestations of the ultimate Devi, or female divine. Since the Paleolithic era more than 22,000 years ago, archaeological evidence shows that devotion to the absolute understood as divine feminine has existed as a major tradition within Indian religion. Today Shaktism continues as a widespread devotional understanding of the divine, and various bhakti devotions, especially to female gods, are practiced as forms of shaktism.

**shruti** Meaning "what is heard," it refers to the status of Hindu sacred texts believed to be authored or inspired by Brahman. Shruti texts are the most authoritative and are earlier than smriti.

**smriti** Variously translated as "tradition," "remembrance," and "remembering," the term refers to Hindu sacred texts that, although important, are considered secondary to shruti (inspired) texts. Unlike shruti texts, smriti texts were not given directly by Brahman. They were all composed after the Vedas, Hinduism's primary sacred texts.

**Upanishads** Philosophical commentary on the Vedas, or revealed knowledge. They are often referred to as "Vedanta" or the end of the Veda.

**Vaishnavism** The form of Hindu practice and worship focusing on Vishnu as the supreme Lord and creator. Like other forms of Hinduism that understand Brahman as personal, Vaishnavism is characterized by regular bhakti devotion both in the home and at festivals, as well as pujas.

**Vedas** The oldest Hindu scriptures, composed in Sanskrit, they are believed to be directly revealed by Brahman and are thus referred to as shruti, or "what is heard."

**yoga** This term can refer to many forms of spiritual, physical, and mental practice, among them bhakti yoga, karma yoga, raja yoga, and jnana yoga. Yoga has been important in Hinduism as a way of centering one's self and attaining moksha, or liberation.

## Annotated Bibliography

Swami Bhaskarananda. *Journey from Many to One: Essentials of Advaita Vedanta.* Seattle: Viveka Press, 2009.

This easygoing introduction to Advaita is written for people wishing to start a Hindu practice. The text is extremely accessible and full of helpful analogies, which draw the reader into the spiritual points being made.

Deutsch, Eliot. *Advaita Vedanta: A Philosophical Reconstruction.* Honolulu: University of Hawaii Press, 1973.

A concise treatment of the concepts of Advaita philosophy, this book approaches Advaita as a comprehensive system of thought that can be studied and understood by any student of philosophy in the East or West. It explains concepts like Brahman, the world, the self, epistemology, ethics, moksha, and jnana.

Flood, Gavin. *An Introduction to Hinduism.* Cambridge: Cambridge University Press, 1996.

A general survey of the historical development and diverse philosophical, narrative, and ritual traditions of Hinduism, this book discusses the significance of yoga and the path of renunciation as well as tantric thought. The text's delineation and comparison of the Visnu, Saiva, and Sakta traditions proves especially helpful.

Hay, Jeff. *Hinduism: Religions and Religious Movements.* Farmington Hills, MI: Greenhaven Press, 2006.

This book exemplifies the trend in recent scholarship to deny Hinduism's status as a unified religion. Instead, it treats various historical and modern beliefs and movements as separate phenomena, sometimes connected by emigration and common source texts.

Klostermaier, Klaus. *Hindu and Christian in Vrindaban.* London: SCM Press, 1969.

Klostermaier, a Catholic priest, details his experience of Hinduism while stationed in the holy Indian city of Vrindaban. He discusses his encounter with the Krishna bhakti traditions there, providing an important example of early comparative theological work.

Knott, Kim. *Hinduism: A Very Short Introduction.* Oxford: Oxford University Press, 1996.

This book, part of Oxford University Press's Very Short Introduction series to the world's major religions, offers a blend of historical, sociological, theological, and political information. Knott's text is an excellent choice for readers looking for a brief but thorough overview of Hinduism.

Lopez, Donald S., ed. *Religions of India in Practice.* Princeton: Princeton University Press, 1995.

This edited volume of short essays studies Hinduism through the lens of particular devotional, ritual, and narrative traditions. Its exploration of different aspects of Hindu practice provides a nice balance to texts that focus on the historical development or philosophical traditions of Hinduism.

Rambachan, Anantanand. *The Advaita Worldview: God, World, and Humanity.* Albany: State University of New York Press, 2006.

Rambachan's systematic treatment of Hindu philosophical religion proves especially useful. Like an insider's perspective, the book teaches readers about the coherency of Hindu doctrines, teachings, and philosophy, rather than focusing on what may be foreign to Western audiences.

Renou, Louis. *Hinduism.* New York: Braziller, 1961.

This text offers a good introduction to the study of Hinduism as a unified phenomenon. Less than current on Hindu monism, the text is nonetheless important for its sociological and historical treatment.

Sharma, Arvind. *The Philosophy of Religion and Advaita Vedanta: A Comparative Study in Religion and Reason.* University Park: Pennsylvania State University Press, 1995.

This is perhaps the authors' favorite text on Hinduism. Sharma proceeds topically, delineating Advaita's treatment of subjects ranging from the nature of God to the problem of evil and epistemology. The book offers much to readers already conversant in Christianity's or other religions' basic tenets who want to proceed comparatively, subject by subject.

Thatamanil, John. *The Immanent Divine: God, Creation, and the Human Predicament—An East-West Conversation.* Minneapolis, MN: Fortress Press, 2006.

Those ready for comparative work between Christianity and Hinduism will find Thatamanil's book essential. Written as a comparison between the modern theology of Paul Tillich and Shankara's Advaita, the book centers on the incipient nonduality of Tillich's theology and the radical nondualism of Shankara.

## Internet Resources

### General Information

*beliefnet.com/Faiths/Hinduism/index_old.aspx*

*britannica.com/EBchecked/topic/665848/sanatana-dharma*

*religioustolerance.org/hinduism.htm*

### Images of Hindu Temples

*binscorner.com/pages/w/wonderful-hindu-temples.html*

*terragalleria.com/pictures-subjects/hindu-temples/index.html*

### Websites of Specific Hindu communities

*chinmayamission.org*

*hinduamericanseva.org*

# PART 4: BUDDHISM

*Peter Feldmeier and Heng Sure*

# CHAPTER 13

# An Outsider's Perspective

*Peter Feldmeier*

## What Makes Buddhism So Interesting?

Westerners have been fascinated with Buddhism since classic Buddhist texts were first translated and disseminated by Western scholars well over a century ago. This interest has only increased over the past fifty years. What might be particularly surprising is that the reasons for such interest are utterly varied and even contradictory.

Some scholars, for example, have noticed Buddhist affinity with some expressions of Christian mysticism. Here both traditions emphasize a kind of self-emptiness as a prelude to either Nirvana or union with God. Both also understand that the problem of the human condition is being attached to things that ultimately do not satisfy, and thus clinging to the very things that keep us spiritually stuck. So, even while Buddhism seems so different, denying both soul and God, it may be fundamentally aligned with Christianity in crucial ways.

Others have become interested in Buddhism precisely because it offers an alternative to a Western or Christian perspective. For them, Buddhism offers ways to systematically develop and purify the mind with little to no appeal to supernatural forces or the need for divine grace. Rather, Buddhism directly and immediately demonstrates both the problem of human suffering and its remedy.

Some of the Western fascination with Buddhism can be attributed to claims that Zen Buddhism can be positively embraced by Christianity. Forty years ago, highly respected Jesuit missionaries recommended Zen insights and practices for Christians. Even more recently, respected Christians have received official designations as *Roshis* (Zen masters) and even claim that the traditions can unite. Such Christians argue that Zen is not about doctrine, but about directly seeing and participating in reality. As Zen's founder, Bodhidharma taught, "A special transmission outside the scriptures, not founded upon words or letters; by pointing directly to one's mind; it lets one see into one's own true nature, and thus attain Buddhahood."[1]

Another reason Buddhism interests many in the West is the enigmatic nature of Nirvana, the term that names Buddhism's objective. Is Nirvana, as the absolute transcendental reference in Buddhism, God? Is it the kingdom of God or heaven? The challenge to make sense of the nature of Nirvana attracts many Westerners.

---

1. Heinrich Dumoulin, *Zen Buddhism: A History*, vol. 1, *India and China*, trans. James Heisig and Paul Knitter (New York: Macmillan, 1999), 85.

# The Buddha's Life and Unique Teaching

According to Hinduism, one's karma, which is derived from the quality of one's moral and spiritual life, determines the quality of one's rebirth. A religiously devout and moral life generates good karmic energy leading to a better rebirth, such as a better human life, or even an existence in a god-like state, while a morally and religiously bankrupt life creates bad karmic energy leading to a painful rebirth. Even the most sublime existences are eventually subject to decay and are ultimately pointless. Finding a way to escape (moksha) the endless wandering (samsara) from one rebirth to another requires higher knowledge, extraordinary virtue, and intensive meditation. Such a vigorous life (or series of lives) enables one to stop identifying with one's body, emotions, or thoughts and discover that the core of one's existence (atman) identifies with ultimate reality (Brahman). When one realizes this identification, one becomes liberated. This is the goal of Hinduism.

The Buddha, who lived in the fifth century BCE, shared this broad Hindu understanding almost entirely. He too believed in karma and rebirth, and he advocated seeking an escape from samsara. But he thought many of his Hindu contemporaries were wrong in important ways, some of which would ensure that adherents would not achieve moksha. First, he (and some others) challenged the caste system and the dominance of Brahmanic rituals. In his view, the real Brahmin was anyone who was enlightened, and enlightenment had nothing to do with Brahmanic rituals or sacrifice. Second, he insisted there was no atman (self) and no Brahman (ultimate reality). Thus, he challenged the ultimate goal of Hinduism.

The Buddha, whose name was Siddhartha Gautama, was a prince of a small kingdom in northern India (today Nepal). According to legend, his father wanted him to grow accustomed to a kingly lifestyle and to avoid whatever might spark religious consciousness. His father tried to ensure he did not encounter unpleasant things, inside the palace or out. By the time Siddhartha reached his late twenties, however, he had experienced four realities. On separate occasions he saw an old man, a sick man, a corpse, and a holy man. That is, he saw the reality of old age, sickness, and death, and then someone devoted to escaping these inevitable realities of life. Surely, it is not as though such possibilities had never occurred to him. Rather, Siddhartha *absorbed* these facts deeply into his consciousness. Ashvaghosha, his biographer, writes, "When he thus gained insight into the fact that the blemishes of disease, old age, and death vitiate the very core of this world, he lost at the same moment all self-intoxication."[2]

Siddhartha left the palace and found a great spiritual master who taught him *Samkhya,* an advanced form of Hindu psychology and metaphysics. After mastering all the subtleties of Samkhya, he learned from another master the most advanced meditation practices of the day, which again he quickly mastered. Finally, he devoted himself to severe asceticism, particularly fasting, as a method of detaching from all things and achieving moksha (escape). He found that none of these, least of all asceticism, gave him true freedom. Siddhartha realized that he had mastered the best philosophy, meditational practices, and ascetic practices of the day and had found them all wanting. After this realization, he accepted a pious woman's offering of boiled rice and milk and determined to sit under a papal tree, known henceforth as a *bodhi* (enlightenment) tree, and to remain there until he achieved moksha. It was here where he

---

2. Edward Conze, ed., *Buddhist Scriptures* (New York: Penguin, 1959), 43.

Siddhartha Gautama attaining Nirvana under the Bodhi tree. This is the occasion when he became the Buddha, or "awakened one."

discovered the core truth about reality and the means to achieve moksha. These are the Four Noble Truths. From that point on, Siddhartha was the *Buddha*, which means "awakened one." The Buddha spent the rest of his life teaching others how to become awakened as well. He called this awakening Nirvana.

## The Canon

The Buddha started a monastic order of men, and later women, who memorized his sermons. After his death, many prominent disciples gathered at the Council of Vesali and recited these sermons. They also discussed rules for monks. There was a great deal of disagreement about both, particularly regarding the material legislating monastic life. This led to a number of schools or subtraditions of Buddhism. The surviving school of this early period is now known as the Theravada tradition, or "way of the elders." It wasn't until the first century BCE that the Theravada tradition developed a canon of written texts. By then the "authentic" teachings of the Buddha were impossible to verify. The canon reflects thinking that developed over centuries, critically examining the nature of the person, psyche, and path. This massive canon has three sections: (1) *vinaya*, which are rules for monastic life; (2) *suttas*, which represent the Buddha's teachings; and (3) *abhidhamma*, which elaborate on and scrutinize those teachings.

The Theravada canon includes some 2,500 suttas (*sutras* in Sanskrit), some of them quite long. Because it is so unwieldy, the tradition focuses on some parts of the canon as most important. A small part of the canon consists of a collection of Buddha's sayings called the Dhammapada. This serves as a kind of canon within a canon and many monastics memorize it. Other important texts include the suttas on Turning the Wheel of Truth, Sublime States, Foundations of Mindfulness, Fire Sermon, and Buddha's Farewell Address.

## Buddhist Holiness: Knowing the Truth and Living the Skillful Life

### The Four Noble Truths

Virtually everything the Buddha taught was grounded in the Four Noble Truths that he learned the night he became awakened. Briefly, the Four Noble Truths are as follows: (1) life is suffering, (2) the cause of suffering is craving,

(3) suffering ends when craving ends, which is Nirvana, and (4) one achieves the end of suffering by following the Eightfold Path of Right Understanding, Right Thought, Right Speech, Right Action, Right Livelihood, Right Effort, Right Mindfulness, and Right Concentration.

To many Western ears, framing the spiritual life in this way and suggesting that everything is suffering sounds negative and even absurd. The word translated here as suffering is *dukkha*, and the concept of dukkha is complex. Dukkha could be translated very differently, such as "dissatisfaction, unease, stress, pain," or even simply "not fully satisfying." There are also different kinds of dukkha. For example, dukkha-dukkha means something literally painful, say, dropping a hammer on your foot. *Viparinama-dukkha* refers to the dissatisfaction that arises when we experience change. Even if an experience is enjoyable, dissatisfaction can arise when the joy diminishes. Finally, there is *sankara-dukkha*, which refers to the fact that all states, except Nirvana, have the liability of lacking any kind of ultimacy. Because these states are not absolute, they cannot provide a place of refuge free of craving.

In Buddhist thought, this is how the craving mind works: We falsely think we have a self, that there is something personal, eternal, and essential about our existence. So we stay attached to our experience. (Conventionally, we can talk about ourselves, which proves useful as long as we realize that there is no *real* self underneath it all.) If an experience is satisfying, we feel attraction; if dissatisfying, we feel aversion. Unless we realize that the idea of an eternal self is a delusion, we are constantly jerked around by feelings of attraction and aversion. While sometimes quite subtle, these nonetheless dominate the mind.

Perhaps the Buddha's message could be considered as follows: We are imprisoned by a reactive mind. We can make the prison cell more comfortable with good karma, but until we address what imprisons us, we will find ourselves forever caught. The Eightfold Path provides the means to escape for good. It is the only way to freedom.

## The Eightfold Path

The categories of the Eightfold Path discussed above fit into three subcategories: virtue, mental discipline, and wisdom. The cultivation of virtue for the Buddhist includes Right Speech, Right Action, and Right Livelihood. Right Speech is speech that must be useful, gentle, edifying, and truthful. In some circumstances, speech can and should be challenging, but even then it would be offered humbly and with the intention of pursuing a wholesome outcome. Right Action resembles speech but applies to activities. It refers to conduct that is peaceful and respectful of life. It would not be unusual for many Buddhists to refrain from killing even an insect that is biting them. Right Livelihood consists of a profession that does not lead to harming others or oneself. Buddhists strive for employment that brings wholesome goods and services to others.

The second subcategory in the Eightfold Path, mental discipline, involves Right Effort, Right Mindfulness, and Right Concentration. Right Effort intends to cultivate wholesome states of mind that lead to a sound psyche as well as possibilities for deep meditation. Right Effort also involves developing a balanced mind, one both focused and open. The Buddha once compared the right mental energy to a stringed instrument. The string should be taut, not loose, but not so tight as to vibrate improperly or even break. Right Mindfulness involves diligent awareness of the dynamics of mind and body. It entails recognizing the qualities of one's experience and one's relationship to that experience. Am I inclining toward it, averting from it? Here one also watches the phenomena of mind and body arise and dissipate. This leads to the realization that there is nothing substantial in any experience (or experiencing self) and thus nothing substantial to be controlled by (indeed, no substantive self to be controlled). Finally Right Concentration cultivates a strong, wholesome mind. One traditional commentator, Buddhaghosa, taught that there are forty meditation subjects. Some counteract negative mental states. So if one were vain about one's looks, a good meditation would consist of contemplating a corpse rotting. The objective of other meditations is the cultivation of positive mental states. A faithful, emotional psyche might do well meditating on the qualities of the Buddha, which would help one both revere the Buddha and appropriate those qualities for oneself. Finally, some meditational objects are meant to develop deep concentration.

The final subcategory, wisdom, includes Right Thought and Right Understanding. Right Thought consists of one's vision or perspective. It includes commitment to not being attached to or identified with our experience. At a basic level, Right Thought means accepting the Buddhist perspective on a notional level. As one gets deeper into the practice of Buddhism, one recognizes how attachments work on the mind and how suffering comes from them. Right Thought intimately aligns with Right Understanding, which is the discovery of the impermanence of all things and the absolute lack of selfhood in what makes up a human being.

# The Self and Nirvana

## What Is the Self?

The Buddha taught that all reality has three characteristics: impermanence, no-self, and suffering (dukkha). His Hindu counterparts cautioned against identifying with or getting lost in a superficial sense of self (one's body and thoughts). But unlike his Hindu counterparts, who taught that there is a core, atman, underneath, he taught there is no atman at all. To believe an atman exists is part of the delusion one suffers from in this life.

The Buddha taught that the *conventional* self is made up of five impersonal aggregates (literally "bundles"): materiality, feeling, perception, mental formations, and consciousness. In a famous dialogue between the Buddhist monk Nagasena and King Melinda, Nagasena asks what a chariot is and the king tells him it is an arrangement of an axle, wheels, a carriage, and so on. Nagasena presses him to identify its essence, and the king replies that the chariot has no essence. This is the same as the self, Nagasena argues; the self has no essence but *self* is the conventional term used to describe the collection of the five aggregates.

One of the most important teachings of the Buddha regarding the self can be translated as "dependent coarising." This refers to all of these impersonal aggregates mutually conditioning each other. They all relate to and affect one another, and in a sense they collectively *cause* existence. Because of dependent coarising, we have a particularly difficult time seeing the impersonal aggregates for what they are. Many of the Buddha's meditations are designed to disentangle our mind so as to see how the aggregates work and that there is no self, and thus identifying with our experience is absurd.

## Karma

Buddhist understanding of how the person is reborn and the quality of that rebirth has everything to do with karma. Karma both produces the condition that causes rebirth and sustains the human being. Ignorance causes karma and gives rise to craving and clinging. So karma is the energy for rebirth and aggregate formation, and it is perpetuated constantly throughout life by craving. All of this ties together in the mind.

© Sheldan Collins / Corbis

A *thangka* is a traditional painting on silk with embroidery, typically Tibetan. This *thangka* depicts the Wheel of Life, or realms of rebirth, with Yama, the god of death, presiding over judgment.

Ignorance of the three characteristics of all reality (impermanence, no-self, and suffering) conditions craving—it makes us want to identify with and cling to our experience. Ironically, the process of craving keeps the mind from seeing these central characteristics clearly.

Such ignorance causes and shapes a craving mind, and thus leads to even more volitions. By *volition* Buddhists mean an "intention involving craving." Someone who is enlightened surely intends things. But this intention is neither caused by nor cultivates an attachment or narcissistic clinging. In this sense, it is as though

wisdom itself acts. There is no-self behind the action, and when one realizes this truth, karma ceases to be produced. Without karma there is no energy for rebirth, and attaining awakening, or Nirvana, is the way to stop karma production.

## Self and Nirvana

This problem of the self raises a lot of questions. What is it that frees the self to see that there is no-self and so attain Nirvana, the ultimate refuge for the self? What happens to an enlightened person after death? Is there a super-secret self that can't be discussed or addressed? Would this survive for some existence after death (final-Nirvana)? Or is final-Nirvana simply extinction? The Buddhist would respond that its teachings only have an instrumental use: they are used only to lead to Nirvana. Additionally, Buddhists speak of two kinds of truth: conventional truth (*sammuti-sacca*) and ultimate truth (*paramattha-sacca*), Nirvana being ultimate. The Buddha was silent about Nirvana and what happens after death for those who have attained it. In one teaching, the Buddha used two similes regarding doctrine. The first involved holding a poisonous snake and the second holding on to a raft to get across the river. Taken together, they describe how a good Buddhist should deal with doctrine. Regarding the snake, you grasp it with great skill, firmly but not tightly. Regarding the raft, once you get to the other side (Nirvana), you let the raft go.

Nirvana references an ultimate truth and therefore cannot be conceptualized very well. It is known as *atakkavacara*, inaccessible to thought, and *avisayasmim*, beyond conceptual range. This holds true, even for the Buddha. That is, even the Buddha himself did not conceptually *understand* Nirvana.

In the end, Buddhists are somewhat dogmatic about what they believe in terms of conventional truth. They have confidence that the Eightfold Path leads to Nirvana. Speculating beyond the teachings that lead to Nirvana distracts one from the path. Indeed, once Nirvana is attained such concerns seem silly.

## Mahayana Shifts in Buddhism

### Introducing the Great Vehicle

The Theravada school, which dominates in Sri Lanka, Thailand, Myanmar, Laos, and Cambodia, probably represents the tradition closest to early Buddhism. This school, however, was only one of perhaps eighteen during the time when the Pali canon was being devised by the Theravada tradition. Other schools of thought and practice represented a contrasting expression of Buddhism, which one can call collectively,

Mahayana or "great vehicle." Mahayana texts claimed an ancient heritage as well and were put down in written form starting in the first century CE. While the Mahayana canon included many of the Theravadin teachings of the Buddha, it also incorporated additional famous teachings, such as the Perfect Wisdom, Diamond, Heart, Vimalakirti, and Lotus sutras. Mahayana also developed philosophical principles not found in Theravada. Arguably the most important of these is that everything is "empty" (*shunyata*) and everything has a characteristic of "suchness" or "thusness" (*tathata*); and these are related. To say that everything is empty—and this would include Nirvana—means that there is nothing separate and absolute. Rather, everything is intrinsically interconnected. This is also to say that everything carries profound truth and

Theravada monks process during the Songkran (water) festival in Sukhothai, Thailand. Even here they carry their "begging bowl," as they depend on the generosity of the laity.

beauty, even Nirvana itself; this is what is meant by "suchness."

The Theravada school has a strong monastic tradition, which tends to emphasize individual liberation, or enlightenment. This can make Theravada Buddhism, especially its monastics, appear self-centered to outsiders. However, monks and lay people see themselves as mutually supportive: lay people give monks material support (*dana*) and monks offer lay people spiritual support (*dhamma dana*). Monks also note the Buddha's strong emphasis on monasticism, and that personal liberation has everything to do with living in the world free from greed and filled with compassion. For them, seeking enlightenment is exactly the opposite of being self-centered.

In contrast, the Mahayana tradition holds great confidence that the lay life can be extraordinarily profound and holy. According to Mahayana, buddha nature permeates the entire universe. One does not have to go off to a monastery to discover this. Rather, since it is right before us and indeed part of us, we can express the Buddha's teaching profoundly here and now. In fact, the lay life could even be better than monasticism.

## Reconceptualizing Dependent Coarising

The differences between Theravada and Mahayana traditions are exemplified by how Mahayana changes the notion of dependent coarising. In the Theravada school this concept described how each person conditions his or her own rebirth. In the Mahayana tradition, the term rarely references this personal preoccupation at all. Rather, it almost always refers to the interconnectedness of everything in the universe. Mahayana believes that the universe is completely interpenetrating. While all Buddhists believe that there is no "I" or atman underneath the aggregates, Mahayana

claims this primarily because there is no such thing as a discretely separate independent being.

Mahayana Buddhism believes that the universe is like an interpenetrating web of life. Everything is interconnected on some level. While this tradition recognizes that everyone has an individual center of consciousness, Mahayana thinkers caution that even one's own center is not isolated from the rest of reality. In Mahayana, compassion and wisdom involve moving beyond the notion of an isolated individual seeking Nirvana. By recognizing the delusion of a separate existence, one also sees that the suffering in the world is really one's own suffering and that the release from suffering in the world is necessary for one's own release. For example, one of the most inspiring practices in Tibetan practice is *tong-len*, a meditation that takes into one's own consciousness the energy of another's suffering in order to heal and purify it by one's own love and compassion. Paradoxically, this practice increases one's own happiness.

## The Bodhisattva Vow

In the Theravada tradition a bodhisattva is a being on the cusp of enlightenment who temporarily renounces enlightenment and vows to train in the spiritual perfections (generosity, morality, renunciation, wisdom, energy, patience, truthfulness, determination, loving-kindness, and equanimity) to the ultimate degree. This being waits to be reborn on earth for the time when, in becoming a buddha, he can lead the most people to enlightenment. This is extraordinary and only applies to those rare individuals throughout eternity who have or will become a buddha. In the Mahayana tradition, the idea of a bodhisattva (and bodhisattva vow) broadens and morphs, referring to anyone on the path who vows to forestall Nirvana until every being in the universe experiences Nirvana. A bodhisattva vow is the promise to take all of one's good karma and apply that merit to the service of all beings and their enlightenment, and this virtually for eternity.

This stunning vow represents something beyond mere heroism. If one were to think about a Mahayana understanding of reality, one might ask: since everything is interrelated, could an individual even attain Nirvana alone? That is, in the absence of an absolute "I" completely distinguished from others, the "I" could not attain Nirvana until all do simultaneously. In one Mahayana text, the Buddha addresses this very point: "All these living creatures are my children to whom I will give equally the Great Vehicle, so that none will gain an individual Nirvana."[3] Mahayana Buddhists would say that the bodhisattva vow expresses proper intention for one's life: serving others by seeking to relieve their suffering and support their enlightenment.

## Buddhist Practices

### The Brahma Viharas

As mentioned above, meditation was central to the Buddha's teaching. Some particularly fruitful meditation strategies occupy a central place in Buddhist practice and spirituality. Among them are those called the Brahma Viharas (Divine Abidings), also known as the Four Sublime States or Unlimitables. These meditations are loving-kindness (*metta*), compassion (*karuna*), sympathetic joy (*mudita*), and equanimity (*upekkha*). Collectively, they represent an ideal way of relating to others, and one that reflects spiritual maturity. The Buddha promised that those who focus on these meditations will enjoy numerous benefits including a serene and happy life, a radiant face, and the protection of

*devas* (godlike beings) and animals. In each of these four meditations, one takes on the particular quality—for example, loving-kindness—as a meditative subject and extends it progressively to all beings in the entire universe.

The four Brahma Viharas balance each other. Compassion balances sympathetic joy and keeps it from degenerating into sentimentality or fanciful optimism. Sympathetic joy keeps compassion from brooding over suffering. The boundless nature of loving-kindness extends conscious care to the whole universe. And equanimity provides balance for the above three. Without practicing equanimity, one can slip into some form of control or attachment around another. In terms of proper relationship with oneself and the world, probably nothing compares to the Brahma Viharas. When deeply ingrained in the psyche, they represent the Buddhist ethos perfectly.

### Devotions and Holy Days

Because Buddhism is so diverse, Buddhist practices, rituals, and celebrations are likewise highly varied. In fact, the religious practices of many Buddhists in Southeast Asia might look rather confusing to Westerners. One could easily find a devout Buddhist in Sri Lanka offering devotion, or puja, to a Hindu god such as Shiva or Ganesh before heading to the local temple to light incense to a statue of the Buddha. Many Thai Buddhists have miniature temples on their roofs dedicated to guardian spirits, to whom they offer food and flowers daily. This may even be the case for Thai monks. They would not see themselves as blurring Buddhism with Hinduism or spirit religions. Rather, they take seriously the Hindu and Buddhist belief in a complex cosmology where spirits and gods are

---

3. E.A. Burtt, ed., *The Teachings of the Compassionate Buddha: Early Discourses, the Dhammapada and Later Basic Writings* (New York: New American Library, 2000), 124.

active in the world, and where merit-making (good karma) is valuable, even if it will not directly lead one to Nirvana.

When Buddhists visit shrines, they are reminded of the qualities of the Buddha and venerate the Buddha as their guide and inspiration. They come with folded hands at the level of the chest, a symbol of reverence. Usually, they prostrate themselves before a statue or image of the Buddha. Venerators also light candles and offer incense, fruit, or flowers. All this, too, is merit-making, and deepens their devotion to the path.

Like most religions, Buddhism has a number of festival days. Buddhist New Year is an important holiday. In Theravadin countries it is celebrated for three days from the first full moon day in April. In Mahayana countries, such as China, Korea, and Vietnam, it is celebrated in late January or early February, according to the lunar calendar. Vesak or "Buddha Day" simultaneously celebrates his birth, enlightenment, and death. It is perhaps the holiest day for Buddhists. Asalha Puja Day marks Buddha's first teaching and is celebrated on the full moon day of the eighth lunar month. There are a number of similar commemorations broadly noted in the Buddhist calendar, as well as specific ones relevant to different countries or traditions, such as Kandy, Sri Lanka's Festival of the Tooth, where a relic of the Buddha's tooth, which is normally kept in a great temple, is paraded through the streets.

On festival days, lay people usually go to local monasteries or temples and offer food to the monks. The laity will renew their moral commitments and might even take on the stricter monastic moral code for the day. They will also distribute food to the poor, listen to dharma talks by monks, and walk around the temple or shrine three times to commemorate their three refuges: the Buddha, the Dharma, and the Sangha (monastic community). Such a festival day typically concludes with chanting and meditation.

A Burmese monk venerates the "reclining Buddha," an expression of the peace of enlightenment, at the Manuha pagoda in Pagan Myanmar.

© Luca I. Tettoni / CORBIS

## Dialogue and the Future

In 1896, at the Parliament of World Religions in Chicago, Mahayana Buddhists introduced themselves to a large Western stage. This may have been the beginning of the modern Buddhist-Christian dialogue. While friendships were made and communication between participants continued throughout their lives, Buddhist-Christian dialogue lay fallow for decades. Then in the 1950s interest reemerged with monastics from both traditions writing and visiting each other, inspiring new possibilities for spiritual understanding. Along with this monastic experience, several books were published that highlighted possible ways to appropriate the spirit of the other tradition, including D.T. Suzuki's *Mysticism: Christian and Buddhist* and Alan Watts's *The Way of Zen*. Some of Christianity's and Buddhism's most influential monastics have engaged in Buddhist-Christian dialogue, including Christians such as Thomas Merton, Wayne Teasdale, and David Steindl-Rast, and Buddhists such as the Dalai Lama, Thich Nhat Hanh, and Ajahn Buddhadasa.

In recent years institutional and structured forms of dialogue have taken place. Such examples include the Monastic Interreligious Dialogue, which focuses on Buddhist-Christian engagement, the Society for Buddhist-Christian Studies, and the Journal of Buddhist-Christian Studies. Each helps Buddhists and Christians better understand both the religious other and their own tradition in light of the other's religious expression.

Some forms of Buddhist-Christian dialogue are less fruitful than others. The least helpful expression of dialogue between Christians and Buddhists focuses on differences and similarities in doctrine. How far can one go comparing and contrasting propositional claims, particularly when these traditions are so dissimilar, and their teachings are used in very different ways?

More fruitful discussions revolve around such questions as how does the belief in no-self *function* in the Buddhist religious tradition? That is, instead of focusing just on the teaching of the impermanent aggregates, how would looking at oneself in this manner allow for a kind of spiritual freedom unknown to the West? Could the Buddhist framing of religious practice associated with no-self provide insights for Christians in rethinking the nature of a soul or the nature of religious practice? Christians might also ask whether Mahayana dependent coarising can open up new ways of thinking about the mystical body of Christ or cosmic Christ. Some Buddhists have been surprised by how much Christians emphasize the passionate love of Jesus Christ and wonder if metta (loving-kindness) as traditionally framed is a bit too flat. They are discovering ways in which deeply passionate love can be spiritually profound, rather than problematic.

Even more fruitful dialogue has been influenced by interreligious practice, particularly Christians who have embraced Buddhist meditation practices. Because Buddhism has no deity, engaging many of its traditions is less compromising than, say, participating in Hindu rituals worshipping Krishna. In focusing on religious practices, one gets inside a religious sensibility in ways that mere conceptual dialogue alone cannot. Meditative practices that focus on Right Understanding, for example, helps one recognize that much of what one would identify as "I" or "mine" is really quite impersonal and impermanent after all.

# CHAPTER 14

# An Insider's Perspective

*Heng Sure*

## A Mahayana Perspective

Buddhism encompasses a wealth of forms and traditions. The last chapter explored the Theravada tradition, and many Westerners have some familiarity with Zen Buddhism, which is part of the Mahayana tradition. Less well known are Buddhist traditions that come by way of China. In fact, Japanese forms of the Zen tradition in many aspects directly copied their Chinese sources: their ritual style, their cultural and linguistic idioms such as parables and koans, their interpretations of the Buddha's teaching, and their formulation of dharma practices were essentially Chinese. Indeed, the Chinese tradition of the Mahayana, "the Northern tradition," includes a wealth of Chinese texts and practices that stretch back 2,000 years. The Chan tradition informed Buddhist East Asia, but few people in America know of it.

For nearly fifty years, from 1949 until the late 1990s, few people had access to the treasures of the Chinese Mahayana. Mao Tse-tung and his version of Marxism viewed religious practice as harmful to a communist utopia. The so-called bamboo curtain made study of the dharma impossible. Scholars could not come and go, and few Chinese monks emerged from China. Those who did faced language barriers that made communication difficult.

Theravada Buddhism from Sri Lanka and Thailand, on the other hand, faced no such obstacles to study, for it had arrived in the West in English translations done largely by scholars and missionaries. Learning about Chinese Buddhism, on the other hand, required mastering Chinese and traveling to Taiwan or Hong Kong or else working from secondary sources. For these reasons Westerners to this day have little knowledge of the flourishing of the Pure Land tradition or the rich resources of the Chinese Buddhist canon. When pioneer monks arrived in the West in 1962 and translated the texts and practices of the Buddha's dharma in China, people finally had access to the living Chan tradition of the Sixth Patriarch, the Pure Land school of Buddhist devotion, the lore of the bodhisattvas, including the inconceivable responses of Guan Shi Yin (the Bodhisattva of Great Compassion), and so many other treasures of the Mahayana. This chapter explores these treasures, examining Buddhist texts and practices from the Mahayana perspective.

## What Makes Buddhism Attractive in the West?

### The Nontheistic Nature of Buddhism

For individuals raised in Christian or Jewish traditions (or other theistic forms of belief), the lack of a creator deity in Buddhism may require some mental adjustment. Is Buddhism simply "godless"? If so, what is the proper role for an aspiring devotee in a tradition without a creator? Newcomers to Buddhist practice report a variety of answers—from relief at the absence of a distant, all-powerful patriarchal authority figure to a certain uneasiness at the lack of a vigilant shepherd watching over his flock. In what ways is the Buddha godlike—and in what ways not godlike at all? When the Buddha in the Avatamsaka Sutra states that "everything is made from mind alone,"[1] is he talking about creation?

Some of the early English writings on Buddhism[2] claim that Buddhism is entirely atheistic, that it believes in no deity at all. This notion, however, needs clarification. The Mahayana sutras mention gods in three different levels of heavens, performing many functions, including on occasion speaking the dharma on behalf of the Buddha. Gods make offerings to buddhas and bodhisattvas, and they appear before practitioners to test their sincerity. They invite the Buddha into their celestial palaces and then serve as his audience for dharma teachings. They intervene in the affairs of humans and hold a space in the Brahma Heavens. An atheistic religion would hardly present gods so frequently or in such vivid detail.

From the Mahayana perspective, then, Buddhism is not atheistic; nor is it monotheistic like the Abrahamic faiths. Instead, Buddhism is nontheistic; the teachings of the dharma did not proceed from a creator deity, nor did they come from prophetic revelation, from truths handed down by a divine being to a prophet. Instead, they came by realization, from a human's transformation of his own consciousness through diligent spiritual cultivation.

## Orthopraxy, Not Orthodoxy

Another quality of Buddhism many find attractive is its emphasis on orthopraxy ("right practice") as opposed to orthodoxy ("right belief"). The Abrahamic traditions of the Bible also invite believers to experience the fruits of practice for themselves, but Buddhism makes this overt. What matters most for Buddhist disciples is not whether they say they believe in or accept a statement made by the Buddha. What matters most is how they practice according to the methods of the Buddha. Belief is important—indeed, the Pure Land devotional tradition has been called "the Buddhism of faith." The difference is this: somebody who works at holding precepts purely, entering profound samadhi (concentration) and activating their inherent wisdom will become a Buddha regardless of their never having said even once, "I believe in what the Buddha said." Professing faith is unimportant; cultivating the dharma correctly is essential.

Orthopraxy matters because the dharma is based on cause and effect. Merely professing belief will not help one move toward liberation. Orthodoxy proves useless if one fails to put that belief into practice. By cultivating the dharma as the Buddha taught it, one can wake up, or become enlightened, regardless of any profession of belief in the Buddha. This is true at all levels of the Buddhist community of believers. Advanced bodhisattvas have mastered pure conduct; they do not grow morally lax because of seniority.

In the Kalama Sutta, the Buddha tells a tribe of disbelievers, the Kalamas, how to deal with their doubts about teachers and their doctrines:

> Kalamas: Don't go by reports, by legends, by traditions, by scripture, by logical conjecture, by inference, by analogies, by agreement

1. Author's unpublished translation.

2. Among them, Walpole Rahula's perennial introduction to Theravada Buddhism: *What the Buddha Taught*, 2nd ed. (New York: Grove Press, 1974).

through pondering views, by probability, or by the thought, "This contemplative is our teacher." When you know for yourselves that, "These qualities are unskillful; these qualities are blameworthy; these qualities are criticized by the wise; these qualities, when adopted and carried out, lead to harm and to suffering"—then you should abandon them.[3]

The Buddha essentially deconstructs his own religious authority. He tells the Kalamas to challenge all truths and ideas by applying these criteria for belief. After giving the Kalama tribe ten sources of information open to analysis, the Buddha concludes with advice on how to discern and accept truth, free of doubts:

> Kalamas, when you know for yourselves that these qualities are skillful, that these qualities are blameless and these qualities are praised by the wise, moreover these qualities, when adopted and carried out, lead to welfare and to happiness, you should undertake them.[4]

In Buddhist practice, teachings come directly from the Buddha's experience. In other words, the fundamentals of the dharma are embedded in the founding story of the Buddha's six years of practice in the forest before his enlightenment. He studied and mastered the various yogas taught by the gurus or adepts in his vicinity and then either discarded or adapted their methods to his own needs. After his meditation carried him to ultimate awakening, the prince (who was now the Buddha) transmitted his methods to anybody who cared to follow him. To this day, one who studies the dharma encounters the very practices the Buddha used along the Path.

One might consider the dharma-teachings as "public domain," that is to say, for the 2,550 years since the Buddha's time, his dharma-methods have always been offered to practitioners without requirement of membership or profession of faith. Catholics, Jews, scientists, atheists, and non-Buddhists of all descriptions are welcome to take up any practices they find suitable and appropriate. Committed believers of any tradition can delve deeply into meditation practice and gain the fruits of insight without compromising their cultural and religious identities. This situation also creates a rich environment for sharing practices among interfaith communities.

## Buddha's Life and Teaching

Prince Siddhartha lived a life of affluence. His future promised the power, authority, wealth, and hedonistic indulgence known only to royalty. Further, the prince had mastered every aspect of his training for the throne: charioteering, archery, wrestling, logic, debate, and statesmanship. No challenge defeated him. However, despite his father's attempts to keep him from asking questions that would lead him to realize the limitations to his freedom, the inevitable happened: Siddhartha woke up to the truth of impermanence. He saw the approach of old age, sickness, and death and realized that all the pleasures and glory of a king's life come to nothing in the end. Seeing the limits to his freedom, he asked himself, "Is this where life leads?" The prince challenged himself to overcome mortality and find freedom from samsara, the endless rounds of birth, death, and rebirth. Finding the Middle Way between extremes of asceticism and sense

---

3. Kalama Sutta: To the Kalamas (AN 3.65) 1994–2012, trans. Thanissaro Bhikkhu, *accesstoinsight.org/tipitaka/an/an03/an03.065.than.html.*

4. Ibid.

pleasure, he succeeded in putting an end to thoughts of desire in his mind. Having identified the source of his afflictions, he became the Buddha, "the Awakened One."

He explained his methods for realizing bodhi, or awakening, for forty-nine years. In the Theravada tradition, these methods included the Four Noble Truths and the Eightfold Path among others. In the Mahayana teachings, the Buddha emphasized the Six Paramitas (Perfections) and the Ten Thousand Practices.

A unique aspect of sharing his Path is that every individual who practices the Buddha's methods has the potential to become a buddha. Anyone who applies himself and replicates the Buddha's own process, as the Buddha exhorted his followers to do, does so fully expecting to replace the Buddha, so to speak, to become identical with the Buddha in wisdom and compassion. This is possible for several reasons: first, buddhas are perfected humans, not divine; and second, the Path is inward, not external. One achieves full awakening by transforming ignorance and afflictions in the mind to bodhi, or enlightened awareness.

## The Canon

It is said the Buddha refused his disciples' requests to write down his teachings, insisting they remain accessible to all. Literacy in the agrarian culture of India was rare; only priests and royalty had the opportunity to learn to read and write. The dharma, however, was meant for use by people in need, so the Buddha gave the task of transmitting the teachings to his monastic *sangha* (community), which maintained the oral tradition. Once written down, scripture becomes the possession of a literate elite, that is, religious professionals who tend the libraries of texts and who are charged with protecting their sacred literature. The ordinary suffering sentient

being, for whom the dharma was spoken, would have to go through the priests to find the principles and learn their healing methods. By keeping the dharma oral and opening up membership in the sangha clergy to anybody, regardless of their caste background, the Buddha democratized access to the scriptures.

From this perspective, the oral tradition is indeed not an inferior medium for transmitting received knowledge. Along with the advantages mentioned above, chanting or singing sacred texts from memory has proven the most reliable vehicle for transmitting tradition through generations. For example, in traditional Hindu communities, the Sanskrit Vedas survive to this day in an oral tradition, carried by pandits, young Brahmins carefully trained for this sacred task. These young men have prodigious memories and astonishing recall of sacred texts and liturgies. In the Buddhist sangha, the fortnightly recitation of the monastic rule, the Pratimoksha (Pattimokha), is ideally done from memory.

The Buddha's sutras were delivered often as solutions to problems, rarely as sermons or philosophical treatises. They offered practical meditation instructions and solutions to disciples' daily concerns. The contents of the Buddhist Tripitaka, or "Three Baskets," are the Sutra (*pitaka*), which contain the Buddha's words; the Shastra (*pitaka*), commentaries appended over the centuries by the Buddha's learned disciples; and the Vinaya (*pitaka*), which contains the rules for regulating the monastic sangha.

The Three Baskets exist in both Pali and Sanskrit compilations. The Pali canon, studied by the Theravada tradition, calls the second basket the Abhidhamma (the highest dhamma), and it functions by and large as the repository for commentarial literature. In the Mahayana canon, the sutras, Shastra, and Vinaya texts came down not through the Pali language but through Sanskrit, which is also the language of the Vedas. Texts from all three baskets are in daily use and a portion has been translated out of Sanskrit and Pali into the world's languages.[5]

Unlike the Ten Commandments and biblical prophetic literature, sutras arise not through revelation but through realization. The source of the realized insights is the mind in *samadhi*, a meditative state of stillness, purity, and awareness. For this reason, the Three Baskets of the Tripitaka is not a closed canon. Potentially, any individual who cultivates the dharma and realizes buddhahood could produce a sutra identical in principle to the Buddha's. Texts have been added to the sutra basket through the Tang Dynasty, in tenth century China.

The sutras of the Mahayana comprise some of the most profound and sublime religious literature in human heritage. They include such famous texts as the Lotus Sutra, the Diamond (Vajra Prajna Paramita) Sutra, the Shurangama Sutra, and the expansive Avatamsaka or Flower Garland Sutra. These texts are voluminous and diverse, containing descriptions of the Buddha's psychological transformation from consciousness to wisdom as well as explanations of the thinking and behavior of bodhisattvas (awakened beings), who live inspiring lives of service to others. The Lotus Sutra explains the path to buddhahood, while the Shurangama describes the methods of cultivating samadhi.

The Avatamsaka Sutra explains the many stages of the bodhisattva path and then follows the theory section with one of Buddhist literature's crowning achievements: an epic story of a young man's successful quest for bodhi

This plaster cast of the original relief from the eighth century depicts the aspirant Sudhana receiving enlightenment from the bodhisattva Samantabhadra.

© Universal History Archive / UIG / Getty Images

---

5. Texts exist in English, Chinese, Korean, Japanese, Vietnamese, Mongolian, Tibetan, and Silk Route scripts, such as Sogdian, Khotanese, and Uighur. Efforts are underway to bring the Tripitaka into English and other languages of the West. The work of the Buddhist Text Translation Society and Dharma Realm Buddhist University are online at *drbu.org*.

(awakening). In the "Gandhavyuha Chapter,"[6] the Youth Sudhana sets out on a pilgrimage at the behest of the bodhisattva Manjushri and visits in succession fifty-three teachers, twenty-one of whom are women. Each teacher asks him if he has brought forth the resolve for bodhi (*bodhicitta*), the "thought for awakening." Sudhana tells each of these accomplished teachers (a list that includes bodhisattvas Avalokiteshvara, Manjushri, Maitreya, and Samantabhadra, a ship's captain, a prostitute, incense makers, kings, non-Buddhist Brahmins, children, and a host of female spirits who rule the night) that he has. Maitreya bodhisattva witnesses Sudhana's enlightenment and then sends him on to his final teachers, the bodhisattvas Manjushri and Samantabhadra. From Samantabhadra, Sudhana learns the essentials of practice and discovers that even after ultimate awakening, because of their altruistic vows, buddhas do not rest, but continue to teach sentient beings how to transform their afflictions and troubles into wisdom and compassion. The story of Sudhana on his successful quest for the Buddha's wisdom can be considered as one of the epic pilgrimages in world literature.

## The Split in Buddhism: The "Multi-yana" Community

The religious world of India during the Buddha's lifetime was full of contending schools, with debate frequently used as a means of recruiting new students and becoming famous. The Buddha, however, did not contend. He taught through a dialectic process, like Socrates, asking questions of sincere students and leading them gradually to make their own conclusions. He never made philosophical statements for their own sake; nor did he make speculative statements about the nature of the universe. In one discourse he likened metaphysical sophistry to a man who, having been shot by an arrow, first discusses the details of the arrow itself—what the wood is made of, what bird gave its feathers to the arrow, and so on—rather than pull out the shaft and seek medical attention. After making the analogy, the Buddha says that ending birth and death is the central issue; his disciples should give full attention to the methods that lead to liberation, not fruitlessly debate issues that do not lead to liberation.

Indeed, within the sangha order the Buddha always taught expediently, directing certain teachings to various individuals according to their capacity for understanding. In this way, dharma is like medicine and the wise teacher is like a healing physician, dispensing the right antidote to cure the illness of each different sentient being. Sometimes the purity of the arhat (an awakened sage) is the ideal role model for one to emulate; at another time the altruism of the bodhisattva is right. The Buddha teaches according to their potential for awakening. Dharma is shared equally by all Buddhist traditions.

Excavations of the early monasteries in India reveal that followers of Mahayana bodhisattvas and Theravada arhats meditated in the same monasteries. Current thinking on the historical origins of the sangha suggests that both Theravada and Mahayana monks coexisted in the same monasteries and that the Buddha's teaching was heard by different individuals, each according to their potential for understanding. However, for a variety of reasons, Buddhism over its 2,550-year history has experienced certain sectarian differences. The tradition broke into two main schools. The Theravada (Teaching of the Elders) school could be described as the "Southern tradition," with the Mahayana or "great vehicle" as the "Northern tradition."

---

6. Published in eight volumes by the Buddhist Text Translation Society as *Chapter 39: Entering the Dharma Realm.*

© Inti St. Clair / Spaces Images / Corbis

A statue of the Buddha serenely meditating in the full lotus position. One sees here that food alms have been placed in his hands as an expression of devotion.

buddhas, Shifu?" Master Hua replied, "To my mind there are no buddhas at all. There is only great wisdom." The driver was delighted with the answer.

Images from the Thai tradition depict the Buddha sitting with legs crossed in half-lotus posture, while Mahayana images always show the Buddha seated in full-lotus, with both legs crossed. Both images depict a meditator sitting quietly, with his body upright and his mind focused and serene. Contemporary Mahayana and Theravada meditators may use different methods, but all alike are disciples of the Buddha and all strive to walk the same Path the Buddha walked to its end.

## Buddhas and Bodhisattvas

One major difference between the traditions is that, unlike followers of the Theravada, Mahayana devotees worship multiple buddhas in their daily liturgies. Buddha(s) is written in the plural to indicate that the Mahayana tradition honors on a daily basis the historical Buddha, Shakyamuni (the former Prince Siddhartha Gautama); Amitabha, the Buddha of Limitless Light, who created the Western Pure Land of Utmost Happiness; and Baisajyaraja, the Healing Buddha, whose Buddha Realm is known as Lapis Lazuli Light in the East. One might add Maitreya, the Buddha to come, and Vairocana, the Teaching Buddha of the Avatamsaka Sutra. The historical Buddha, Shakyamuni (Siddhartha Gautama), later on in his teaching career introduced these other buddhas and their dharma-methods. The sutra collections in the Pali canon contain the teachings spoken during the years of peripatetic teaching. These particular buddha figures rarely appear in the Pali canon.

What is different, then? The scriptural languages are different, as are the scriptures.[7] Thus, interpretations of the buddhas and the sages who model success are different. Is there one Buddha or many buddhas? A Buddhist layman in Kuala Lumpur driving Venerable Master Hsuan Hua to the airport seized his chance with the senior monk to ask a question that had troubled him: "Here in Malaysia we have both Mahayana and Theravada practitioners, and they disagree. In the end is there just one Buddha or many

---

7. The text and commentary chapter that follows presents the Dhammapada, which belongs to the Pali canon, as well as a section from the Lotus Sutra, which introduces Guan Shi Yin Bodhisattva, lore held sacred by the Mahayana, but that would never appear in the Pali tradition.

The figure of the bodhisattva, however, is so well developed in the Mahayana that to the average Chinese or Vietnamese devotee, attention to and worship of bodhisattva figures rivals worship of buddhas in importance. Avalokiteshvara (the bodhisattva Guan Shi Yin, or Guan Yin) is the only figure in the Mahayana pantheon with three official celebration days in the calendar year. Guan Shi Yin is the Awakened Being of Great Compassion. In her female form she is without doubt the most popular figure for worship in East Asia. Other bodhisattva figures include Ksitigarbha (the Bodhisattva Earth Treasury), Manjushri (the Bodhisattva of Great Wisdom), and Samantabhadra (the Bodhisattva of Great Practices). These four, often referred to as "Celestial Bodhisattvas," function as paragons of altruistic service to all sentient creatures.

### The Bodhisattva Vows

The two signature features of bodhisattvas are their practices and their vows. Each bodhisattva, indeed each buddha, has a distinctive set or number of vows. All Mahayana bodhisattvas adhere to what are known collectively as "The Four Great Bodhisattva Vows":

1. Sentient beings are beyond numbering; even so, I vow to save them all.
2. Afflictions are infinite; even so, I vow to transform them all.
3. Methods of practice are beyond measuring; even so, I vow to master them all.
4. The Buddha's Way is the highest Path; even so, I vow to realize it.

Inherent in each lies a contradiction, which the Awakened Being acknowledges: "This is an impossible task; even so, I set my heart on accomplishing the impossible." What moves the bodhisattva forward at all times is the bodhi resolve or *bodhicitta*, the "thought for enlightenment."

This is a heartfelt, two-part thought in the bodhisattva's deepest mind that says, "My highest aspiration is to realize my potential for ultimate wisdom and compassion, and I will realize that awakening by 'taking across' to awakening all sentient creatures."

Bodhisattva practices center around personal, societal, and universal vows. The Avatamsaka Sutra (Flower Garland Sutra), among the longest of all the Buddha's discourses, provides detailed explanations of the bodhisattva path from start to finish. The bodhisattva Samantabhadra, known as the "Bodhisattva of Great Practices," plays a major role in explaining a bodhisattva's practices and vows. Samantabhadra has a group of ten practices and vows associated with his name. In the sutra he teaches a bodhisattva pilgrim named Sudhana how to cultivate all ten vows to perfection. There are four personal vows (to bow in respect to every buddha, to praise the Tathagatas, to make extensive offerings, and to repent of karma offenses and reform), four social or relational vows (to offer joyful support for other's meritorious conduct, to request that the Buddha turn the wheel of dharma, to request that the buddhas stay in the world, and to always learn from the buddhas), and the universal vows (to ever accord with beings' abilities to respond, and to transfer merits everywhere to all beings). In chapter 39 of the Flower Garland Sutra, Sudhana masters these ten vows and realizes buddhahood.

### 84,000 Dharma-Doors (or the Myriad Practices)

Just as arhats, the role models of the Theravada school, observe the Four Noble Truths and the Eightfold Path, likewise in the Mahayana tradition bodhisattvas cultivate the Six Perfections and Myriad Practices. They are the hallmark quality of bodhisattvas. So many practices exist because sentient beings in all their diversity require different methods to "cross over the ocean of troubles" from this shore of samsara to the other shore of Nirvana. Each method is geared for a specific being's propensities, and the bodhisattva's job is to employ skillful, expedient means to teach and inspire those beings to wake up and make the bodhi resolve for themselves.

# Buddhist Holiness

## The Four Noble Truths

The Buddha's first teaching was the turning of the dharma-wheel of the Four Noble Truths. Each of these four profound insights can expand one's awareness of the nature of the world and the proper role of humanity in the world.

Some consider Buddhism pessimistic, claiming that the first Noble Truth, the teaching on the unsatisfying nature of all compound things, is joyless and life-denying. In fact, pointing to the transient nature of phenomena provides a keen insight into the reality of all things that are made up of other things. In its essence, the First Noble Truth says that things that come together will later come apart; as much as we develop emotional attachments to transient, impermanent things is how much we will suffer when they come apart.

Even more startling than this profound insight is the Third Noble Truth, which reveals the result of the Buddha's six years of ascetic discipline in the forest. Stating that suffering can end, it brings a message of hope, not defeat. Suffering can end, and the Eightfold Path is the road to suffering's end. Moreover, this salvation from suffering does not come at the hands of an external agency, nor is it the exclusive reward of a chosen one. The path to suffering's end is open to all. The human individual who claims that, by

using his method, anybody can transcend mortality and reach a state where all suffering ends offers a startlingly simple and direct promise. It is immanent and not transcendent. Diligent application of the dharma brought a result that took him beyond rebirth entirely, and he offers this method to all comers.

The Avatamsaka Sutra celebrates the Four Noble Truths, dedicating an entire chapter to their exposition. However, this Mahayana version of the Four Noble Truths also relates them to the bodhisattva's Four Great Vows:

1. In accordance with the first truth of dissatisfaction/suffering, I vow to save all suffering living beings.

2. In accordance with the second truth of suffering's accumulation, I vow to cut off all afflictions.

3. In accordance with the third truth of cessation, I vow to learn all the immeasurable methods of practice.

4. In accordance with the fourth truth of the Path, I vow to realize Buddhahood.

## The Eightfold Path

The Mahayana, like the Theravada, teaches the Eightfold Path, but in the Mahayana tradition one would be more likely to hear about the Ten Wholesome and Unwholesome Deeds than the Eightfold Path. The Mahayana embraces that profound teaching, but integrates it into a different formulation.

In the Ten Grounds chapter of the Avatamsaka Sutra,[8] the Second Ground explains the causes and effects of Ten Unwholesome Deeds. Avoiding these creates ten wholesome deeds. The ten consist of three unwholesome deeds

---

8. Tripitaka Master Hua, commentary, *Flower Adornment Sutra: The Ten Grounds*, ch. 26, pt. II, DRBU (Burlingame, CA: Buddhist Text Translation Society, 1981).

done with the body (killing, stealing, and adultery or promiscuity) as well as four unwholesome deeds done with the mouth (lying, gossip or schism-making, profanity, and frivolous prattle) and three done with the mind (greed, anger, and delusion). By avoiding those ten unskillful actions one purifies body, mouth, and mind and thereby creates wholesome karma.

The Mahayana tradition teaches that when one's ethical conduct accords with the Five Precepts (avoiding killing, lying, sexual misconduct, intoxicants, and stealing) and the Ten Wholesome Deeds, then the resulting blessings will lead one to rebirth in the heavens in a future life, as well as provide the foundation for deep samadhi and wisdom, should one choose not to aim for rebirth as a god. This formulation of dharma is the Mahayana equivalent of the Eightfold Path, in that it answers the question for practitioners, "How shall I live that is in accord with the dharma?" At the same time it depicts the realm of gods as a station of rebirth attainable by anybody through cultivation of an ethical lifestyle. Living wisely and harmlessly can take one to a divine state, although the Buddha warned against such a choice, for rebirth in the heavens remains subject to samsara, or birth and death. A much better goal would be Nirvana, transcending entirely the wheel of rebirth.

## The Self and Emptiness

### What Is the Self?

"Truth in the primary sense" is the Buddha's name for the teaching of "not-self." The understanding that all phenomena have no separate, distinct core of being, that all things are like onions, simply layers around an empty core, was the key insight that brought him to liberation.

Having seen this truth, the Buddha still had to verify it through meditation until his mind was pure and still. After awakening he explained how phenomena came about through a process of dependent coarising (*pratitya-samutpada*): that all things arise when conditions come together and vanish when conditions disperse. The term refers to the mutually interdependent links that bring phenomena into being in the mind and in the world. Here the Buddha "lifted the hood," so to speak, on the engine of the universe to reveal not only how phenomena arise from ignorance but also how they can be untied or unlinked and, when ignorance is illuminated through wisdom, how the chain of conditioned existence can be reversed and cast off.

In the Mahayana tradition, this fundamental insight was articulated in the Prajna Paramita texts for meditators whose skill had matured. The Vajra Prajna Paramita Sutra[9] contains this famous quote: "All things arising from the coming together of conditions resemble dreams, illusions, dewdrops, shadows and flashes of lightening; we should contemplate in that way."

Dependent coarising further created the basis for the Buddha's disciples to assert the nonultimate status of the various gods of the Brahmanic pantheon and the other divinities prevalent in India. All things in the universe have no inherent nature, but instead come together and disperse based on temporary adhesion of conditions. If they arise through a process of dependent coarising and disappear the same way, then there is no basis for asserting the existence of a creator deity. Not surprisingly, this caused consternation among the various Hindu schools and sects in India. The Buddha neither debated nor asserted otherwise, he simply invited all seekers to meditate correctly and see for themselves the truth of his observation.

9. Tripitaka Master Hsuan Hua, *The Vajra Prajna Paramita Sutra: A General Explanation* (Burlingame, CA: Buddhist Text Translation Society, 2003), 161.

## Self and Nirvana

Nirvana is the ending of further becoming. If rebirth is likened to a flame leaping from one candle to the next, then Nirvana is the blowing out of the flame, with the smoke rising up, extinguished forever. In the Mahayana tradition buddhas do not explain Nirvana as an end; the word *extinction* does not accurately convey this vision of Nirvana. The Buddha's perspective extends beyond the world of duality. The sutras give the average reader, bound by discriminating consciousness, access to the Buddha's unitive consciousness, which sees beyond duality. Reading about the Buddha's insights into ultimate truth, however, does not bestow that truth on the reader or grant him or her license to speak with that religious authority until he or she actually does the work of purifying body, mouth, and mind, entering samadhi, and realizing wisdom.

# Buddhist Practices

## Buddhist Pure Land Devotion

Mahayana Buddhist literature incorporates the teachings on Pure Land Buddhism. Upon entering Buddhist monasteries from Kuala Lumpur to Beijing, from Ho Chi Minh City to Taipei, one rarely finds meditation cushions or people meditating. Instead, one sees bowing benches set before tall images of Amitabha and lines of devotees circling the hall with recitation beads in their hands, chanting "Namo Amitofo," meaning "I return in refuge to the Buddha of Limitless Light."

The Pure Land form of devotion has been the dominant practice in East Asia for centuries—a reality that often surprises those who identify Buddhism with meditation. Seeing monks and laity alike praising Amitabha, reciting scriptures devoted to his Pure Land paradise, and chanting his name hundreds or thousands of times a day may seem "un-Buddhist" to those

whose knowledge of the dharma is limited to insight (*vipashyana*) meditation or studying Zen koans. East Asian Buddhists by and large prefer devotion to meditation because the full lotus posture, with both legs crossed over the thighs, requires flexibility and patience. A popular saying in Chinese Mahayana Buddhist circles says, "When one hundred practitioners do Chan (Zen) meditation, not even one can expect success; when one hundred devotees recite the Buddha's name, one hundred will be reborn in Amitabha's Pure Land."

The figure of Amitabha can seem like a Buddhist god, waiting for the faithful devotee to return to a home in the Western Land. For those familiar with the solitary Buddha of Theravada Buddhist culture, both the idea of faith and devotion to another numinous buddha can seem quite novel.

### Source of the Pure Land Teaching

Pure Land devotional practice dates back to a fabled monk, Fazang (*dharma-kara* or "Treasury of Dharma"). While practicing throughout eons of lifetimes, Fazang dedicated all of his accumulated merit to the creation of a Pure Land, a paradise where no suffering was allowed. Animals, ghosts, and the hell realms would not exist. Monk Fazang made forty-eight vows, which stated in essence that whoever recited his name with sincerity, even ten times, could at the end of life leave the endless cycle of samsara and be reborn in a pure lotus flower in the Land of Utmost Happiness. There one would rest in the lotus until one's karma was purified and then emerge into an inspiring environment conducive to spiritual practice and free of any obstacles.

The Avatamsaka Sutra relates that new immigrants to the Pure Land learn all the means for teaching those beings still stuck in samsara. After being instructed in the skills of a bodhisattva, the newly trained buddhas-to-be return to

Buddhist monks circling a statue of Amitabha Buddha, himself surrounded by Buddhas, at Fo Guang Shan Monastery in Kaohsiung, Taiwan. Amitabha ("boundless light") is the Buddha of the Western Paradise and the main focus of Pure Land Buddhism.

the worlds where their affinities lie, reach their final incarnation, become buddhas, and teach those beings who can hear their dharma. It is not surprising that such an extraordinary salvific tale sounded attractive to an Asian populace that was, for the most part, poor, uneducated, agrarian, and beset with cruel sufferings: harsh and catastrophic climate, incessant war or violent revolution, little difference between bandits and soldiers, exorbitant imperial taxes, forced labor, and disease. It is said that three types of individuals—those with dull wits, people with middling intelligence, and even skeptical intellectuals—need only recite the name of Amitabha to be reborn in the Pure Land, free of samsara's incessant rounds of incarnation. There they can cultivate bodhisattva practices undisturbed by the vicissitudes of the turbid world. The promise of

such unalloyed bliss awaiting those who believed in Amitabha's vows, wished to be reborn in his Pure Land, and who then recited his name with sincerity and vigor, makes a strong case for the rise of Amitabha's devotional practices as the most popular form of Buddhist practice for millions upon millions of East Asian Buddhists.

# Dialogue and the Future

## Buddhism and the West

Buddhism has successfully reinvented itself for 2,500 years, jumping cultures, languages, continents, and generations, as its principles and practices hybridize and renew in each new country. Wherever it goes, the Buddha's dharma not only influences the new culture but also is transformed by each new religious environment. After Indian Buddhist pilgrims arrived in China, it took roughly 200 years for fully indigenous Chinese Buddhist forms and followers to evolve, following uniquely Chinese perspectives and practices of the dharma. If history repeats itself, then Buddhism in the West has another century before deeply rooted, distinctly Western practices of the dharma will emerge.[10] In the meantime, contemporary Western Buddhists live on a bridge. They gain inspiration and knowledge of traditional dharma from Asia as interpreted by the few authentic dharma pioneers who introduced the living traditions to North America and to Europe, and then they integrate what they learn into Western cultural modes and into the English language.

The job for Western students of first generation Asian Buddhist pioneers consists of distinguishing the purely cultural elements of the practices they have absorbed from what is genuinely Buddhist, that is to say, taught by the sutras and by the various practices that have come down through the monastic tradition. Keeping alive Chinese, Japanese, Korean, Thai, Tibetan, or Vietnamese cultural norms is a priority for first-generation Buddhist immigrants from those cultures. But that generation's religious practices often matter little to their children and less to others outside their linguistic and cultural communities.

Bringing Buddhism into the twenty-first century is the challenge of those dedicated to absorbing the Buddha's teaching. Practitioners strive "to cultivate the dharma," that is, to apply the Middle Way to body, mouth, and mind and relearn many of the viewpoints and mind-sets regarding humanity and the world.

## Four Aspects of Western Culture's Interaction with the Dharma

Buddhism has the potential to influence the culture of the West most markedly in the areas of psychology, science, egalitarian social structures, ethical environmental interdependence, and the reanimation of nature. The four aspects of the Buddha's teachings that could have the biggest impact are Buddhism's egalitarian nature, psychological orientation, science-friendly attitude, and contribution to discovering appropriate responses to technological advances.

### Buddhism's Egalitarian Nature

The Buddha described all sentient beings in the Ten Dharma Realms as equally possessing the buddha nature; therefore, all beings share equal access to the fruits of cultivation. Goodness and virtue, along with vigor in cultivating the dharma, determines one's progress in the Buddha's Path, not birth or influence, gender, class, bank account, or age.

Buddhist practice appeals to the democratic nature of modern individuals, especially with regard to access to the teachings and the status of women in the Mahayana. This democratic aspect of the dharma has great significance. The Buddha welcomed all sincere practitioners, regardless of caste. He instructed that his teachings be kept in the vernacular, not in the language of priests or scribes, so that the purpose of the dharma—ending suffering—remained clear and available to all people, literate and illiterate alike. Likewise, he opened up the dharma for half the human population at a time and in a culture where women were little more than property; their primary value was their reproduction of

---

10. Organized Buddhism arrived in North America at the end of the nineteenth century with the establishment of the San Francisco Buddhist Church. In 1969, five American men and women from Gold Mountain Monastery became the first Americans to leave the home-life as fully ordained, celibate monastics.

© Karen Kasmauski / National Geographic Society / Corbis

Buddhist nuns in prayer at Dong Thuyen pagoda, established in the eighteenth century in the village of Duong Xuan, Vietnam.

male children. The women's sangha was established in the Buddha's lifetime; his own foster mother became the first ordained nun, Mahaprajapati, and established the female (Bhikshuni) sangha. In the Mahayana tradition, women have been ordained and have taken vows for 2,500 years. The Buddha taught that liberation is possible not only for all humans, but for beings in all the realms of rebirth.

## Buddhism's Psychological Orientation

Professor Huston Smith, celebrated educator and writer on religion, believed that one of the major avenues for Buddhist interest and acceptance in the West would be psychology and that the dialogue between psychology and Buddha dharma would shape Western Buddhism in the twenty-first century. Buddhism's orientation toward psychology has already paved a broad highway of East-West exchange and mutual learning.

Since Freud, Jung, Adler, and the rise of secular humanism in Europe, individuals have largely defined themselves through the vocabulary and perspectives of psychology. Many lay Buddhist teachers and disciples in America were initially attracted to Buddhism by its attitude toward the mind. Students of psychology often report that advancing in the study of psychology required training in statistics, demographic studies, and experimentation with lab animals. When addressing human experience, training too often focused on pathology and chemical therapies. Buddhist meditation allowed them to experience the healthy human mind with a theoretical model—that is, the Buddha's description of the mind available both through Abhidharma texts and through the sutras' discourses on meditative states.

Two levels of inquiry are emerging now from the dialogue between psychology and Buddhism. The first consists of a meditative therapeutic model that uses the sutras' description of the mind as a methodology for self-understanding. The Buddha's sutras serve as blueprints of his awakened consciousness. He directed them to those whose meditations carry them through the same territory and along the same paths that the Buddha traversed to their end.[11] The second area investigates the interaction between Buddhist theories of mind and neuroscience.[12]

### Buddhism's Science-Friendly Nature

The Buddha's methodical practice in the forest for six years fits the paradigm of proper scientific investigation. He worked from a theoretical hypothesis—that suffering can end—and employed a variety of methodologies in his research, discarding those that led to extremes. He left a paper trail in the sutras, and he bequeathed the fruits of his research for testing to anyone who might seek answers on their own. His model has been tested by subjects East and West for two and a half millennia.

Popular awareness of the conversation between Buddhism and post-Newtonian physics started with Fritjof Capra's book *The Tao of Physics* and Gary Zukov's *The Dancing Wu Li Masters*. This conversation is now working back into the life sciences, with researchers in the fields of psychology, health, genetics, and biological engineering looking into Buddhist models of interdependence and conditioned arising.

### Buddhism's Contribution to Discovering Appropriate Responses to Technological Advances

Buddhism offers a potential ethics-based solution to a current crisis created by advances in technology. It suggests that humans, as stewards for the planet, have a duty to think on behalf of not only all beings who share the natural environment but also unborn of generations to come. This emphasis on virtue and compassion, on giving and ethical integrity, can reshape our priorities as a society.

Contemporary Buddhists advocate the use of traditional ethics, or ancient wisdom tools, to review appropriate technology. This approach is not based on abstract predetermined laws or rights, but on cause and effect between you and yourself, you and society, and you and nature. In short, to discern the moral choices on an issue, one need not buy into the entire cosmology of the Buddhist faith to receive the benefits. Cause and effect operate independent of faith in a doctrinal creed.

Bill Joy, a former science officer at Sun Microsystems, has written extensively about humanity's lack of commonly agreed-upon standards to evaluate advances in technology. In a

---

11. The pilgrimage of Sudhana, the Buddhist pilgrim in the "Gandhavyuha Chapter" of the Avatamsaka Sutra, can be explained as the Buddha's description of meeting and integrating the archetypes of the anima and the shadow into a holistic conscious awareness. The Buddhist language for this process says that Sudhana, the pilgrim, experiences and cultivates to success his wisdom and great compassion through progressive encounters with fifty-three Good Spiritual Friends.

12. Formal studies are ongoing in University of Wisconsin at Madison, UCLA, and Stanford (B. Alan Wallace Contemplative Science), among other research institutions. There has been evolution, too, of the dimensions of humanistic psychology, and the theories of Fritz Perls, Abraham Maslow, Carl Rodgers, and others, vis-à-vis their contact with Buddhist practice and theory of mind.

talk at Stanford University he said, "I have a copy of the Bible and also His Holiness the Dalai Lama's *Ethics for a New Millennium* here in my briefcase, and frankly I don't find either one offering much in the way of concrete guidelines for addressing the dangerous situation humanity finds itself in today."[13]

The Buddhist awareness of interdependence and the value of basic human kindness actually provide good starting points for a conversation dedicated to evolving those standards. Further, the Buddha's sutras, which can be understood as maps of the mind and blueprints for perfecting awareness, offer a means toward developing the sense of enlightened responsibility that Joy suggests is humanity's next step, a necessary step to survive the challenges of the twenty-first century.

---

13. Quotation from unpublished talk attended by the author in May 2000.

# CHAPTER 15

# Texts and Commentary

*Peter Feldmeier and Heng Sure*

## Introduction to the Canonical Selections

The following selected texts are central in both the Theravada and Mahayana canons. They highlight important features in each of these traditions. The Dhammapada is a collection of aphorisms principally from the Buddha, and the text offered here is its first chapter. As couplets, these verses frame two ways to engage life, either skillfully where life is happy and contented or unskillfully where life becomes a burden. The emphasis is on the quality of one's mind. The second text is the Metta Sutta or teaching on loving-kindness. This small classic emphasizes the importance of desiring universal flourishing for all beings. As we shall read, "As a mother would risk her own life to protect her only child, cultivate this same boundless heart for all beings."

The Heart Sutra reflects a Mahayana teaching that all reality carries two additional qualities (along with impermanence, no-self, and dissatisfaction); these being "emptiness" and "suchness." Here one finds that emptiness has an intrinsic relationship to form where all things exist in a constant interpenetrating flow. Further, there is a transcendental quality to it all, a suchness, that is sometimes understood as "buddha nature." The second Mahayana text is a portion of the Lotus Sutra, which many Mahayana Buddhists believe to represent the fullest expression of the Buddha's teaching. In this portion, one encounters the Bodhisattva named Gwan Shr Yin (or Guan Shi Yin) who has devoted her ministry to bringing compassion, healing, and blessings to those who call upon her. In the Mahayana vision, the universe is alive with spiritual forces that support one's life and practice.

## Text 1: The Dhammapada— Chapter 1: Twins

### Text

1. All phenomena are preceded by the mind, created by the mind, and have the mind as their master. If one speaks or acts from a corrupted mind, suffering follows as the cart-wheel follows the ox's foot.

2. All phenomena are preceded by the mind, created by the mind, and have the mind as their master. If one speaks or acts with a pure mind, happiness follows as an ever-present shadow.

3. He insulted me; he struck me; he robbed me; he defeated me. For those

who dwell on such resentments, enmity never ceases.

4. He insulted me; he struck me; he robbed me; he defeated me. For those who do not dwell on such resentments, enmity subsides.

5. Enmities are never appeased by enmity. They are appeased by peace. This is an eternal law.

6. Many do not realize: We all must die. Those who see this appease their quarrels.

7. One focused on pleasant things and unrestrained in the senses, who is immoderate in food, who is listless and lazy: Māra overcomes him, as wind overcomes a weak tree.

8. One focused on unpleasant things and restrained in the senses, who is moderate in food, who has faith and diligence: Māra cannot overcome him, just as wind cannot overcome a rocky mountain.

9. Whoever would take on the yellow robe, while hampered by defilement, being unrestrained and without truth, is unworthy of that yellow robe.

10. Whoever has thrown off defilement and is established in virtue, is truly worthy of the yellow robe.

11. Those who deem the worthless as valuable, and see the valuable as worthless: they do not attain the valuable; they roam in the field of wrong thought.

12. Those who have known the valuable as valuable, and the worthless as worthless: they attain the valuable; they roam in the field of right thought.

13. Just as rain penetrates a poorly thatched house, so passion enters an uncultivated mind.

14. Just as rain does not penetrate a well-thatched house, so passion fails to enter a well-cultivated mind.

15. Here he grieves, following death he grieves; in both states the evil-doer grieves. He grieves, he is afflicted, having seen the defilement of his deeds.

16. Here he rejoices, following death he rejoices; in both states he who does good rejoices. He rejoices, he delights, having seen the purity of his deeds.

17. Here he is tormented, following death he is tormented; in both states the evil-doer is tormented. He is tormented knowing, "I have done evil." Reborn to a miserable state, he is tormented all the more.

18. Here he rejoices, following death he rejoices; in both states he who does good rejoices. He rejoices knowing, "I have done good deeds." Reborn to a blissful state, he rejoices all the more.

19. One who recites much scripture, but, being negligent, does not act accordingly, is like a cowherd counting others' cows. He has no share in the fruits of monastic life.

20. One who recites little scripture, but lives in truth according to the teaching, having abandoned lust, ill will, and delusion, having right knowledge and a well-emancipated mind, not clinging in this world or the next: he has great share in the fruits of monastic life.[1] ■

## Outsider Commentary
### Feldmeier

The Dhammapada is an anthology of the Buddha's teachings in the form of aphorisms collated under twenty-six themes as chapters. This

1. Translation by Peter Feldmeier. Originally published in Leo D. Lefebure and Peter Feldmeier, *The Path of Wisdom: A Christian Commentary on the Dhammapada* (Louven: Peeters, 2011), 29–32.

collection is the most revered and quoted part of the Pali canon. In fact, Theravada monks typically memorize the entire 423-verse text as part of their formal training, and chant many of its verses daily.

This first chapter provides a perfect example of how Buddhism frames itself. The twin verses pose one possibility against its opposite. One represents happiness and the other affliction. One can also see this kind of framing in the Judeo-Christian tradition. For example, according to Deuteronomy, when God lays out the Torah (law or way) for Israel, he frames it thusly: "See, I have set before you today life and prosperity, death and adversity" (30:15).[2] Also, the classic early Christian text, the *Didache*, begins, "There are two ways, one of life and one of death, and there is a great difference between these two ways."[3]

The Dhammapada begins with the twin verses that describe how all phenomena are preceded and controlled by the mind. Thus, a corrupted mind conditions suffering, while a pure mind conditions happiness. The contrasting images are insightful as well. The afflicted quality of one's experience makes one feel like a beast of burden dragging a heavy cart. In contrast, for those of pure mind, happiness lightly dances around as a shadow in the sun.

These two verses highlight the Buddhist understanding of how the mind works. The Pali term is *mano*, which represents the rational functioning of consciousness. *Mano* directs how one perceives and interprets reality. It is in this sense that "phenomena are preceded by the mind . . . and have mind as their master." A mind filled with passions actually misinterprets reality and so makes one's engagement with it unwholesome. This is why verses 11 and 12 contrast those who can and cannot distinguish between what is worthless and valuable.

The issue gets even more complex. Past karma actually affects not just how one perceives reality but also phenomena itself. The universe is interconnected, with karmic laws always in play. This verse emphasizes perceptions of immediate experience, but past mental states and engagement with the world also influence the phenomena encountered in the present.

At its core, Buddhism takes people back to themselves and the imperative to cultivate their minds well. No one can save another person, but individuals can save themselves, teaches the Buddha. Personal responsibility is a dominating theme in the Theravada Buddhist tradition. In the Buddha's farewell address, he insisted, "You should live as islands unto yourselves, being your own refuge, with no one else as your refuge."[4]

The Dhammapada includes a number of verses that highlight the difference between substance and appearance or surface and deep truth. Verses 9–10 reference this crucial truth regarding who is a true monk who can legitimately wear the yellow robe. There is a pun in the text, missed in English. The term for *defilement* (or mental stain) is *kasāva* and the term for yellow is *kāsāva* (adjective derived from *stained*). So one who is stained is unworthy of the stained robe, while one who is without stain is worthy of the stained robe. The chapter ends emphasizing the distinction between appearance and reality. One can be devout in reciting the scriptures, but if one hasn't appropriated their wisdom, it means nothing. In contrast, one who has integrated the

---

2. All biblical quotes in this chapter are from the New Revised Standard Edition.

3. Michael Homes, ed., *The Apostolic Fathers*, trans. J.B. Lightfoot and J.R. Harmer, 2nd ed. (Grand Rapids, MI: Barker House, 1989), 149.

4. Digha Nikaya, *Thus Have I Heard: The Long Discourses of the Buddha*, trans. Maurice Walsh (London: Wisdom, 1987), 245.

truth of the scriptures into one's life is truly holy, even if he recites little.

Can the Dhammapada challenge the way Christians think about or engage religious concerns? Most authentic spiritualities have an ultimate horizon that guides and inspires the aspirant. Buddhists call this Nirvana and Christians call this heaven, though they need not be considered the same. A danger in focusing on such a horizon is that one can be overly directed to reaching the endgame and miss the importance of the quality of the moment. That is, focusing on the future can lead to less attention on the present.

Biblical texts are dominated by considerations of an ultimate horizon, which for Christians is about final destiny in heaven or hell. Christians recognize the importance of life in the spirit. Even so, the Christian scriptures regularly describe the presence of the spirit in conjunction with ultimate salvation as not yet fully present, for example, "We ourselves, who have the first fruits of the Spirit, groan inwardly while we await for adoption, the redemption of our bodies" (Rom. 8:23, see also Eph. 1:12–13). Even the many exhortations to virtue and holiness in the New Testament are posed in terms of salvation or damnation. For example, Paul's long exhortation to holiness at the end of Romans that encourages purity of mind and body, unity among members, and love for all, ends with "each one will be held accountable to God" (12:1–14:12).

The New Testament and other Christian writings do speak of the devout life leading to happiness in the present, but they give more attention to the discussion of end times and heaven and hell. This differs from the Dhammapada, which speaks of Nirvana but places more emphasis on the quality of life in the here and now. Further, it is concerned less with the nature of experience and more with the quality of one's mind in the midst of experience.

The First Noble Truth in Buddhism is that life is painful or dissatisfying. The second is that life is afflictive because of one's grasping, craving mind. Perhaps the biggest craving has to do with one's sense of self. Humans identify with experiences and thoughts and create a persona or conventional self that needs protection. From a Christian point of view that self is a false-self, because the truest self is hidden in God. St. Paul writes, "I have been crucified with Christ; and it is no longer I who live, but it is Christ who lives in me" (Gal. 2:19–20). Such "dying to oneself" is something of a relocation of oneself within God, the true center of all reality. The experience of this "dying" is really great inner liberty and an infusion of great spiritual joy. In that same letter, Paul writes, "For freedom Christ set us free" (5:1). Buddhism teaches that there is no self. This is different from a Christian sense of finding oneself in God. But, perhaps there are striking similarities. Like spiritually advanced Buddhists, Christian saints are typically extremely self-possessed, aware and nonreactive. With no ego to protect or advance, they live freely and wholesomely. Happiness naturally follows, "like an ever-present shadow."

## Insider Commentary

### Heng Sure

The Dhammapada is one of the few texts that finds adherents in both the Pali and the Sanskrit traditions. Although identified primarily with the Theravada Buddhist world, Mahayana practitioners embrace it for the simple reason that it is a memorable and profound teaching delivered in pithy, bite-sized aphorisms. The title in Chinese is *Faju Jing* or (The Sutra of Dharma Phrases).

The Buddha taught the dharma for more than forty-nine years. Once it was recorded in print and collected, the canon of his teachings was subsequently divided into "three baskets and twelve divisions." The three baskets include sutra discourses, or the Buddha's words; *shastra*, commentaries on the Buddha's words by erudite monks and scholars; and *vinaya*, rules for organizing the monastic community. The twelve divisions include, among others, the three baskets as well as stories of the Buddha's past lives, predictions of buddhas to come, and several sutras unique because they alone, among all the other discourses, were spoken spontaneously without request.

The Buddha stipulated that the Dhammapada— and all his discourses—should be kept in the vernacular and thus preserved in spoken transmission (oral tradition) and not written down. His reason may have been that, in a society structured around four castes, once the sutras were committed to writing then only the literate castes would have access to them. Since the sutras' main purpose was to provide methods to end suffering for anybody who endeavored to follow them, keeping the sutras in the public domain was a decision consistent with the egalitarian nature of the Buddha's dharma teachings. And in the Buddha's monasteries illiterate monks who came from among the Untouchables could memorize and recite the texts sitting next to and, if they were ordained first, sitting in front of monks who had grown up in the Brahmin caste.

Sutras were memorized and chanted, and as anybody who has tried memorization knows, it is aided by metric measure and concrete images. Hence the Dhammapada, with its pithy, essential phrases, lends itself to memorization. Its images drawn from nature and human society are readily grasped and universally applicable. Some of the stanzas are autobiographical, such as Dhammapada 154 where the Buddha characterizes his own liberation from the endless and painful rounds of rebirth as a victory over craving. He describes craving as a "house-builder" and exults, "House-builder you are seen! You will build no more! Your rafters are broken, the roof destroyed. The mind, having gone to the Unconditioned, has attained the destruction of craving."[5]

According to the Theravada school, the Buddha at first was reluctant to teach; he had decided to enter Nirvana and not attempt to teach others the Path. He feared the cultivation of discipline was too difficult for most and, further, that nobody would understand it. Some gods from the Brahma Heavens appealed to the Buddha's kind heart and his past vows and implored him to talk about the Path to awakening. After three weeks of walking around the bodhi tree and contemplating the challenges, the newly awakened Buddha left the spot on the riverbank and went looking for five companions who had been with him in the forest at various times during his practice. Each had abandoned the prince for different reasons and had gone their own ways.

He found the five cultivators together in the Deer Wilds Park. His former companions now recognized that something was different about their former guru. He was now radiant and serene. The Buddha then explained the Four Noble Truths to his five ascetic brothers and one of them, Ajnatakaundinya ("First to Awaken"), woke up on the spot and became the first arhat. The other four sequentially woke up as well. For the next forty-nine years, the Buddha walked through India and parts of what is now Nepal speaking to the various conditions and potentials for understanding of the assemblies he met. After the Buddha attained Nirvana under the bodhi tree, and for the next several centuries, his followers wrote down his words and translated them into the world's languages. The Taisho edition of the Mahayana

---

5. Lefebure and Peter Feldmeier, *The Path of Wisdom*, 158.

canon lists more than 1,300 separate texts in the sutra category alone!

Faced with so many sutra discourses, the Buddha's followers in China proposed systems for categorizing and organizing them. One system, known as the Tientai Teachings, divided the sutras into five periods of teaching. According to the Mahayana tradition, the Buddha first spoke the Avatamsaka Sutra while seated beneath the bodhi tree for the benefit of the gods and the bodhisattvas. That teaching conveyed his vision of the universe directly and free of any interpretations. Understanding that this vision was going to be unpalatable for ordinary people still caught up in duality, the Buddha taught the second category, the *agamas*. The Dhammapada belongs to this category of discourse. Its teachings are basic, easily digested, and universally true; moreover, they are accessible to all mentalities. Even the Buddha's most faithful disciples were not initially ready for the more profound teachings that were to come, in sync with their progressively deeper states of meditation. Later on in his teaching career the Buddha spoke about *vaipulya* (expansive) teachings, which bridged the *agama* period and the more profound *prajna* (wisdom) teachings. Vaipulya sutras expand the basic principles expounded in the agamas and connected them with the wisdom to come.

As Buddhist followers, particularly his sangha of monks and nuns, gradually adapted their habits and viewpoints to those of the Buddha and began to restructure their awareness into the methods of the dharma, their precepts grew more pure and their meditative states of absorption deepened. To guide their new awarenesses, the Buddha spoke the prajna teachings, including the Heart Sutra addressed below, for twenty-one years. This was the fourth period of discourses.

Finally, near the end of his teaching career, the Buddha explained a class of texts known as the Lotus-Nirvana teachings. Unlike any of the preceding teachings, the Lotus Sutra says that anybody who recited the Buddha's name even once or who raised even a single hand toward the Buddha's image in salute, planted a seed in their consciousness that in the future would result in buddhahood for that individual. The tradition says that when the Buddha delivered this teaching on Vulture Peak, 5,000 irate disciples stormed out in protest. They were upset that everything they had learned was not ultimately true but only conventionally helpful and that the renunciations they had made were now characterized as unnecessary. Having believed that extraordinary measures were necessary, they now find the Buddha guaranteeing perfect enlightenment to anyone who simply saluted the Buddha. They felt this was unfair and left the assembly in protest. The Buddha, far from sympathetic, scolded this group as "sterile seeds in the Buddha's garden"; he criticized the stingy measure of their minds and considered them selfish and far from the boundless, giving heart of the dharma.

Sutras came about for a variety of reasons. Leaders of spiritual communities would ask about the deeper causes of a situation, or they would inquire about doubts they had regarding a certain teaching. Often the Buddha taught his monastic disciples when they were ready to take the next step in their meditations. He also spoke when requested to solve problems and to heal conflicts the way doctors prescribe medicine for each different illness. In his travels the Buddha might encounter a variety of circumstances that required resolution: warring armies about to go into battle, mothers with broken hearts whose infant sons had just died, or kings wishing to create merit or blessings for the prosperity of their reign. And often the Buddha spoke the dharma for ordinary people who in the course of their days encountered situations of grief, pain, and seemingly insoluble troubles. His disciples would remember the Buddha's words and pass them on. The Dhammapada is a perfect example of this kind of teaching.

# Text 2: The Metta Sutta

## Text

1. The one who is skilled in well-being, who wishes to advance to the state of tranquility, must be capable and upright—utterly upright—easy to instruct, gentle and humble.

2. This is one content and easy to support, with few responsibilities, living simply, with senses calmed, prudent, modest, and unattached to families.

3. He should not do the smallest thing which the wise might reprove. [He contemplates:] May all beings be glad and secure. May all beings be happy.

4-5. Whatever living beings there may be—frail and strong; long, large, medium, and small-sized; visible and not; dwelling near and far; those born and those awaiting birth—may all beings be happy.

6. Deceive no one, nor despise another anywhere. Wish no one suffering, neither by anger nor by ill will.

7. As a mother would risk her own life to protect her only child, cultivate this same boundless heart for all beings.

8. Radiate a boundless love throughout the whole universe—above, below, and all around with no obstructions—with no taint of ill will or resentment.

9. When standing, walking, sitting or lying down, as long as you are awake, devote yourself to this mental state. It is a divine abiding here and now.

10. Not clinging to *views* and freed from sensual desire, filled with virtue and perfect insight, never would one be reborn in the womb.[6] ■

---

6. Unpublished translation by Peter Feldmeier.

7. Digha Nikaya, 99.

## Outsider Commentary

### *Feldmeier*

The first chapter of this section discussed the practice of metta or loving-kindness, which is one of the four "divine abiding" meditations. Along with compassion, sympathetic joy, and equanimity, metta helps one cultivate a wholesome, balanced psyche and a kind of perfect posture toward the world. Imagine your whole mind utterly saturated with loving-kindness toward the entire universe. Imagine also filling the entire universe with your loving-kindness. This is what the Metta Sutta draws us to.

Metta is not love in the typical sense of the term. It is more like "good will." *Love* is a tricky word, particularly in Theravada Buddhism, where this text comes from. The term *love* in Western terms evokes some sense of particularity, attraction, and bonding. This understanding rests on the edge of danger, according to the classical Buddhist perspective. Obviously, Buddhists enjoy some people more than others. And, of course, even in the Buddha's day, most followers were "householders," and thus loved their families.

Being a householder is not a bad thing per se, but is it an excellent thing? It is clear from the Pali canon that the Buddha strongly encouraged believers to become monks and nuns. In the Samannaphala Sutta, the Buddha defends this preference. He compared the difference between a lay life and a monastic life as that between a slave and a free person. He described the lay lifestyle as "close and dusty [while] the homeless life is free as air."[7]

Two other Pali words that seem something like Western notions of love are *piya* and *pema*. They refer to a relationship to something dear, pleasant, or agreeable. What may seem strange to Western sensibilities is that Buddhists usually use these terms in the context of problems with craving and attachment.

In and of themselves experiences of attraction and aversion are not problems. It is one's relationship to these experiences that matters utterly. To protect metta from attachment, equanimity is considered the best balancing posture. Equanimity is not uncaring or disengagement with the world, nor is it a kind of listless apathy. Quite the opposite, being free from one's attachments means being free from craving, pursuing, and fearing the loss of something that cannot satisfy. This frees up enormous psychic and physical energy to direct toward the Path and to engage the world in the most wholesome ways. Bhikkhu Nyanasobhano, a highly respected Theravadin voice in America, contrasts romantic love and the dynamics of human affections. He writes,

> Buddhism, of course, teaches such an ideal, which is nothing less than deliverance from all sorrow, called Nibbana [Nirvana]. While worldly joys are mutable and fleeting, Nibbana is established, sorrowless, stainless, and secure. . . . The Dhamma [dharma] puts the delights and torments of love into perspective so that we can break the illusion of love as the highest of aspirations and most essential of desires. . . . The Dhamma purges the grasping, selfish qualities of our love and makes them purer and nobler. . . . This is *metta*—loving-kindness devoid of selfishness.[8]

Another text, *A Happy Married Life: A Buddhist Perspective* by Sri Dhammananda, encourages couples to let go of any attached love and focus one's energy on metta, a loving-kindness that seeks the good of the other. This, he claims, is the only way to flourish in a marriage without suffering. This sounds strikingly odd to modern Western ears. Taken at face value, it would suggest the following dialogue: Wife: "Do you love me?" Husband: "Yes, I love you unboundedly, with the very same universal love that I hold for our dog, our turtle, and the tree in the neighbor's front yard."

What might be a surprise is that many of the great leaders of early Christianity would have aligned themselves completely with these Buddhist sensibilities. They too highly recommended celibacy and for the same reasons—namely, that it would condition greater service, deeper prayer, a simpler life, and a freedom from the passions.[9]

The early church referred to an advanced spiritual posture as *apatheia*, which literally means "no suffering." *Apatheia* refers to a spiritual state of being in which one is neither grasping at attractions nor blanching at aversions. One is free from all reactivity so as to pursue the truth. Apatheia was considered necessary to come to a deep contemplative encounter with God. It is exactly the equanimity that Buddhism preaches. Early Christians also thought that apatheia was the best posture for love, because then love would be free from self-interest and clinging.[10] Then love could freely focus on the good of the other. This aligns with Buddhist sensibilities exactly. Interestingly, it is also a sensibility largely abandoned by Christianity in the modern world.

8. Bhikkhu Nyanasobhano, *Nothing Higher to Live For: A Buddhist View of Romantic Love* (Kandy: Buddhist Publication Society, 1985), 3–6.

9. Such representatives included possibly every great church father, from Origen, Athanasius, Gregory of Nyssa in the East to Ambrose, Jerome, and Augustine in the West.

10. See Michael Casey, "Apatheia," in *The New Dictionary of Catholic Spirituality*, ed. Michael Downey (Collegeville, MN: Liturgical Press, 1993), 50–51.

The tradition of "forest dwelling" is deep in the Theravada tradition, as it represents austerity and undistracted practice.

Christianity has always considered love, whether understood as apatheia or not, to be utterly important. Interpersonal communion with God, recognizing that "God is love" (1 John 4:8), is central to Christian faith. Christian discipleship is about not only knowing the love of God but also radiating that love to others: "As the Father has loved me, so I have loved you; abide in my love. . . . This is my commandment, that you should love one another as I have loved you" (John 15:9–12).

Bridal or sexual metaphors are widely used in the tradition to signal the passionate experience of love the soul enjoys with God. Consider the following from the medieval mystic Hadewijch: "The beloved and lover penetrate each other in such a way that neither of the two can distinguish oneself from the other. . . . They abide in one another in fruition, mouth in mouth, heart in heart, body in body, and soul in soul, while one sweet divine nature flows through them both, and they are both one thing through each other."[11]

Buddhist insight into metta helps keep one grounded in universal, nonexclusive, nongrasping loving-kindness. But it still strikes Christian ears as somewhat flat in terms of spiritual possibilities.

## Insider Commentary

### Heng Sure

The Buddha gave the Metta Sutta (Sutra on Loving-Kindness) to his monks as a power-tool that would act on their hearts, to make them

---

11. Hadewijch, *The Complete Works*, trans. Mother Columba Hart (New York: Paulist Press, 1980), 66.

kinder and allow them to cope with obstacles and distress. There is a story behind the text. A group of the Buddha's young monastic disciples wanted to imitate their teacher's experience and go on a forest retreat. They asked the Buddha's permission to spend a night in the jungle out beyond the safe perimeter of the monastery. The Buddha granted their wish and told them they could come back, if necessary, at any time. The inexperienced monks set off with their bowls and umbrellas and when they reached some trees in the woods that looked suitable for meditation and shelter, they stopped and set about making camp. As the sun set they realized, however, that none of the comforts they were used to in the monastery were available. Before long they started to complain, then find faults, and then bicker among themselves. The local tree spirits, who had originally been awed by the presence of the Buddha's monks, saw them fighting among themselves and lost their heart of respect. "These are just ordinary, common men," they said, "what are they doing in our forest?" The tree spirits began to drop coconuts and ripe fruit onto the heads of the monks, greatly increasing their discomfort and anxiety.

As night fell, the monks, unaccustomed to living outdoors, grew frightened by the sounds from the dark woods. They shivered through a miserable night and as soon as the sun rose, trudged back to the monastery feeling defeated and dejected. The Buddha asked for a report, and they shamefacedly related their experience beneath the trees. The Buddha, full of empathy, said, "I suspected something like that might have happened. Now I want you to go right back to the woods this very day after your alms-round. Don't be alarmed because this time I'm going to give you an expedient method, a monk's power-tool. I want you to keep this tool at hand whenever anything arises that doesn't go your way. This is a magic text that can turn any uncomfortable or inauspicious state into loving-kindness, gratitude, and well-being."

Then the Buddha recited for them the text of the Metta Sutta: "The one who is skilled in well-being, who wishes to advance to the state of tranquility. . . ." He had the monks recite the text until they had memorized it and then sent them back. They retraced their steps and settled in under the same trees as before. This time the tree spirits, coconuts in hand, noticed a difference in the attitude of the monks, how they recalled the Buddha's instructions and treated each other with kindness and respect. Most impressed with the monks' demeanor and by their kind hearts, the spirits presented them with fruit and coconuts as offerings instead of throwing them as projectiles.

At the end of the week, the monks sent a representative back to get the Buddha's permission for a longer stay. It was the Metta Sutta's spirit of compassion that made all the difference. Keeping loving-kindness in mind, the monks were able to maintain a serene state toward all circumstances, be they gratifying or afflictive.

This sutra is divided into three sections: a personal, a social, and a universal section. The refrain that divides the sections is the line, "May all beings be glad and secure. May all beings be happy." The first section comprises the Buddha's personality inventory. It gives his prescription for qualities of character required by one who is "skilled in well-being"; that is, one who is preparing well to leave the world through transcending samsara.

"[One] must be capable and upright—utterly upright—easy to instruct, gentle and humble." Here the Buddha emphasizes that the spiritual path begins with character and ethical goodness. After relating the qualities of the ideal personality, the teaching then describes how to express personal goodness in the social realm.

"Deceive no one, nor despise another anywhere. Wish no one suffering, neither by anger nor by ill will." This section gives guidelines for interaction between disciples and the people in their lives. It includes a wish for well-being and loving-kindness for all creatures, including people yet to come, and even one's enemies.

Next is an analogy of a mother who is protective of her child even at the cost of her own life: "As a mother would risk her own life to protect her only child, cultivate this same boundless heart for all beings." This is genuine great compassion. How difficult to look at evil people, at rivals, or at criminals with the same loving eyes that a mother uses to gaze upon her own child! Yet this is the Buddha's description of genuine loving-kindness. Not easy at all.

Then in the third part the Buddha describes how to send the heart of loving-kindness throughout the entire world: "Radiate a boundless love throughout the whole universe . . . with no obstructions—with no taint of ill will or resentment."

The Buddha says in the closing lines that this is the state where gods in the Brahma Heavens dwell. In other words, genuine loving-kindness is a divine state, transcending human experience. Someone who can stay in the state of loving-kindness can become an arhat, "never would one be reborn in the womb."

This state differs greatly from a sticky and unexamined "I love everybody" feeling of overflowing emotional attachment. The Buddha's description of world-transcending loving-kindness requires a foundation in character and wholesome behavior, decisions for *ahimsa*—harmlessness in deeds, words, and thoughts—and the fierce, uncompromising devotion and service to all beings that a mother feels for her child.

The Metta Sutta is a power-tool of the heart and mind and a living spiritual text, as relevant and useful in the twenty-first century as it was in the Buddha's time, 2,550 years ago.

# Text 3: The Heart Sutra

## Text

Bodhisattva Avalokiteshvara, while deeply immersed in *prajna paramita* [perfection of wisdom], clearly perceived the empty nature of the five skandhas, and transcended all suffering. [Speaking to the monk Shariputra before him]

Shariputra! Form is not different from emptiness, emptiness is not different from form. Form is emptiness, emptiness is form. So it is with feeling, conception, volition, and consciousness.

Shariputra! All dharmas [realities] are empty in character; neither arising nor ceasing, neither impure nor pure, neither increasing nor decreasing.

Therefore, in emptiness, there is no form; there is no feeling, conception, volition, or consciousness; no eye, ear, nose, tongue, body, or mind; no form, sound, smell, taste, touch, or dharmas; no realm of vision, and so forth, up to no realm of mind-consciousness; no ignorance or ending of ignorance, and so forth, up to no aging and death or ending of aging and death.

There is no suffering, no cause, no extinction, no path. There is no wisdom and no attainment. There is nothing to be attained.

By way of prajna paramita, the bodhisattva's mind is free from hindrances. With no hindrances, there is no fear; freed from all distortion and delusion, ultimate nirvana is reached.

By way of prajna paramita, Buddhas of the past, present, and future attain anuttara-samyak-sambodhi [supreme-perfect-awakening].

Therefore, prajna paramita is the great powerful mantra, the great enlightening mantra, the supreme and peerless mantra. It can remove all suffering. This is the truth beyond all doubt.

And the prajna paramita mantra is spoken thus: *Gate gate paragate parasamgate bodhi svaha* [Gone, gone, gone over, gone fully over. Awakening! Hail!][12] ∎

## Outsider Commentary
### Feldmeier

The Heart Sutra is part of a much larger text called the Prajna Paramita, which translates to "Perfection of Wisdom." The first chapter of part 4 discussed the Buddhist idea that all things are impermanent, without a core self, and dissatisfying. Mahayana Buddhism added two additional categories that it found to be necessary implications. The first is that everything is "empty" and, secondly, everything carries the quality of "suchness" or "thusness." These were described earlier, where emptiness referred to nothing having an absolute, eternal substance, even Nirvana, and where everything carried with it a kind of transcendental quality of buddha nature.

Some Buddhist texts describe the dynamic of the constant flux of "emptiness" and "form." The claim "form is emptiness and emptiness is form" is not Buddhist double-speak, but a way to point to a universe in perpetual flow where samsara does not stand in contrast to Nirvana.

This thinking grounds the Heart Sutra, which presents a teaching by bodhisattva Avalokiteshvara, the bodhisattva of compassion and one of the most important figures in Mahayana cosmology. It begins by stating that Avalokiteshvara was immersed in the perfection of wisdom, thus seeing with perfect insight. He looks at the five "parts" of the human being and declares them "empty." Then he declares that all "dharmas" (things) are empty, thus "neither arising nor ceasing." This contrasts greatly with the Theravada framing of reality. Theravada Buddhists would say that all things are real, even if impermanent. So, they do in fact arise and dissipate. Not so, says Avalokiteshvara. From the perspective of emptiness, there is no essence, thus no real thing. So emptiness teaches "no suffering, no cause, no extinction [Nirvana], no path . . . no wisdom and no attainment."

From a Western point of view, this may seem absurd or little more than metaphysical nonsense. Taking it seriously, however, could lead one to profound insights. Conventionally, there are skillful and unskillful behaviors; there are lessons to learn; there is still the Eightfold Path, and so on. But the conventional perspective must give way to the ultimate perspective. Here, seeking Nirvana as though it were something "out there" is exactly what keeps one from Nirvana. In this ultimate perspective, seeking wisdom as though it is some kind of rarefied "thing" to cling to or some kind of trophy is also what keeps one from wisdom. This leads to the next part of the sutra that relates how in perfect wisdom the bodhisattva's mind is free from hindrances, distortions, delusions, and indeed "Nirvana is reached." It is a mystery, for sure, but not one that boasts of intellectual inanity. Rather, it is a mystery that leads one into the perfection of wisdom, not as a claim on some "thing," but as self-emptying, unhindered immersion into the absolute truth of a dynamic universe.

While this may seem foreign to Westerners, the same paradox is reflected in Christianity. St. Paul encourages his readers to take on the same mind as Christ, "who, though he was in the form of God, did not regard equality with God as something to be clung to, but he emptied himself" (Phil. 2:5–7). In a later

---

12. *The Heart of Prajna Paramita Sutra,* trans. Chung Tai Translation Committee (from the Chinese translation by Tripitaka Master Xuan Zang, seventh century), *ctzen.org/sunnyvale/enUS/index.php?option=com_content&task=view&id=145&Itemid=57.*

part of that passage Paul references the sacrifice of Christ as the absolute expression of this emptiness. Paradoxically, his very emptying himself in self-offering is what draws the Christian to proclaim "Jesus Christ is Lord" (vv. 9–11). John's Gospel refers to the same dynamic where his glory and even identification with God is revealed exactly in his self-offering on the cross: "When you have lifted up the Son of Man [on the cross], then you will realize that I AM" (8:28). There is something about the cross that makes it both an icon of God and a magnet for the soul for Christians. While Avalokiteshvara would say that emptiness is form and form is emptiness, Jesus might say emptiness is glory and glory is emptiness. Here emptiness might be an interpretive tool to understand something really profound about Jesus and the nature of salvation.

The mystery of emptiness and its relation to absolute truth is revealed in Christian mysticism as well. St. John of the Cross characterized his path to union with God as though climbing a mountain. "The path of Mount Carmel, the perfect spirit: nothing, nothing, nothing, nothing, nothing, nothing, and, even on the Mount, nothing."[13] So it is not simply that the path is one of self-emptying. Even radical union with God is described as "nothing." One becomes lost in the mystery of the divine and there is not only nothing there to locate as if separate from God, but one cannot locate anything of oneself. Obviously, conventionally, John of the Cross knew his name, his friends, and carried on in the world quite well. But, just like the Buddhist conventional perspective, a conventional sense of self only goes so far for Christians and ultimately needs to be rejected as an impediment to experiencing what Christians regard as the ultimate truth.

## Insider Commentary

### Heng Sure

One key to understanding the Heart Sutra is to consider its purpose: it is a discourse taught primarily to meditators. The signature teaching of all the Prajna Paramita sutras, that of *sunyata*, or emptiness, offers practical guidance for the process of "emptying out of both self and dharmas." When advanced meditators begin to experience changes in body and mind from their practice of deep mental absorption, they need instruction in navigating the states that arise. None of the Buddha's disciples were ready to appropriate this teaching during the early stages of his instruction. The Buddha delivered the discourses on emptiness during the second half of his career and, according to the Tientai school's explanation, did so for more than twenty-one years to develop the meditation skills of his advanced disciples. From this perspective, "emptiness" is clearly not a philosophical proposition. It is not a deliberate self-contradicting conundrum; nor is it mystical Zen banter meant to sound esoteric or cryptic. The Buddha presents emptiness as an existential state of mind that can occur when the ego-bound self begins to break down its rigid categories of self and others, rights and wrongs, loves and hates.

Because the teaching of emptiness is such a compelling, radical notion, the Chinese referred to the Buddhist religion as *kong men*, translated as "the school of emptiness." People often react superficially to logical conundrums, either rejecting them out of hand or misinterpreting them as confusing mysticism for its own sake or as esoteric license to let go of conventional standards of behavior, a sort of, "anything goes" nihilism. Nothing could be further from the truth.

---

13. John of the Cross, *The Collected Works of St. John of the Cross*, trans. Kieran Kavanaugh and Otilio Rodriguez (Washington, DC: Institute of Carmelite Studies, 1991), 111.

It is helpful to see the Heart Sutra in its context among the larger category of Prajna Sutras. There are forty texts in this category, and they range from 100,000 stanzas, the longest, to a single syllable ("A"), which is said to contain the entirety of the wisdom of emptiness. The version known as the Heart is among the shortest. It consists of an abstract of the principles explained at length in Prajna Paramita sutras of 5,000, 8,000, 25,000, and 100,000 stanzas.

The Heart Sutra contains the famous Sanskrit mantra: *Gate gate paragate parasamgate bodhi svaha* (Gone, gone, gone over, gone fully over. Awakening! Hail!). This mantra has long been considered powerful and able to generate auspicious energy, to protect from harm, and to neutralize unwholesome situations. When Master Xuanzang conducted his difficult journey from Chang'an, China, to India and back, he traversed forbidding deserts and crossed the world's highest mountains. His biography recounts that in a demon-infested stretch of the Taklamakan Desert, he relied on recitation of the Heart Sutra's mantra to protect him from harm and to keep his mind free from fear.

At no time did the Buddha seek to establish metaphysical truths. He did not debate, claim ownership of his teachings, or attempt to set up a school with doctrines. He taught solely to share with others the path to liberation that he had walked. Ending suffering was his purpose, and teaching others how to reach that goal according to their abilities was the application of that purpose.

From this perspective, when the Buddha speaks about emptiness, it seems clear that he is not making a metaphysical assertion. He is instead guiding those meditators who had already experienced an awareness of the transient, insubstantial nature of the material and spiritual worlds through the dissolution and reformation of their own bodies and minds. Meditation as the Buddha taught it investigates the

five *skandhas*, or aggregates, of which the body is the first. When the meditator actually experiences his aggregates loosening their solidity, then having a teacher guide one's investigation into the nature of the self is necessary; hence, the purpose of the Prajna Sutra's teaching on emptiness. Meditation begins to yield the insight that the self is merely a construct, a shifting, multilayered, fluid entity with neither permanence nor fixed boundaries. At that point the meditator is more ready to accept that "form and emptiness are not different." Interestingly, the book of Ecclesiastes begins, "Vanity of vanities, says the Teacher, vanity of vanities! All is vanity" (1:2).

In this regard emptiness is better understood as a verb than a noun: the Buddha encouraged his meditators to continue emptying out the self and what pertains to the self, to empty out the body, feelings, thoughts, mental formations, and consciousness. The apparent logical contradictions of the prajna teachings encourage the meditator not to stop at emptying out the false self but to empty out emptiness as well.

By taking that next step and refusing to establish emptiness as a thought or position to cling to, both subject and object are returned to the mind that sets up nowhere; the dynamic nonduality of the true nature is revealed. Thus, the Heart Sutra presents in abstract the single essential message of the prajna category of sutras: "There is no wisdom and no attainment. There is nothing to be attained."

The great Buddhist synthesizer, Nagarjuna (c. 150–250 CE), based his watershed interpretations of the Buddha's teachings, the Middle Way Teaching, on the formula "empty, false, and the middle." This dialectical formula describes the experience of meditators in absorption on their way to the Buddha's liberation. The Middle Way Teaching was rooted in actual practice, and Nagarjuna was known as a profound meditator. He described the Path as a process of analysis that begins by emptying out language and thought, then applying the same analysis by letting go of the "falseness" of the one who meditates. This is the step that "empties out emptiness." Having let go of attachment to both self and dharmas, one integrates body and mind back to the Middle Way. Only this awakened individual finds his identity grounded in the wisdom of emptiness.

As the often-quoted closing stanza of the Diamond Sutra says, "All things made of conditions are like dreams, like illusions, like bubbles, like shadows, like dew drops, and like flashes of lightning. You should contemplate them in this way."[14]

# Text 4: The Universal Door of the Bodhisattva Who Listens to the Sounds of All the World

The following verses are excerpted from the Complete Universal Door Chapter 25, from the *Sutra of the Lotus Flower of the Wonderful Dharma.*

## Text

At that time, Bodhisattva Infinite Resolve rose from his seat, bared his right shoulder, joined his palms, and facing the Buddha, said, "O World Honored One, how did Gwan Shr Yin Bodhisattva get the name Gwan Shr Yin?"

The Buddha answered Bodhisattva Infinite Resolve,

"Good Man, if all the countless hundreds of thousands of millions of living beings tormented by misery and pain hear of Gwan Shr Yin Bodhisattva, and with all their hearts invoke his name, Gwan Shr Yin Bodhisattva will immediately respond to their prayers and set them free.

"If those who hold the name of Gwan Shr Yin Bodhisattva should fall into a great fire, the fire will not burn them, because of Gwan Shr Yin Bodhisattva's awesome spiritual power. If they are being tossed about in deep and treacherous waters and call his name, they will quickly reach the shallows. . . .

"Even if the entire three-fold, great, thousand-world system were teeming with Yakshas and Rakshashas [nature and demon spirits] bent on vexing men, when the evil demons hear the name of Gwan Shr Yin Bodhisattva called out by these men, they will not be able to see them with their wicked eyes, much less do them in! . . .

"Infinite Resolve! How imposing is the awesome spiritual power of the Great Bodhisattva Who Listens to the Sounds of All the World!

"If any living being with weighty desires can constantly revere and keep in mind Gwan Shr Yin Bodhisattva, his passions will subside. If someone with much anger can constantly revere and keep in mind Gwan Shr Yin Bodhisattva, then his anger will subside. If someone dull and foolish can constantly revere and keep in mind Gwan Shr Yin Bodhisattva, he will leave stupidity behind. . . .

"Therefore, every single living being should hold Gwan Shr Yin Bodhisattva's name in mind. Infinite Resolve! Suppose someone held the names of Bodhisattvas to the number of grains of sand in sixty-two million Ganges Rivers, and for this person's entire life, made offerings to them all of food and drink, clothes, bedding, and medicine. What is your opinion? Would the merit and virtue accrued by that good man or woman be abundant?"

Infinite Resolve replied, "Extremely abundant, World Honored One, very great indeed!"

---

14. Tripitaka Master Hsuan Hua, commentary, *The Vajra Prajna Paramita Sutra: A General Explanation* (Burlingame, CA: Buddhist Text Translation Society, 2003), 190.

The Buddha said, "Yet if someone else held the name of Gwan Shr Yin Bodhisattva, bowed and made an offering but one time, the blessings of these two people would be identical, the same in every way, and would endure for quadrillions of aeons.

"Infinite Resolve! Holding the name of Gwan Shr Yin Bodhisattva brings blessings and benefits as limitless and boundless as these."

Again, the Bodhisattva Infinite Resolve asked the Buddha, "World Honored One, how does Gwan Shr Yin Bodhisattva wander in this Saha World? How does he speak Dharma for living beings, and what manner of resourcefulness does he command?"

The Buddha answered Bodhisattva Infinite Resolve, "If there is a living being in some country who can be liberated by a Buddha, Gwan Shr Yin Bodhisattva appears as a Buddha and teaches him the Dharma. If someone can be liberated by a Pratyeka Buddha, he appears as a Pratyeka Buddha and teaches him the Dharma. If someone can be liberated by a Sound-hearer, he appears as a Sound-hearer and teaches him the Dharma. If someone can be liberated by a Brahma-heaven King, he appears as a Brahma-heaven King and teaches him the Dharma.

"If someone can be liberated by Shakra, he appears as Shakra and teaches him the Dharma. If someone can be liberated by the God of Comfort, he appears as the God of Comfort and teaches him the Dharma. If someone can be liberated by a mighty General of the Gods, he appears as a mighty General of the Gods and teaches him the Dharma. If someone can be liberated by the God Vaisravana, he appears as Vaisravana and teaches him the Dharma." [The sutra continues with Bodhisattva Infinite Resolve breaking into verses of praise.][15] ■

## Outsider Commentary
### *Feldmeier*

The Lotus Sutra has become a central Mahayana text because of the meritorious power of this section and the extraordinary promises it offers. As this selection shows, even the smallest act of piety can condition the bodhisattva's extraordinary boons of protection, wealth, safety, and so on. To the possible challenge that the boons given are out of proportion to the devotion offered, Buddhists might say that it is exactly as intended. Such a contrast helps us recognize the limited and even meager quality of our spiritual lives, and places that realization in the context of a spiritual universe that is holy, powerful, and deeply caring about the plight of sentient creatures like ourselves.

This chapter of the Lotus Sutra describes and praises the ministry of Avalokiteshvara, who has also been named Gwan Shr Yin Bodhisattva or "Bodhisattva Who Listens to the Sounds of All the World." While this may seem quite a clumsy name, it well represents the extraordinary ministry of Avalokiteshvara. Originally, this bodhisattva was masculine, but as the tradition developed in China and Japan, one now finds her as feminine. She listens to the suffering, cries, and appeals of the whole universe.

As mentioned, the power of this bodhisattva and her universal desire to help, heal, and support those in need are extraordinary. This short section of the chapter shows that her very name (as Gwan Shr Yin) confounds evil spirits, that her presence quells passions, and that those in grave danger who call on her are rescued. Most extraordinary is the claim that even the slightest devotion will gain the same karmic fruit as those who have offered the most extraordinary devotions throughout their lives.

---

15. *The Lotus Sutra*, trans. Dharma Realm Buddhist University, online only, *drba.org/dharma/universaldoor.asp*.

How can this be? One response might be to point out that in all Buddhist schools the karmic consequences of one's actions tend to be framed in extravagant terms, both good and bad. So, for example, a greedy person in life could get a rebirth of many thousands of years as a "hungry ghost" or *preta*. Here the greedy person is imagined born in a spiritual world with an extraordinarily large body, but only a pinhole of a mouth. Thus, he or she is always hungry, always seeking, and never satisfied—an exaggerated version of a life of greed. In counterpoint, the Metta Sutta includes the promise that one would be reborn in the Divine World. This would be an existence higher than the gods (*devas*) and a realm that is extraordinarily sublime. Indeed, this could be for as much as 64,000 years.

While the idea that karmic fruit has a kind of exponential quality to it exists throughout all of Buddhism, this doesn't completely answer the question. How is it that a small act of devotion to Gwan Shr Yin can gain the same karmic fruit as an extraordinary life of devotion? One answer would be that Gwan Shr Yin shares her own karma, usually called "transfer of merit." Merit transfer works like this: because the universe is radically interconnected and because my merit (karmic fruit) is under my control, I can transfer that merit to another via the web of an interpenetrating universe. Gwan Shr Yin has deeply practiced the dharma for so many lifetimes and has accumulated so much merit that she can transfer her merit to others even without their deserving it as an expression of her infinite compassion.

How shall a Westerner consider such claims? At first blush, many might see this as preposterous. Yet, what do most Christians believe about intercessory prayer? Does it work, and if so, why? Some might say that it works because one asks God to do something; it is nothing like a transfer of merit. But why would God need insight into what God should do? Furthermore, why would having many people pray on one's behalf be better than simply one person doing so? It can't be because this gets a better chance at access to God or that God is vulnerable to the bandwagon effect.

In the New Testament, Paul frequently asks for prayers on his behalf. Would God have otherwise not supported Paul's ministry? The Letter of James includes some fascinating claims: "Therefore, confess your sins to one another, and pray for one another, so that you may be healed. The prayer of the righteous is powerful and effective. . . . My brothers and sisters . . . you should know that whoever brings back a sinner from wandering will save the sinner's soul from death and will cover a multitude of sins" (James 5:16–20).

Here James suggests there is something powerful about the holy person that effects the prayer or spiritual intention of that holy person, including covering a multitude of sins. Perhaps Christians might consider this: would you rather have a saint or a sluggish, mediocre Christian pray for you at a time of need? Could it be that people really are so interconnected that spiritual power moves across an interpenetrating spiritual web that connects us to all and allows us to have meritorious impact on others? This needn't be imagined in contrast to God, since God undergirds both the web and the spiritual power. But could it be that we are actual players in this dynamic? It may make Christians rethink what really happens in intercessory prayer.

## Insider Commentary

### Heng Sure

The Universal Door Chapter appears near the end of the Lotus Sutra and relates the story of Guan Shi Yin Bodhisattva (Avalokiteshvara), the Awakened Being of Great Compassion. Guan Shi Yin ("She Who Contemplates the World's Sounds") may be the most recognized religious figure in all of East Asia. Buddhists

Guan Yin, the bodhisattva of compassion, has many faces and hands to assist the masses of suffering beings who seek her help.

and non-Buddhists alike know her name. She fulfills the same role in many respects as the Mother Mary, the Holy Blessed Virgin of Roman Catholicism and Eastern Orthodoxy. The awesome purity and radiant perfection of the buddhas can seem to some extra-human and difficult to approach. Guan Yin Bodhisattva of the Universal Door Chapter stands ready to lend a hand as she responds to calls from every side.

Her story, chapter 25 in the Lotus Sutra, describes Guan Yin's vows to rescue sentient beings. She will respond to all those who recall her strength in times of trouble and who then call her name: "Namo Guan Shi Yin Bodhisattva." The sutra first introduces the Inexhaustible Intention Bodhisattva, who asks the Buddha the source of Guan Shi Yin's name, "Awakened Being Who Contemplates the Sounds of the World." In answering his question, the Buddha describes seven situations of mortal danger from which Guan Shi Yin will rescue beings if they remember to call out her name. Further, Guan Yin will remove three kinds of poisons: greed, anger, and delusion from anybody who sincerely requests this healing. The Buddha also promises that Guan Yin will bestow sons or daughters on childless couples who make a sincere request.

Then Inexhaustible Intention asks the Buddha to know how Guan Shi Yin Bodhisattva uses expedient means to teach the dharma. The Buddha relates thirty-two appearances that Guan Yin can make in order to get close to beings who can accept the teachings from that particular form: "If someone can be liberated by a Brahma-heaven King, he appears as a Brahma-heaven King. . . . If someone can be liberated by Shakra, he appears as Shakra. . . ." The account of Guan Yin's expedient skill in the Universal Door Chapter is one of the most detailed and marvelous descriptions of bodies projected by transformation in all of Buddhist sacred literature. From the body of a buddha to the body of a layman, a public official, a Brahmin priest, or even the terrifying form of a *vajra*-wielding spirit, Guan Yin knows how to show up and speak for individuals in a way each can understand.

In the next scene of the text, the interlocutor wishes to make an offering to Guan Yin of a priceless rosary of precious beads. Guan Yin declines twice but the Buddha intervenes and instructs her to accept it not for her sake, but rather for the sake of the donor and those who will gain merit from her receiving their gift. She accepts in order to grant the donor's wish, but she then becomes a donor herself by separating the beads into two strands and handing one to Shakyamuni Buddha and offering the other as a gift to the stupa (Buddhist reliquary) of the Buddha Many Jewels. The Buddha praises her lack of greed and her generosity. Then begins the section of verses that reiterate the principles from the prose section. This brief chapter of the popular Lotus Sutra has galvanized the faith of millions of Buddhists for centuries and if asked why, they would answer, "Because Guan Yin really responds."

This text describes Guan Shi Yin not only as an ideal or supernatural deity, but also as one with the ability to save those in need in real life. Guan Yin has been responding to those believers who call on her name for thousands of years. There is a literary tradition of Guan Yin response stories, originating in Mount Potala, the island in the South China Sea between Shanghai and Ningbo. The list of famous people and ordinary citizens who have recited Guan Yin's name and have received miraculous rescues numbers in the millions. For each of the seven types of rescue listed in the text, there are many thousands of stories testifying to Guan Yin's efficacy. When one recites the name of Avalokiteshvara with sincere gratitude, she will extend one of her thousand hands and respond in a transformation body to effect a rescue.

A curator at the Shanghai City Museum, for example, was "struggled against" during the Cultural Revolution in China. Authorities confiscated his personal collection of more than 300 Buddha images, and he was thrown into a labor camp. It was well known that any overt display of religious practice would result in beatings or execution, so devout Buddhists had to conceal their faith or stop their devotions. I asked the curator how he survived the ordeal and he pulled out a cheap metal keychain—the kind you can get at the five-and-dime—with the tiny metal sticks and balls. He said that by day it was his keychain. At night when he was alone it became his recitation beads. He continued to secretly call on the name of Guan Yin Bodhisattva. She gave him the courage not to give up and not to despair when times were really hard. In the end, he said, he survived without any injuries and all his Buddhist art works and images were finally returned. He felt sure that Guan Yin's protection brought him through the ordeal. It was his conclusion that those who didn't have the support of religious faith didn't survive.

Guan Yin appears in many of the major Mahayana sutras, and her image as the "Maiden in the White-robe" is one of the most recognizable images of the universal religious pantheon. The manifestations of the Blessed Virgin as the Black Madonna in Barcelona's Monserrat Benedictine Monastery resemble images of Guan Yin in remarkable ways. Both appear as women holding young baby boys, both hold pearl-like orbs, both grasp the stem of a tree branch, and both display profoundly compassionate expressions and postures. The Black Madonna of Monserrat has been receiving petitions for help from those in need (including messages in bottles) for centuries, just as Guan Yin has been hearing the cries of the world for thousands of years.

Fascinatingly, two great world religions with minimal contact across the eastern and western hemispheres witness to a powerful spiritual being in a compassionate female form. She comes as a nurturing mother, a wise sister, and a powerful and resourceful friend who can be counted on to lend a hand when times get tough.

One might conclude that some wholesome impulse in our hearts reaches for a compassionate and wise female figure to whom we can call and who inspires us to try our best. Guan Yin responds to those in need; she shows up in the pounding waves of the high seas; she opens a gate when there is no way ahead; she delivers the last-minute rescue; she keeps us cool when the pressure would overwhelm us. She bestows courage. In anxious situations, Guan Yin can remove the terror from a frightened mind: "Good Man, if all the countless hundreds of thousands of millions of living beings tormented by misery and pain hear of Gwan Shr Yin Bodhisattva, and with all their hearts invoke his name, Gwan Shr Yin Bodhisattva will immediately respond to their prayers and set them free." Through her Universal Door, Buddhists recall their better side and find the courage to go on.

# CHAPTER 16

# Concluding Reflections

*Peter Feldmeier and Heng Sure*

## Reflections of an "Outsider"

*Peter Feldmeier*

Comparing my description of Buddhism in the introductory chapter with Heng Sure's as well as our commentary on several classic texts, I appreciate the real differences in approach. These are not merely because we are distinct scholars and personalities. Many of the dissimilarities arise precisely because I am an outsider and he an insider. I trust that readers can actually *feel* the difference. There is a kind of clinical distance that I bring. So, while I don't think anything I wrote is inaccurate; nonetheless, I provided a kind of classical description based on standard references and standard ways of framing Buddhism.

## General Reflections on Living Outside the Tradition

I've experienced Buddhism with some depth of practice personally. So, for example, I've not only taken graduate courses in Buddhist teachings and practices, I've also practiced vipashyana (insight) meditation for years and taken a number of retreats, including a three-month-long intensive meditation retreat. Still, my training and experience comes from Westerners and mostly in academic and retreat forums.

Because of this, Heng Sure's disinterest in the Eightfold Path and Nirvana came as a surprise. These appear not at all to be part of Mahayana Buddhist day-to-day consciousness. The reader should see how much of my framing of Buddhism has to do with doctrine, with interests in such things as the self that is no-self and the nature of Nirvana. Even my wrestling with the Heart Sutra is one of metaphysics, while Heng Sure's complete interest is in seeing how the sutra provides an interpretive strategy for deep meditation and wisdom.

While Heng Sure is a scholar (we graduated from the same PhD program), he also guides a Buddhist community. Our work reflects this difference. For example, I describe the Metta Sutta in the context of the four divine abiding meditations, reflecting a classical presentation from the fifth century great Buddhaghosa. In contrast, Heng Sure exhorts us with the image of a "power-tool," something that inspires one to take it up in order to turbocharge one's spiritual practice. I also noticed that he spent a good deal of time sharing the wonderful story of why the Buddha taught it. Such stories stay in one's imagination. He didn't simply tell us that practitioners with a poor attitude can really turn this around by practicing metta, he brought us into a world of tree spirits who went from throwing coconuts on monks' heads to offering them food that they might stay. It would be interesting to see whose way of description it would have more impact on the reader. Surely, one who is already a Buddhist would find Heng Sure's description far more interesting.

A second clear example of the pastoral nature of Heng Sure's insider approach is his obvious love for bodhisattva Guan Yin. I've spent some time at a local dharma center and the incredible love for Guan Yin is everywhere evident. My description of Guan Yin in the preceding chapter is virtually clinical. I describe the theory of how and why merit can be transferred and Guan Yin's claimed participation in this. Rev. Heng Sure tells us that his own Buddhist experience confirms that she cares for those who come to her.

## Seeing Things Differently

An outsider clearly has a limited perspective. Consider the following image: There are two architects discussing a house whose plans, materials, and even furniture both know well. The difference between them is that one of them has been actually living in that house and raising a family there for the last twenty years. This one has a feel of the house the other never could. On the other hand, it could be that the *outsider* architect doesn't have the same blind spots, and so recognizes mold that the other has grown used to or even benefits (that great bay window!) that the other now takes for granted.

With the above in mind, let me as an outsider raise some questions regarding particular assumptions from our insider, which he can then respond to as he wishes. As an outsider, one thing that strikes me as odd is the broad Buddhist insistence on focusing almost exclusively on orthopraxy or right practice with little consideration of orthodoxy (right belief). As an outsider I question this in two ways. First, consider the claims by Mahayana practitioners

that insights found say in the Heart Sutra on emptiness represent advanced teaching that the Buddha reserved for those who had deeply appropriated the earlier teachings. I see these same claims in the Lotus Sutra, where "expedient means" is the reason why the Buddha taught lower-level teachings to most of his adherents. Theravadin believers, however, consider these texts and their claims unacceptable. These texts provide doctrines Theravadins consider "wrong view" and even insulting, as they suggest that the Theravada understanding of the way to Nirvana is ultimately limited and unsuccessful.

Second, as an outsider who has studied many other religions and belongs to a religion in which doctrine is highly important, I wonder how one can make such a distinction between practice and doctrine. Often, the practice is based on the doctrine and reaffirms that same doctrine. So, for example, one could say, "Practice mindfulness and watch the arising and dissipation of thoughts, feelings, and sensations. See for yourself that there is no *self* there." If you do this intensely, it does indeed confirm the "no-self" teaching. But a Christian might say, "Look deeply within and recognize a spiritual presence that calls you to holiness. This is the Divine dwelling within speaking to your soul." Christian contemplatives practicing this way do seem to discover God and their soul; experiences that confirm the doctrine. To this outsider, I would say that doctrine and practice necessarily imply and condition each other. Doctrine frames one's experience and helps to form one's interpretation of that experience.

Related to all of the above is Heng Sure's confidence that there is not much conflict between Theravada and Mahayana expressions of Buddhism. Of course, he recognizes that some exploit the differences contentiously. But still, I think he argues that these traditions are as sisters or like fingers on a hand. As an outsider, it seems as though this appears both true and false. On the one hand, it is true in that I've never heard of Buddhist wars. And, since most Buddhists take a view that this is just one lifetime in eons of lifetimes, getting it exactly right is not crucial. It also seems to me that most Buddhists from different schools simply don't talk to each other. So, while this allows for mutual coexistence, it may simply be mutual snubbing. Further, as an outsider I've had some contacts with Buddhists who feel free to tell an outsider what they think of other schools' understanding of the dharma. And their assessments often come down to, "That's *false view*." This can even come from inside the same tradition. I once shared with a Sri Lankan monk and scholar, a Thai monk and scholar's opinion about Nirvana. His reply was, "Who told you that? I bet he was Thai. Thai monks are not good scholars."

A final issue as an outsider that I find fascinating and would ask Heng Sure to comment further on, is the issue of an open canon. The canon is closed in Christianity. This provides an objective reference to an ongoing, changing tradition. For the Christian faith to be relevant and not some religious museum, it must constantly reconsider itself anew. This constitutes tradition, that dynamic life of the church, including her prayer, doctrine, history, leadership, and lived experience. It represents the spirit-led church being church. The scriptures, the canon, is set as a reference for orthodoxy as well as that which provides an apostolic imagination. It's the glue to the fundamental witness, which Christians continue to carry on. Obviously, the interpretation of scripture changes as Christians change and as the questions put to the text change. But scripture, particularly because it is closed, grounds the faith.

One of the most fascinating claims by Heng Sure is that the canon is as open as there are enlightened minds who can contribute to it. How does this work, and who decides if a text deserves to be rendered as equal to texts already

embraced? What ensures a grounded continuity with the original dharma? What keeps the Buddhist tradition authentically grounded?

## Reflections of an "Insider"
*Heng Sure*

I have been a Buddhist monk for nearly four decades, longer than I was "other than" Buddhist. Yet it is important to clarify that in this chapter I have presented these ideas not for Buddhism but only for myself as a Buddhist. I trust the reader has grasped how varied and multifaceted the Buddhist world is in the twenty-first century. After all, how many 2,550-year-old human institutions still flourish on the planet? In all that time there have been so many understandings about what the Buddha taught that the only honest representation one can make is to acknowledge one's sources and keep a humble and respectful attitude. Afflictions are infinite and dharma-doors are likewise infinite.

In this dialogue I have responded to Peter Feldmeier's questions differently than I would have as a young monk. The dharma works on the mind the way nature grows trees. If you stare directly at the trunk you don't see much change. If you look away and then look back you realize the tree has grown and changed. There are no shortcuts to wisdom. Plus, when younger I couldn't really absorb the depth of the First Noble Truth that all things comprised of component conditions change and move on. As much as I'm attached to things being a certain way, that's how much I'll suffer when things shift, as they always will. And this includes *Buddhism*!

The Eightfold Path is a fundamental formula in the Buddha's teaching; these eight factors answer the question, "How does one bring suffering to an end?" But it doesn't come up as a primary teaching to cultivate in the Chan

School's daily exhortations. Other factors that answer the same question from a Mahayana perspective do come up. Master Hua recited the list of eight and we memorized it, but always in the context of "what the Theravada learned," along with the Four Noble Truths and the Twelve Links of Dependent Coarising. These are essential teachings, and we certainly learned them. But they were considered superseded by a Mahayana version—in fact several versions—of how to cultivate the mind to end suffering for oneself and for all sentient beings.

For example, Chan monks hear about the Six Paramitas (Perfections) all the time. Daily we chant the Ten Practices and Vows of Samantabhadra in our morning liturgy. The Ten Practices and Vows do not replace the Eightfold Path, but represent a daily mental cultivation even more essential to the Bodhisattva Path. While we are encouraged to hold on to "correct views" and avoid "false views," our emphasis is decidedly toward skillful activity.

Like the Theravada, the Mahayana tradition strongly emphasizes the Five Lay Precepts as the first answer to the question, "How do I begin my cultivation?" In the Mahayana, one officially becomes a Buddhist when one "Takes Refuge with the Three Treasures" of Buddha, Dharma, and Sangha. At that time there is the option to commit to the Five Precepts. In the Precept Transmission Ceremony one vows to uphold the Five Precepts (refraining from killing, stealing, sexual misconduct, lying, and intoxicants) for the remainder of one's life. One takes these precepts with solemnity, as they only work with earnest intentionality. All buddhas began their commitment to the Path with these five precepts. These precepts are a commitment to stepping up one's practice, beginning with one's character and personal behavior. Someone who has been through the ceremony is honored in the community and walks and sits in front of other laity during ceremonies and assemblies.

## Gently Responding to an Outsider
### Orthodoxy and
### Orthopraxy Clarified

Peter Feldmeier asked about orthodoxy and orthopraxy and, yes, these are not absolute distinctions within Buddhism either. In Pure Land Buddhism, devotion to and faith in the Buddha Amitabha is essential to making his vows work. To go to the Pure Land, one must believe in the description of Amitabha's vows and call on his name with single-minded concentration. Then at death one is reborn into a pure lotus flower in the Land of Utmost Happiness. So Pure Land Buddhism is one place where teaching completely blends practice and understanding. Right belief and right practice are inseparable. Scholars of the Avatamsaka Sutra have divided its teachings into four divisions: Faith, Understanding, Practice, and Realization. Faith is crucial: "They all had certain faith in the sublime truth. . . ."[1]

Pointing out Buddhism's relative stress on right practice highlights how right belief is not enough. Those who do not make the profession of faith but who still hold the precepts, meditate deeply, and make a transformation in their deep consciousness will make it all the way to buddhahood, regardless of verbal approval of the Buddha's teachings. While scholarship requires attending to doctrine cultivation requires watching the mind and attending to motives. Nobody asks, "Do you believe in the Buddha and accept what he said?" They do ask, "Did you follow the precepts and watch your mind? Did you transform your polluted thoughts of greed,

---

1. 2.fodian.net/world/0279_01.html.

anger, delusion, pride, and doubt?" Around Gold Mountain Monastery, Master Hua rarely if ever asked his disciples about doctrine or their own enlightenment. He knew better! But every day he would test us to see if he could make us angry. Purging one's reactive mental states was essential for actual awakening, not parroting any formula for enlightenment.

### Buddhism's Openness

The worldwide Buddhist community has its share of narrow-minded fundamentalists, but nowhere does a prejudice for one school or group appear in the Buddha's sutras. The Buddhist world holds millions of people, many of whom are provincial folks who only know their own flavor of food, incense, and prayer and have no interest at all in any variant forms or flavors. This is true in Sri Lanka, Thailand, Tibet, China, Japan, Korea, and perhaps your neighborhood Zen center. People are people after all and tend to interpret any new or different ways as "other" and suspicious. Buddhists are no different. There is much mutual ignorance in any religion.

Because the dharma only arrived in the West a century ago, we seem to have avoided those tribal antipathies here; much of the baggage of ignorance has been set down. The North American Monastic Sangha gathering has been meeting annually for nearly two decades; men and women in red, brown, gray, black, and saffron robes are always present and nearly always supportive and in harmony. Of course, even here some Buddhists can be as full of self-importance and fear as any other religious group. This is a human failing, and certainly does not represent the Buddha's wisdom.

### The Canon Witnesses to Awakening

Regarding the open canon question, I may be missing the point but I thought the Hebrew scriptures were a closed canon because they represent a collection of historical documents, spoken by God or given by revelation to prophets. Certainly the various councils and text editions put their stamp on the various books including the Gospels and the New Testament. Then there are the Apocrypha and marginalized texts to consider. Peter Feldmeier says the canon is closed in Christianity because it then provides an objective reference to an ongoing, changing tradition. But doesn't tradition actually precede the canon and determine it?

The idea that the canon remains open for Buddhists is grounded in the very nature of the canon, that is, witness to the path toward, experience of, and nature of awakening. The Buddha spoke the sutras from his human nature, which had been freed of ignorance. In the Mahayana tradition, he is reported to have said that all living beings have the buddha nature and all can become buddhas. Only because of polluted thinking and attachments do they fail to realize the virtues and wisdom of their buddha nature. Anybody who wakes up to the purity of his or her nature can speak sutras of equal value to those Buddha Shakyamuni spoke. There is no difference.

The basic sutra is wordless. When the Buddha wanted to pass on the dharma to the next patriarch, Mahakasyapa, he held up a flower and Kasyapa smiled. Mahakasyapa got the whole teaching wordlessly because the wisdom that allows one to speak the dharma with the same authority as the Buddha does not come from above or from without, but from within one's own nature. The dharma is the teaching discovered by realization, not by revelation. As the sutras say, to wake up you rely on the teachings of nobody else. When one transforms the illusion of a separated ego, one drops the ignorance that kept one apart from all sentient beings in substance and in nature. When one realizes the absolute, universal truth (*dharmakaya*), then all of the teachings are available to that person to speak expediently in whatever way living beings can understand. The source of the sutras is simply the calm, concentrated mind of samadhi. There, all the sutras then appear as maps, as blueprints, as medicine for the illness of greed, anger, and delusion. When you wake up, the core experience is yours, identical with the Buddha's. So my point is not that we are waiting for another sutra to appear any minute, but rather that, in principle, anybody who replicates the Buddha's awakening can deliver teachings of equal value to the Buddha's; they point us back to our own nature and teach us how to awaken. It's an open canon.

# Resources for Further Study

## Review Questions

1. Where does Buddhism agree with Hinduism and where are there decisive differences?
2. What are the Buddha's Four Noble Truths, and how do they relate to his assessment of the three conditions of all reality?
3. Why is Buddhism described as radically egalitarian? What are the qualities of the religion that make it so?
4. How does each author understand the Heart Sutra's message that form is emptiness and emptiness is form? How are their interpretations alike and different?
5. Buddhism's First Noble Truth is that life is suffering. Why did both authors argue that Buddhism is far from a negative, life-rejecting religion?

## Questions for Reflection and Discussion

1. Dr. Feldmeier has questioned Rev. Heng Sure's de-emphasis of orthodoxy in favor of orthopraxy. Do you think there can be a religion that has relatively little interest in doctrine? How would Christianity be different if this were the case?
2. Rev. Heng Sure has made an association between the bodhisattva Avalokiteshvara (Guan Shi Yin) and the Virgin Mary in Catholicism and Orthodoxy. Do you see them playing the same spiritual roles in both religions?
3. Consider the image of two architects discussing the same house, the second being a resident of that house. How does this shed light on understanding a given religion (outsider and insider)?
4. How would you distinguish Dr. Feldmeier's description of Buddhism from Rev. Heng Sure's description of Buddhism?
5. What do you think of Buddhism's emphasis on the monastic life? Does this make it an elitist religion? Do you think you would have a better chance of being holy if you were a monastic?
6. Consider Dr. Feldmeier's comments about metta (loving-kindness) and how different this view of love is to Western and even Christian sensibilities. Can you have love without attachments? Are all attachments problematic?

## Glossary

**anatman**   Sanskrit for "no-self" (Pali: *anatta*). In contrast to Hinduism's assumption of an eternal self (atman), Buddhism posits that the self is made up of five aggregates, all of which are impersonal and without an absolute eternal self.

**anitya** Sanskrit for "impermanence" (Pali: *anicca*). Refers to a quality of all phenomenal existence; everything is impermanent and thus an unsatisfactory refuge.

**arhat** Sanskrit for "worthy one" (Pali: *arahant*). Refers to a fully enlightened one who has attained Nirvana.

**Avalokiteshvara** The bodhisattva of compassion. One of the main bodhisattvas and one most beloved in the Mahayana tradition. Also known as Gwan Sri Yin (Chinese) and Kwan Yin (Japanese).

**Bodhidharma** (c. 470–543 CE) The twenty-eighth patriarch of the Buddha and first patriarch of Chan (Zen) Buddhism in China.

**buddha** Sanskrit for "awakened one." The standard reference is to Siddhartha Guatama, who began the religion of Buddhism. It also refers to all the buddhas who have preceded or will follow the historical Buddha throughout the universe's history.

**buddha nature** The foundational reality and pure truth of all beings in Mahayana Buddhism.

**conditioned mind** An unenlightened mind is reactive due to three conditions: lust, ill will, and delusion. These are also framed as desire, anger, and ignorance.

**dependent coarising** A Buddhist descriptive of the interconnected arising of all physical and mental formations. Each part of the person depends on the arising of every other part. To break the chain of rebirth (samsara), one has to conquer the ignorance that perpetuates the mutual dependence.

**The Dhammapada** A canonical compilation primarily of the sayings of the Buddha in 423 verses. The Dhammapada is the most read, meditated on, and cited material in the canon.

**dharma** Sanskrit for "teaching" or "truth" (Pali: *dhamma*). The collective term for the spiritual truths of Buddhism.

**dukkha** Pali for "suffering" or "dissatisfaction" (Sanskrit: *duhkha*). The pain or dissatisfaction that is endemic to all of life is dukkha and the fact of dukkha is the First Noble Truth.

**Eightfold Path** The last of the Four Noble Truths, constituting the path to enlightenment. The Eightfold Path represents (1) Right Understanding, (2) Right Thought, (3) Right Speech, (4) Right Action, (5) Right Livelihood, (6) Right Effort, (7) Right Mindfulness, and (8) Right Concentration.

**Four Noble Truths** The Buddha's fundamental message: (1) life is dissatisfying, (2) the cause of dissatisfaction is craving, (3) there is an end to craving, which is Nirvana, and (4) the way to Nirvana is the Eightfold Path.

**karma** Sanskrit for "action" (Pali: *kamma*). This refers to action and the result of action. When one acts while identifying with the action, there are karmic consequences that follow the person. Morally good and bad actions produce karmic fruit that affects one's current life and future lives.

**Mahayana** Sanskrit for "great vehicle." A school of Buddhism that arose in the first century CE that emphasizes the possibility of liberation for a great number of people in various lifestyles. *Mahayana* is a collective term referring to various schools of Buddhism, including Tibetan, Zen (Chan), Pure Land, and in India, Madyamika and Yogacara schools.

**Maitreya** The expected next Buddha to come to the earth and renew the dharma.

**moksha** Sanskrit for "release." The liberation from the cycle of rebirth. For Buddhists, it marks attaining Nirvana.

**Nagarjuna** (c. 150–2550 CE) Considered the most influential Buddhist philosopher in the Mahayana tradition, particularly on his insistence that Nirvana and samsara are one.

**Nirvana** Sanskrit for "blowing out" (Pali: *Nibbana*). The goal of Buddhists, it refers to the extinction of all karmic formations and breaking the chain of the cycle of rebirths (samsara).

**Pali Canon** The first written canon in Buddhism and the central texts of the Theravada school. The Pali Canon consists of three collections or baskets (*tripitaka*): *vinaya*—monastic rules; *suttas*—teachings of the Buddha; and *abhidhamma*—philosophy and psychology.

**Prajna Paramita** Sanskrit for "perfection of Wisdom." This is a main sutra in the Mahayana tradition, the core of which is the Heart Sutra.

**samsara** Sanskrit for "wandering." The succession of rebirths that all beings go through within various modes of existence until they become fully enlightened and achieve moksha (escape).

**satori** In Zen, it refers to an enlightened experience whereby the truths of Zen are realized dramatically in the mind.

**shunyata** Sanskrit for "emptiness." A universal quality of all phenomena that relates to impermanence and no-self, but also involves the notion that it has an intrinsic relationship with "fullness"; that is, everything is both empty and full simultaneously.

**Siddhartha Gautama (c. 566–486 BCE)** The name of the historical Buddha who founded Buddhism. He was born in present-day Nepal as a prince in the Shakya clan, was enlightened at the age of thirty-five, and led the Buddhist movement until he died at the age of eighty.

**sutra** Sanskrit for "teaching" (Pali: *sutta*). This term could refer to any teaching, but most typically refers to a teaching of the Buddha.

**tathata** Sanskrit for "thusness" or "suchness," a universal, spiritual quality of all phenomenal reality.

**Theravada** Pali for "teaching of the elders." The only surviving school from the early period of Buddhism. Theravada Buddhism is widespread in the countries of Southeast Asia, such as Thailand, Burma, Sri Lanka, Cambodia, and Laos.

**Trikaya** Mahayana Buddhism's doctrine of the three "bodies" of the Buddha, which are

(1) *dharmakaya*—the cosmic Buddha nature;
(2) *nirmanakaya*—historical Buddhas; and
(3) *sambhogakaya*—celestial Buddhas.

**vipashyana** Sanskrit for "insight" (Pali: *vipassana*). This refers to clear seeing or the recognition of the three marks of all existence: impermanence, no-self, and suffering. It is also a term for the meditational practice of mindfulness in order to recognize these marks.

**Zen** Japanese for "meditation" (Chinese: *Chan*). Begun by Bodhidharma, this represents the school of Mahayana Buddhism that emphasizes enlightenment through meditation and the realization of a non-attaining mind.

## Annotated Bibliography

Bailey, Greg and Ian Mabbett. *The Sociology of Early Buddhism*. Cambridge: Cambridge University Press, 2003.

This text describes the early religious and cultural development in Theravada Buddhism.

Buddhaghosa, and Ñāṇamoli. *The Path of Purification [Visuddhimagga]*. 5th ed. Kandy, Sri Lanka: Buddhist Publication Society, 1991.

This synthesis of Buddhist practice and philosophy is considered the most influential text in Theravada Buddhism.

Burtt, E.A., ed. *The Teachings of the Compassionate Buddha: Early Discourses, the Dhammapada, and Later Basic Writings*. New York: New American Library, 2000.

This text is a compendium of classic Buddhist teachings from various canons and traditions of Buddhism.

Buswell, Robert and Robert Gimello, eds. *Paths to Liberation: The Marga and Its Transformation in Buddhist Thought*. Honolulu: University of Hawaii Press, 1992.

This volume examines a variety of systematic approaches to enlightenment.

Collins, Steven. *Nirvana and Other Buddhist Felicities: Utopias of the Pali Imaginaire*. Cambridge: Cambridge University Press, 1998.

This is a challenging and important guide to understanding the relationship between the pursuit of gratifying rebirth and that of Nirvana.

Collins, Steven. *Selfless Persons: Imagery and Thought in Theravada Buddhism*. Cambridge: Cambridge University Press, 1982.

This is a highly accessible, scholarly introduction to Theravada Buddhism.

Conze, Edward, ed. *Buddhist Scriptures*. New York: Penguin, 1959.

This text provides many short, classic expressions of Buddhism from various canons and traditions.

Dhammadana, Sri. *A Happy Married Life: A Buddhist Perspective*. Lumpur: Buddhist Missionary Society, 1978.

This short work illustrates the high honor given to loving-kindness as well as the suspicion of sexual passion, even in marriage.

*Digha Nikaya: Thus Have I Heard: The Long Discourses of the Buddha*. Maurice Walsh, trans. London: Wisdom, 1987.

This is a translation of the Pali Canon's lengthy teachings of the Buddha.

Gombrich, Richard. *Theravada Buddhism: A Social History from Ancient Benares to Modern Columbo*. London: Routledge, 1988.

This text details the development of Theravada Buddhism in countries where it is the principal religion, from its origins to today.

Hadewijch. *Hadewijch: The Complete Works*. Mother Columba Hart, trans. New York: Paulist Press, 1980.

This text acts as a medieval representative of the passionate love of God.

John of the Cross. *The Collected Works of St. John of the Cross*. Kieran Kavanaugh and Otilio Rodriguez, trans. Washington, DC: Institute of Carmelite Studies, 1991.

This work expresses a classic understanding of Christian mysticism, including the path toward it and the experience of union with God.

Kugler, Peter. "The Logic of Nirvana: A Contemporary Interpretation." In *International Journal for Philosophy of Religion* 53 (2003): 93–110.

This article describes the modern challenge in understanding the experience and reality of Nirvana, as well as the complexity of language for what is beyond words or conception.

Nyanasobhano. *Nothing Higher to Live For: A Buddhist View of Romantic Love*. Kandy, Sri Lanka: Buddhist Publication Society, 1985.

This short text provides an example of the "monastic priority" in Theravada Buddhism, and its traditional suspicion of the possibilities of a holy life in marriage.

Rahula, Walpola. *What the Buddha Taught*. Rev. ed. New York: Grove Press, 1974.

This is a classic synopsis of the basic teachings of Buddhism, particularly in the Theravada school.

Ratnayaka, Shanta. "The Bodhisattva Ideal of Theravada." *Journal of the International Association of Buddhist Studies* 8, no. 2 (1985): 85–110.

This article investigates the distinct understanding of a bodhisattva from the Theravada perspective.

Samuels, Jeffrey. "Buddhist Theory and Practice: A Re-evaluation of the Bodhisattva-Shravaka Opposition." *Philosophy East and West* 47, no. 3 (1997): 339–415.

This article considers the logic of taking the bodhisattva vow and controversies about its meaning.

Shantideva. *The Way of the Bodhisattva*. Padmakara Translation Group, trans. Boston: Shambala Press, 1997.

This classic expression of Mahayana holiness is among the most beloved and meditated on texts in the Buddhist tradition.

Silva, Lily de. *Nibbana as a Living Experience*. Kandy, Sri Lanka: Buddhist Publication Society, 1996.

This short work describes how Nirvana is expressed in this world, and how this distinguishes one who is enlightened from one who is not.

Silva, Lily de. *The Problem of Self in Buddhism and Christianity*. Columbo, Sri Lanka: Study Centre for Religion and Society, 1975.

This volume investigates, both theoretically and culturally, how Theravada Buddhists wrestle with the vexing problem of claiming they have no actual self underneath the impersonal "aggregates" that make up a "conventional" self.

Suzuki, D.T. *The Essentials of Zen Buddhism*. Bernard Phillips, ed. Westport, CT: Greenwood Press, 1962.

Bernard Phillips gathers many of the best essays of noted Zen philosopher D.T. Suzuki in a volume intended to introduce the West to the Kyoto School of Zen Buddhism.

Suzuki, D.T. *An Introduction to Zen Buddhism*. New York: Grove Press, 1964.

Noted philosopher of Zen, D.T. Suzuki, provides for the English-speaking audience a quick introduction to the fundamental ideas of Zen from the Kyoto School.

Yoshinori, Takeuchi, ed. *Buddhist Spirituality: Indian, Southeast Asian, Tibetan, Early Chinese*. New York: Crossroads, 1995.

This text traces Buddhist doctrine and spirituality from its Indian context, focusing on Theravada Buddhists teachings and spirituality to early Mahayana developments in philosophy and practice in India and China.

Yoshinori, Takeuchi. *Buddhist Spirituality: Later China, Korea, Japan, and the Modern World*. New York: Crossroad, 1999.

This volume traces the development of Mahayana Buddhist teachings, practices, and spirituality as it continued to develop in East Asia and how various Mahayana traditions traveled to Europe and the United States.

## Internet Resources

*Buddhanet.net*

*Buddhistelibrary.org*

*Dharmanet.org*

*thebuddhistsociety.org*

# CONCLUSION

# Learning World Religions by Encountering Religious Others

*Pim Valkenberg*

## The Dialogical Approach

The discussions of Judaism, Islam, Hinduism, and Buddhism in this text aim to offer accurate information much like any other book about world religions. The authors explain concepts and texts, provide historical information, and explore theological insights. In addition, the text's dialogical approach, with its emphasis on insider and outsider voices, models a way to learn about world religions that moves beyond mere information to real encounters with religious others. It aims to facilitate deep understanding by learning *with* and *from*—not just *about*—members of a different religious tradition.

First, the outsider perspectives on religious practices and foundational texts raise awareness of how people approach new religious phenomena from a specific point of view, often one determined by a particular religious tradition. Categories and concepts, some dating back to one's upbringing, inevitably impact one's view of the world. For example, even scholars who want to distance themselves from a "confessional" approach often unconsciously rely on Christian categories. For this reason, the outsider voices in the sections on Judaism, Islam, Hinduism, and Buddhism try to be mindful of the Christian background that informs their perspective. Although outsiders to the religions discussed in this book, they are insiders as well, drawing on their religious background to better understand other religions. This gives these outsiders a double function: on the one hand, they are facilitating the understanding of those who stand outside these traditions; and at the same time, they are facilitating a deeper understanding of these traditions by approaching them from another religious viewpoint. Insofar as the outsider can understand the religion discussed from a different religious viewpoint, the dialogue between insider and outsider becomes a dialogue between two insiders in two different religious traditions, and therefore is a form of comparative theology and interreligious dialogue. For example, the dialogue between the Christian scholar of Buddhism and the Buddhist monk, who was raised as a Christian, highlights the fascinating interplay between those characteristics of Buddhism that many in the West find so appealing and other characteristics that remain utterly strange to the Western mind-set. It also highlights how Christian theological categories can serve to sometimes hinder and sometimes facilitate a better understanding of Buddhism.[1]

---

1. Peter Feldmeier, one of the dialogue partners in this book, recently addressed these issues in his book *Encounters in Faith: Christianity in Interreligious Dialogue* (Winona, MN: Anselm Academic, 2011).

Second, the insider perspectives on religious practices and foundational texts open a new window into the religious worlds of Muslims, Jews, Hindus, and Buddhists. The process of dialogue allows outsiders to encounter new voices and gain insight into the different approaches of these religious others. The Jewish author, for instance, demonstrated how a rabbinical approach to Torah differs from what is usually described as the role of "law" in the Jewish religion. This distinction, a matter of style and specific wording, can often be lost in an "objective" survey of Judaism.

The third and perhaps most important way this approach allows for a deeper understanding of religious others is through its dialogic nature. The exchange between "outsider" and "insider" constitutes a conversation, a back and forth, a shift in perspective between a Christian theological approach to these religions on the one hand and an insider theological approach to them on the other. As the dialogue between the two authors writing on Hinduism shows, such a dialogue can sometimes lead to surprising commonalities in style and content. Where outsiders and insiders share not only terminologies but also experiences and religious sensibilities, deep friendships may develop that give rise to fuller understandings of the religions involved.

The three components of the dialogical approach developed in this book offer all the usual instruments for learning *about* religious others, but they also move toward a model of learning *from* and *with* religious others. In other words, they strengthen the idea that religious insiders can serve as important teachers of world religions. This final chapter elaborates on this insight, proposing that experiential learning offers perhaps the most fruitful way to learn from religious others.

## Experiential Learning

The process of writing this book provided the authors with ample opportunity to learn from religious others. While scholars of religion and credentialed practitioners often have occasion to engage in dialogue with individuals of other religious traditions, those without such backgrounds may have to create those opportunities for themselves. Experiential learning offers a good way to achieve that goal.

Experiential learning fosters education not only through reading and studying books but also (and sometimes even mainly) by experiencing what has been studied. Books, films, works of art, and objects of worship can convey much good and worthwhile information about a religious tradition, but learning about a religion from someone who actually practices it has even greater value. This type of learning offers an important entry point for understanding religion as "lived experience."[2]

Traditionally, the study of a world religion has involved scrutinizing its classical texts and observing religious practitioners in other parts of the world. Today, adherents of the four world religions discussed in this book can be found in most every major city in the West, which makes this "lived experience" more accessible than ever.[3] Those who want to learn from religious others can find them if they know where to look. Indeed, students of world religions can find opportunities to learn from and with religious others quite easily and perhaps even integrate these experiences into their studies.

---

2. See Paul O. Myrhe, "What Is Religion?" in *Introduction to Religious Studies,* ed. Paul O. Myrhe (Winona, MN: Anselm Academic, 2009), 13.

3. See *World Religions in America: An Introduction*, ed. Jacob Neusner, 4th ed. (Louisville, KY: Westminster John Knox Press, 2009).

An experiential form of learning can take the form of "observations of rituals" or "visits to local religious communities."[4] It can also be achieved using simple techniques, such as interviewing religious leaders or volunteers or observing religious rituals. The main point is facilitating a serious encounter with the religious other. This chapter suggests two important avenues for such experiential learning, namely, (1) mapping religious pluralism by encountering religious others in their own faith communities, and (2) service-learning in organizations and communities of other faiths. Both forms function as extensions of the dialogic approach to world religions used in this book.

For those studying world religions as part of an undergraduate introductory class, institutions of higher education may facilitate such forms of experiential learning, especially if forging relationships with other religious communities comprises an important part of their institutional mission.[5] Yet experiential learning is not limited to an institutional context—it can be fruitfully pursued by individuals, church-affiliated groups, cultural associations, and other community organizations.

To show how such diverse forms of experiential learning might work, this text discusses these in the context of courses on world religions, drawing on personal experiences in the classroom, as well as presenting some ideas on how this might work in other contexts.[6]

## Encountering Religious Others in Their Faith Communities

One way to engage in experiential learning is through the process of "mapping," that is, trying to gain an insight into the proportions and dimensions of the plurality of world religions in one's vicinity. As Diana Eck has shown in her book *A New Religious America,* every city and state in the country is now more religiously plural than ever.[7] This diversity makes it possible to experience religious others everywhere—if one knows where to look and is prepared to step out of the comfort of the familiar.

Some of my students who undertook a mapping project emphasized how being forced out of their comfort zones constituted an important

---

4. See Debra Majeed, "How Is Religion Studied?" in *Introduction to Religious Studies,* ed. Paul O. Myrhe (Winona, MN: Anselm Academic, 2009), 16.

5. This is specifically true of the many private institutions of higher education in the United States that have been founded and often still operate with specific ideals about education from a religious point of view. Though it is quite possible to integrate elements of encountering religious others in an "objective" approach to the study of world religions, such integration is much easier when the basic learning aims and the mission of an institution of higher education favor such an experiential form of learning. See Fred Glennon, "Service-Learning and the Dilemma of Religious Studies: Descriptive or Normative?" and Charles R. Strain, "Creating the Engaged University: Service-Learning, Religious Studies, and Institutional Mission," in *From Cloister to Commons: Concepts and Models for Service-Learning in Religious Studies,* ed. Richard Devine, Joseph A. Favazza, and F. Michael McLain (Washington, DC: American Association for Higher Education, 2002), 9–24 and 25–39.

6. Most data in this chapter derive from teaching at Loyola University Maryland during the academic years 2009–10 and 2010–11. In each year, the course *Christianity and World Religions* was taught in two different forms: one section (with a total of 31 students in 2 years) had a compulsory service-learning component, while the other section (with a total of 48 students in 2 years) contained the "Religious Map of Baltimore" project instead of the service-learning. As part of the course, I asked the students to write about their experiential learning and told them their answers might be used for this book unless they indicated they did not want them to be published. I am aware that the in-class setting of this questionnaire may result in a higher percentage of positive reactions; yet, I think the general tone of the answers reflects the experiences of the students. To protect their identities, I use first names only.

7. Diana L. Eck, *A New Religious America: How a "Christian Country" Has Become the World's Most Religiously Diverse Nation* (New York: Harper Collins, 2002).

element of the learning experiences. Michael, for instance, said,

> Leaving the shell of a classroom and using the world of real people as a textbook from which to learn makes for a much more personal and therefore much more lasting, accurate, education. [Without this,] we would miss the dancing at the Shabbat services, we would miss the personal stories from Holocaust survivors. . . . It is the personal stories that we remember and learn from the most.

Julia added, "Because I would NEVER go visit a Buddhist meditation center on my own, a class that requires me to provides me with an experience I would not otherwise have had."

## Mapping Religious Pluralism

The first step in the process of mapping religious pluralism in one's own neighborhood consists of selecting a religion—or religions—to concentrate on. In many cases, it proves helpful to select a specific subtradition within a religion, for instance, "I am mainly interested in Buddhist meditation centers—if possible Zen Buddhism or Tibetan Buddhism" or "I would like to know more about indigenous forms of Islam, such as the Nation of Islam." The next step entails doing basic research on the specific tradition to get a sense of its beliefs and practices and to identify particular aspects one hopes to experience when visiting the local community. It often helps to focus on a specific subject matter important to that religious community, for instance, prayer or meditation. The third step is finding a local community to visit. Many local phone directories and city guides provide contact information for religious communities, although they may not list them under the heading "religion" but rather under a variety of categories such as "churches" or "cultural centers."

Internet versions of these guides sometimes contain links to websites, which aid in the process of gathering information. A local interfaith organization may be able to provide information about its member communities as well.

Some religious communities may seem hesitant when first contacted by an outsider; this may occur because of security concerns. Personal experience has shown that most religious communities welcome guests who sincerely want to learn more about their religious tradition. Cultural differences may give rise to some initial difficulties making arrangements, but once a meeting is arranged, the religious community often turns out to be quite welcoming. One student, Karla, wrote,

> I had expected that Hindus would not be open to people of another religion interrupting their service. However, . . . the head of the temple welcomed us with open arms and made us feel welcome. He even made copies of handouts for us and read and explained everything with us.

Bethel admitted, "I felt almost silly that of all the Muslim friends [I have,] . . . I never asked one of them if it was OK to go to the mosque with them because I thought that Islam didn't permit me to."

## The Religious Map of Baltimore

In some of my world religions courses, students took on an experiential learning project called the "Religious Map of Baltimore." The project was designed to help students acquire a basic idea of the religious diversity of Baltimore. Each student focused on one religion taught in the course and prepared a group presentation to teach classmates about that community, especially as it related to a specific topic. To get an overview of the religious communities they could visit, students consulted the website of the Harvard-based Pluralism Project, which provides a list of religious organizations for every state in the United States.[8]

After collecting this information and selecting a specific community to visit, the class discussed different groups in the Baltimore area and their most important characteristics. As part of the project, students would connect the contents of the course with the group visit by studying some specific aspects of the religion concerned, writing about these in an essay, and preparing questions for interviews or observations at their selected site. Many of the students who wanted to visit a Buddhist community, for instance, chose to write on meditation or the Buddhist concept of consciousness, while quite a few students who wanted to visit a Muslim community were interested in the place of women in the religion. One of the main questions posed by those visiting Hindu temples was the relation between the one divine reality in the world and the many images through which this reality can be worshipped. Finally, questions for Jewish communities often focused on the changes in Jewish identity because of the experiences of the Holocaust and the foundation of the State of Israel.

Usually, students made the first contacts with the religious communities, such as synagogues, mosques, temples, and meditation centers. In some cases, especially where there was a preexisting relationship between the community and the university, this was easy; however, sometimes cultural and other differences made this a challenging part of the process.

Generally speaking, students evaluated this Religious Map of Baltimore project as a considerable broadening of their horizons. Here are comments by Victoria, Stephanie, and Katie, respectively:

One can be in a classroom and learn endless accounts from other historians and theologians, but to go out and experience doctrine in action adds a level of understanding unattainable in the classroom alone. . . . One can learn about ceremony and services, but the emotional and spiritual connection can only be experienced through action. . . . It is like the learning of a language. One can learn all of the grammar and syntax and vocabulary, but to go to a native-speaking country adds a whole new flavor to the mix.

Being able to connect what you have learned in class to real people, places, and faces refocuses you and gives you the energy to do what the religions call you to do. You become more open and accepting of others by limiting the distance between you and them by leaving the security of a book or classroom and immersing yourself in someone else's life. With this experience I have grown, matured, and become wiser.

The Religious Map of Baltimore project took something on a piece of paper and made it come alive. In many classes, it is easy to overload on facts, basically regurgitate them on your test papers and simply walk out unchanged. Something may spark your interest, but I think it's unlikely that something will really move a student. . . . In contrast, I cannot see how my visit to the mosque could have left someone *unchanged*. Seeing their prayers in action also helped me have a greater conceptual understanding of a process such as the afternoon Muslim prayer which is so foreign to me. I am very glad I took the course for this aspect but am especially glad I chose to study Islam for my Map of Baltimore project.

---

8. See *pluralism.org/resources/map/index.php*.

Some students who connected a topic studied in class to their experiential learning visit (by, for instance, interviewing a member of the religious community about the topic) received unexpected insights. This proved particularly true if their initial view of the religion had been shaped by its portrayal in the popular media. The role of women in Islam is a case in point, as Lisa explains,

> Upon arriving at the mosque I was adamant in my disapproval of the Muslim treatment of women. It did not even occur to me to bring it up because I was sure that nothing could change my mind. However, after we had finished asking questions, our host, Jamir, felt the need to bring it up. His explanation emphasized that women are separated from men in order to avoid distractions. I was completely shocked because I had never thought of it that way. I always assumed it was part of the patriarchal society in which women were oppressed.

Another student noted,

> Going into this project, . . . I signed up for studying Islam to sort of "bust open" this unfair treatment of women that the religion promotes. In studying the texts, I was unconvinced that I was entirely wrong in my preconceived notion. What truly changed my opinion was visiting the Muslim community center. Yes, things were as my textbook said, the women and men separated and the women wore loose clothing. The women sat behind the men during prayer, which I had always viewed as a sign of submission to men because of things I'd read or seen in the news. But the women laughed and chatted and mingled with men before the service just like any Catholic Mass. But the real moment for me was in conversation with one woman. She said women sat in the back so men would not get distracted by the women bending over to kneel in front of them, and they could remain modest during prayer. It sounds funny because it was. She said, "You know we don't care what they are doing up there but if we were in front of them bending over like that, prayer would not be on their minds." I instantly had to smile at the thought of the men I knew, and I knew that at least in this way I understood a tradition I thought was hateful to women in a new, more positive light.

Students also frequently remarked that the practitioners of other religions were often more like themselves than they expected. Daniel writes,

> When I visited the Shambala Meditation Center, I came in there with thoughts of a really uptight traditional-looking pagoda, with structural prayers and meditations. However, what I got was a rather casual religion that focused on clearing any distractions in life rather than escape from the rebirthing cycle. After the Samatha breathing exercise I felt the way I did after my first reconciliation. I felt like weight had been lifted off my shoulders, and I could breathe easy. It was really nice.

Rita adds,

> I visited my Islamic community . . . thinking this would be somewhat of a cult-like theology like that we see on the news all the time for their "terrorist" behaviors, but I was proved wrong. They are normal, everyday people with a devout and beautiful faith. Their beliefs were actually shockingly similar to how I was raised.

Not every interreligious experience is a positive one, and experiential learning has not corrected every biased opinion. Sometimes it even confirms rather than refutes preconceived

The Muslim Community Cultural Center of Baltimore is located in the Bergner mansion in Leakin Park (West-Baltimore). The building contains a prayer room, classrooms, a community bookstore, and a computer lab.

notions—and that can be a good experience as well. Matthew describes this as follows:

> One preconceived notion I had about Islam, which was endorsed by my experiences with this visit, was that the adherents were very sincerely devout, even more so than most other religions . . . and I was quite impressed by this. I felt like when the majority of Muslims recite the shahada or performed their daily prayers, they truly *wanted* to do this in devotion to God. They were not just going through the ritual motions, at least not to the degree I feel is present in many other religions I have encountered.

Finally, students not only learned about other religious communities but also reflected on their own religious backgrounds, thus initiating an interior dialogue process. Matthew wrote,

> The Religious Map of Baltimore component of the course set the class far apart from all other theology courses I have taken in my life, including all twelve grades of Catholic schooling. The experiential aspect brings up an empathetic sense of a connection between the person experiencing the worship and a religion not previously practiced, which adds a tremendous sense of compassion to the other field of faith. Going out and participating in the faith, which for me was Buddhism, not only gave me an appreciation for that faith but for the faith I hold as well.

And Lisa:

> Due to my lack of religion, I was initially overwhelmed by this assignment. However, it gave me the opportunity to see how important it is to understand your religion and beliefs. Without understanding these teachings, you will have nothing to challenge or support in interreligious dialogue. I thought that I would have an advantage walking in as a blank slate. However, this causes the tendency to then absorb everything you hear without truly considering and challenging it. Now, I will make more of an effort to distinguish my beliefs with the hope of utilizing them in my next dialogue experience.

These experiences forced many students to rethink traditional Christian approaches to other religions. Daisy, for instance, writes,

> My ideas about Catholicism have not essentially changed. I do believe it to be a wonderful religion but what has changed is my view on other religions. I'm sure everyone who has a religion believes theirs to be great, but by taking this course I have learned why people who are part of these other religions believe their religion is so great. Although this course was just as hard as my Organic Chemistry II course, it challenged me to think more. It challenged me to think outside the box. For me, Catholicism is not the only religion that will lead to salvation. There are plenty of other religions out there with believers who share similar truths.

And finally Megan:

> I was relieved to discover an inclusivist point of view in theological approaches. I now realize that it is not abnormal to find yourself within other religions. When I studied Hinduism, I often found myself believing in some of their values as well; for instance, I related to their value of "ahimsa" or nonviolence. . . . I now realize that Hinduism is not as distant and different from Christianity as I once thought.

The encounter with religious others in their faith communities can take many forms. It can emphasize obtaining information about religious others in interviews or observations, and thus be used mainly as another way to gather information alongside reading books and listening to expert opinions. The dialogic approach taken in this book, though, fits in well with a more interactive form of encounter, one in which prior study of religious traditions is tested through dialogue with adherents of these religious traditions. This has the advantage of adding an extra source of information as well as facilitating a different kind of contact with members of local religious communities. As the quotations from students show, often this dialogic encounter with religious others not only readjusts one's perception of another religion but also causes a reconsideration of one's own religious background.

# Encountering Religious Others through Service-Learning

## Service-Learning in Religious Communities

A more intense form of experiential learning is known as service-learning. A recent book series published by the American Association for Higher Education gives the following definition:

> Service-learning is a type of experiential education in which students participate in service to the community and reflect on their involvement in such a way as to gain

further understanding of course content and of the discipline and its relation to social needs and an enhanced sense of civic responsibility.[9]

While the idea of service-learning is quite common in secondary and higher education, combining it with religious diversity is less so. Yet the notion that service-learning might promote an awareness of religious diversity that allows one to learn about and from religious others is not new.

Many Jesuit universities and colleges, for example, define their mission as forming "men and women for others," who develop solidarity with others and "let the gritty reality of this world into their lives."[10] Thus, contact with the less privileged becomes an important part of Jesuit education and has in many cases led such institutions to establish offices for social justice and service-learning, often connected to campus ministry. Other Christian, Jewish, Muslim, Hindu, and Buddhist institutions share this focus on learning through interfaith dialogue and particularly interfaith service. The Chicago-based InterFaith Youth Core, founded by the Muslim Eboo Patel, for example, stimulates the formation of interfaith student groups on many campuses with the aim of promoting a wide array of intercultural and interfaith community-based and immersion projects.[11]

## Service-Learning at Loyola University in Baltimore

When I started integrating service-learning into my classes on world religions at Loyola University in Baltimore, this Jesuit institution already had an excellent support system for such efforts. Service-learning falls under the purview of the Center for Community Service and Justice, which works together with Campus Ministry on a number of projects. The center has compiled a comprehensive list of community service sites whose focuses range from literacy, advocacy, environment, and development to health, homelessness, housing, and youth education. Yet almost all of these community sites were either Catholic or secular, requiring the addition of a considerable number of newer, religiously diverse sites. Although establishing new sites for service-learning was a laborious process, these efforts often developed valuable partnerships, both for the university and the religious communities.

Together with a staff member of the Center for Community Service and Justice, I prepared a list of sites for service-learning. Students in my course on world religions could either first choose a religion and then look at the sites corresponding with this religion, or directly choose a specific site for their service-learning. Some of these sites directly related to a religious community, but at

---

9. This definition (by Julie Hatcher and Robert Bringle) is quoted in the introduction to *From Cloister to Commons: Concepts and Models for Service-Learning in Religious Studies*, ed. Richard Devine, Joseph A. Favazza, and F. Michael McLain (Washington DC: American Association for Higher Education, 2002), 1.

10. The first quotation is a famous statement by then Superior General Pedro Arrupe, SJ, in 1973. See Pedro Arrupe, "Men and Women for Others: Education for Social Justice and Social Action Today," in June Ellis et al., *Commitment to Justice in Jesuit Higher Education* (Baltimore: Apprentice House, 2006), 1–18. The second quotation is from his successor as Superior General of the Jesuits, Peter-Hans Kolvenbach, who told a conference of American Jesuits in 2000 that the measure of Jesuit universities "is not what our students do but who they become and the adult Christian responsibility they will exercise in future towards their neighbor and their world." He connects the Jesuit ideal of educating the whole person with the idea of solidarity that is learned through "contact" rather than "concepts." See Peter-Hans Kolvenbach, SJ, "The Service of Faith and the Promotion of Justice in American Jesuit Higher Education," Ellis, *Commitment*, 21–41.

11. See *Building the Interfaith Youth Movement: Beyond Dialogue to Action*, ed. Eboo Patel and Patrice Brodeur (Lanham, MD: Rowman & Littlefield, 2006). Patel gives autobiographical backgrounds in his *Acts of Faith* (Boston: Beacon Press, 2007).

other sites religion played a different role. The list consisted of nine possible sites:

- a Jewish geriatric center and hospital
- a Muslim community cultural center
- a preschool and daycare center connected to a Jewish temple
- a Jewish museum
- a Buddhist meditation center
- a Muslim school connected to a religious community
- the Baltimore Jewish Council
- an interfaith building program, part of Habitat for Humanity
- the Civilizations Exchange and Cooperation Foundation, an interfaith youth program

As with the Religious Map of Baltimore project, students not only chose a religion to focus on and a site for their service-learning but also a topic for further study related to their service-learning. Students reported on their service-learning experiences regularly and reflected on them in essays and class presentations. Some of their experiences paralleled those of students in the Religious Map of Baltimore project, for instance, in the difference found between experiential learning and other forms of learning. Daniel wrote,

> The service learning aspect of this course adds a lot to the course and really sets it apart from just the instructional courses. It is easy to read and write about a religion from the comfort of your classroom seat but when you must go out and interact with the people of the religion, there is an array of mixed emotions. . . . [M]any students nowadays just memorize material only to be able to regurgitate it back on a quiz or exam but by being involved in this service-learning aspect of the course what you can learn can potentially stay with you for life.

Many of the students involved in service-learning noted that Jewish or Muslim children were much like other children they knew and that they often shared much in common. Erin observed,

> I think that the moments in which the kids were simply kids most changed my preconceived ideas about the religion. Though the school often gives a very isolated image, the students would periodically discuss pop culture with me. Somehow the juxtaposition of such a current conversation with so many of the school's more traditional practices always seemed to remind me of today's context so that the Qur'an and Arabic classes were only one part of these kids' lives. Just this past week, one of the third graders started singing Justin Bieber!

Another student noticed cultural similarities as follows:

> I think the experience in my service-learning that most changed my preconceived ideas about the religion I encountered was when I . . . attended the [temple's] tot Shabbat for the kids and the lady was singing the songs. . . . [A]t one point in the ceremony she had bread and put it up and then grape juice that symbolized the wine they use. I always thought Judaism was completely different. Yes they have different beliefs and traditions, but they are also similar in some aspects and this ritual reminded me of communion and the Eucharist in my religion.

Adults of other faiths turn out to be normal people, which even holds true for Buddhist meditation teachers, as Marash tells,

> I remember one of the first days at the Vikatadamshtri Buddhist Center, I had a conversation with a young Kelsang about

my accounting major in school. He told me how much he used to dislike mathematics, but he was the one in charge of the accounting books for the center. For one, I never imagined a Buddhist Kelsang would perform accounting, however naïve that might have been. It was a reality check that although many people are devout followers of ancient religions, they are still living in the modern world.

Another recurring student theme was how different people within the same faith could be. William observed,

> One day at my site, two of the museum workers and I had a conversation about a disagreement the two other employees had earlier that day. . . . I realized from this that Judaism is not as united a religion as depicted. Judaism is constantly portrayed as a religion whose adherents stick up for each other no matter what. I believe that the worldwide Jewish support for the state of Israel contributes to this idea. I was surprised to find just how fractious such a religion could be.

While these experiences related to persons of other faiths, most students discussed their experiences of the religious communities they visited. Students working at one of the mosques in Baltimore, for instance, wrote,

> This course was so fulfilling because it featured a service-learning component. It is one thing to read about a religious practice like Jumah prayer but to be able to sit through it and talk one-on-one with Muslim attendants afterwards is enlightening. You can't ask a book why ablution is necessary before prayer. . . . Everything I've read from the World Religions reader and lectures came to life when I volunteered at the Muslim

Cultural Community Center of Baltimore. I was able to see a pluralistic approach to other faiths at its finest when Elizaveta and I were so warmly welcomed.

World religions is probably one of the more complex and involved classes that I have taken over the last year at Loyola. The course challenges not only your understanding of the material presented but also the understanding of your own identity and religion. . . . I can say that I have learned so much more from visiting MCCCB [the Muslim Cultural Community Center of Baltimore] and just having a chat with the members of the community, than I had learned in books. The classroom gives you the knowledge base; however, the service and exposure gives you a deeper connection to the religion of study. It is as if there is an intuitive understanding when you are immersed in the community.

One of the strongest experiences was building houses with Jewish and Muslim students for a Habitat for Humanity project. Rebecca, a student who stayed to work with the organization after her service-learning ended, said the following:

> At my service-learning site I worked and spoke with individuals of the Jewish and Muslim faith. From my research and studies in class of other religions, I learned the traditional beliefs and practices of Jews and Muslims. Never once did I stop to consider that not all individuals within a religion practice and hold beliefs in accordance to these textbook definitions. This is something my class readings did not teach me: about the variability between individuals. I learned from my service that each person relates to God in their own personal and unique way and

An intercultural group of students participating in a "Better Understanding for a Better World – BUBW" conference, organized by the Civilizations Exchange and Cooperation Foundation, in front of the inner harbor in Baltimore.

that there are many different levels of devotion and practice among worshipping individuals of any faith. I encountered some that were extremely devoted and practiced by-the-book tradition, and I also encountered individuals that although they held strong beliefs, didn't practice their religious traditions as often.

The Civilizations Exchange and Cooperation Foundation (CECF), led by Imam Bashar and his wife, Kim, provided another source of inspiration for many students, as the following quote shows:

Through CECF I was able to see the loving, caring, and humanitarian roots that exist in Islam. Islam is a religion of accepting, of helping God's people. The religion does not discriminate who they help, . . . the press media only gives them negative coverage. But through this CECF it is clear to see that the media is manipulative and wrong. I now view the Islamic tradition with high

esteem and respect their mission to help the world and its people.

The final point shared in student reflections was how service-learning had changed their way of looking at religion, including their own religious backgrounds.

I think that my service-learning experiences have impacted my spirituality and person. Listening to the Qur'an and Arabic classes made me want to learn the language, while hearing about their prayer made me grateful for my own flexible spirituality. I do not think, though, that it changed in any huge ways my ideas about the lack of religion that I grew up with. However, it did allow me to see the value in practicing religion in community, because of how that can intensify the experience.

Engaging with the Buddhist lifestyle contributed greatly to my way of thinking about God and Catholicism. Gandhi once said that he would have become a Christian if he had ever met one. Indeed, it is difficult to find someone adhering to the faith who is completely genuine and sincere. However, all the monks and nuns I met at the [Buddhist] center literally blew my mind with their serene content. The physical presence of their satisfaction forced me to consider my earlier teachings, ingrained during twelve years of Catholic schooling, that Christianity was the only way. I began to find it difficult to believe that every other religion was just a failed attempt.

Quite a few students expressed a new awareness of religious pluralism, even though they may have derived different lessons from that awareness.

The experience has taught me to be more conscientious and dedicated to my own faith. I guess [it] has strengthened my spirituality but has allowed me to open up to other religions and not judge them based on appearance and hearsay.

Through what I have learned from studying Buddhism in class and experiencing it at the Kadampa Center, I feel that I have become even fonder of the religion. Despite being a product of 12+ years of Catholic education, . . . I have not been the most devout Catholic. Although I was a member of two youth groups, took part in retreats,

and was both an altar server and Eucharistic minister, I have lately found myself becoming more doubtful and straying from the ideals I've held for the majority of my life. Although I will remain a Catholic, I have increased respect for the Buddhist way of life and have adopted some of it for myself.

This conclusion has sketched two dialogic ways of encountering religious others as an integral part of learning about world religions. The dialogic approach to other religions exemplified in this book highlights how learning *from* religious others provides an important complement to learning *about* these religious others. Such an approach offers an interplay between outsider and insider views of these religions in which religious others as insider-scholars form an important part. As the examples of mapping religious pluralism in one's neighborhood and of service-learning in religious communities show, encounters with religious others can correct misconceptions that often develop unconsciously. That does not mean that every such encounter is truthful; some adherents may have skewed opinions about their own religions as well. But encounters with religious others often serve as powerful means to learn about these others in new and unexpected ways—and perhaps to learn more about oneself and one's religious background as well. In this manner, encountering religious others allows one to use what one has learned about world religions in one's daily life.

# CONTRIBUTORS

**Philip A. Cunningham, PhD,** is director of the Institute for Jewish-Catholic Relations of Saint Joseph's University in Philadelphia, where he is professor of theology in the Department of Theology and Religious Studies. He serves as a vice-president of the International Council of Christians and Jews and as secretary-treasurer of the Council of Centers on Jewish-Christian Relations. He is the author or coeditor of numerous articles and books, including the recently published *Christ Jesus and the Jewish People Today: New Explorations of Theological Interrelationships* (William B. Eerdmans, 2011) and an article with Jan Katzew in 2001, "Do Jews and Christians Worship the Same God?" (Westview Press).

**Peter Feldmeier, PhD,** is the Murray/Bacik Professor of Catholic Studies at the University of Toledo. He earned his doctorate at the Graduate Theological Union in Berkeley, California. Dr. Feldmeier has published widely in Christian spirituality, comparative studies, and Buddhist-Christian dialogue. His most recent publications include *The Path of Wisdom: A Christian Commentary on the Dhammapada* (Peeters, 2011) and *Encounters in Faith: Christianity in Interreligious Dialogue* (Anselm Academic, 2011).

**Rita George-Tvrtković, PhD,** is assistant professor of theology at Benedictine University in Illinois. Before completing her doctorate in historical theology at the University of Notre Dame, she served as associate director of the Archdiocese of Chicago's Office for Ecumenical and Interreligious Affairs, where she focused on Catholic-Muslim relations. Her new book, *A Christian Pilgrim in Medieval Iraq: Riccoldo da Montecroce's Encounter with Islam,* is forthcoming from Brepols Press.

**Rabbi Jan Katzew, PhD,** serves as the director of service-learning at the Hebrew Union College–Jewish Institute of Religion in Cincinnati, Ohio, the oldest rabbinical seminary in the United States. Rabbi Katzew's teaching reflects his academic interests in education and moral philosophy in addition to interfaith relations. His scholarly publications include textbooks, juried journal articles, book chapters, and essays in Jewish thought. Coincidentally, Rabbi Katzew's interest in Jewish-Christian relations began in 1965, the year in which *Nostra Aetate* was promulgated. He has been in dialogue with Philip A. Cunningham for more than a decade.

**Aimee Upjohn Light, PhD,** received her doctorate in philosophy of religion from Yale University, with specialization in interreligious work and Catholic feminist theology. She teaches courses in theologies of religion, interreligious dialogue, comparative theology, and feminist theologies at Duquesne University and serves as the executive editor of the *Journal of Inter-Religious Dialogue.* She has authored journal articles on postmodernity, religious pluralism, and negative theology, and presented numerous papers at conferences including the American Academy of Religion, Call to Action, and Lewis and Clark's Symposium on Religion and Gender. Her new book on interreligious thought and feminist theology is forthcoming from Anselm Academic.

**Zeki Saritoprak, PhD,** has held the Nursi Chair in Islamic Studies at John Carroll University since 2003. He has also taught and conducted research at Harran University in Turkey, Georgetown University, the Catholic University of America, and Berry College in Rome, Georgia. He is the founder and former president of the Rumi Forum for Interfaith Dialogue in Washington, DC. He is the author of several books in Turkish, English, and Arabic. He has more than thirty academic articles on topics in Islam and has served as guest editor for issues of the journals *Islam and Christian-Muslim Relations* and *Muslim World*.

**Rev. Heng Sure, PhD,** became a Buddhist Bhikshu (monk) in 1976 and currently serves as director of the Berkeley Buddhist Monastery. He holds a doctorate in religion from the Graduate Theological Union, Berkeley, California, where he co-teaches a class on Buddhist-Christian dialogue. Reverend Heng Sure has represented Buddhism on the Global Council of the United Religions Initiative and served on the board of directors of the Interfaith Center at the Presidio. He speaks widely on such diverse topics as human values in the high-tech world; eating a harmless, plant-based diet; and translating Buddhist music for Western audiences. An accomplished folk musician and storyteller, Reverend Heng Sure interprets traditional insights for contemporary seekers of the path to liberation.

**Pim Valkenberg, PhD,** is ordinary professor of religion and culture at the Catholic University of America's School of Theology and Religious Studies, where he directs the Institute for Interreligious Study and Dialogue. Born in the Netherlands, he studied theology and phenomenology of religions in Utrecht and taught dogmatic theology and theology of religions for twenty years in Nijmegen before coming to the United States in 2006. With a background in medieval Christian theology, he has been involved in dialogue between the Abrahamic religions since the 1990s and has published about past and present forms of dialogue in numerous books in Dutch and English including *The Polemical Dialogue* (Verlag für Entwicklungspolitik Saarbrücken, 1997), *The Three Rings* (Peeters, 2005), and *Sharing Lights on the Way to God* (Rodopi, 2006). While teaching courses in Christian theology and world religions at Loyola University Maryland between 2006 and 2011, his involvement in comparative theology and service-learning brought him to the approach to world religions in dialogue exemplified in this book.

**Madhuri M. Yadlapati, PhD,** has been teaching courses in faith and doubt, modern Christian thought, and world religions at Louisiana State University since earning her doctorate in philosophy of religion from Yale University. Concerned with furthering productive interreligious dialogue and comparative theology, Dr. Yadlapati is involved with the *Journal of Inter-Religious Dialogue* and the newly formed group of the American Academy of Religion, "Interreligious and Interfaith Studies." She is the author of *Against Dogmatism: Dwelling in Faith and Doubt* (University of Illinois Press, forthcoming), as well as several articles engaging comparative religious thought.

# INDEX

Illustrations, captions, footnotes, and charts are indicated with i, cap, n, and c, respectively.